EXCUSE ME WHILE I WAG

Other DILBERT books from Boxtree

Dilbert-A Treasury of Sunday Strips: Version 00
ISBN: 0-7522-7232-2

Random Acts of Management
ISBN: 0-7522-7174-1

Dilbert Gives You the Business
ISBN: 0-7522-2394-1

Don't Step in the Leadership
ISBN: 0-7522-2389-5

Journey to Cubeville
ISBN: 0-7522-2384-4

I'm Not Anti-Business, I'm Anti-Idiot
ISBN: 0-7522-2379-8

Seven Years of Highly Defective People
ISBN: 0-7522-2407-7

Casual Day Has Gone Too Far
ISBN: 0-7522-1119-6

Fugitive from the Cubicle Police
ISBN: 0-7522-2431-X

Still Pumped from Using the Mouse
ISBN: 0-7522-2265-1

It's Obvious You Won't Survive by Your Wits Alone
ISBN: 0-7522-0201-4

Bring Me the Head of Willy the Mailboy!
ISBN: 0-7522-0136-0

Shave the Whales
ISBN: 0-7522-0849-7

Always Postpone Meetings with Time-Wasting Morons
ISBN: 0-7522-0854-3

EXCUSE ME WHILE I WAG

A DILBERT® BOOK
BY **SCOTT ADAMS**

B⊞XTREE

First published 2001 by Andrews McMeel Publishing, an Andrews McMeel Universal company,
4520 Main Street, Kansas City, Missouri 64111, USA

This edition published 2001 by Boxtree
an imprint of Pan Macmillan Ltd
Pan Macmillan, 20 New Wharf Road, London N1 9RR
Basingstoke and Oxford
Associated companies throughout the world
www.panmacmillan.com

ISBN 0 7522 2399 2

9 8 7 6 5 4 3

A CIP catalogue record for this book is available from the British Library

Printed by the Bath Press, Bath

"This book contains no cilantro."

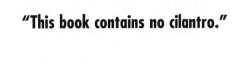

Introduction

The other day I was at Sears, enjoying the intoxicating fragrance of fresh tools and marveling at the fact that there isn't one best way to rotate a bolt. I think Sears has a whole division of wrench developers who sit around asking questions like, "What if the bolt is in a dark place, around a corner, slightly stripped, guarded by a trained raccoon?" Then someone in the wrench division makes a tool that's part wrench, part flashlight, and part tranquilizer dart gun. All I know is that when they're done, I'll buy three of them—one for the tool bench, one for the car and one in case I lose one.

None of this has anything to do with my point; I just like tools.

Anyway, as I was leaving Sears, I passed a naughty lingerie store and pressed my face to the window hoping to catch a glimpse of some more tools. They didn't have any. But what I saw was very disturbing. It was an employee who, in my opinion, was not the very best fit for the lingerie-selling profession.

Now, before I tell you about this employee, and you judge me to be unkind, let me set the stage with some politically correct self-deprecation: I would like to be a linebacker in the NFL. But because I weigh 155 pounds and have legs like chopsticks I consider myself unsuited for that profession. The list of jobs for which I am not physically suited is very long, including anything that involves lifting heavy objects or having direct sunlight come in contact with my skin.

If I worked at a health club the customers might worry that regular exercise causes people to look like me. If I were a policeman, crooks would take turns beating me up.

This is all a very long way of saying that if you happen to measure your panty size in hectares, maybe you're not the very best choice to work in a lingerie store.

I blame the strong economy. Companies are desperate to fill jobs. They're lowering the bar and tolerating more insolence and disobedience than ever. That's the inspiration behind the title of this book, *Excuse Me While I Wag*. It's an anthem for the new millennium, and it's an attitude you'll notice in Dilbert and his co-workers lately. They're more sassy and sarcastic than in the past.

Speaking of attitude, when Dogbert conquers the planet and becomes supreme ruler, everyone who subscribes to the free Dilbert Newsletter will form the New Ruling Class and make everyone else our domestic servants. The totally free Dilbert newsletter comes out whenever I feel like it, usually four times a year.

To subscribe, send a blank e-mail to dilbert-text-on@list.unitedmedia.com.

To unsubscribe, send a blank e-mail to dilbert-off@list.unitedmedia.com.

If you have problems with the automated subscription method, write to newsletter@unitedmedia.com.

S.Adams

Scott Adams

Scottadams@aol.com
Dilbert.com

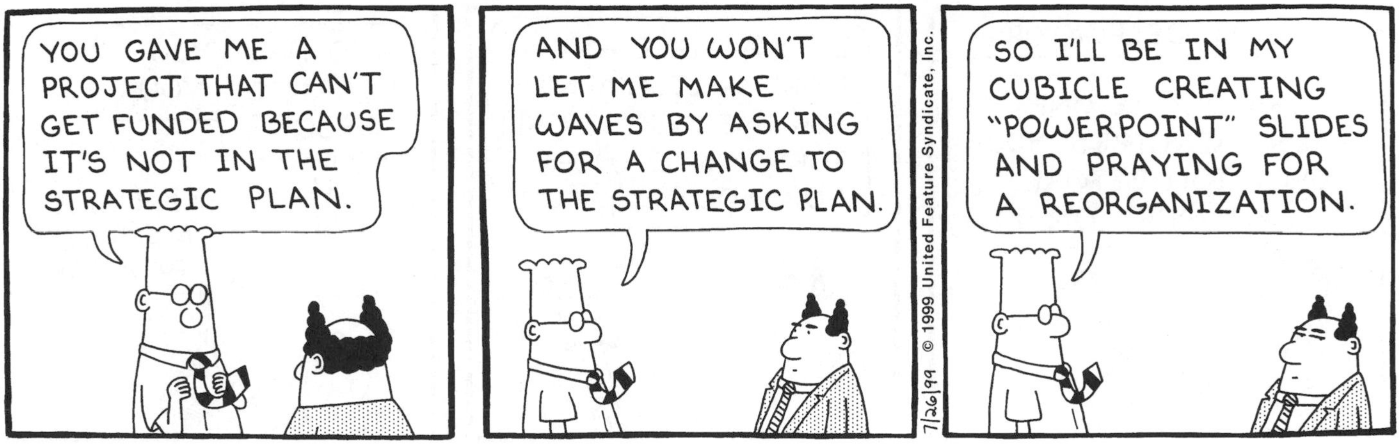
YOU GAVE ME A PROJECT THAT CAN'T GET FUNDED BECAUSE IT'S NOT IN THE STRATEGIC PLAN.
AND YOU WON'T LET ME MAKE WAVES BY ASKING FOR A CHANGE TO THE STRATEGIC PLAN.
7/26/99 © 1999 United Feature Syndicate, Inc.
SO I'LL BE IN MY CUBICLE CREATING "POWERPOINT" SLIDES AND PRAYING FOR A REORGANIZATION.

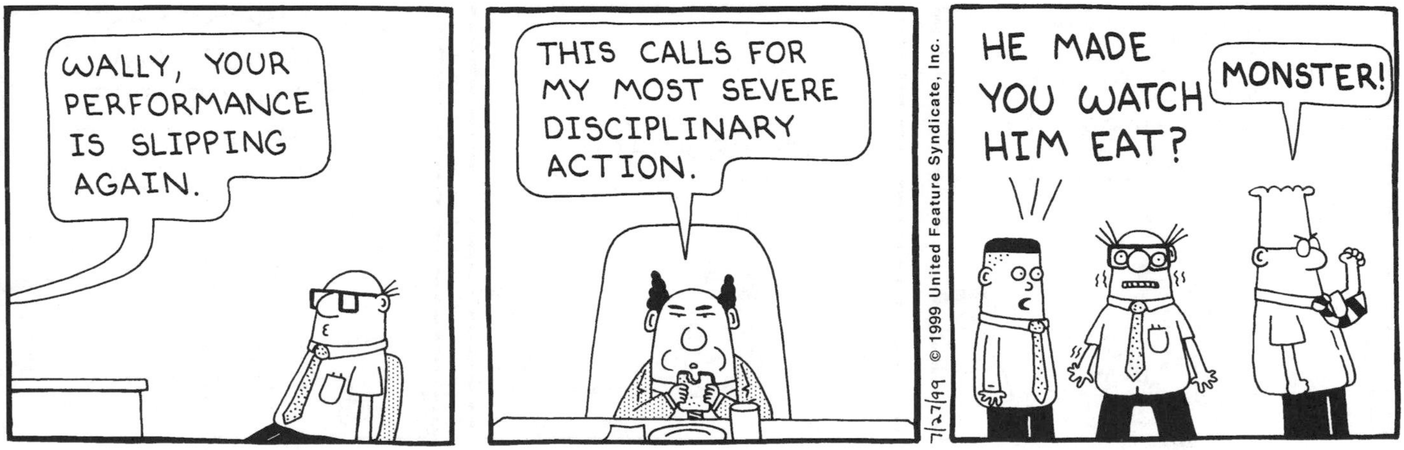
WALLY, YOUR PERFORMANCE IS SLIPPING AGAIN.
THIS CALLS FOR MY MOST SEVERE DISCIPLINARY ACTION.
7/27/99 © 1999 United Feature Syndicate, Inc.
HE MADE YOU WATCH HIM EAT?
MONSTER!

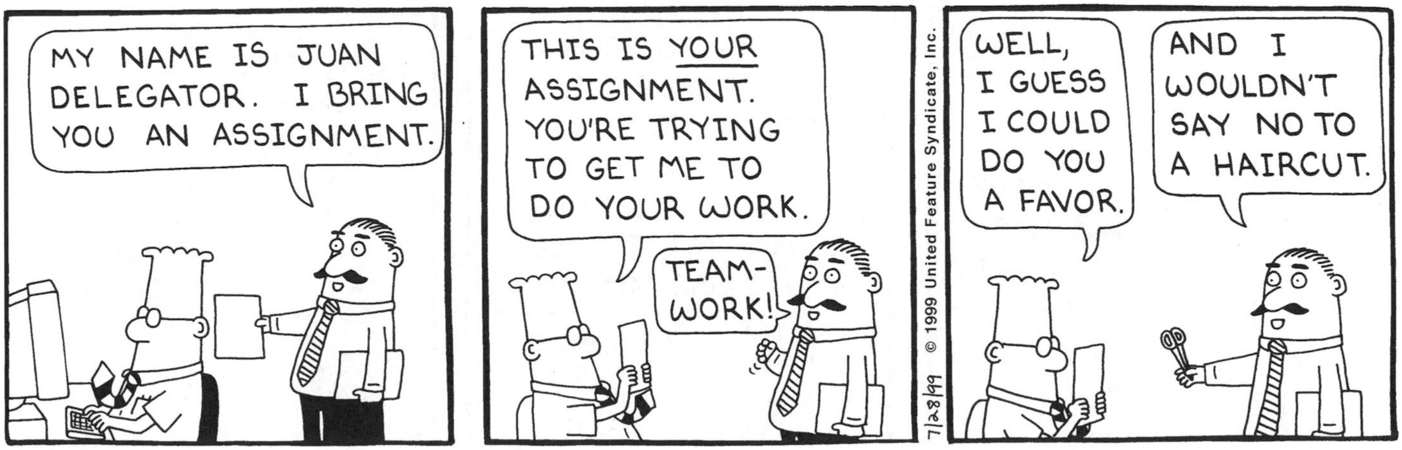
MY NAME IS JUAN DELEGATOR. I BRING YOU AN ASSIGNMENT.
THIS IS YOUR ASSIGNMENT. YOU'RE TRYING TO GET ME TO DO YOUR WORK.
TEAM-WORK!
7/28/99 © 1999 United Feature Syndicate, Inc.
WELL, I GUESS I COULD DO YOU A FAVOR.
AND I WOULDN'T SAY NO TO A HAIRCUT.

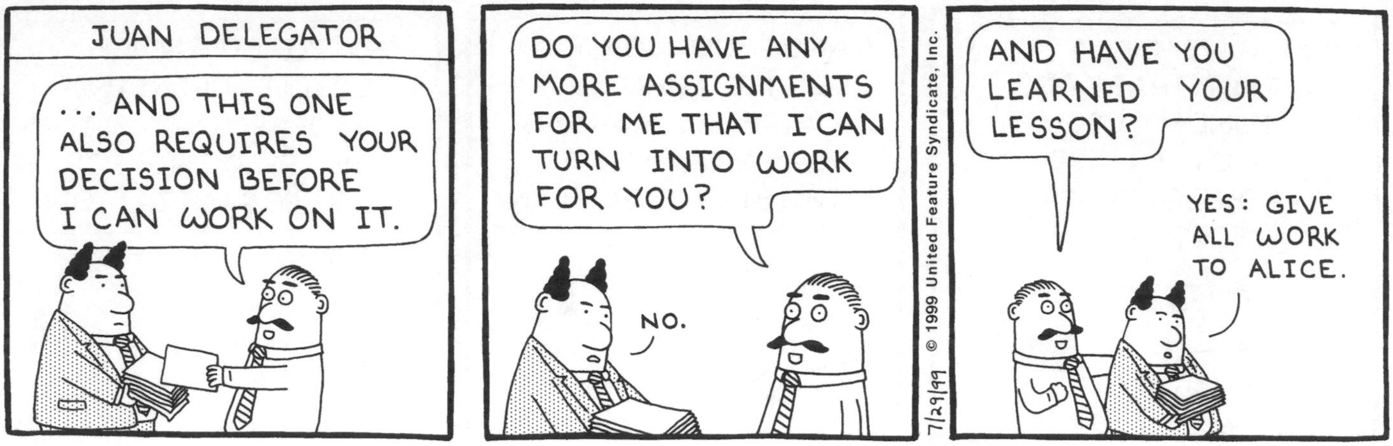
JUAN DELEGATOR
... AND THIS ONE ALSO REQUIRES YOUR DECISION BEFORE I CAN WORK ON IT.
DO YOU HAVE ANY MORE ASSIGNMENTS FOR ME THAT I CAN TURN INTO WORK FOR YOU?
NO.
7/29/99 © 1999 United Feature Syndicate, Inc.
AND HAVE YOU LEARNED YOUR LESSON?
YES: GIVE ALL WORK TO ALICE.

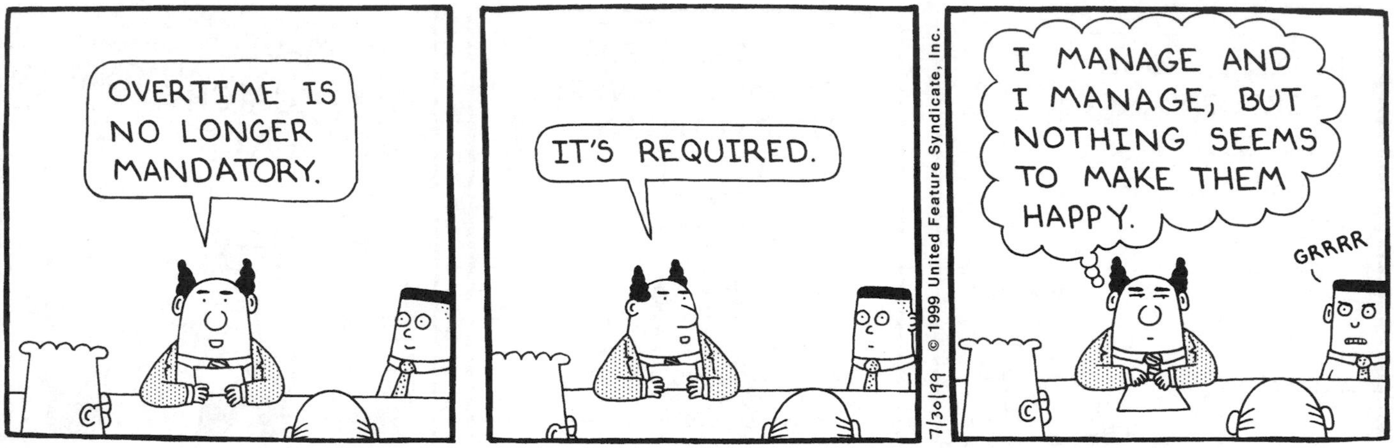
OVERTIME IS NO LONGER MANDATORY.
IT'S REQUIRED.
7/30/99 © 1999 United Feature Syndicate, Inc.
I MANAGE AND I MANAGE, BUT NOTHING SEEMS TO MAKE THEM HAPPY.
GRRRR

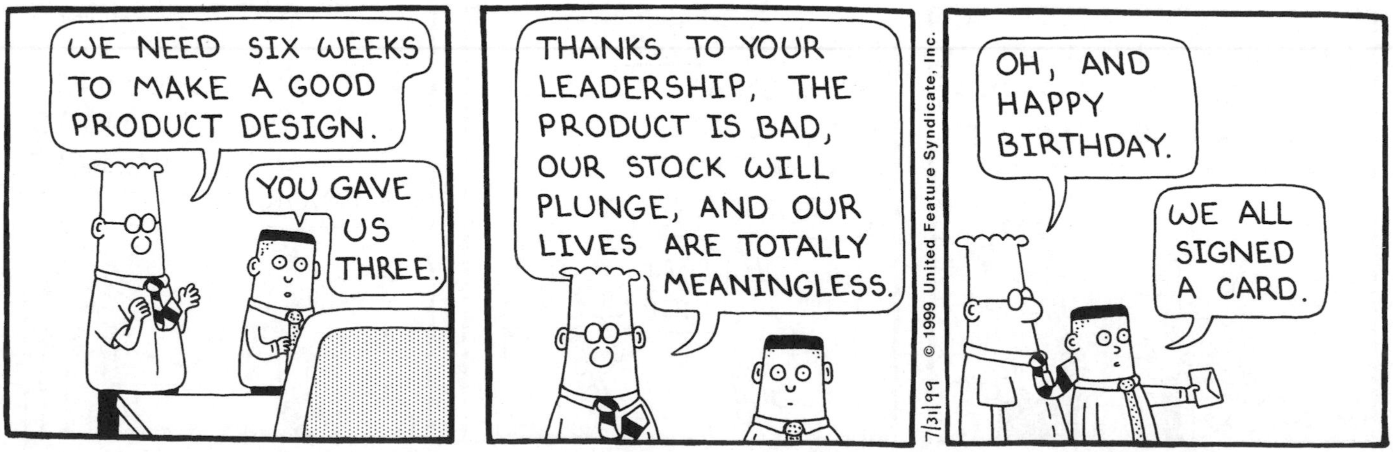
WE NEED SIX WEEKS TO MAKE A GOOD PRODUCT DESIGN.
YOU GAVE US THREE.
THANKS TO YOUR LEADERSHIP, THE PRODUCT IS BAD, OUR STOCK WILL PLUNGE, AND OUR LIVES ARE TOTALLY MEANINGLESS.
7/31/99 © 1999 United Feature Syndicate, Inc.
OH, AND HAPPY BIRTHDAY.
WE ALL SIGNED A CARD.

THE NEW POLICY FROM OUR CEO BANS COFFEE FROM CUBICLES.
BECAUSE, HE SAYS, "IT CAUSES A DISTRACTION" AND CAN "MESS UP DESKS."
HOW DID...
HOLD IT, DILBERT.
IT'S ALICE'S TURN.
YOU GET THE NEXT EASY ONE.
MAKE US PROUD.
AHEM, AHEM.
HOW DID HE BECOME A CEO...
...IF HE'S TOO STUPID TO DRINK COFFEE AND WORK AT THE SAME TIME?
CLAP
CLAP
OUR CEO ALSO DISCUSSED UNNECESSARY EXPENSES.
LUCKY!
AHEM.

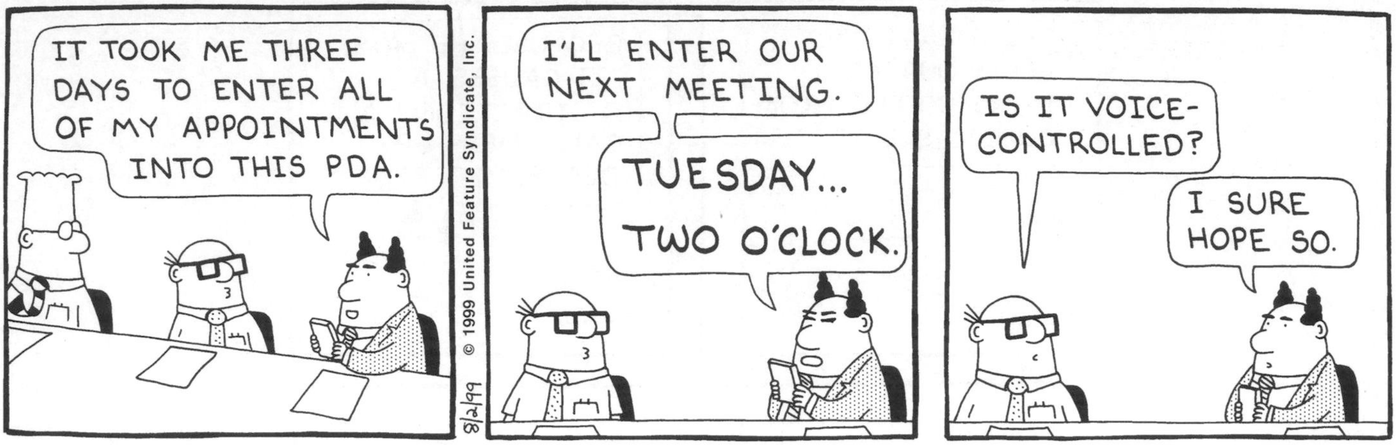
IT TOOK ME THREE DAYS TO ENTER ALL OF MY APPOINTMENTS INTO THIS PDA.
8/2/99 © 1999 United Feature Syndicate, Inc.
I'LL ENTER OUR NEXT MEETING.
TUESDAY... TWO O'CLOCK.
IS IT VOICE-CONTROLLED?
I SURE HOPE SO.

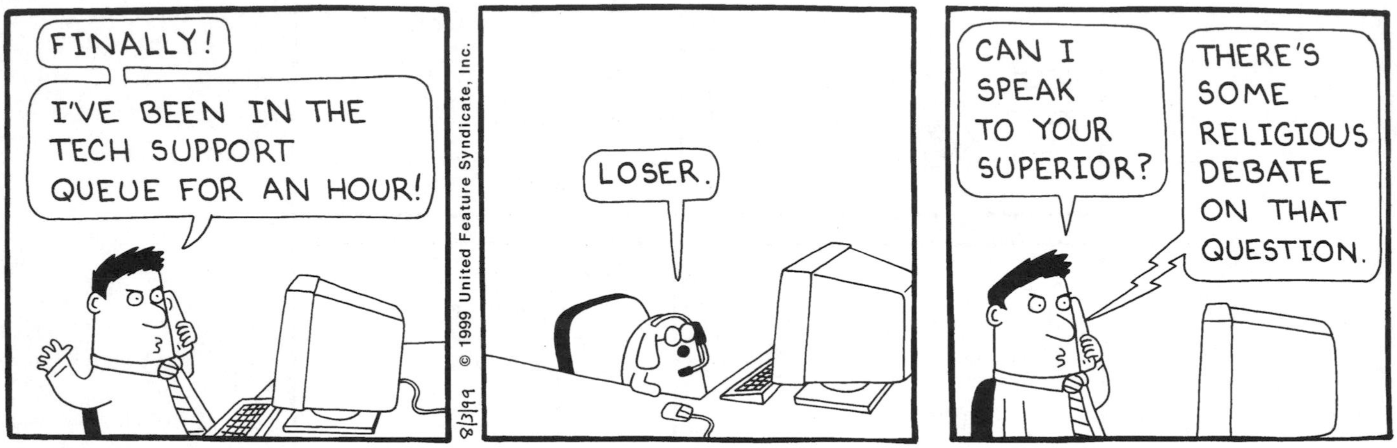
FINALLY!
I'VE BEEN IN THE TECH SUPPORT QUEUE FOR AN HOUR!
8/3/99 © 1999 United Feature Syndicate, Inc.
LOSER.
CAN I SPEAK TO YOUR SUPERIOR?
THERE'S SOME RELIGIOUS DEBATE ON THAT QUESTION.

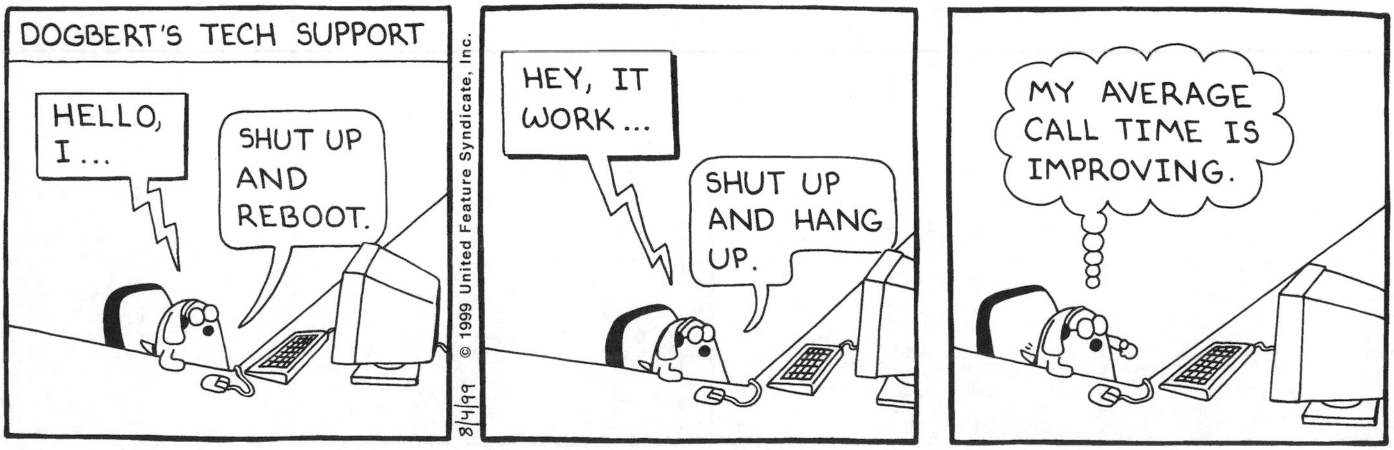
DOGBERT'S TECH SUPPORT
HELLO, I...
SHUT UP AND REBOOT.
8/4/99 © 1999 United Feature Syndicate, Inc.
HEY, IT WORK...
SHUT UP AND HANG UP.
MY AVERAGE CALL TIME IS IMPROVING.

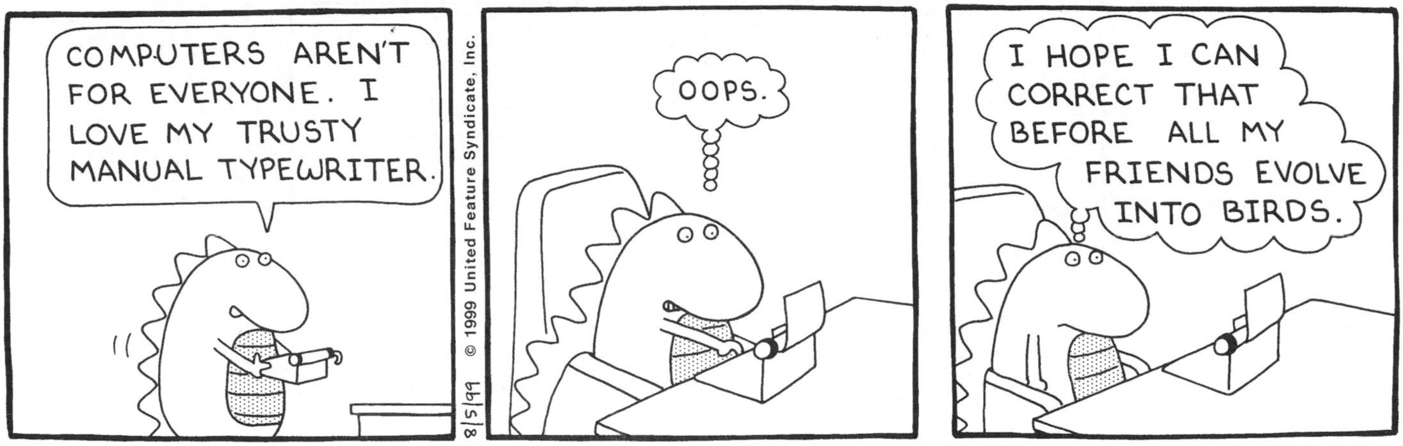
COMPUTERS AREN'T FOR EVERYONE. I LOVE MY TRUSTY MANUAL TYPEWRITER.
8/5/99 © 1999 United Feature Syndicate, Inc.
OOPS.
I HOPE I CAN CORRECT THAT BEFORE ALL MY FRIENDS EVOLVE INTO BIRDS.

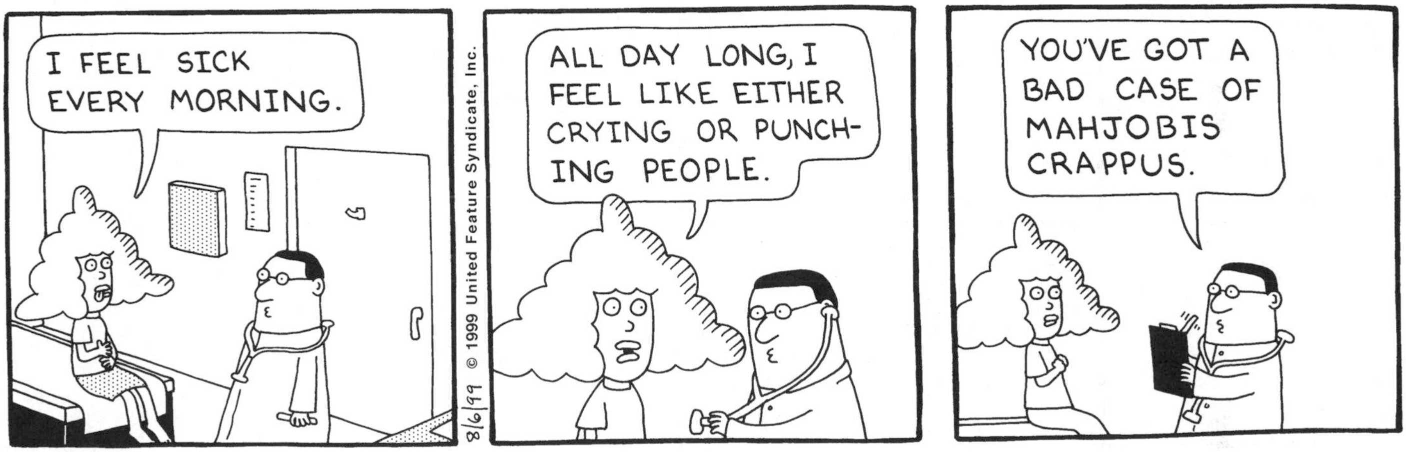
I FEEL SICK EVERY MORNING.
8/6/99 © 1999 United Feature Syndicate, Inc.
ALL DAY LONG, I FEEL LIKE EITHER CRYING OR PUNCH-ING PEOPLE.
YOU'VE GOT A BAD CASE OF MAHJOBIS CRAPPUS.

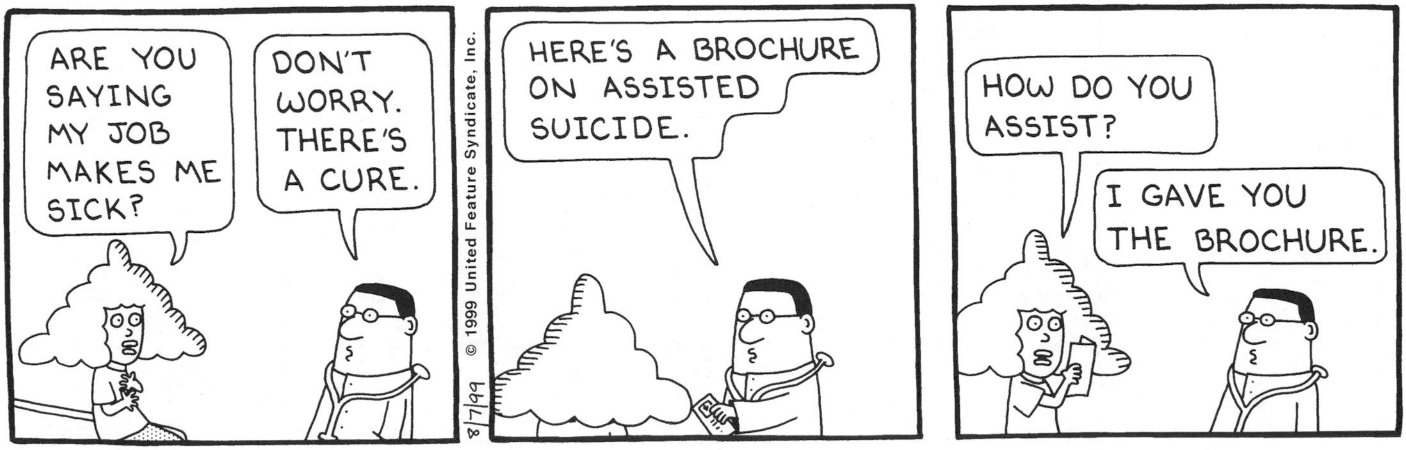
ARE YOU SAYING MY JOB MAKES ME SICK?
DON'T WORRY. THERE'S A CURE.
8/7/99 © 1999 United Feature Syndicate, Inc.
HERE'S A BROCHURE ON ASSISTED SUICIDE.
HOW DO YOU ASSIST?
I GAVE YOU THE BROCHURE.

YOU'RE A TOUGH NEGOTIATOR, BUT I THINK WE HAVE A DEAL.
JUST SIGN THE CONTRACT AND WE'LL DELIVER THE EQUIPMENT.
THIS CONTRACT IS TOTALLY DIFFERENT FROM WHAT WE AGREED.
MUST ACT SURPRISED.
REALLY?
WHY ARE YOU SPRINGING ALL THESE CONDITIONS ON ME AT THE LAST MINUTE?
© 1999 United Feature Syndicate, Inc.
3/8/99
NO ONE HAS EVER COMPLAINED BEFORE.
MAY I BORROW YOUR BRIEFCASE FOR A MINUTE?
UM... OKAY.
THAT WASN'T NICE.
NO ONE HAS COMPLAINED BEFORE.

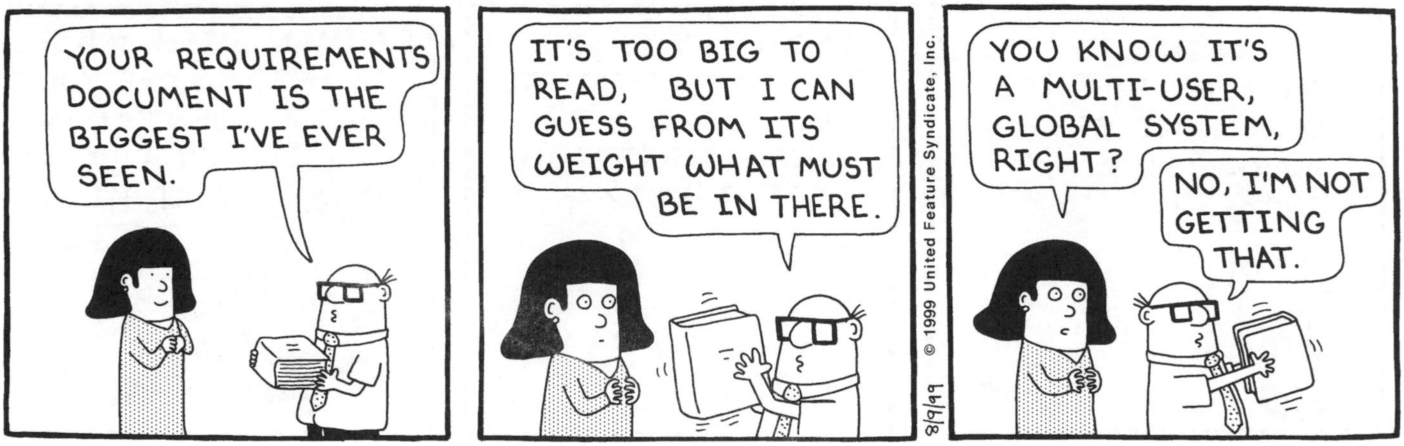
YOUR REQUIREMENTS DOCUMENT IS THE BIGGEST I'VE EVER SEEN.
IT'S TOO BIG TO READ, BUT I CAN GUESS FROM ITS WEIGHT WHAT MUST BE IN THERE.
YOU KNOW IT'S A MULTI-USER, GLOBAL SYSTEM, RIGHT?
NO, I'M NOT GETTING THAT.
8/9/99 © 1999 United Feature Syndicate, Inc.

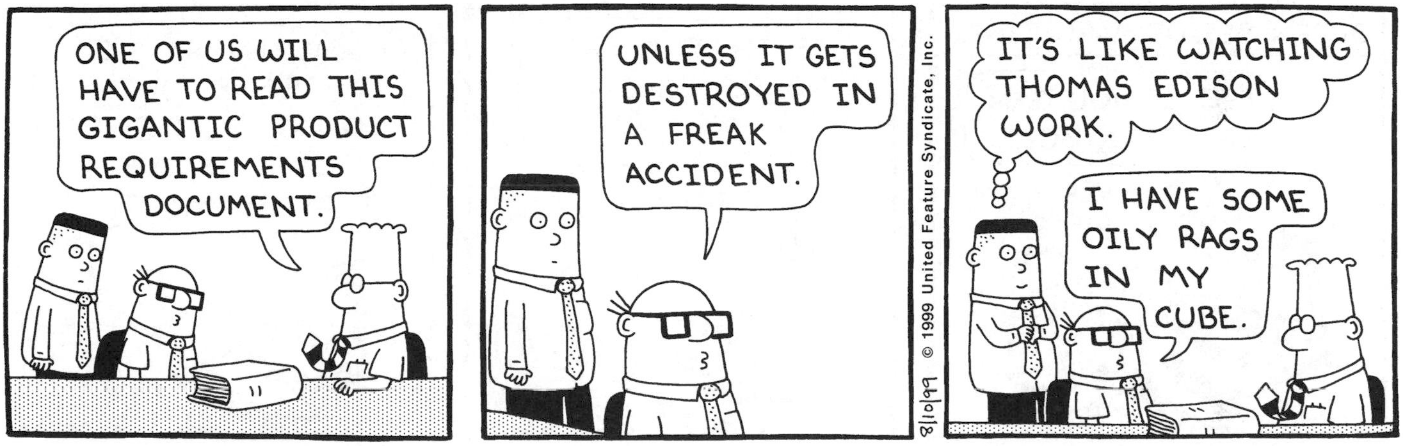
ONE OF US WILL HAVE TO READ THIS GIGANTIC PRODUCT REQUIREMENTS DOCUMENT.
UNLESS IT GETS DESTROYED IN A FREAK ACCIDENT.
IT'S LIKE WATCHING THOMAS EDISON WORK.
I HAVE SOME OILY RAGS IN MY CUBE.
8/10/99 © 1999 United Feature Syndicate, Inc.

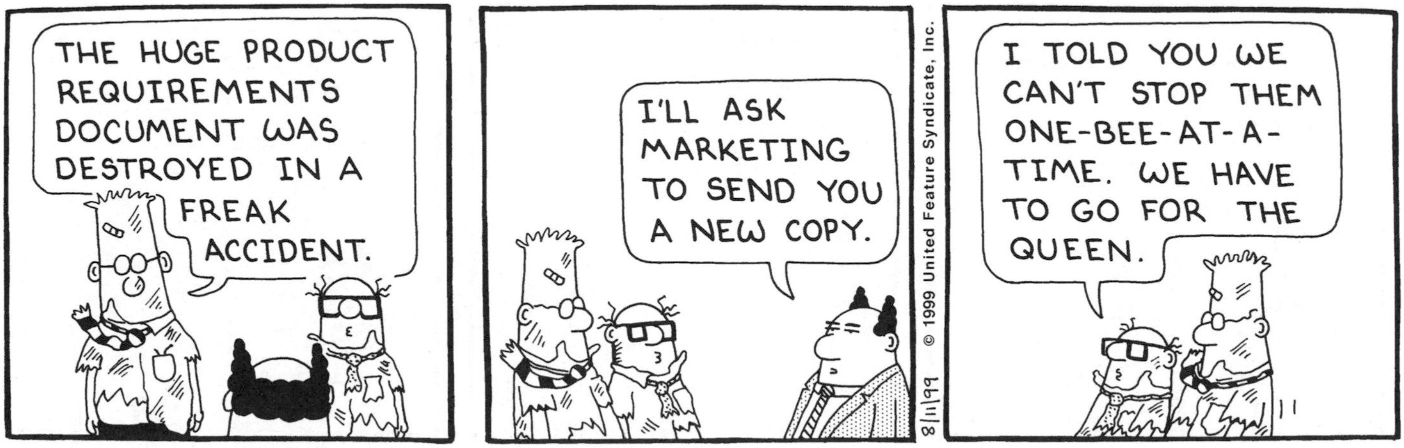
THE HUGE PRODUCT REQUIREMENTS DOCUMENT WAS DESTROYED IN A FREAK ACCIDENT.
I'LL ASK MARKETING TO SEND YOU A NEW COPY.
I TOLD YOU WE CAN'T STOP THEM ONE-BEE-AT-A-TIME. WE HAVE TO GO FOR THE QUEEN.
8/11/99 © 1999 United Feature Syndicate, Inc.

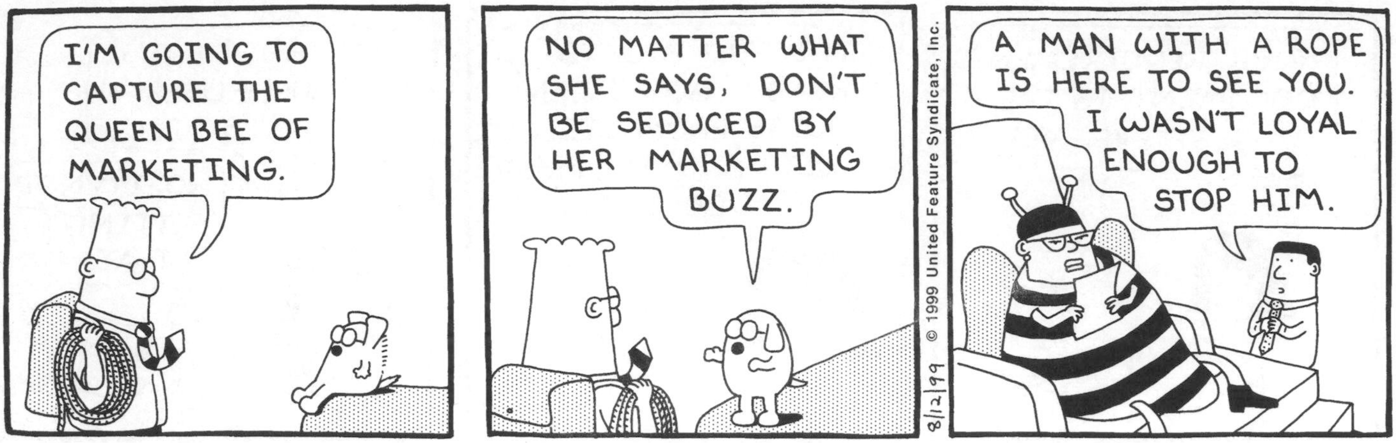
I'M GOING TO CAPTURE THE QUEEN BEE OF MARKETING.
NO MATTER WHAT SHE SAYS, DON'T BE SEDUCED BY HER MARKETING BUZZ.
8/12/99 © 1999 United Feature Syndicate, Inc.
A MAN WITH A ROPE IS HERE TO SEE YOU.
I WASN'T LOYAL ENOUGH TO STOP HIM.

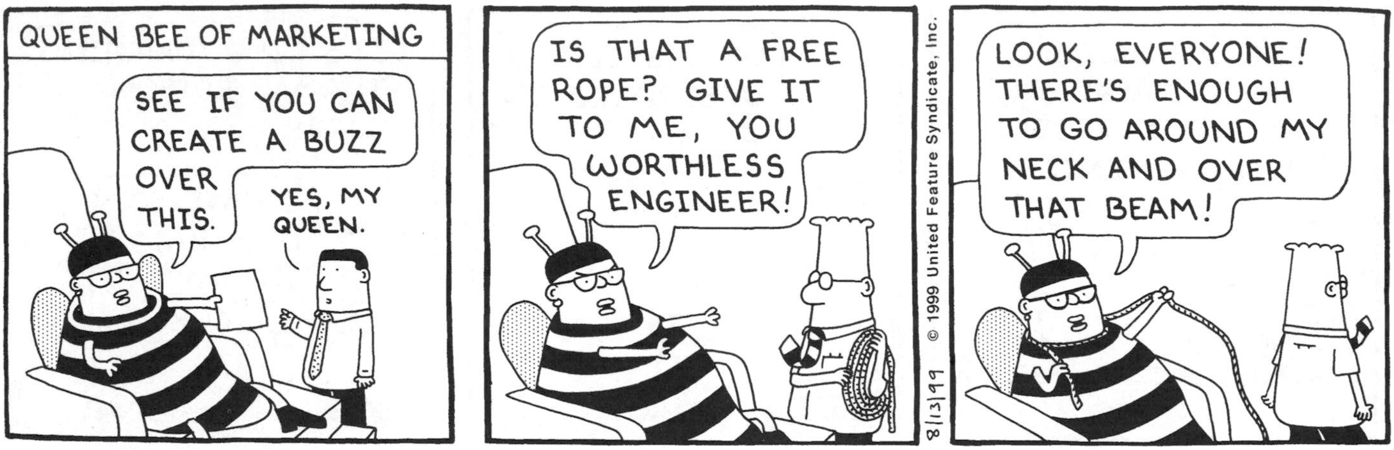
QUEEN BEE OF MARKETING
SEE IF YOU CAN CREATE A BUZZ OVER THIS.
YES, MY QUEEN.
IS THAT A FREE ROPE? GIVE IT TO ME, YOU WORTHLESS ENGINEER!
8/13/99 © 1999 United Feature Syndicate, Inc.
LOOK, EVERYONE! THERE'S ENOUGH TO GO AROUND MY NECK AND OVER THAT BEAM!

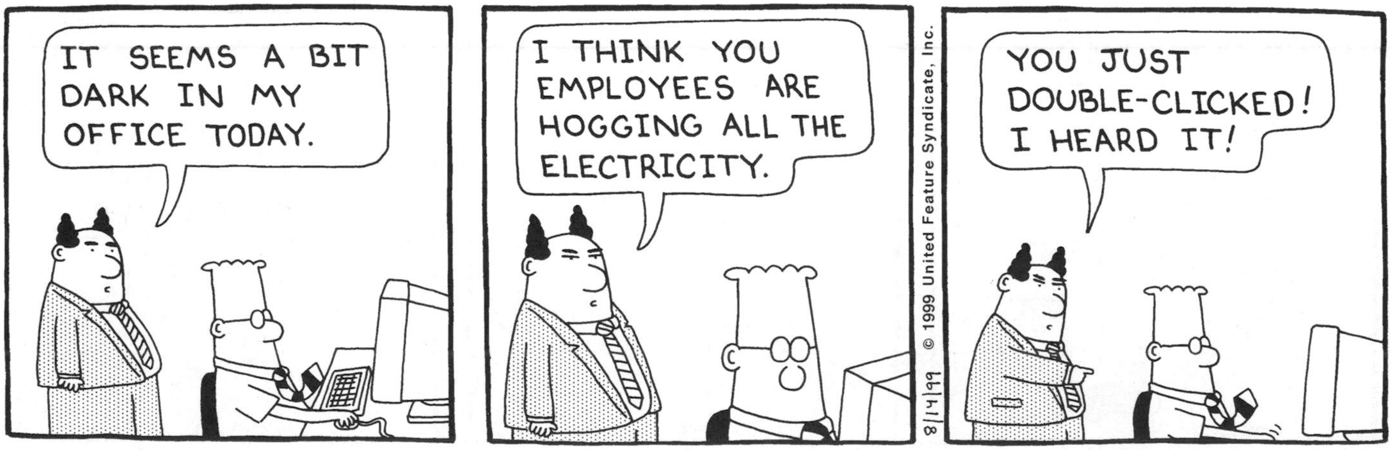
IT SEEMS A BIT DARK IN MY OFFICE TODAY.
I THINK YOU EMPLOYEES ARE HOGGING ALL THE ELECTRICITY.
8/14/99 © 1999 United Feature Syndicate, Inc.
YOU JUST DOUBLE-CLICKED! I HEARD IT!

THE POINTY-HAIRED BOSS WANTS TO SEE YOU.
HE TRIED TO REACH YOU BY PHONE, E-MAIL, AND PAGER.
BUT YOU RESISTED HIS ELECTRONIC ATTEMPTS TO RUIN YOUR PRODUCTIVITY.
SO HE DECIDED TO SEND IN THE GROUND TROOPS.
DON'T MAKE ME USE THIS!
8/5/99 © 1999 United Feature Syndicate, Inc.
COULD YOU WAIT OUTSIDE WHILE I RETURN SOME PHONE CALLS?
GET TO THE BACK OF THE LINE.
DOES ANYONE WANT TO HAVE A CONVER-SATION?
I HAVE A MAGAZINE.

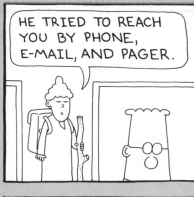

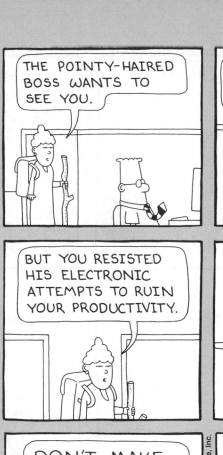

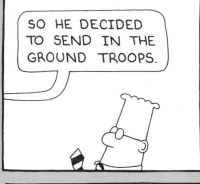

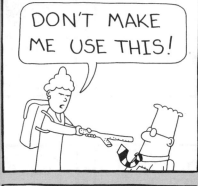

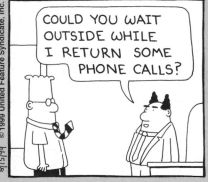

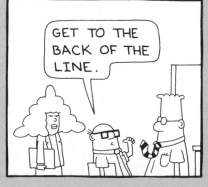

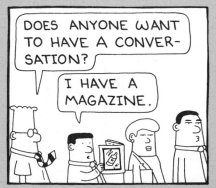

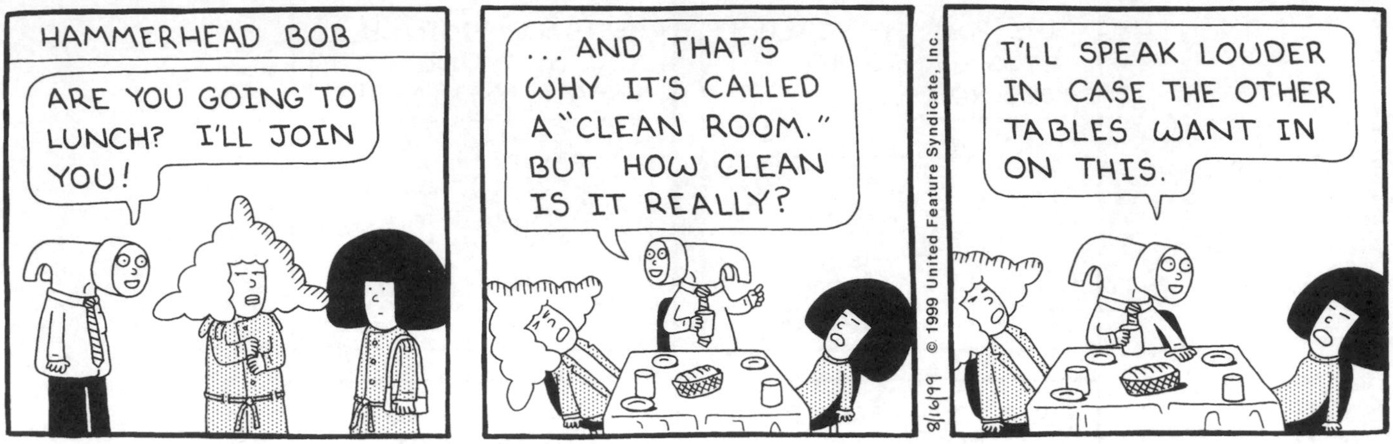
HAMMERHEAD BOB
ARE YOU GOING TO LUNCH? I'LL JOIN YOU!
... AND THAT'S WHY IT'S CALLED A "CLEAN ROOM." BUT HOW CLEAN IS IT REALLY?
8/16/99 © 1999 United Feature Syndicate, Inc.
I'LL SPEAK LOUDER IN CASE THE OTHER TABLES WANT IN ON THIS.

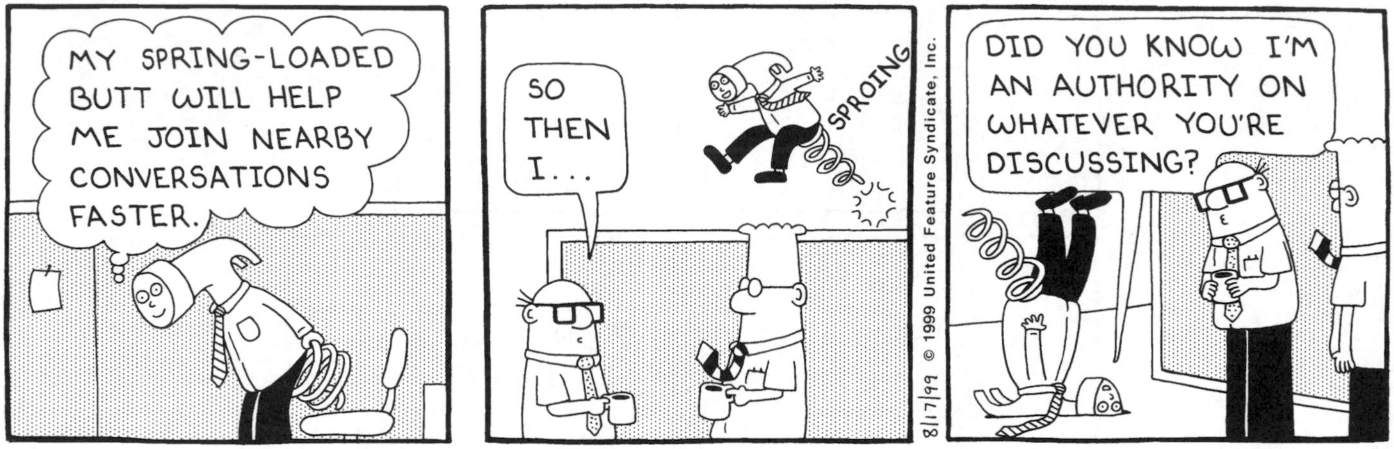
MY SPRING-LOADED BUTT WILL HELP ME JOIN NEARBY CONVERSATIONS FASTER.
SO THEN I...
SPROING
8/17/99 © 1999 United Feature Syndicate, Inc.
DID YOU KNOW I'M AN AUTHORITY ON WHATEVER YOU'RE DISCUSSING?

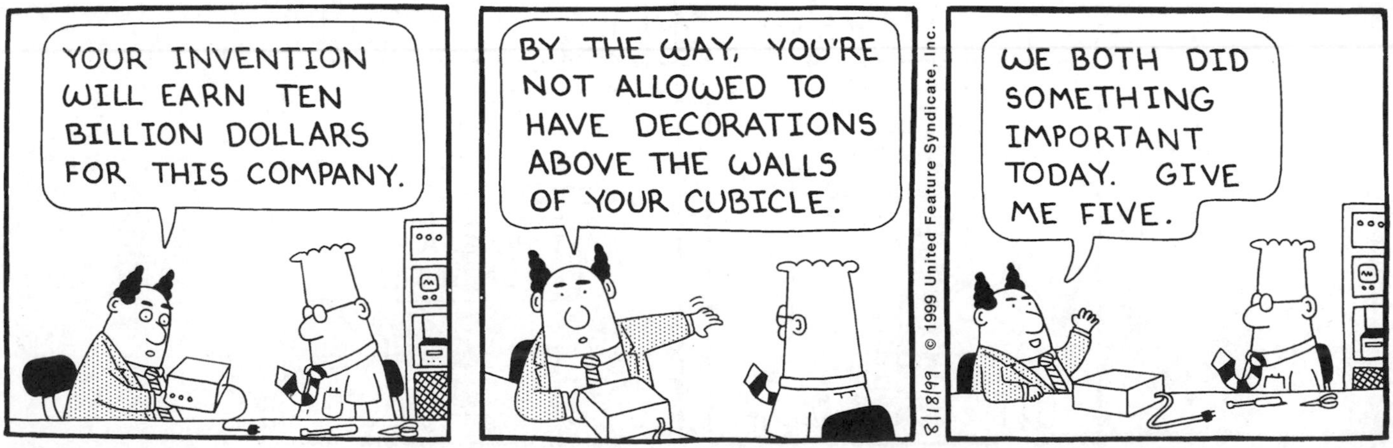
YOUR INVENTION WILL EARN TEN BILLION DOLLARS FOR THIS COMPANY.
BY THE WAY, YOU'RE NOT ALLOWED TO HAVE DECORATIONS ABOVE THE WALLS OF YOUR CUBICLE.
8/18/99 © 1999 United Feature Syndicate, Inc.
WE BOTH DID SOMETHING IMPORTANT TODAY. GIVE ME FIVE.

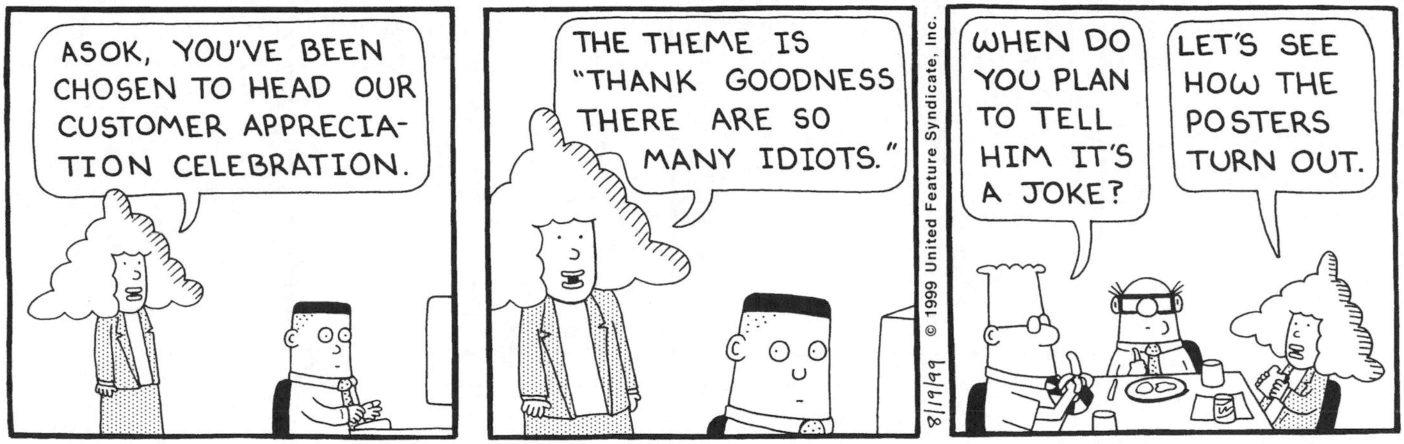
ASOK, YOU'VE BEEN CHOSEN TO HEAD OUR CUSTOMER APPRECIATION CELEBRATION.
THE THEME IS "THANK GOODNESS THERE ARE SO MANY IDIOTS."
8/19/99 © 1999 United Feature Syndicate, Inc.
WHEN DO YOU PLAN TO TELL HIM IT'S A JOKE?
LET'S SEE HOW THE POSTERS TURN OUT.

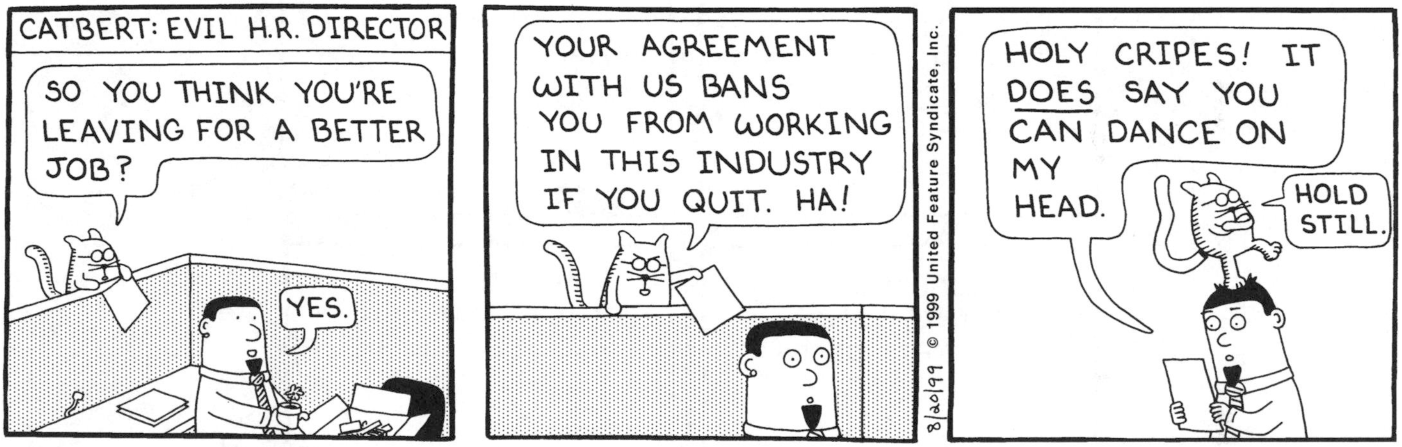
CATBERT: EVIL H.R. DIRECTOR
SO YOU THINK YOU'RE LEAVING FOR A BETTER JOB?
YES.
YOUR AGREEMENT WITH US BANS YOU FROM WORKING IN THIS INDUSTRY IF YOU QUIT. HA!
8/20/99 © 1999 United Feature Syndicate, Inc.
HOLY CRIPES! IT DOES SAY YOU CAN DANCE ON MY HEAD.
HOLD STILL.

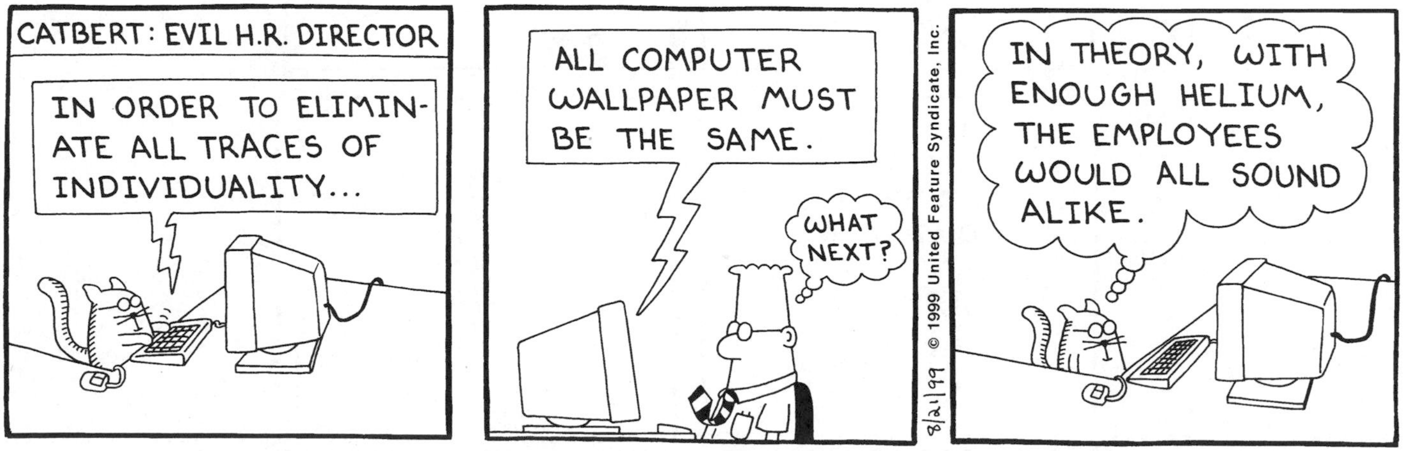
CATBERT: EVIL H.R. DIRECTOR
IN ORDER TO ELIMINATE ALL TRACES OF INDIVIDUALITY...
ALL COMPUTER WALLPAPER MUST BE THE SAME.
WHAT NEXT?
8/21/99 © 1999 United Feature Syndicate, Inc.
IN THEORY, WITH ENOUGH HELIUM, THE EMPLOYEES WOULD ALL SOUND ALIKE.

THERE'S NO REASON TO BE STRESSED, ALICE.
ALLOW ME TO BE YOUR ROLE MODEL.
I REMAIN CALM DESPITE THE PRESSURE OF IMPOSSIBLE DEADLINES.
THAT'S BECAUSE YOU HAVE NO PRIDE AND NO AMBITION!
I'VE WORKED DAY AND NIGHT TO MAKE THIS DEAD-LINE!
AND WHEN I SUCCEED, THE GLORY WILL BE MINE!
OUR NEW VP JUST CANCELED THE PROJECT SO THE LAST VP WOULD LOOK BAD.
THEY SAY THAT WHEN THE STUDENT IS READY, THE MASTER WILL APPEAR.

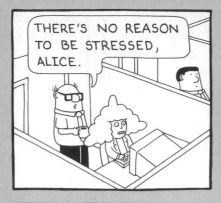

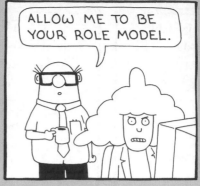

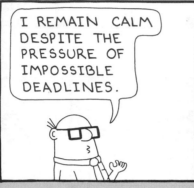

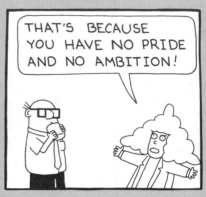

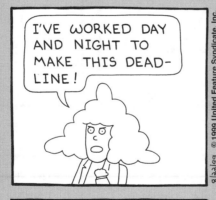

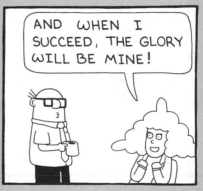

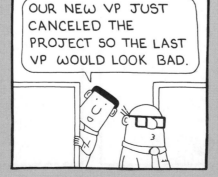

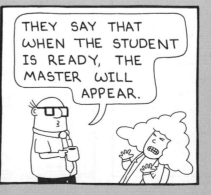

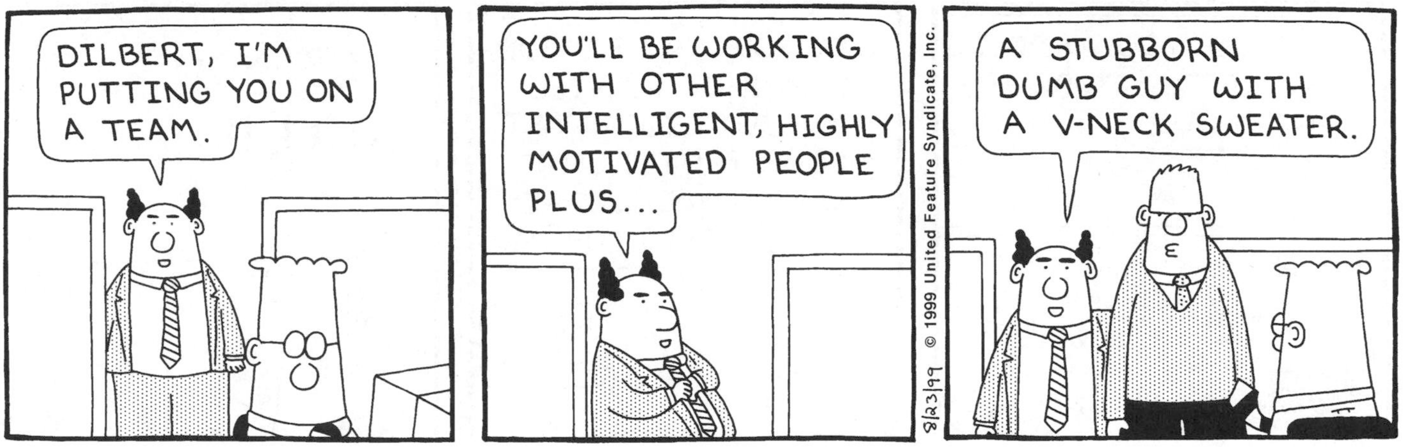
DILBERT, I'M PUTTING YOU ON A TEAM.
YOU'LL BE WORKING WITH OTHER INTELLIGENT, HIGHLY MOTIVATED PEOPLE PLUS...
8/23/99 © 1999 United Feature Syndicate, Inc.
A STUBBORN DUMB GUY WITH A V-NECK SWEATER.

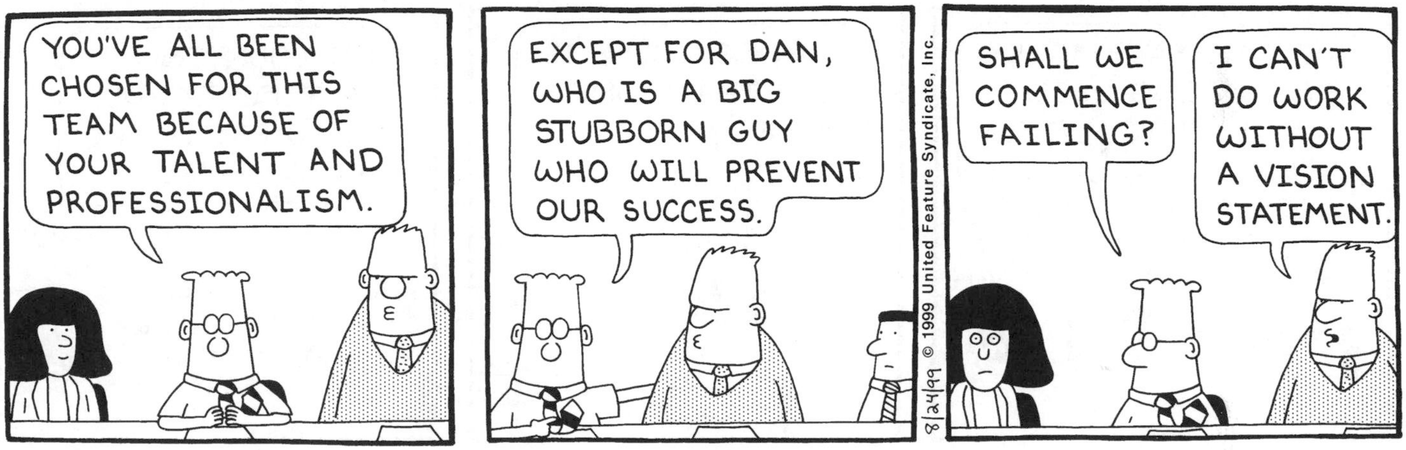
YOU'VE ALL BEEN CHOSEN FOR THIS TEAM BECAUSE OF YOUR TALENT AND PROFESSIONALISM.
EXCEPT FOR DAN, WHO IS A BIG STUBBORN GUY WHO WILL PREVENT OUR SUCCESS.
8/24/99 © 1999 United Feature Syndicate, Inc.
SHALL WE COMMENCE FAILING?
I CAN'T DO WORK WITHOUT A VISION STATEMENT.

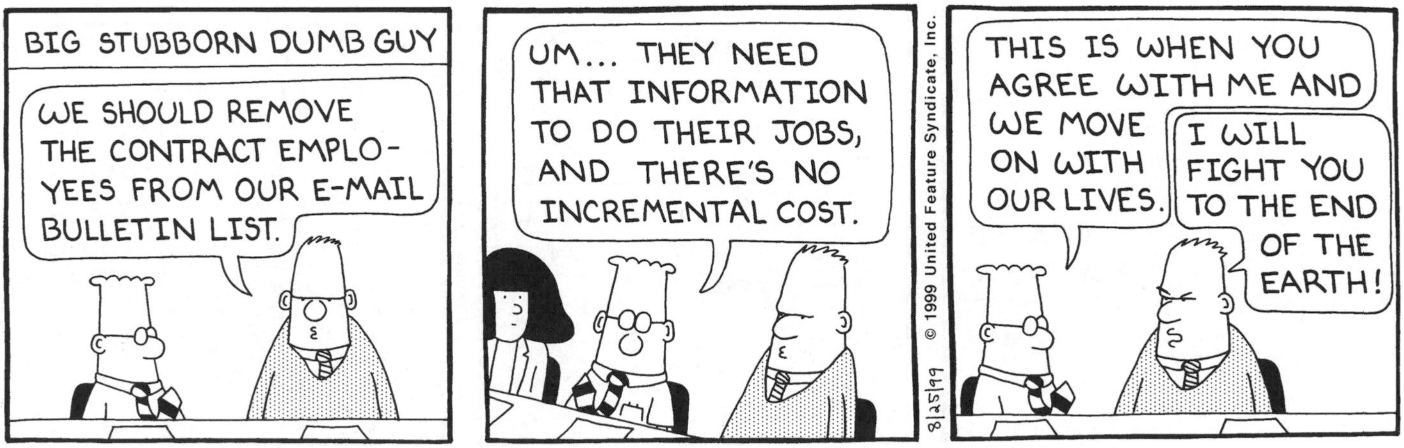
BIG STUBBORN DUMB GUY
WE SHOULD REMOVE THE CONTRACT EMPLO-YEES FROM OUR E-MAIL BULLETIN LIST.
UM... THEY NEED THAT INFORMATION TO DO THEIR JOBS, AND THERE'S NO INCREMENTAL COST.
8/25/99 © 1999 United Feature Syndicate, Inc.
THIS IS WHEN YOU AGREE WITH ME AND WE MOVE ON WITH OUR LIVES.
I WILL FIGHT YOU TO THE END OF THE EARTH!

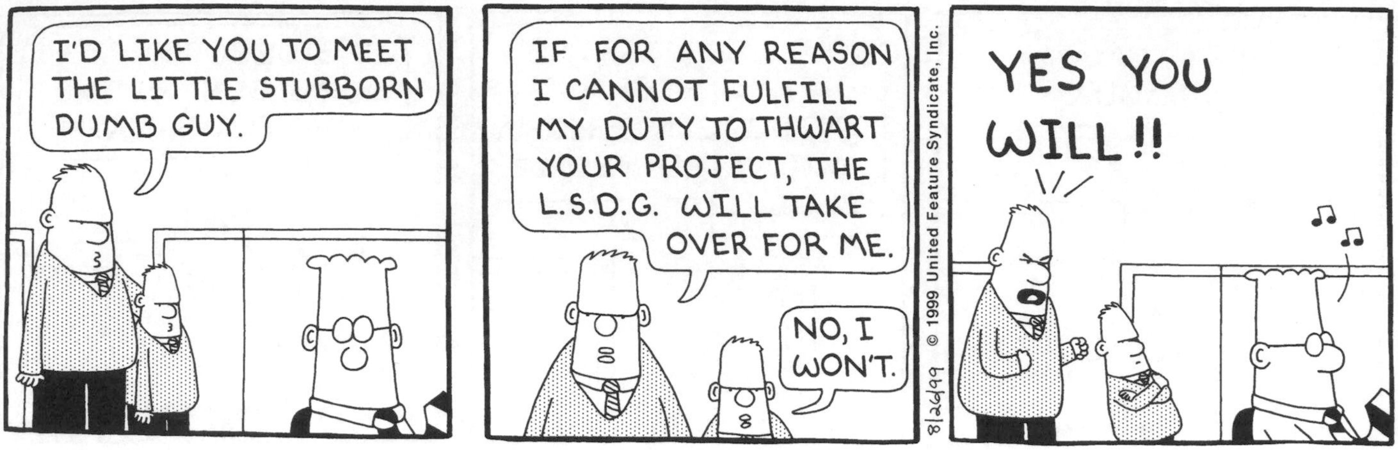
I'D LIKE YOU TO MEET THE LITTLE STUBBORN DUMB GUY.
IF FOR ANY REASON I CANNOT FULFILL MY DUTY TO THWART YOUR PROJECT, THE L.S.D.G. WILL TAKE OVER FOR ME.
NO, I WON'T.
8/26/99 © 1999 United Feature Syndicate, Inc.
YES YOU WILL!!

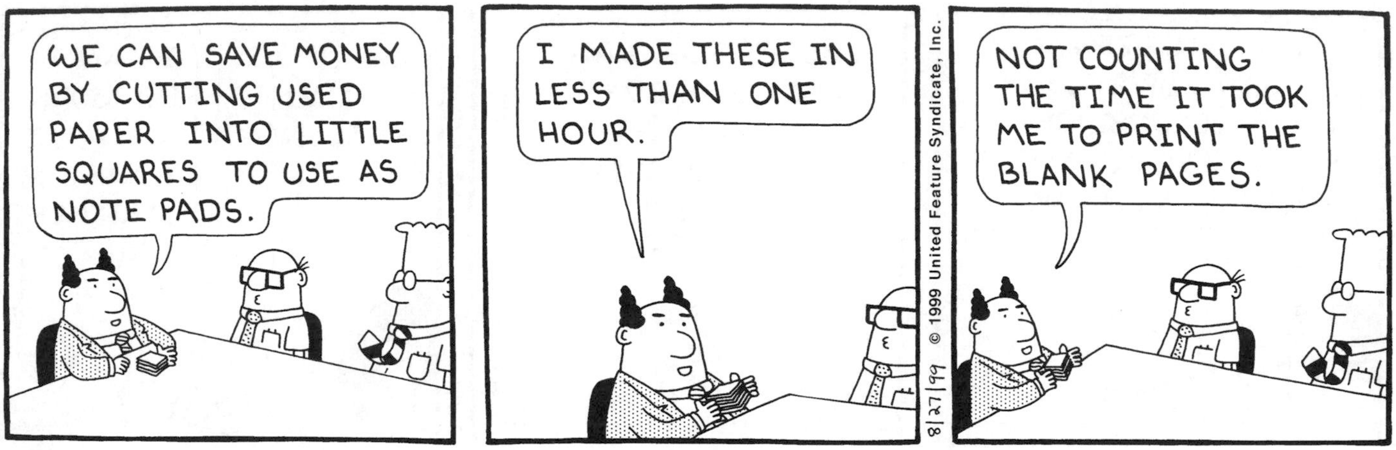
WE CAN SAVE MONEY BY CUTTING USED PAPER INTO LITTLE SQUARES TO USE AS NOTE PADS.
I MADE THESE IN LESS THAN ONE HOUR.
8/27/99 © 1999 United Feature Syndicate, Inc.
NOT COUNTING THE TIME IT TOOK ME TO PRINT THE BLANK PAGES.

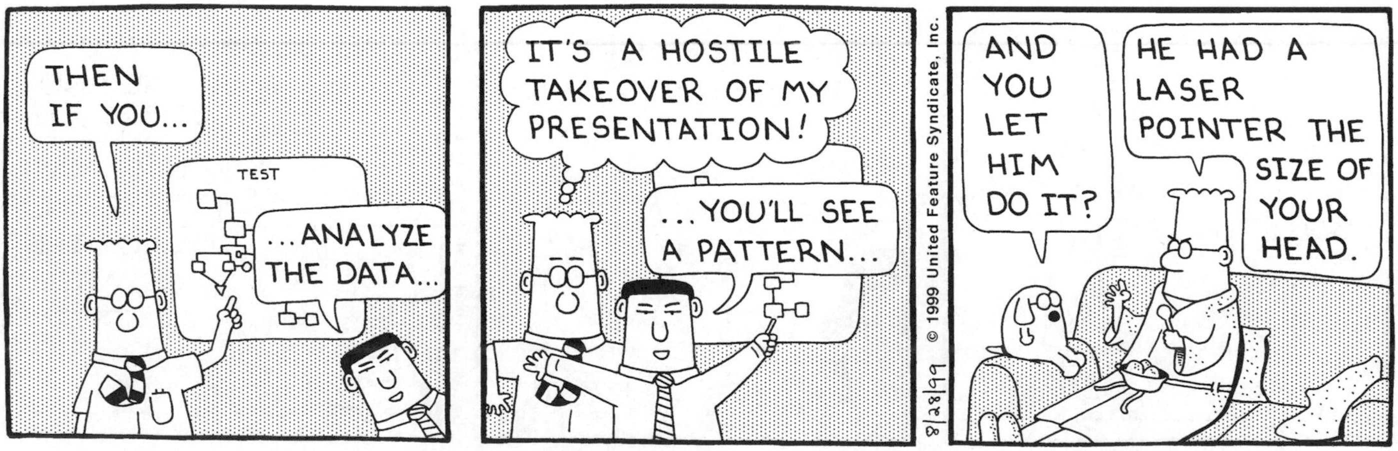
THEN IF YOU...
TEST
...ANALYZE THE DATA...
IT'S A HOSTILE TAKEOVER OF MY PRESENTATION!
...YOU'LL SEE A PATTERN...
8/28/99 © 1999 United Feature Syndicate, Inc.
AND YOU LET HIM DO IT?
HE HAD A LASER POINTER THE SIZE OF YOUR HEAD.

REMOVE THAT LAST BULLET POINT. IT'S STUPID.
GASP
YESTERDAY YOU TOLD ME TO ADD THAT BULLET POINT.
SO EITHER YOU WERE WRONG TODAY OR YOU WERE WRONG YESTERDAY.
EVERYONE COME QUICKLY! HE HAS TO ADMIT HE'S WRONG!
8/29/99 © 1999 United Feature Syndicate, Inc.
SAY IT.
ALICE HEARD ME WRONG YESTERDAY.
IT TAKES A BIG MAN TO ADMIT ALICE IS WRONG.
CAN YOU HEAR US, ALICE?

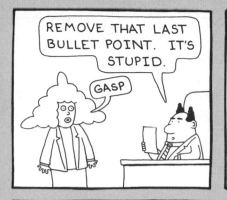

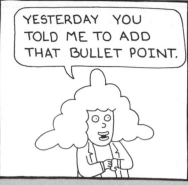

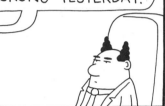

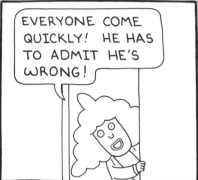

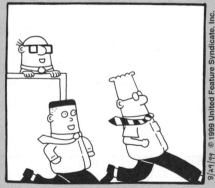

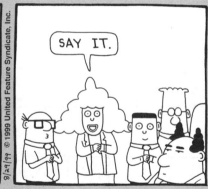

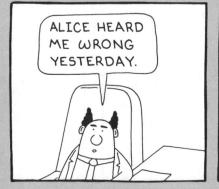

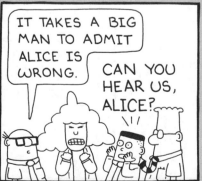

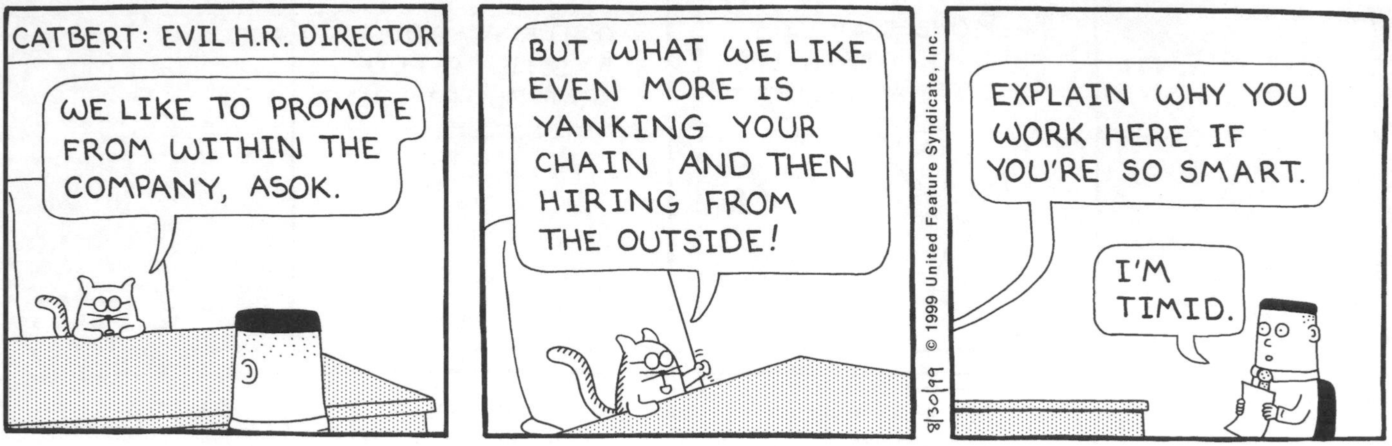
CATBERT: EVIL H.R. DIRECTOR
WE LIKE TO PROMOTE FROM WITHIN THE COMPANY, ASOK.
BUT WHAT WE LIKE EVEN MORE IS YANKING YOUR CHAIN AND THEN HIRING FROM THE OUTSIDE!
8/30/99 © 1999 United Feature Syndicate, Inc.
EXPLAIN WHY YOU WORK HERE IF YOU'RE SO SMART.
I'M TIMID.

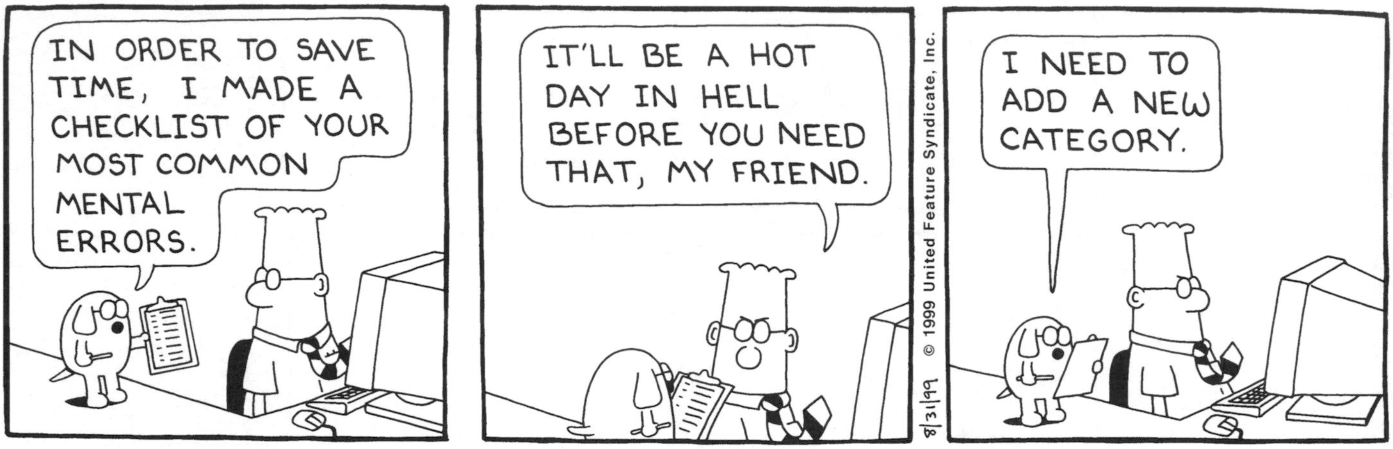
IN ORDER TO SAVE TIME, I MADE A CHECKLIST OF YOUR MOST COMMON MENTAL ERRORS.
IT'LL BE A HOT DAY IN HELL BEFORE YOU NEED THAT, MY FRIEND.
8/31/99 © 1999 United Feature Syndicate, Inc.
I NEED TO ADD A NEW CATEGORY.

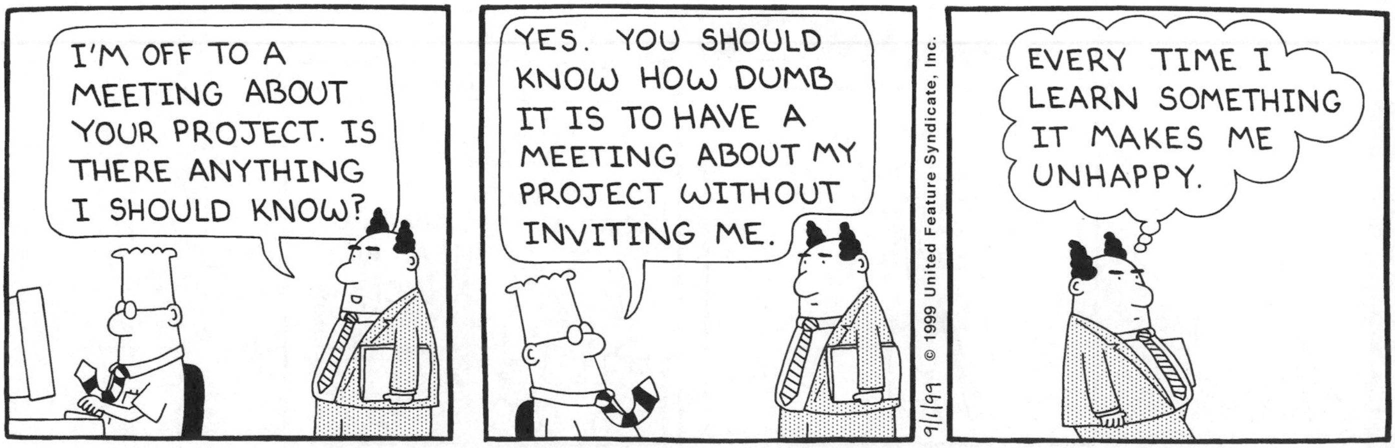
I'M OFF TO A MEETING ABOUT YOUR PROJECT. IS THERE ANYTHING I SHOULD KNOW?
YES. YOU SHOULD KNOW HOW DUMB IT IS TO HAVE A MEETING ABOUT MY PROJECT WITHOUT INVITING ME.
9/1/99 © 1999 United Feature Syndicate, Inc.
EVERY TIME I LEARN SOMETHING IT MAKES ME UNHAPPY.

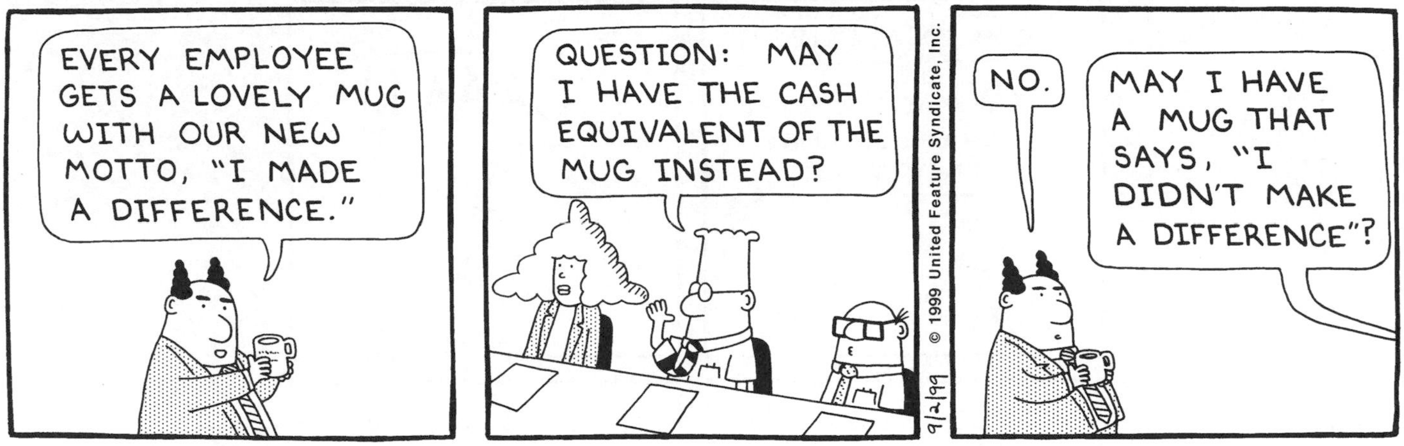
EVERY EMPLOYEE GETS A LOVELY MUG WITH OUR NEW MOTTO, "I MADE A DIFFERENCE."
QUESTION: MAY I HAVE THE CASH EQUIVALENT OF THE MUG INSTEAD?
9/2/99 © 1999 United Feature Syndicate, Inc.
NO.
MAY I HAVE A MUG THAT SAYS, "I DIDN'T MAKE A DIFFERENCE"?

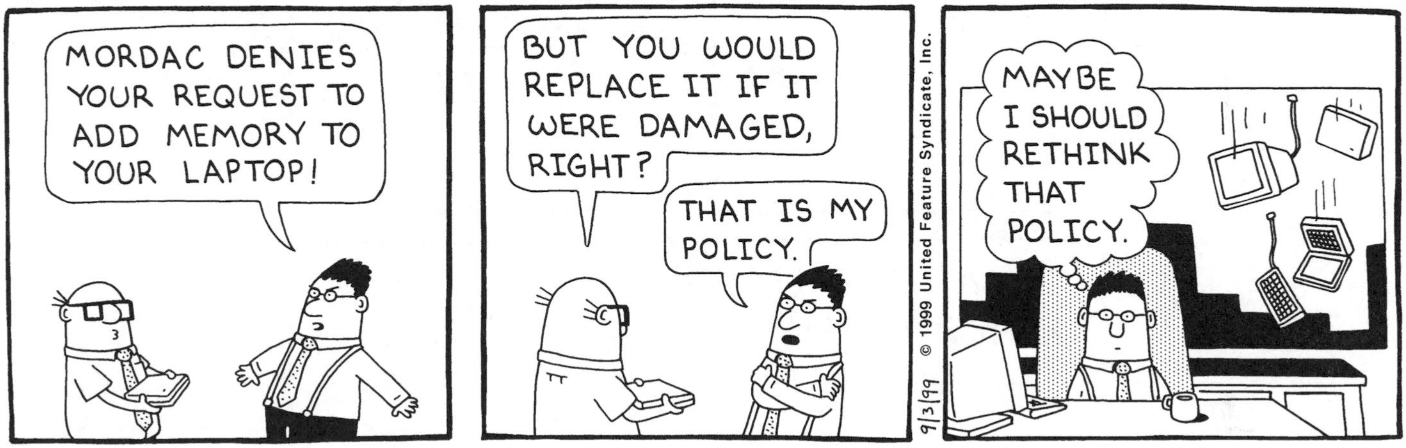
MORDAC DENIES YOUR REQUEST TO ADD MEMORY TO YOUR LAPTOP!
BUT YOU WOULD REPLACE IT IF IT WERE DAMAGED, RIGHT?
THAT IS MY POLICY.
9/3/99 © 1999 United Feature Syndicate, Inc.
MAYBE I SHOULD RETHINK THAT POLICY.

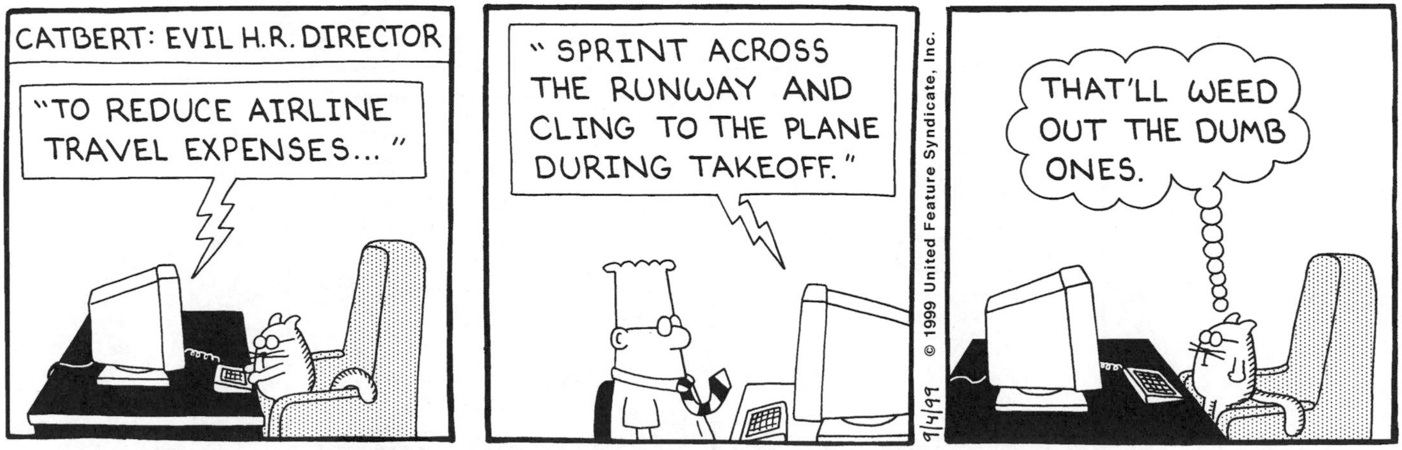
CATBERT: EVIL H.R. DIRECTOR
"TO REDUCE AIRLINE TRAVEL EXPENSES..."
"SPRINT ACROSS THE RUNWAY AND CLING TO THE PLANE DURING TAKEOFF."
9/4/99 © 1999 United Feature Syndicate, Inc.
THAT'LL WEED OUT THE DUMB ONES.

GOOD IDEA, DILBERT.
I MADE A FEW CHANGES AND SENT IT OUT.
GAAA!
YOU REMOVED THE PARTS THAT MADE IT A VISIONARY IDEA!
NOW IT'S JUST AN UNIMAGINATIVE RETREAD OF AN IDEA THAT HAS BEEN WIDELY DISCREDITED.
GAAA! AND IT HAS MY NAME ON IT!
9/5/99 © 1999 United Feature Syndicate, Inc.
THAT IDEA WAS THE ENERGIZING FORCE THAT GAVE ME STRENGTH TO WORK.
NOW IT'S DEAD! YOU KILLED IT!
I'D LOVE TO CHAT BUT I HAVE TO MANAGE SOMEONE ELSE NOW.
GURGLE

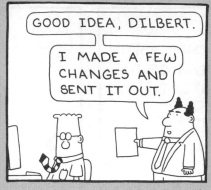

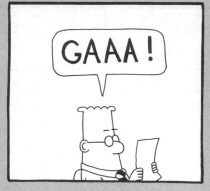

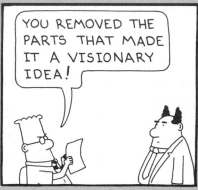

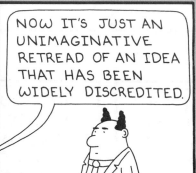

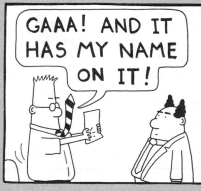

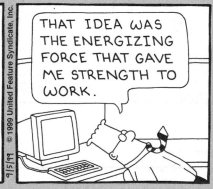

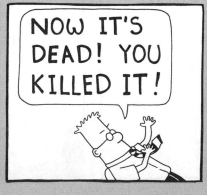

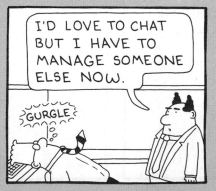

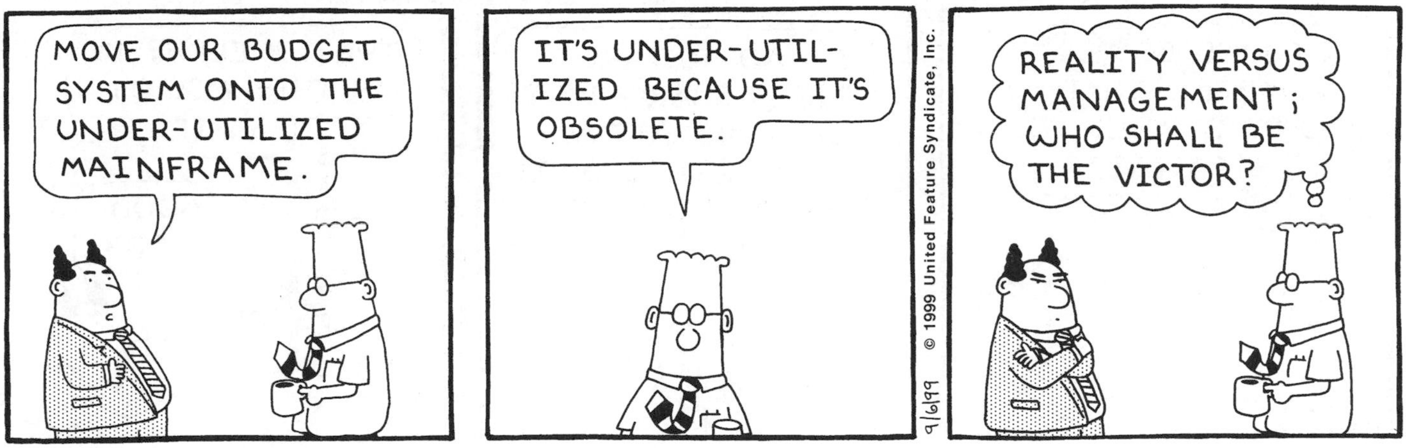
MOVE OUR BUDGET SYSTEM ONTO THE UNDER-UTILIZED MAINFRAME.
IT'S UNDER-UTILIZED BECAUSE IT'S OBSOLETE.
9/6/99 © 1999 United Feature Syndicate, Inc.
REALITY VERSUS MANAGEMENT; WHO SHALL BE THE VICTOR?

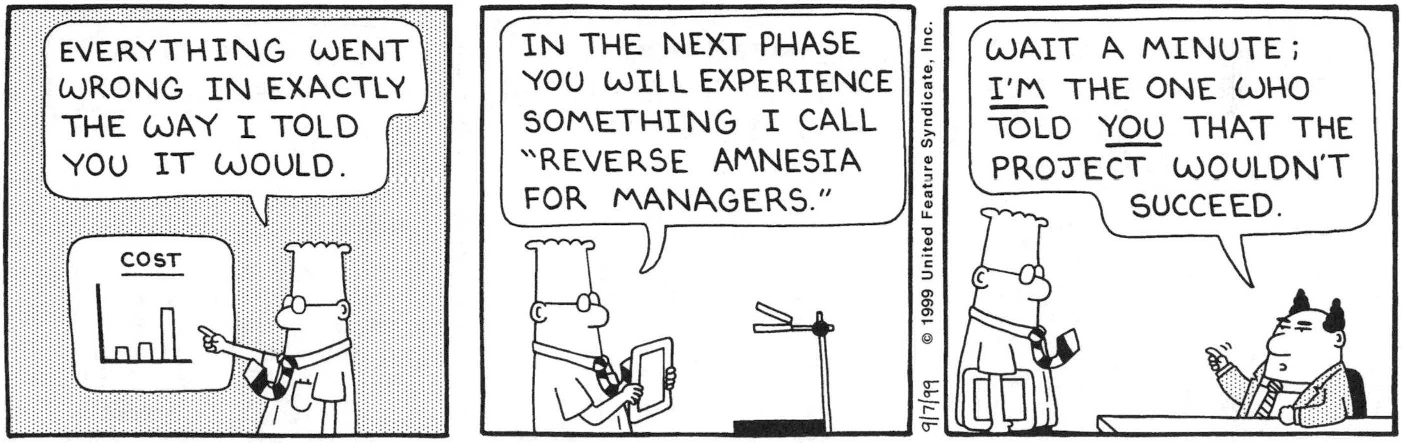
EVERYTHING WENT WRONG IN EXACTLY THE WAY I TOLD YOU IT WOULD.
COST
IN THE NEXT PHASE YOU WILL EXPERIENCE SOMETHING I CALL "REVERSE AMNESIA FOR MANAGERS."
9/7/99 © 1999 United Feature Syndicate, Inc.
WAIT A MINUTE; I'M THE ONE WHO TOLD YOU THAT THE PROJECT WOULDN'T SUCCEED.

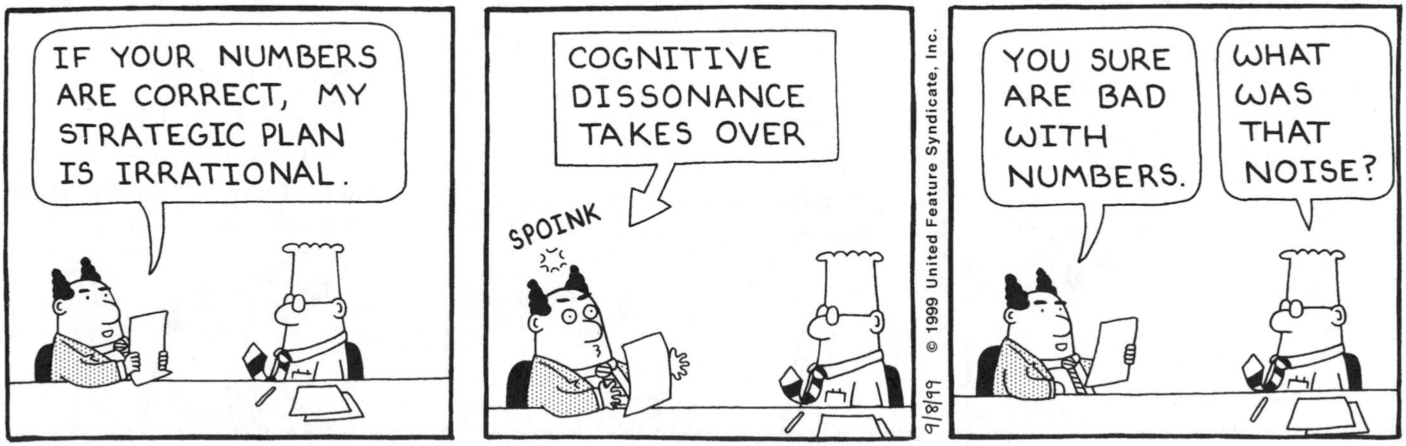
IF YOUR NUMBERS ARE CORRECT, MY STRATEGIC PLAN IS IRRATIONAL.
COGNITIVE DISSONANCE TAKES OVER
SPOINK
9/8/99 © 1999 United Feature Syndicate, Inc.
YOU SURE ARE BAD WITH NUMBERS.
WHAT WAS THAT NOISE?

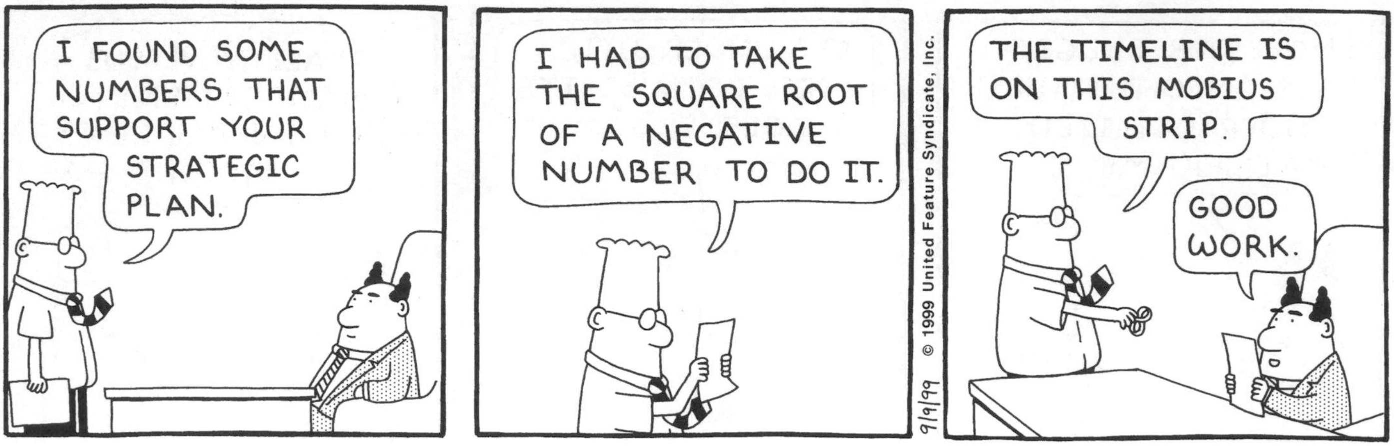
I FOUND SOME NUMBERS THAT SUPPORT YOUR STRATEGIC PLAN.
I HAD TO TAKE THE SQUARE ROOT OF A NEGATIVE NUMBER TO DO IT.
9/9/99 © 1999 United Feature Syndicate, Inc.
THE TIMELINE IS ON THIS MOBIUS STRIP.
GOOD WORK.

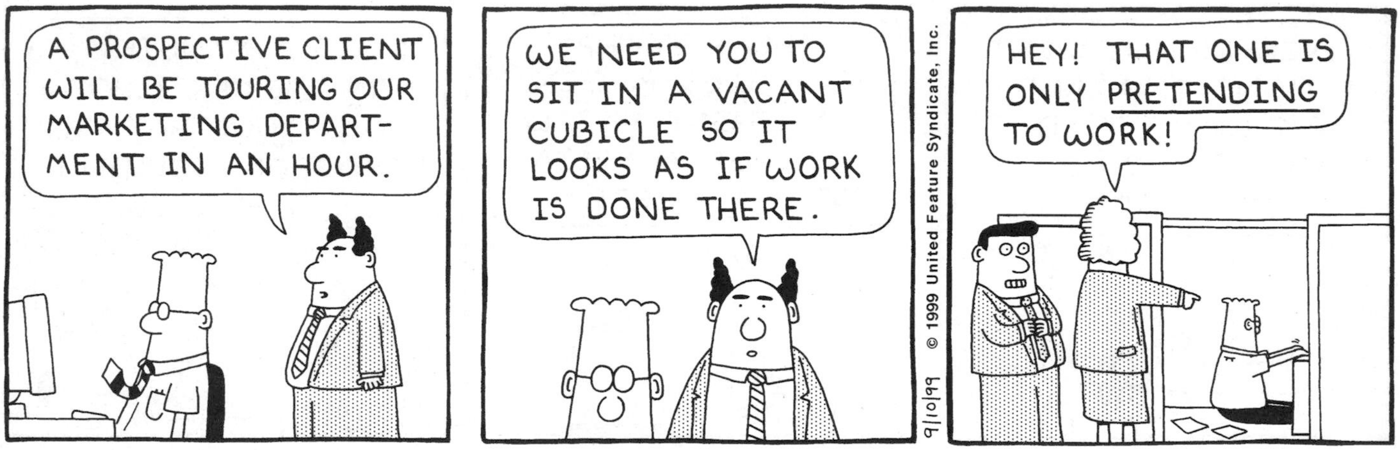
A PROSPECTIVE CLIENT WILL BE TOURING OUR MARKETING DEPART-MENT IN AN HOUR.
WE NEED YOU TO SIT IN A VACANT CUBICLE SO IT LOOKS AS IF WORK IS DONE THERE.
9/10/99 © 1999 United Feature Syndicate, Inc.
HEY! THAT ONE IS ONLY PRETENDING TO WORK!

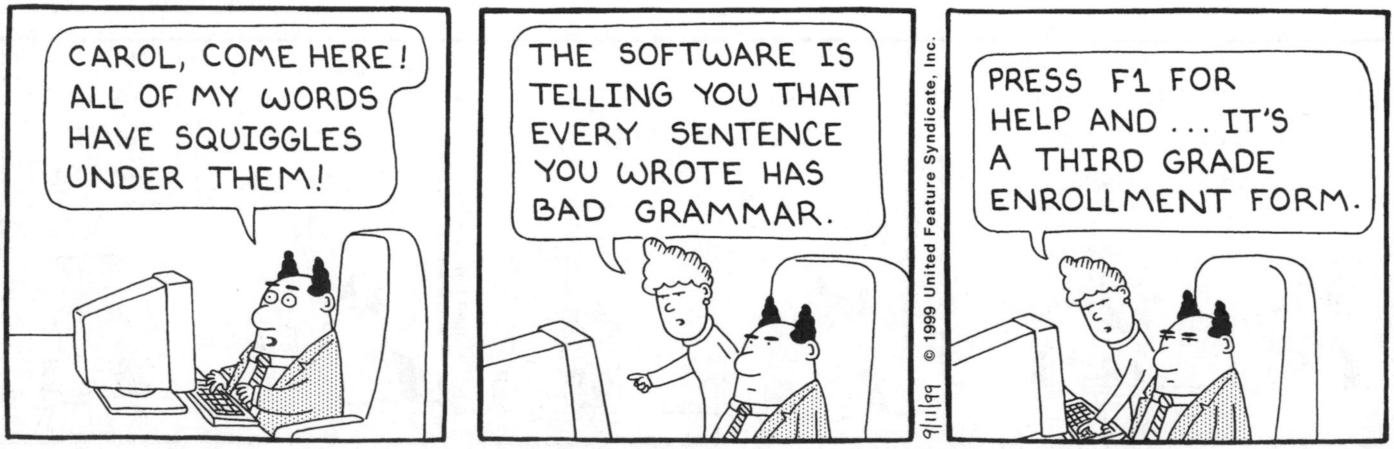
CAROL, COME HERE! ALL OF MY WORDS HAVE SQUIGGLES UNDER THEM!
THE SOFTWARE IS TELLING YOU THAT EVERY SENTENCE YOU WROTE HAS BAD GRAMMAR.
9/11/99 © 1999 United Feature Syndicate, Inc.
PRESS F1 FOR HELP AND . . . IT'S A THIRD GRADE ENROLLMENT FORM.

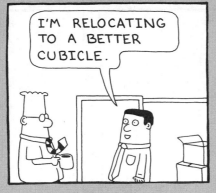

I'M RELOCATING TO A BETTER CUBICLE.
TONIGHT A TEAM OF MOVERS WILL TAKE MY BOXED POSSESSIONS TO AN UNDISCLOSED LOCATION.
THEY'RE ALSO GOING TO LAMINATE MY COMPANY I.D.
I'M SUPPOSED TO LEAVE IT WITH THE GUARD ON THE WAY OUT.
AND I GOT PAID TWO DAYS EARLY!
IT'S ALL BECAUSE MANAGEMENT APPRECIATED THE CONSTRUCTIVE CRITICISM I POSTED ON THE MESSAGE BOARD.
AS I HOPED, MY CONDESCENDING TONE HELPED THEM TO SEE THEIR FOLLY.
DO YOU MIND IF I RIFLE THROUGH YOUR BOXES AND TAKE OFFICE SUPPLIES?
9/12/99 © 1999 United Feature Syndicate, Inc.

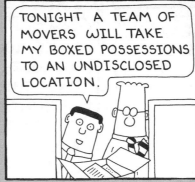

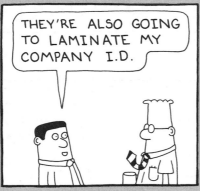

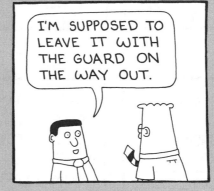

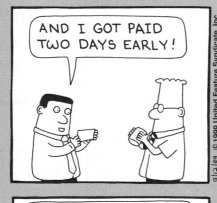

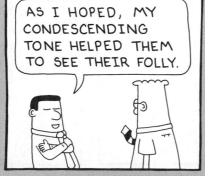

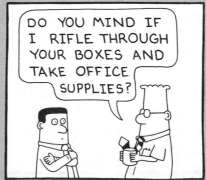

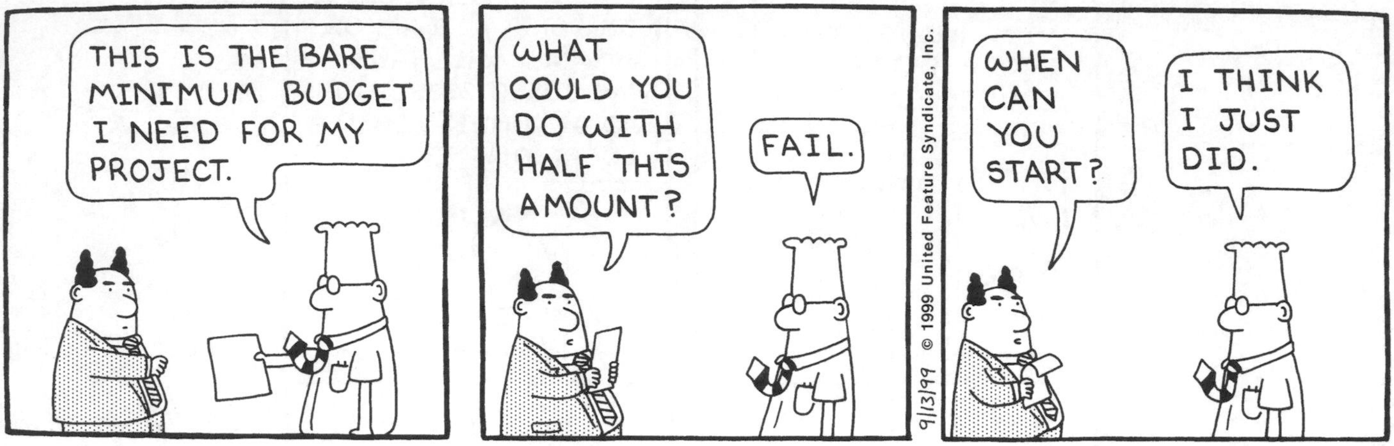
THIS IS THE BARE MINIMUM BUDGET I NEED FOR MY PROJECT.
WHAT COULD YOU DO WITH HALF THIS AMOUNT?
FAIL.
9/13/99 © 1999 United Feature Syndicate, Inc.
WHEN CAN YOU START?
I THINK I JUST DID.

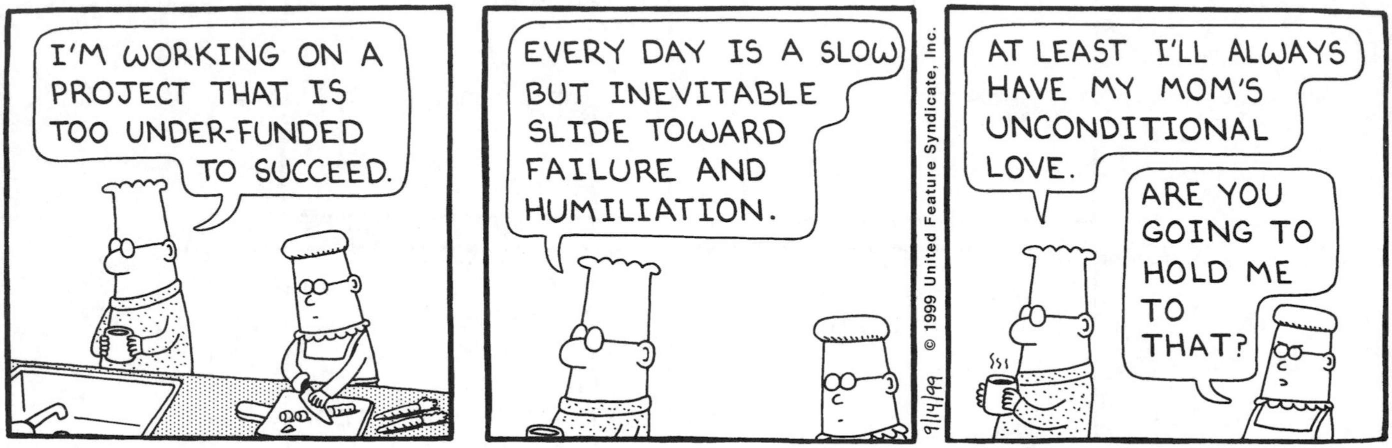
I'M WORKING ON A PROJECT THAT IS TOO UNDER-FUNDED TO SUCCEED.
EVERY DAY IS A SLOW BUT INEVITABLE SLIDE TOWARD FAILURE AND HUMILIATION.
9/14/99 © 1999 United Feature Syndicate, Inc.
AT LEAST I'LL ALWAYS HAVE MY MOM'S UNCONDITIONAL LOVE.
ARE YOU GOING TO HOLD ME TO THAT?

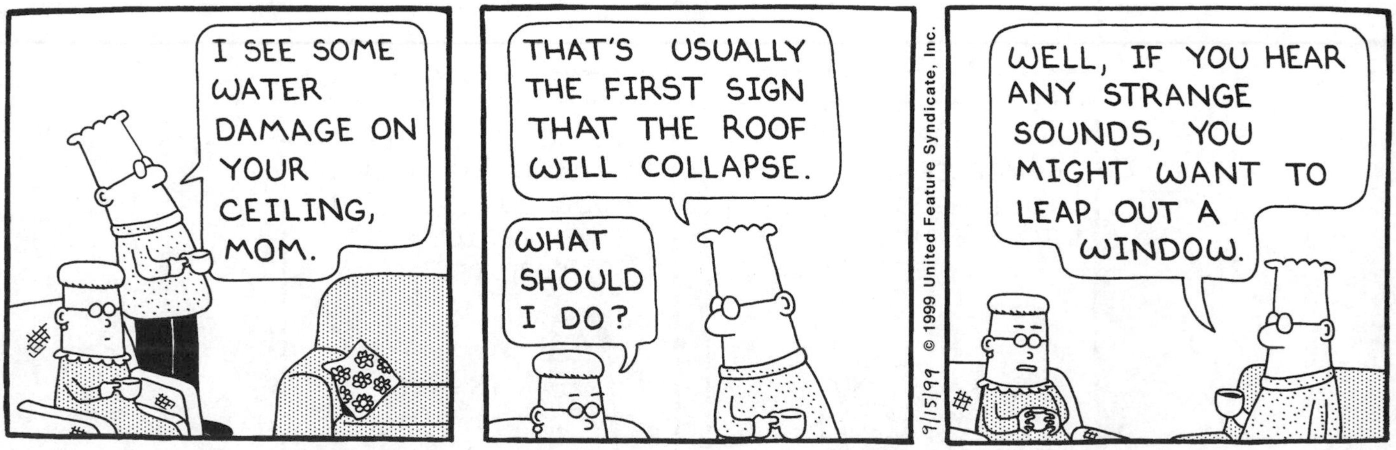
I SEE SOME WATER DAMAGE ON YOUR CEILING, MOM.
THAT'S USUALLY THE FIRST SIGN THAT THE ROOF WILL COLLAPSE.
WHAT SHOULD I DO?
9/15/99 © 1999 United Feature Syndicate, Inc.
WELL, IF YOU HEAR ANY STRANGE SOUNDS, YOU MIGHT WANT TO LEAP OUT A WINDOW.

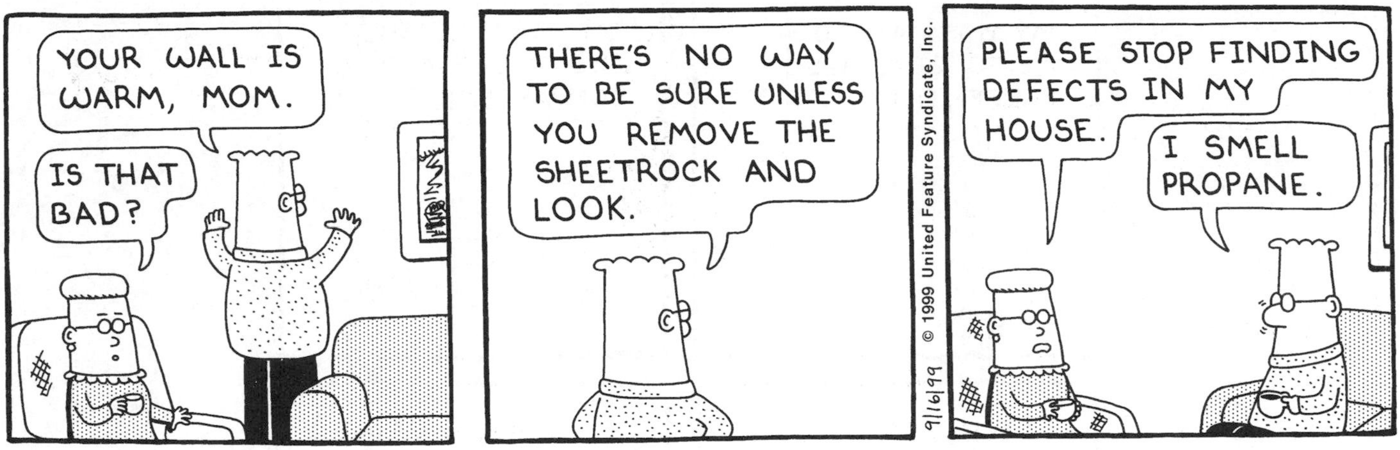
YOUR WALL IS WARM, MOM.
IS THAT BAD?
THERE'S NO WAY TO BE SURE UNLESS YOU REMOVE THE SHEETROCK AND LOOK.
PLEASE STOP FINDING DEFECTS IN MY HOUSE.
I SMELL PROPANE.
9/16/99 © 1999 United Feature Syndicate, Inc.

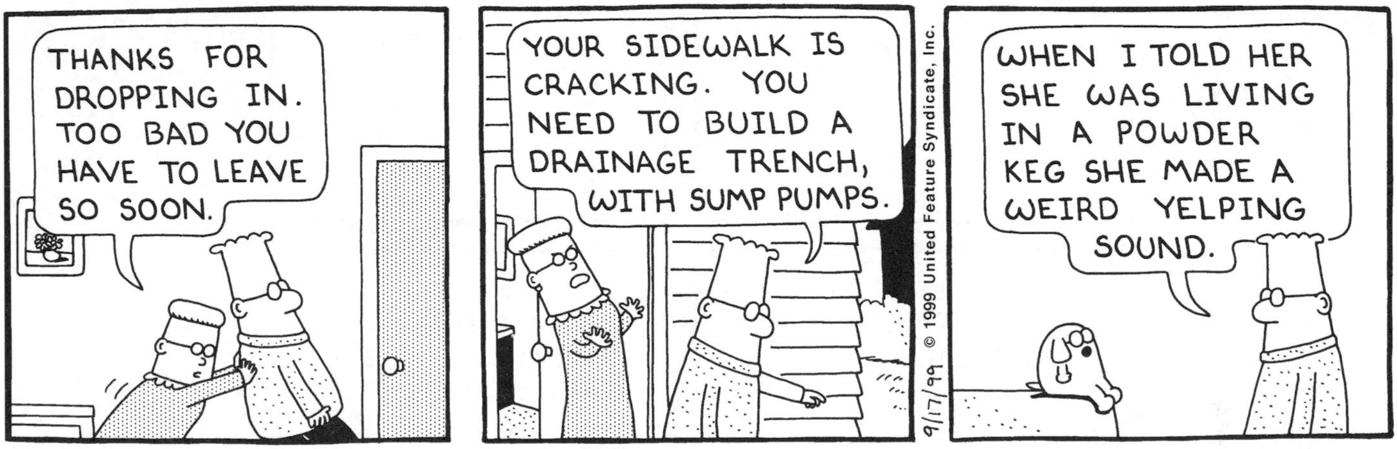
THANKS FOR DROPPING IN. TOO BAD YOU HAVE TO LEAVE SO SOON.
YOUR SIDEWALK IS CRACKING. YOU NEED TO BUILD A DRAINAGE TRENCH, WITH SUMP PUMPS.
WHEN I TOLD HER SHE WAS LIVING IN A POWDER KEG SHE MADE A WEIRD YELPING SOUND.
9/17/99 © 1999 United Feature Syndicate, Inc.

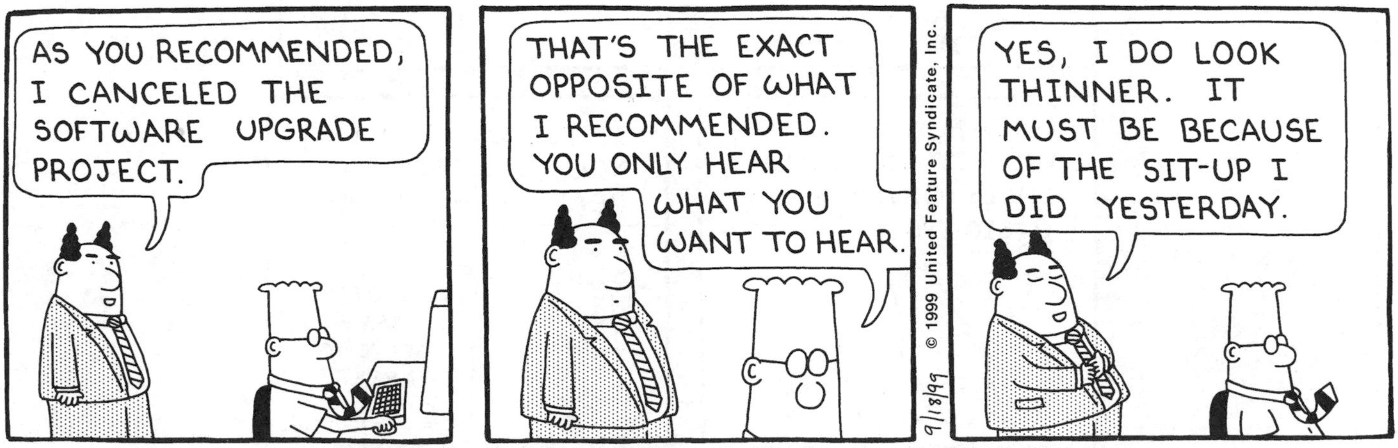
AS YOU RECOMMENDED, I CANCELED THE SOFTWARE UPGRADE PROJECT.
THAT'S THE EXACT OPPOSITE OF WHAT I RECOMMENDED. YOU ONLY HEAR WHAT YOU WANT TO HEAR.
YES, I DO LOOK THINNER. IT MUST BE BECAUSE OF THE SIT-UP I DID YESTERDAY.
9/18/99 © 1999 United Feature Syndicate, Inc.

MY BOSS ASKED ME TO GIVE HIS PRESENTATION.
I'LL START WITH HIS IRRELEVANT COMPARISONS.
OUR BUDGET IS LOWER THAN LAST YEAR...
... WHEN WE HAD COMPLETELY DIFFERENT PROJECTS.
OUR AVERAGE PRODUCT DEVELOPMENT TIME IS LESS...
... THAN THE AVERAGE FOR COMPANIES WHO MAKE DIFFERENT PRODUCTS.
LET'S MOVE ON TO HIS LIST OF BLIND-INGLY OBVIOUS INSIGHTS.
IF IT'S OKAY WITH YOU, I WON'T READ THEM ALOUD.
COMPUTERS ARE GETTING FASTER!
9/9/99 © 1999 United Feature Syndicate, Inc.

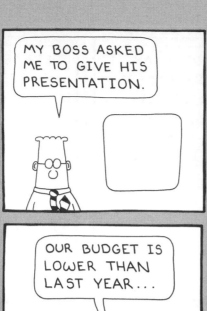

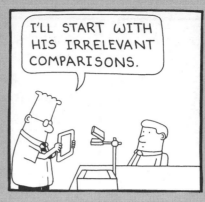

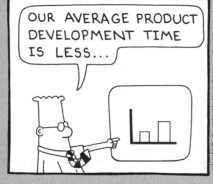

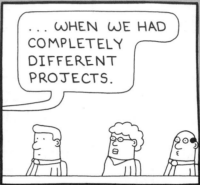

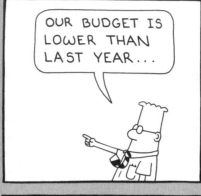

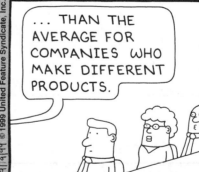

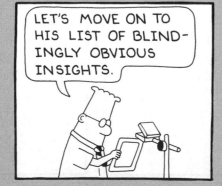

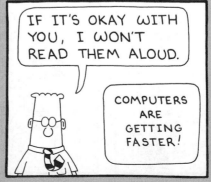

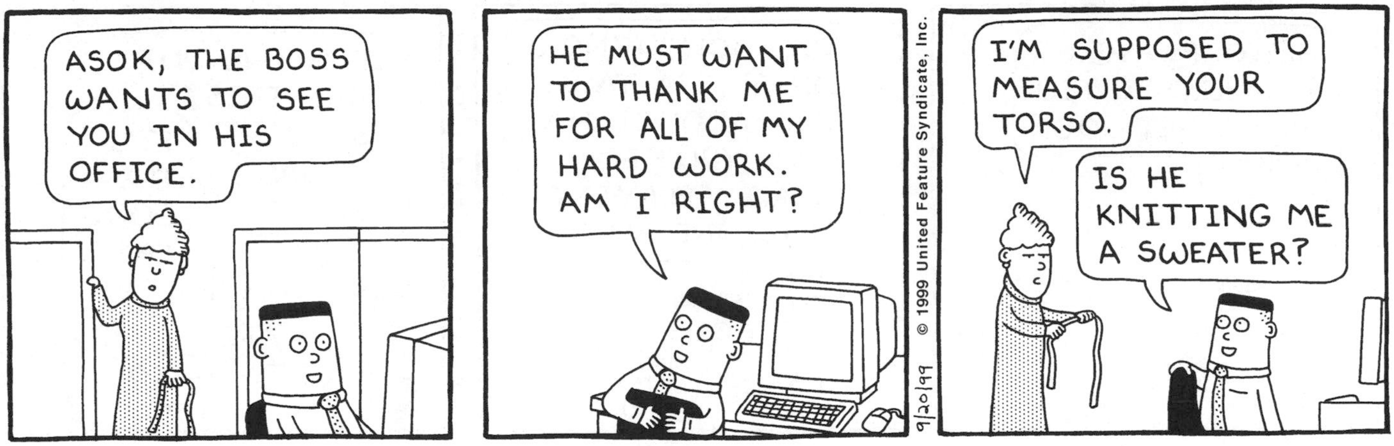
ASOK, THE BOSS WANTS TO SEE YOU IN HIS OFFICE.
HE MUST WANT TO THANK ME FOR ALL OF MY HARD WORK. AM I RIGHT?
9/20/99 © 1999 United Feature Syndicate, Inc.
I'M SUPPOSED TO MEASURE YOUR TORSO.
IS HE KNITTING ME A SWEATER?

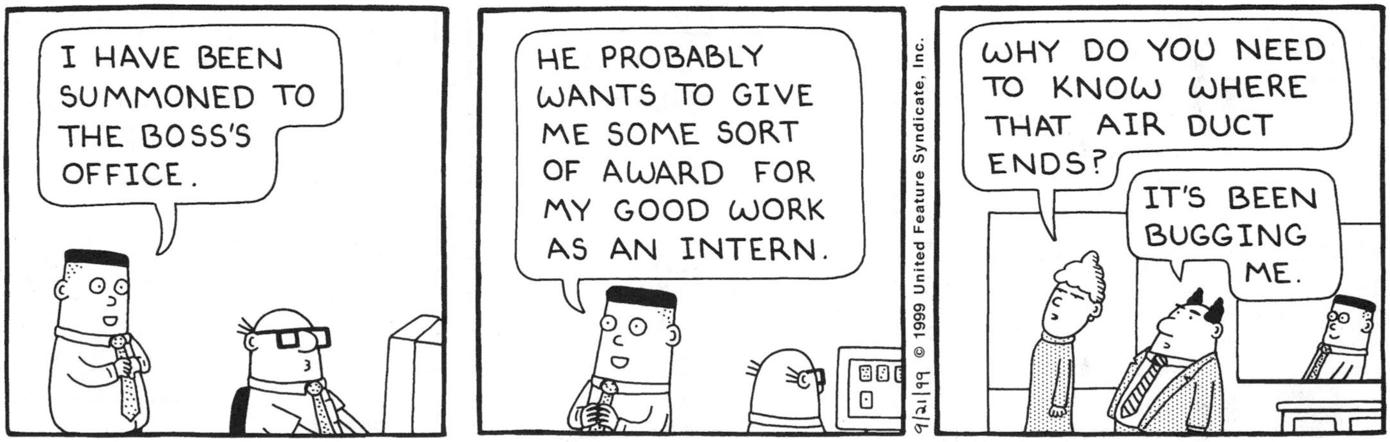
I HAVE BEEN SUMMONED TO THE BOSS'S OFFICE.
HE PROBABLY WANTS TO GIVE ME SOME SORT OF AWARD FOR MY GOOD WORK AS AN INTERN.
9/21/99 © 1999 United Feature Syndicate, Inc.
WHY DO YOU NEED TO KNOW WHERE THAT AIR DUCT ENDS?
IT'S BEEN BUGGING ME.

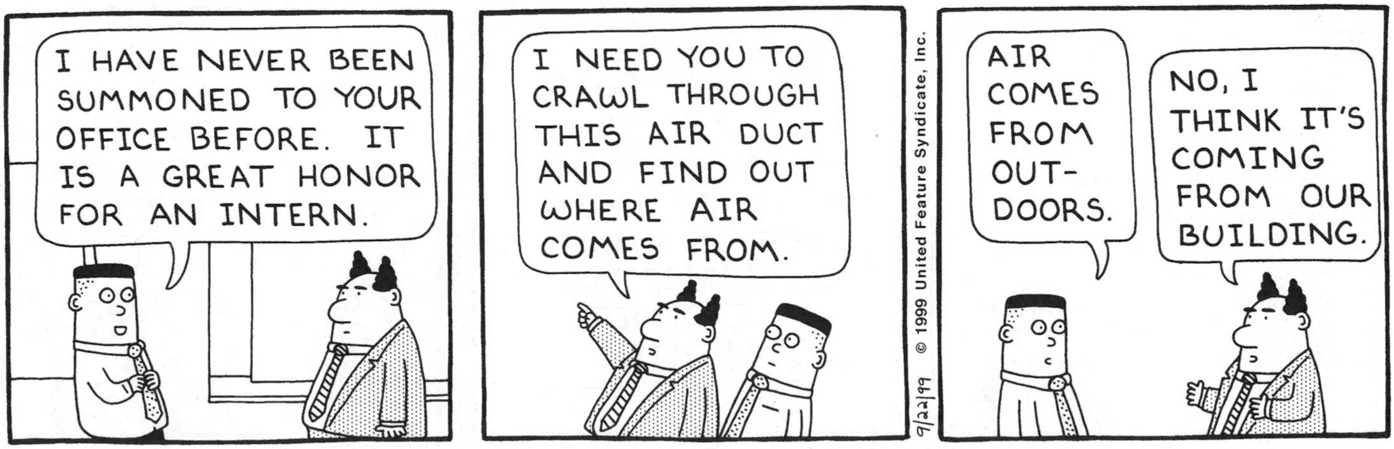
I HAVE NEVER BEEN SUMMONED TO YOUR OFFICE BEFORE. IT IS A GREAT HONOR FOR AN INTERN.
I NEED YOU TO CRAWL THROUGH THIS AIR DUCT AND FIND OUT WHERE AIR COMES FROM.
9/22/99 © 1999 United Feature Syndicate, Inc.
AIR COMES FROM OUT-DOORS.
NO, I THINK IT'S COMING FROM OUR BUILDING.

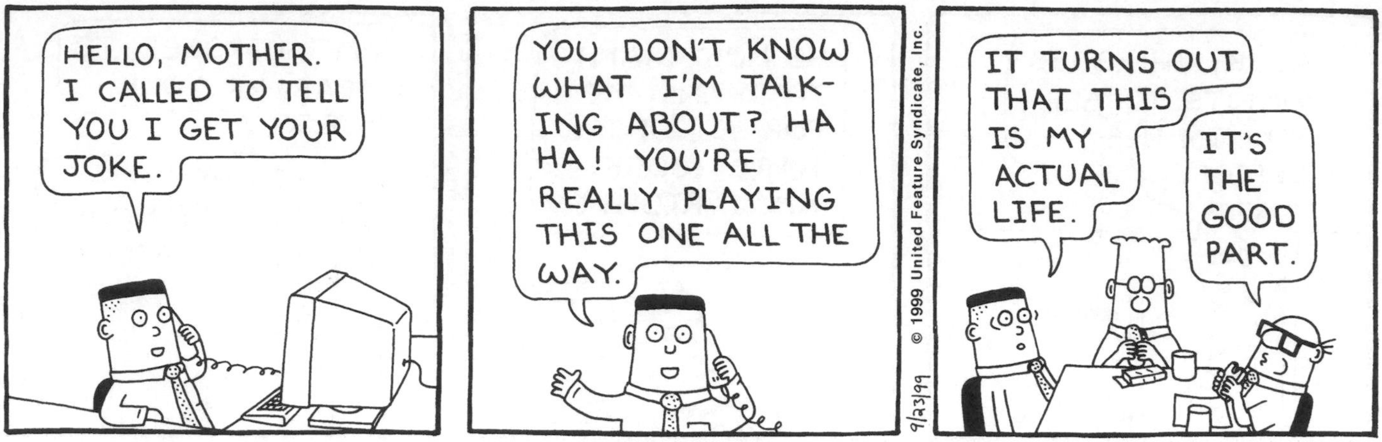
HELLO, MOTHER. I CALLED TO TELL YOU I GET YOUR JOKE.
YOU DON'T KNOW WHAT I'M TALKING ABOUT? HA HA! YOU'RE REALLY PLAYING THIS ONE ALL THE WAY.
9/23/99 © 1999 United Feature Syndicate, Inc.
IT TURNS OUT THAT THIS IS MY ACTUAL LIFE.
IT'S THE GOOD PART.

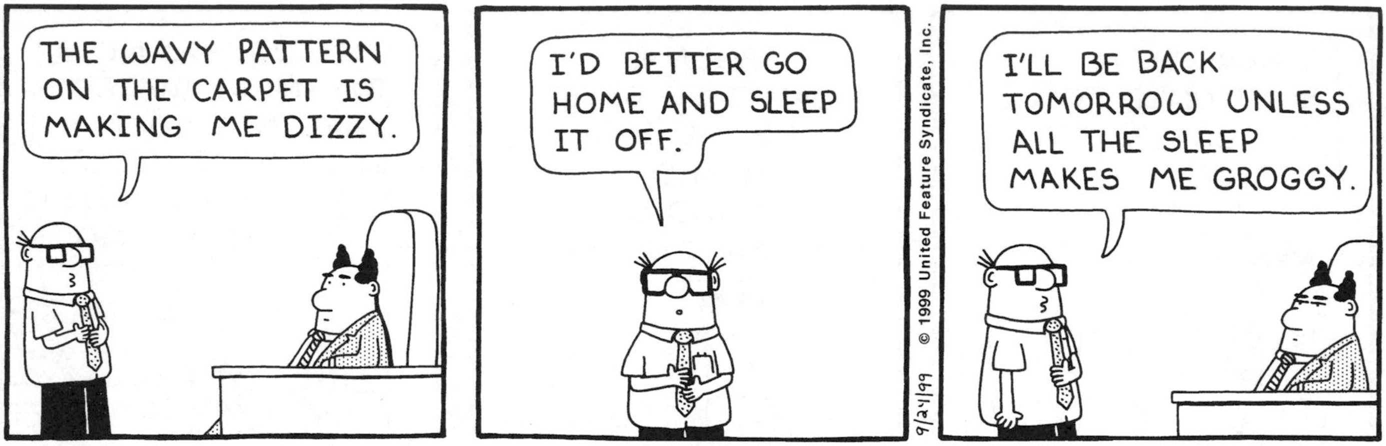
THE WAVY PATTERN ON THE CARPET IS MAKING ME DIZZY.
I'D BETTER GO HOME AND SLEEP IT OFF.
9/24/99 © 1999 United Feature Syndicate, Inc.
I'LL BE BACK TOMORROW UNLESS ALL THE SLEEP MAKES ME GROGGY.

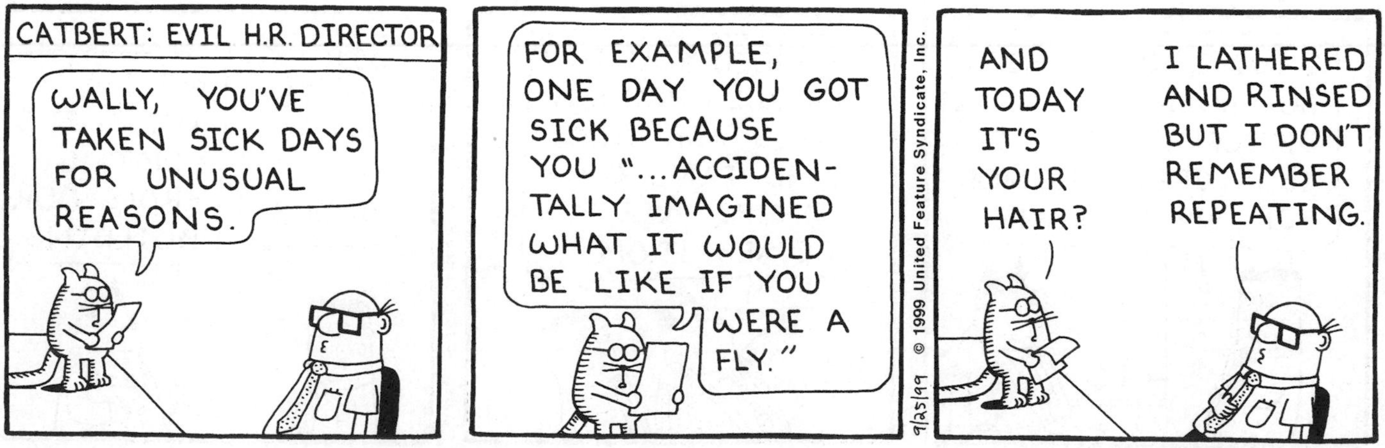
CATBERT: EVIL H.R. DIRECTOR
WALLY, YOU'VE TAKEN SICK DAYS FOR UNUSUAL REASONS.
FOR EXAMPLE, ONE DAY YOU GOT SICK BECAUSE YOU "...ACCIDENTALLY IMAGINED WHAT IT WOULD BE LIKE IF YOU WERE A FLY."
9/25/99 © 1999 United Feature Syndicate, Inc.
AND TODAY IT'S YOUR HAIR?
I LATHERED AND RINSED BUT I DON'T REMEMBER REPEATING.

DOGBERT THE CONSULTANT
THIS IS MY FINAL REPORT.
I'M RECOMMENDING BIG, BIG CHANGES...
BECAUSE I KNOW YOU'RE TOO COWARDLY TO IMPLEMENT THEM.
SO... IT WILL BE OUR FAULT IF NOTHING IMPROVES.
EXACTLY.
AAAGH!!
WE CAN'T DO ALL OF THIS!
© 1999 United Feature Syndicate, Inc.
9/26/99
COULDN'T WE JUST CHANGE THE NAMES OF ALL OUR DEPARTMENTS?
THOSE IMBECILES! HOW DARE THEY IGNORE MY ADVICE!
YOU'RE SUPPOSED TO SAY THAT BEHIND OUR BACKS LATER.
I'M IN A HURRY.

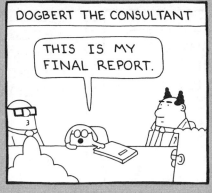

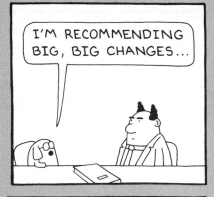

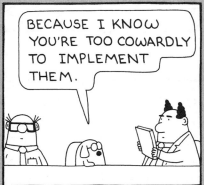

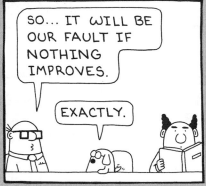

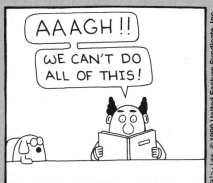

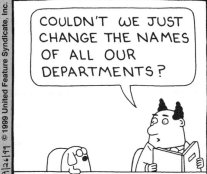

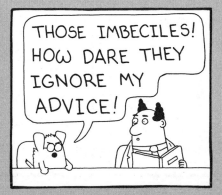

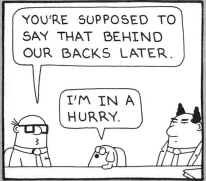

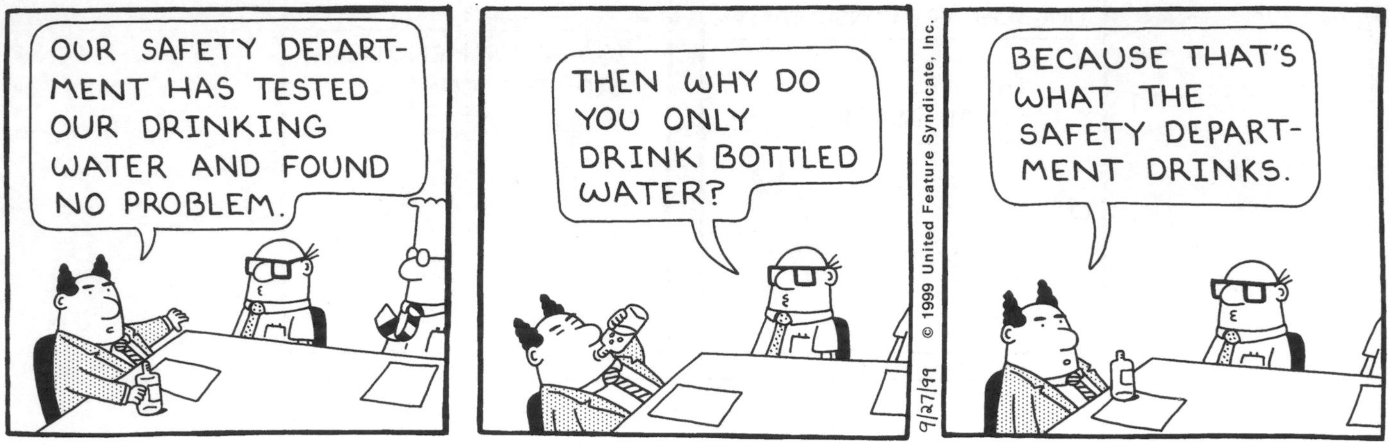
OUR SAFETY DEPARTMENT HAS TESTED OUR DRINKING WATER AND FOUND NO PROBLEM.
THEN WHY DO YOU ONLY DRINK BOTTLED WATER?
BECAUSE THAT'S WHAT THE SAFETY DEPARTMENT DRINKS.
9/27/99 © 1999 United Feature Syndicate, Inc.

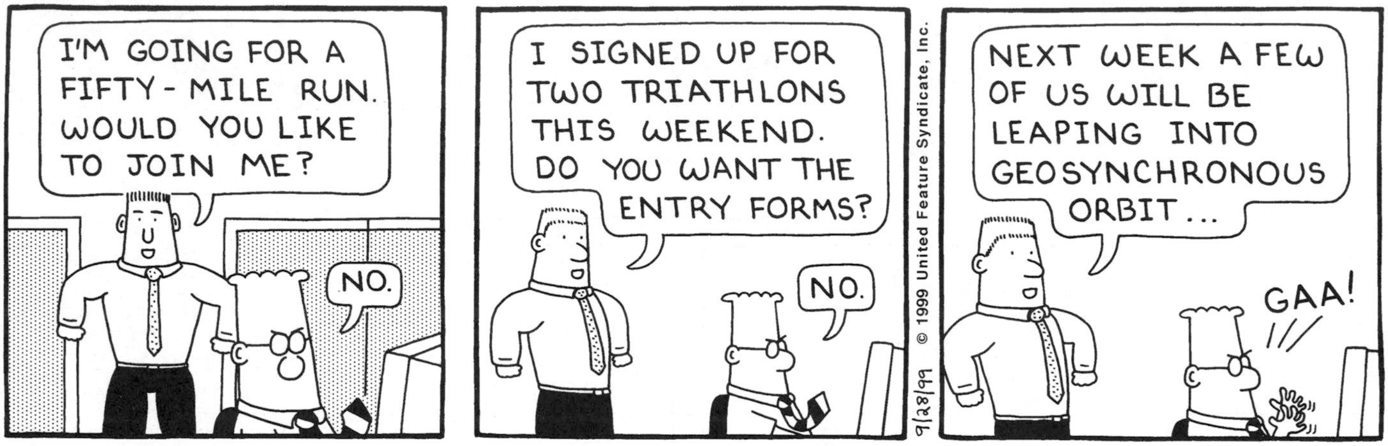
I'M GOING FOR A FIFTY-MILE RUN. WOULD YOU LIKE TO JOIN ME?
NO.
I SIGNED UP FOR TWO TRIATHLONS THIS WEEKEND. DO YOU WANT THE ENTRY FORMS?
NO.
NEXT WEEK A FEW OF US WILL BE LEAPING INTO GEOSYNCHRONOUS ORBIT...
GAA!
9/28/99 © 1999 United Feature Syndicate, Inc.

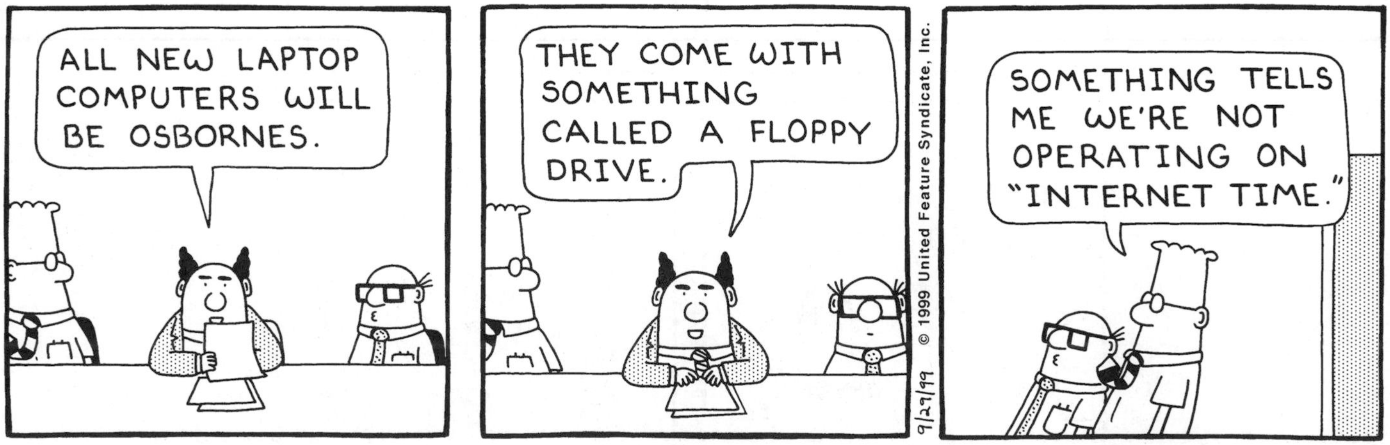
ALL NEW LAPTOP COMPUTERS WILL BE OSBORNES.
THEY COME WITH SOMETHING CALLED A FLOPPY DRIVE.
SOMETHING TELLS ME WE'RE NOT OPERATING ON "INTERNET TIME."
9/29/99 © 1999 United Feature Syndicate, Inc.

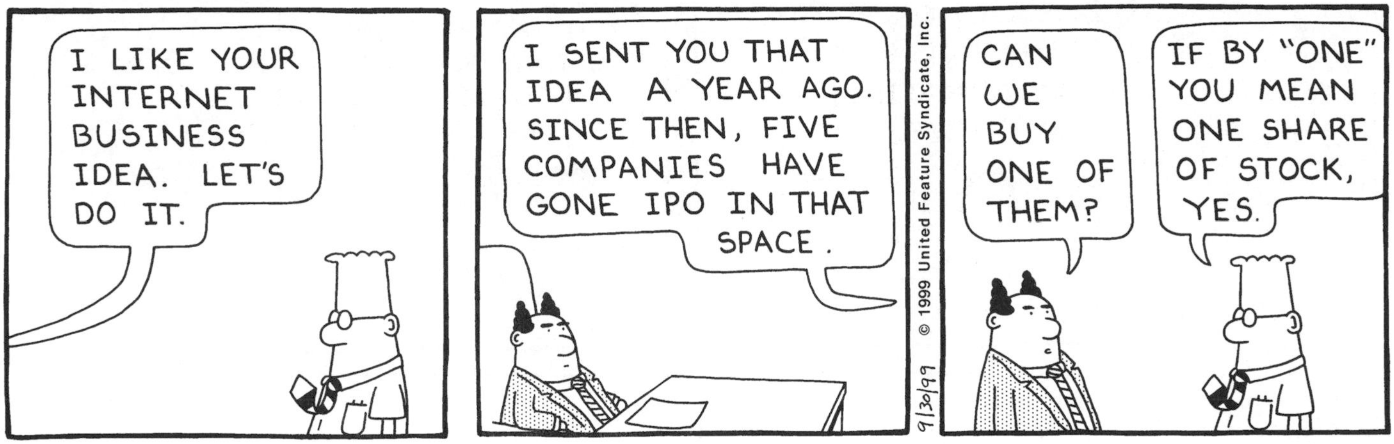
I LIKE YOUR INTERNET BUSINESS IDEA. LET'S DO IT.
I SENT YOU THAT IDEA A YEAR AGO. SINCE THEN, FIVE COMPANIES HAVE GONE IPO IN THAT SPACE.
CAN WE BUY ONE OF THEM?
IF BY "ONE" YOU MEAN ONE SHARE OF STOCK, YES.
9/30/99 © 1999 United Feature Syndicate, Inc.

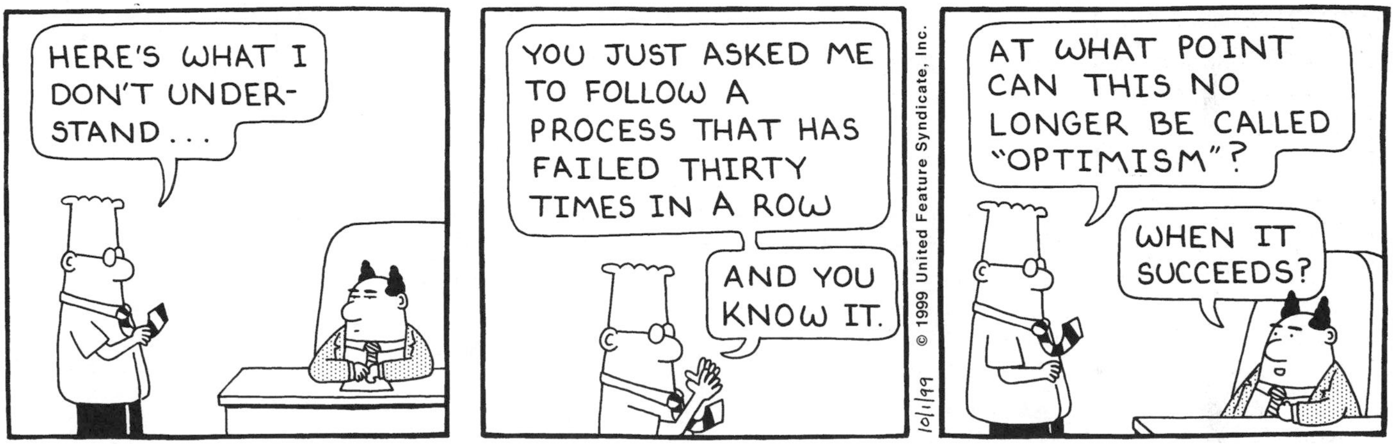
HERE'S WHAT I DON'T UNDERSTAND...
YOU JUST ASKED ME TO FOLLOW A PROCESS THAT HAS FAILED THIRTY TIMES IN A ROW
AND YOU KNOW IT.
AT WHAT POINT CAN THIS NO LONGER BE CALLED "OPTIMISM"?
WHEN IT SUCCEEDS?
10/1/99 © 1999 United Feature Syndicate, Inc.

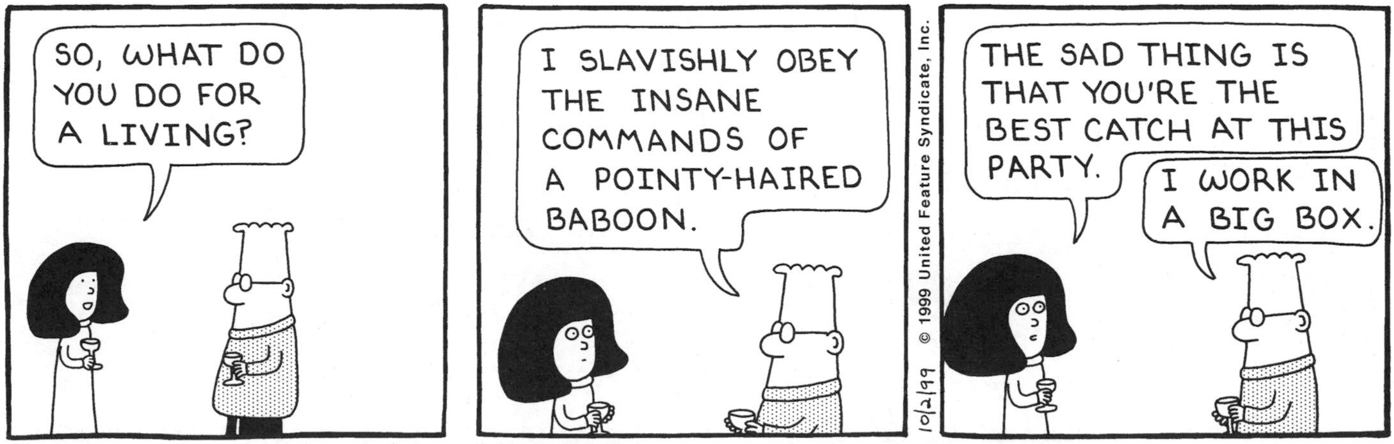
SO, WHAT DO YOU DO FOR A LIVING?
I SLAVISHLY OBEY THE INSANE COMMANDS OF A POINTY-HAIRED BABOON.
THE SAD THING IS THAT YOU'RE THE BEST CATCH AT THIS PARTY.
I WORK IN A BIG BOX.
10/2/99 © 1999 United Feature Syndicate, Inc.

I AM MORDAC, THE PREVENTER OF INFORMATION SERVICES!!
YOU HAVE EXCEEDED YOUR ALLOCATION OF DISK SPACE ON THE SERVER!
I SENTENCE YOU TO ONE WEEK WITHOUT E-MAIL.
NO PROBLEM.
NO PROBLEM?
HOW CAN AN ENGINEER SURVIVE WITHOUT E-MAIL?
UP AGAINST THE WALL!!
WHERE IS IT?
HE FOUND THE MODEM TAPED TO MY ANKLE BUT HE MISSED MY WIRELESS PEN MODEM.
© 1999 United Feature Syndicate, Inc.
10/3/99

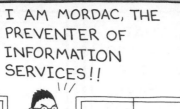

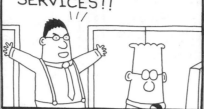

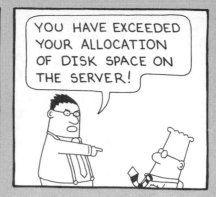

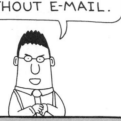

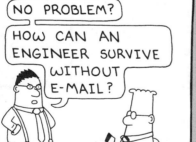

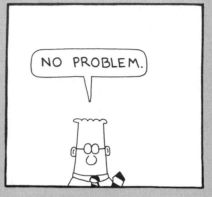

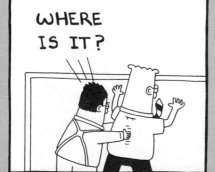

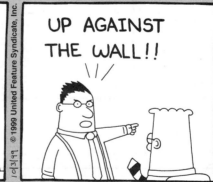

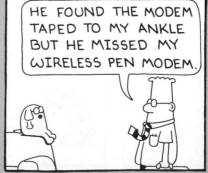

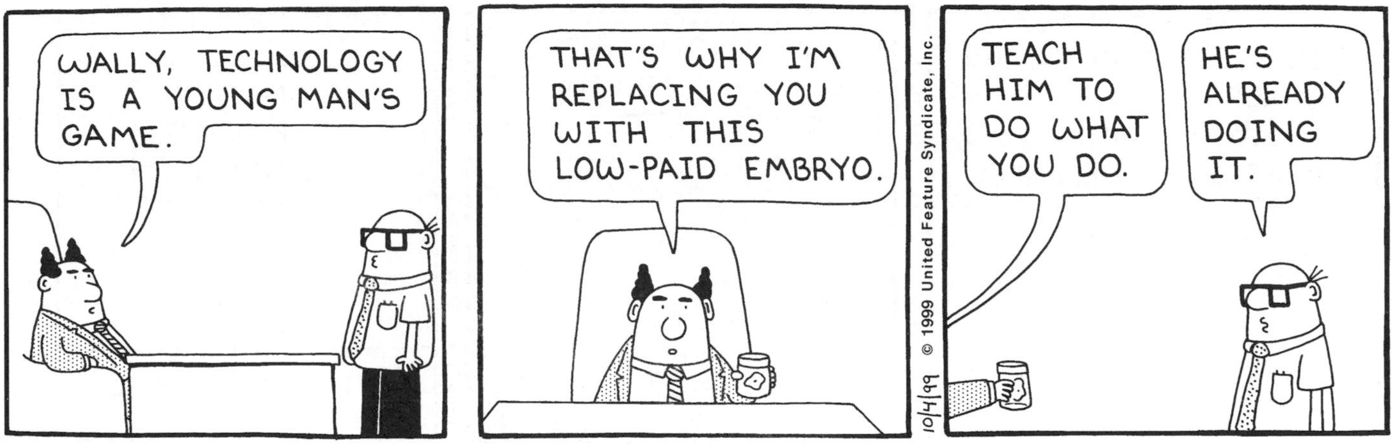
WALLY, TECHNOLOGY IS A YOUNG MAN'S GAME.
THAT'S WHY I'M REPLACING YOU WITH THIS LOW-PAID EMBRYO.
10/4/99 © 1999 United Feature Syndicate, Inc.
TEACH HIM TO DO WHAT YOU DO.
HE'S ALREADY DOING IT.

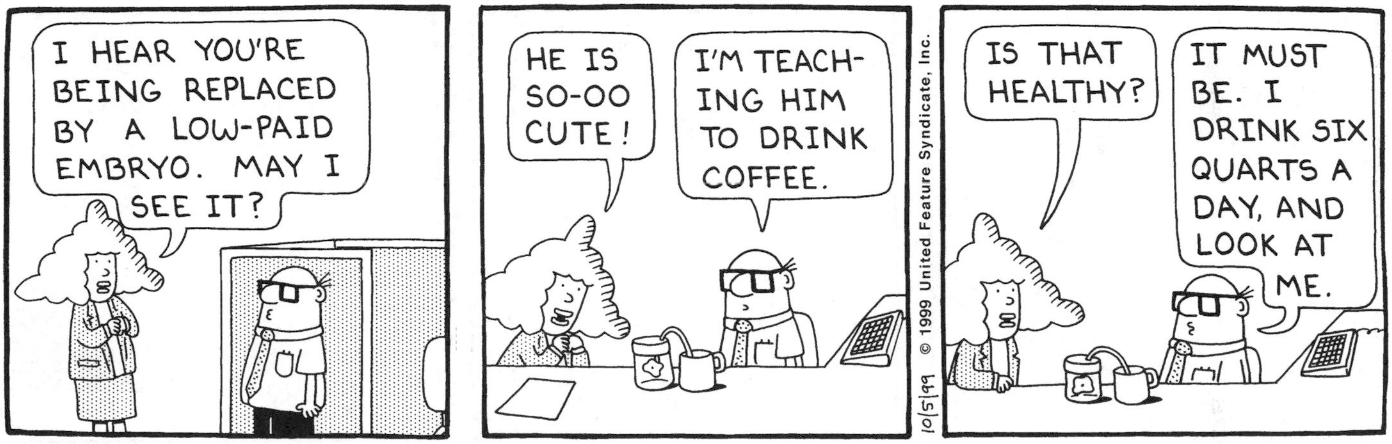
I HEAR YOU'RE BEING REPLACED BY A LOW-PAID EMBRYO. MAY I SEE IT?
HE IS SO-OO CUTE!
I'M TEACHING HIM TO DRINK COFFEE.
10/5/99 © 1999 United Feature Syndicate, Inc.
IS THAT HEALTHY?
IT MUST BE. I DRINK SIX QUARTS A DAY, AND LOOK AT ME.

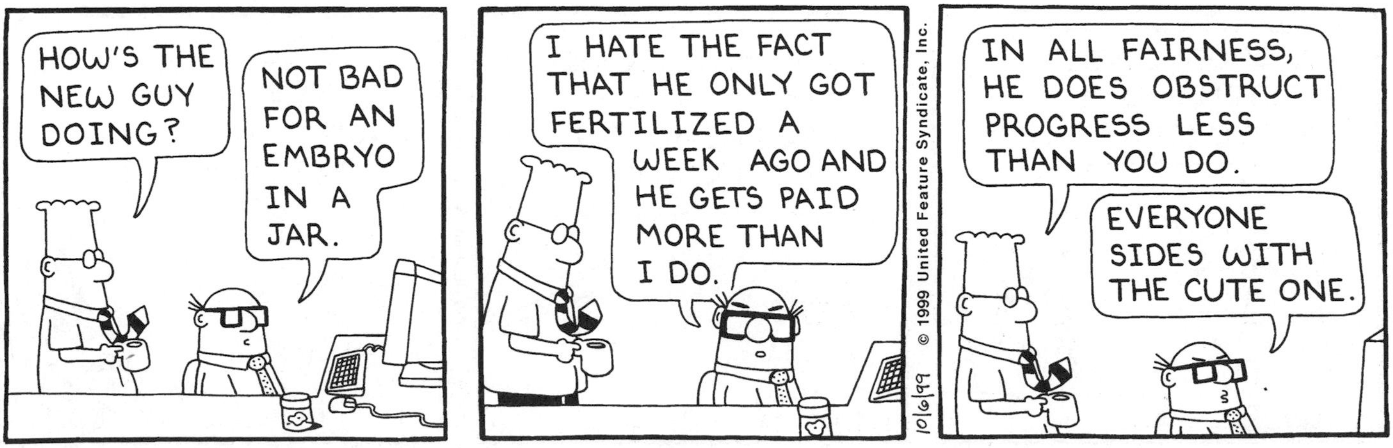
HOW'S THE NEW GUY DOING?
NOT BAD FOR AN EMBRYO IN A JAR.
I HATE THE FACT THAT HE ONLY GOT FERTILIZED A WEEK AGO AND HE GETS PAID MORE THAN I DO.
10/6/99 © 1999 United Feature Syndicate, Inc.
IN ALL FAIRNESS, HE DOES OBSTRUCT PROGRESS LESS THAN YOU DO.
EVERYONE SIDES WITH THE CUTE ONE.

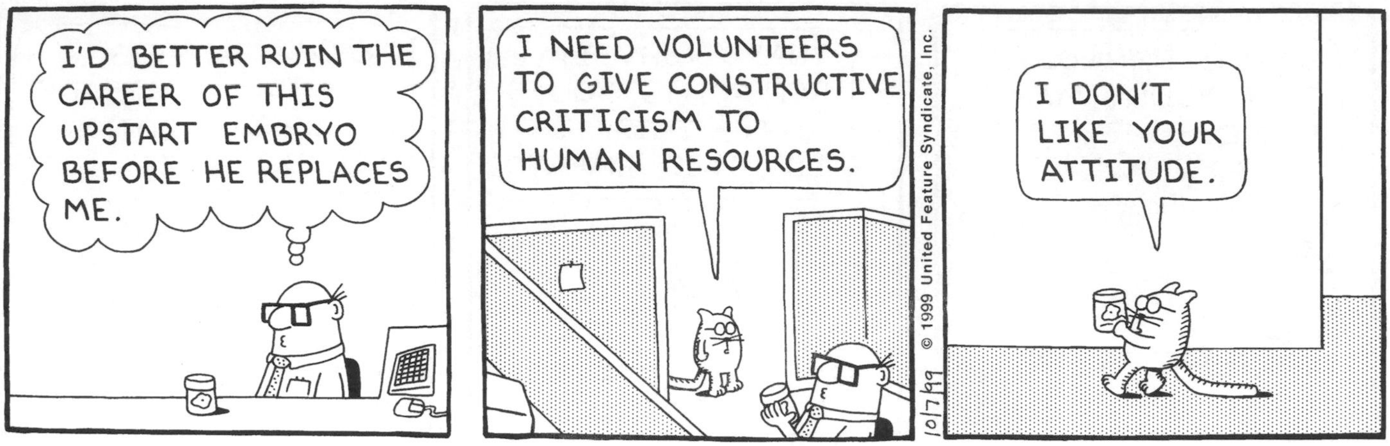
I'D BETTER RUIN THE CAREER OF THIS UPSTART EMBRYO BEFORE HE REPLACES ME.
I NEED VOLUNTEERS TO GIVE CONSTRUCTIVE CRITICISM TO HUMAN RESOURCES.
I DON'T LIKE YOUR ATTITUDE.
10/7/99 © 1999 United Feature Syndicate, Inc.

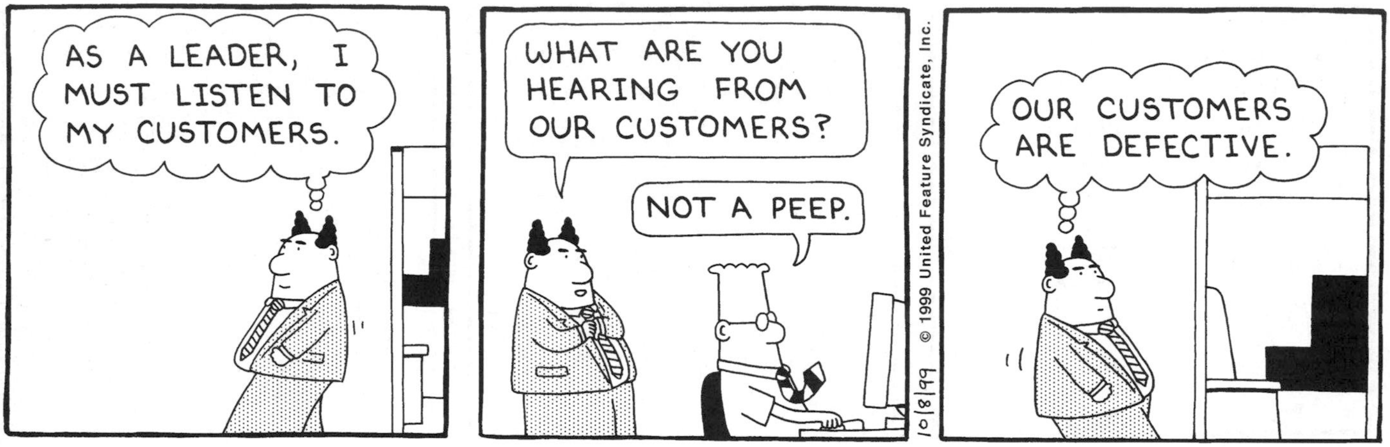
AS A LEADER, I MUST LISTEN TO MY CUSTOMERS.
WHAT ARE YOU HEARING FROM OUR CUSTOMERS?
NOT A PEEP.
OUR CUSTOMERS ARE DEFECTIVE.
10/8/99 © 1999 United Feature Syndicate, Inc.

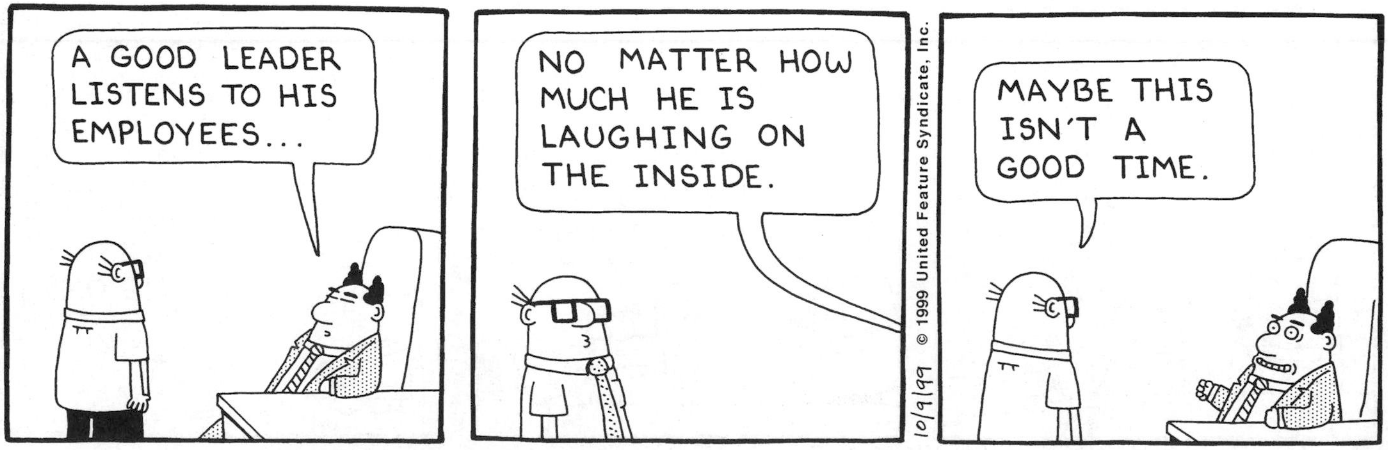
A GOOD LEADER LISTENS TO HIS EMPLOYEES...
NO MATTER HOW MUCH HE IS LAUGHING ON THE INSIDE.
MAYBE THIS ISN'T A GOOD TIME.
10/9/99 © 1999 United Feature Syndicate, Inc.

IT'S "POSITIVE ATTITUDE WEEK," ALICE.
IF YOU SEE A CO-WORKER WITH A POSITIVE ATTITUDE...
...GIVE HIM THE POSITIVE ATTITUDE PAPERWEIGHT.
THERE'S ONE!
IT WORKED. HE'S BACK TO NORMAL.
#☆!! *
HA HA HA!!
UH-OH.
#☆!! *
ONE MORE! QUICK!!
10/10/99 © 1999 United Feature Syndicate, Inc.

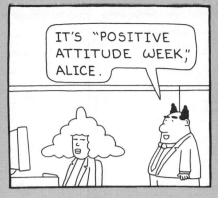

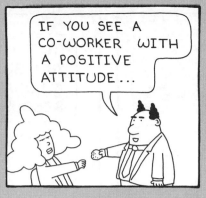

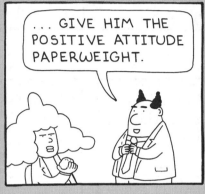

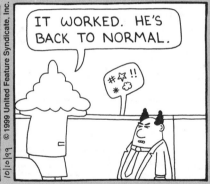

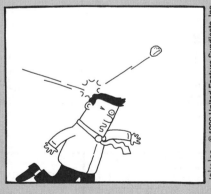

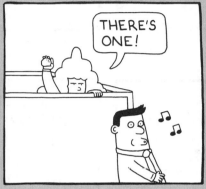

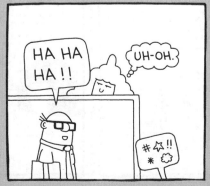

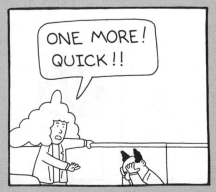

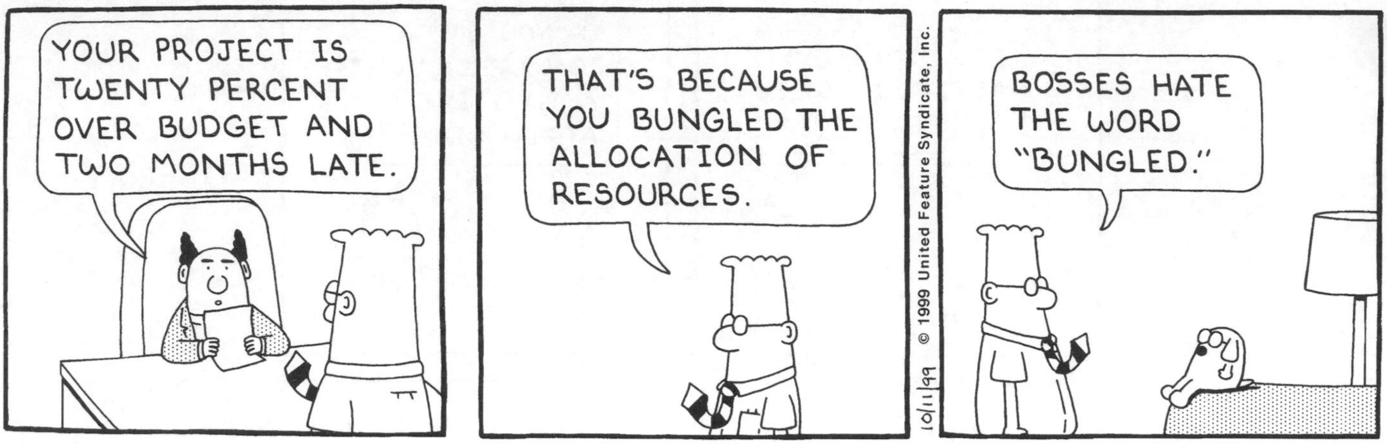
YOUR PROJECT IS TWENTY PERCENT OVER BUDGET AND TWO MONTHS LATE.
THAT'S BECAUSE YOU BUNGLED THE ALLOCATION OF RESOURCES.
10/11/99 © 1999 United Feature Syndicate, Inc.
BOSSES HATE THE WORD "BUNGLED."

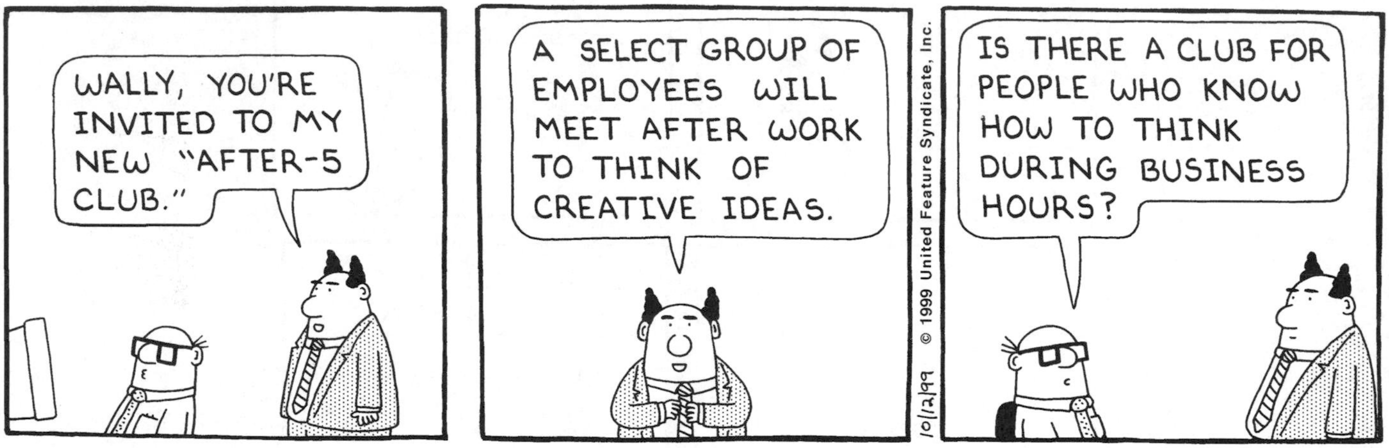
WALLY, YOU'RE INVITED TO MY NEW "AFTER-5 CLUB."
A SELECT GROUP OF EMPLOYEES WILL MEET AFTER WORK TO THINK OF CREATIVE IDEAS.
10/12/99 © 1999 United Feature Syndicate, Inc.
IS THERE A CLUB FOR PEOPLE WHO KNOW HOW TO THINK DURING BUSINESS HOURS?

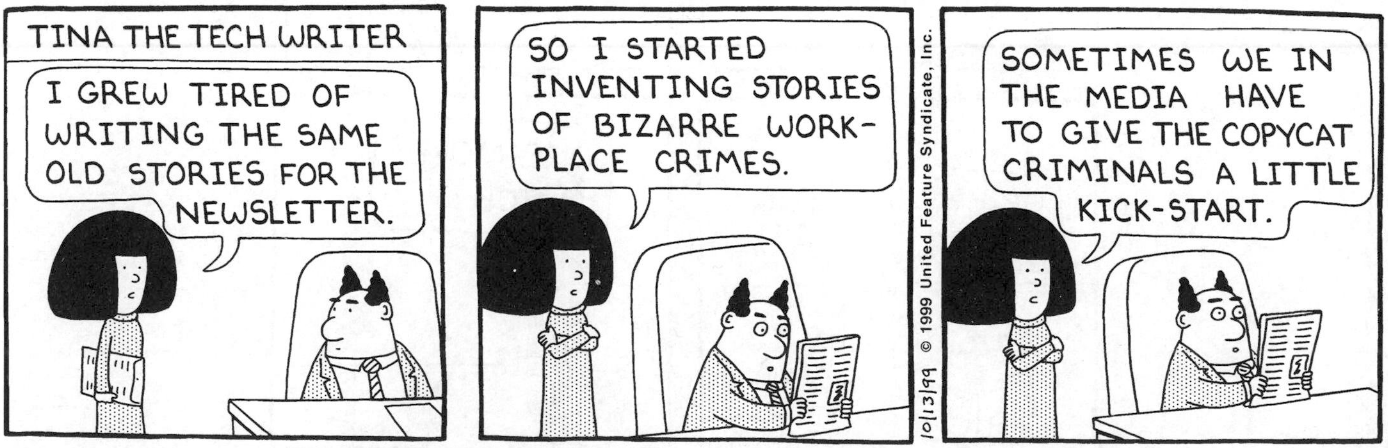
TINA THE TECH WRITER
I GREW TIRED OF WRITING THE SAME OLD STORIES FOR THE NEWSLETTER.
SO I STARTED INVENTING STORIES OF BIZARRE WORK-PLACE CRIMES.
10/13/99 © 1999 United Feature Syndicate, Inc.
SOMETIMES WE IN THE MEDIA HAVE TO GIVE THE COPYCAT CRIMINALS A LITTLE KICK-START.

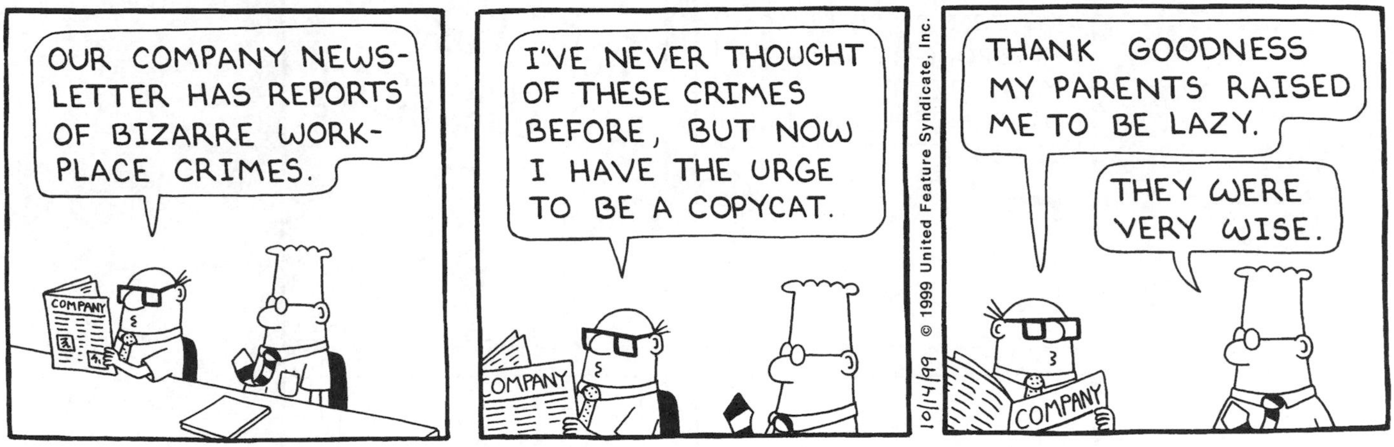
OUR COMPANY NEWSLETTER HAS REPORTS OF BIZARRE WORKPLACE CRIMES.
COMPANY
I'VE NEVER THOUGHT OF THESE CRIMES BEFORE, BUT NOW I HAVE THE URGE TO BE A COPYCAT.
COMPANY
10/14/99 © 1999 United Feature Syndicate, Inc.
THANK GOODNESS MY PARENTS RAISED ME TO BE LAZY.
THEY WERE VERY WISE.
COMPANY

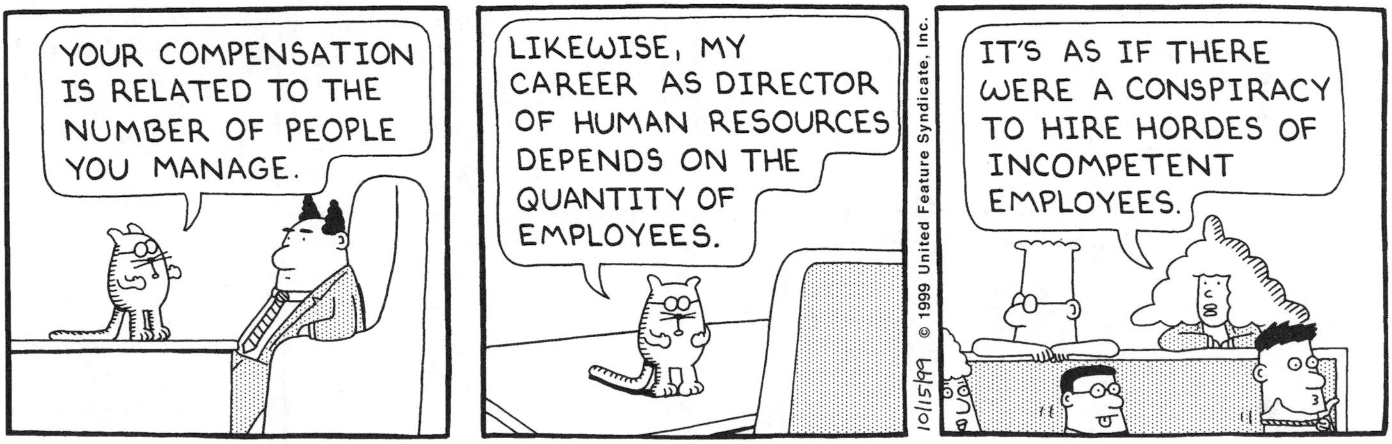
YOUR COMPENSATION IS RELATED TO THE NUMBER OF PEOPLE YOU MANAGE.
LIKEWISE, MY CAREER AS DIRECTOR OF HUMAN RESOURCES DEPENDS ON THE QUANTITY OF EMPLOYEES.
10/15/99 © 1999 United Feature Syndicate, Inc.
IT'S AS IF THERE WERE A CONSPIRACY TO HIRE HORDES OF INCOMPETENT EMPLOYEES.

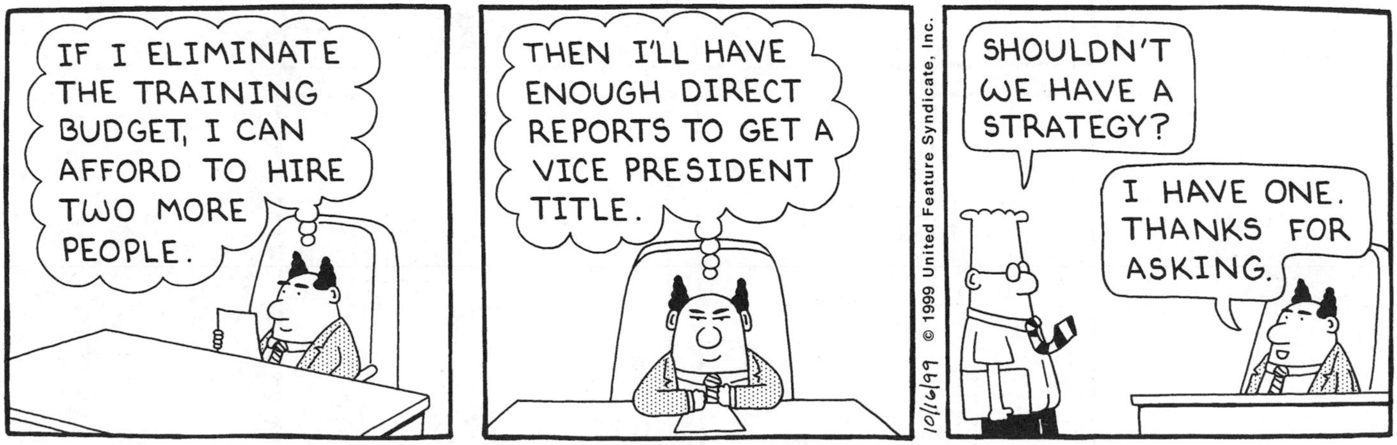
IF I ELIMINATE THE TRAINING BUDGET, I CAN AFFORD TO HIRE TWO MORE PEOPLE.
THEN I'LL HAVE ENOUGH DIRECT REPORTS TO GET A VICE PRESIDENT TITLE.
10/16/99 © 1999 United Feature Syndicate, Inc.
SHOULDN'T WE HAVE A STRATEGY?
I HAVE ONE. THANKS FOR ASKING.

MY BOSS IS SO DUMB, HE BROUGHT A TAPE MEASURE TO A DISTANCE LEARNING CLASS.
HA HA HA HA HA!
MY BOSS IS SO DUMB...
HE PUTS POSTAGE STAMPS ON HIS E-MAIL.
NOW HE CAN'T SEE HIS PC SCREEN.
HA HA HA HA HA HA
HOW ABOUT YOU, DILBERT? DO YOU HAVE ANY DUMB BOSS JOKES?
DILBERT, MY PC IS WARM. I THINK OUR FIRE WALL IS ACTING UP.
WE'RE SORRY.
WE DIDN'T KNOW.
10/17/99 © 1999 United Feature Syndicate, Inc.

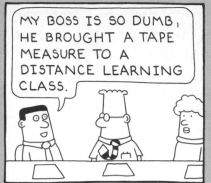

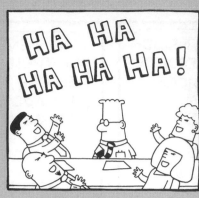

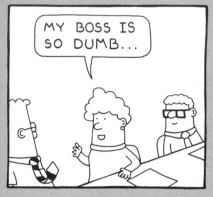

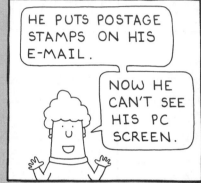

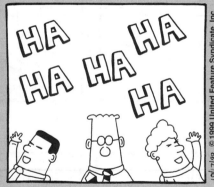

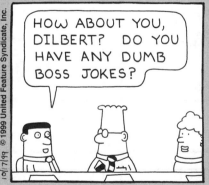

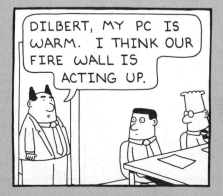

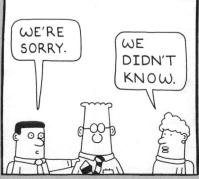

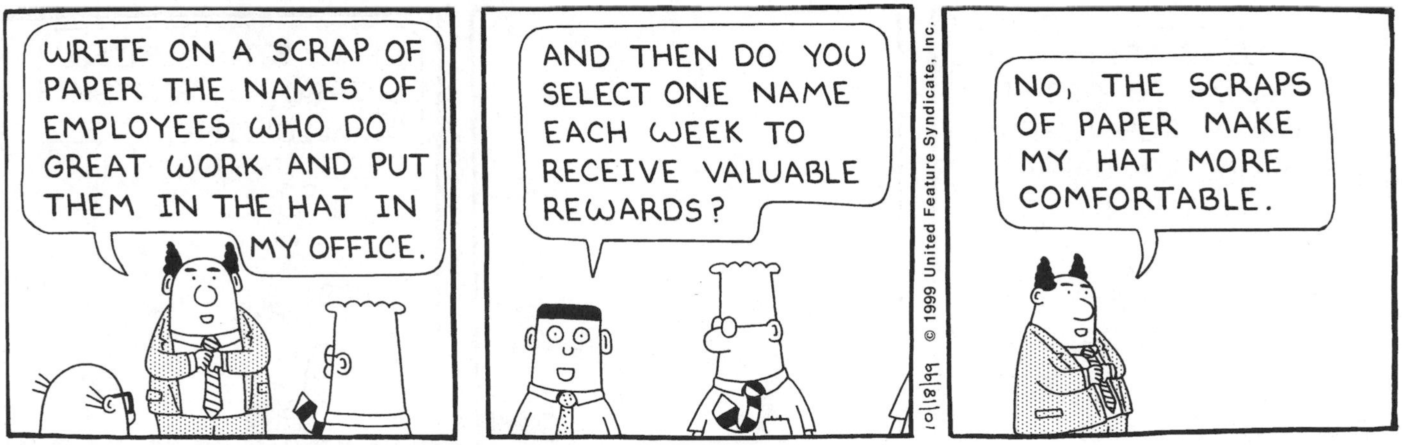
WRITE ON A SCRAP OF PAPER THE NAMES OF EMPLOYEES WHO DO GREAT WORK AND PUT THEM IN THE HAT IN MY OFFICE.
AND THEN DO YOU SELECT ONE NAME EACH WEEK TO RECEIVE VALUABLE REWARDS?
10/18/99 © 1999 United Feature Syndicate, Inc.
NO, THE SCRAPS OF PAPER MAKE MY HAT MORE COMFORTABLE.

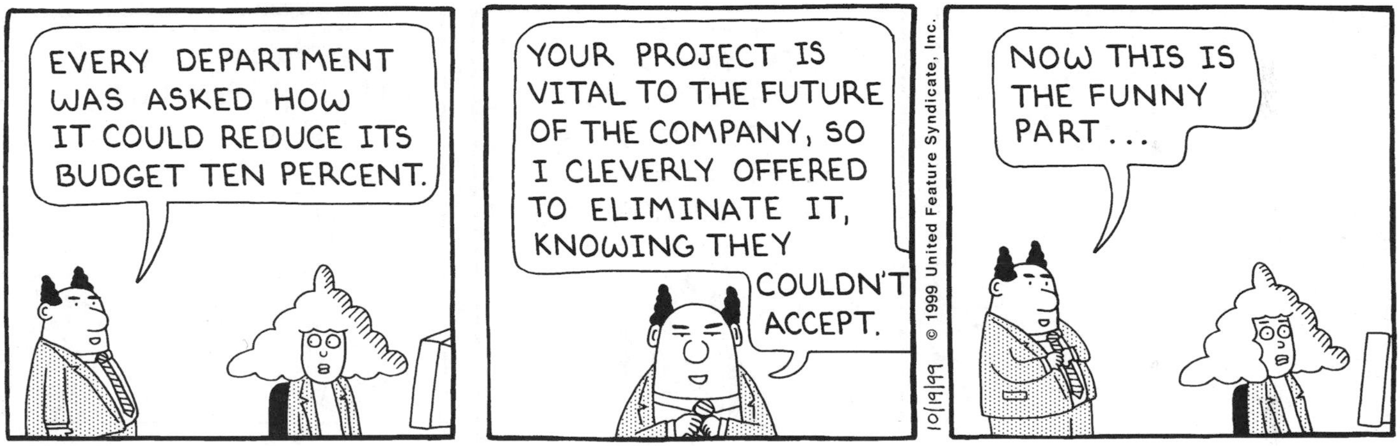
EVERY DEPARTMENT WAS ASKED HOW IT COULD REDUCE ITS BUDGET TEN PERCENT.
YOUR PROJECT IS VITAL TO THE FUTURE OF THE COMPANY, SO I CLEVERLY OFFERED TO ELIMINATE IT, KNOWING THEY COULDN'T ACCEPT.
10/19/99 © 1999 United Feature Syndicate, Inc.
NOW THIS IS THE FUNNY PART...

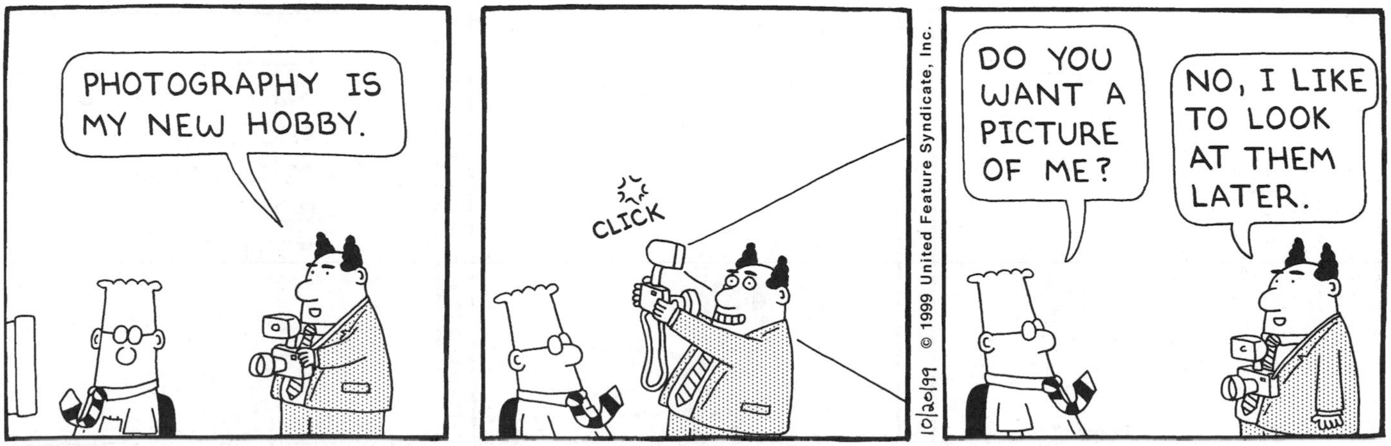
PHOTOGRAPHY IS MY NEW HOBBY.
CLICK
10/20/99 © 1999 United Feature Syndicate, Inc.
DO YOU WANT A PICTURE OF ME?
NO, I LIKE TO LOOK AT THEM LATER.

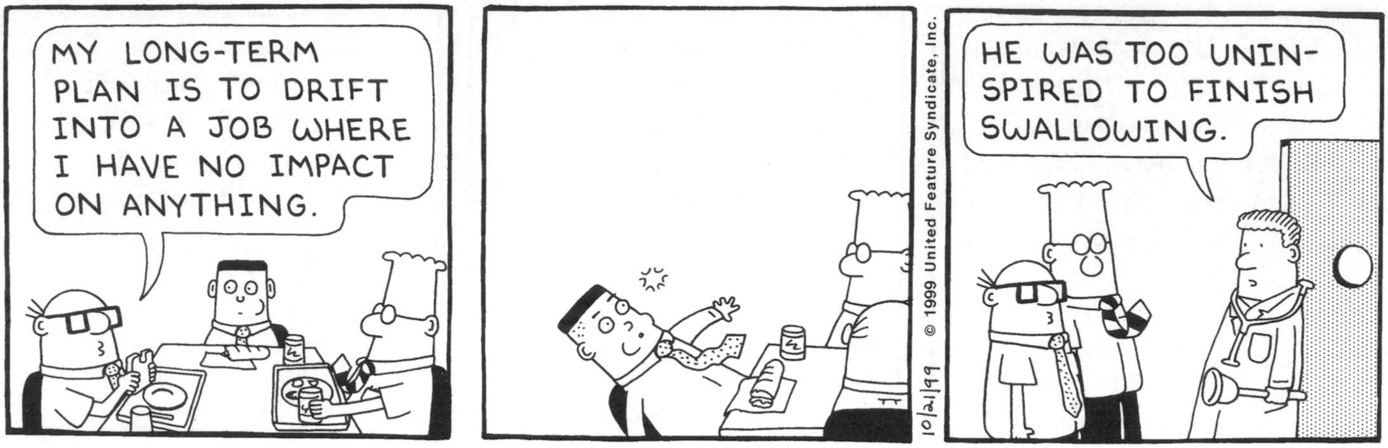
MY LONG-TERM PLAN IS TO DRIFT INTO A JOB WHERE I HAVE NO IMPACT ON ANYTHING.
10/21/99 © 1999 United Feature Syndicate, Inc.
HE WAS TOO UNIN-SPIRED TO FINISH SWALLOWING.

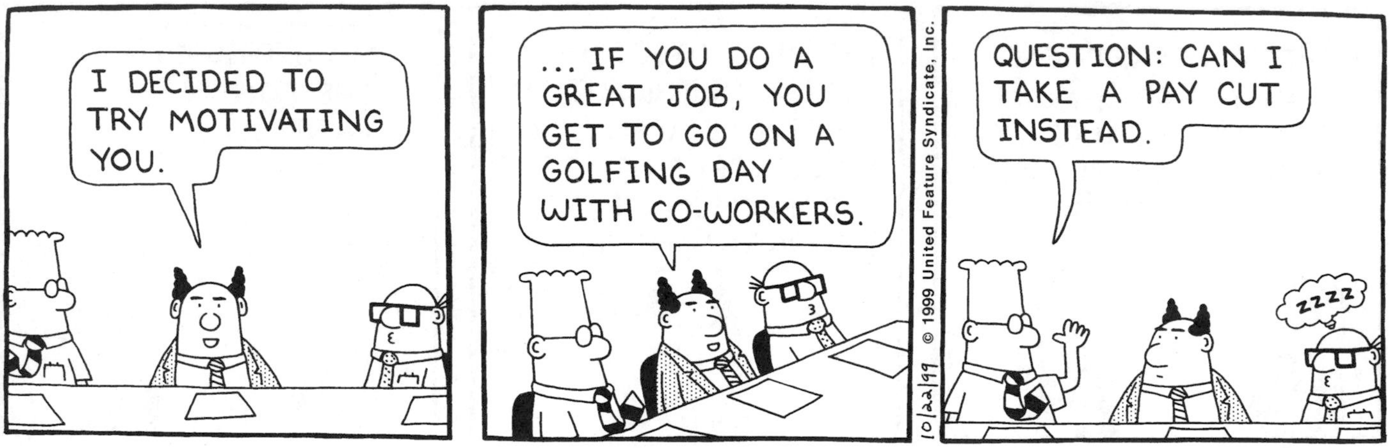
I DECIDED TO TRY MOTIVATING YOU.
... IF YOU DO A GREAT JOB, YOU GET TO GO ON A GOLFING DAY WITH CO-WORKERS.
10/22/99 © 1999 United Feature Syndicate, Inc.
QUESTION: CAN I TAKE A PAY CUT INSTEAD.
ZZZZ

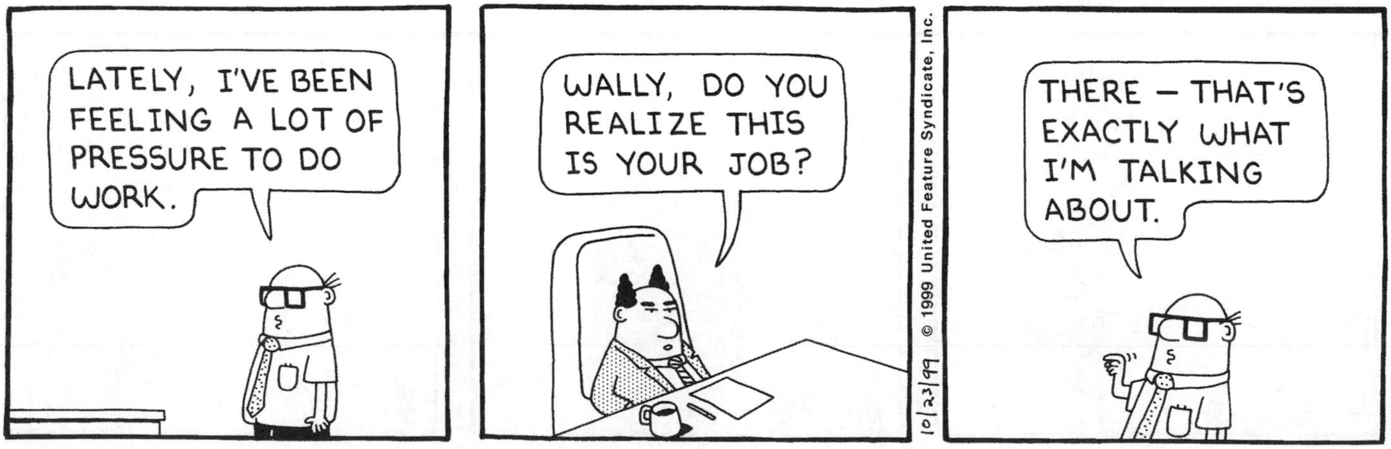
LATELY, I'VE BEEN FEELING A LOT OF PRESSURE TO DO WORK.
WALLY, DO YOU REALIZE THIS IS YOUR JOB?
10/23/99 © 1999 United Feature Syndicate, Inc.
THERE – THAT'S EXACTLY WHAT I'M TALKING ABOUT.

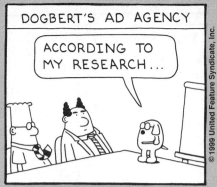

DOGBERT'S AD AGENCY
ACCORDING TO MY RESEARCH...
© 1999 United Feature Syndicate, Inc.
...PEOPLE DON'T USE YOUR PRODUCTS WHEN THEY ARE OUTDOORS.
SOMEHOW WE MUST KEEP PEOPLE INDOORS.
I RECOMMEND AN INTENSIVE AD CAMPAIGN...
FEATURING THIS SLOGAN...
OUTDOORS IS FOR LOSERS
10/24/99
THE TV SPOT WILL SHOW HUMMING-BIRDS ATTACKING A MAN IN HIS GARDEN.
QUESTION: WOULDN'T THAT DESTROY THE HAPPINESS OF GULLIBLE PEOPLE?
WE'LL TELL THEM IT DOESN'T.

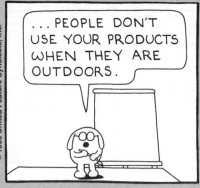

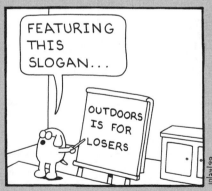

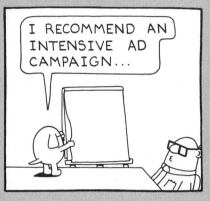

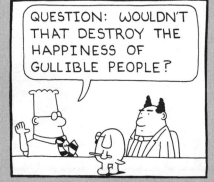

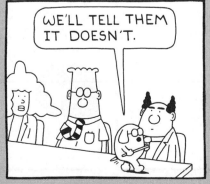

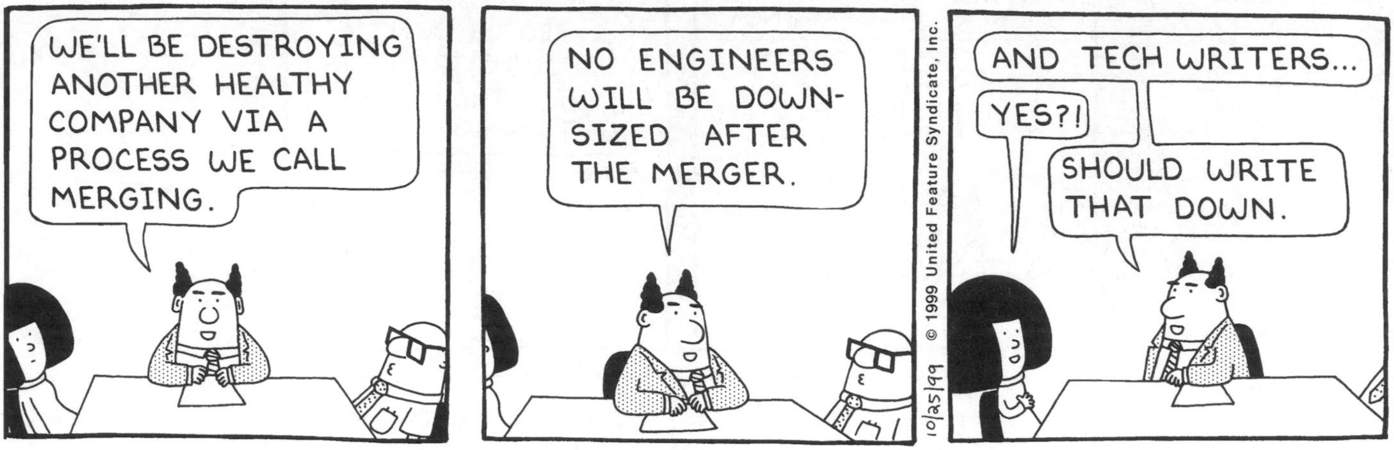
WE'LL BE DESTROYING ANOTHER HEALTHY COMPANY VIA A PROCESS WE CALL MERGING.
NO ENGINEERS WILL BE DOWN-SIZED AFTER THE MERGER.
10/25/99 © 1999 United Feature Syndicate, Inc.
AND TECH WRITERS...
YES?!
SHOULD WRITE THAT DOWN.

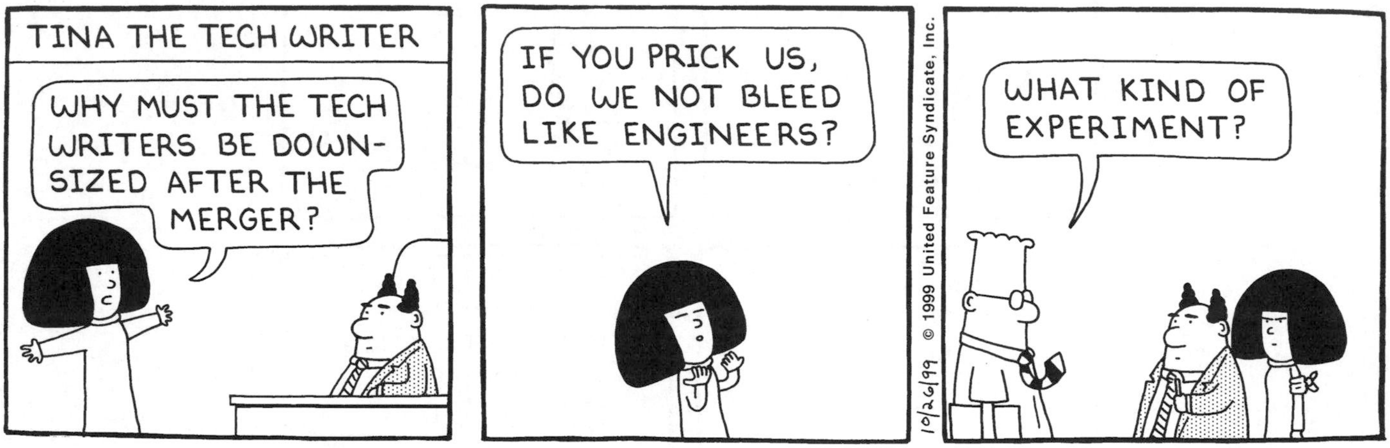
TINA THE TECH WRITER
WHY MUST THE TECH WRITERS BE DOWN-SIZED AFTER THE MERGER?
IF YOU PRICK US, DO WE NOT BLEED LIKE ENGINEERS?
10/26/99 © 1999 United Feature Syndicate, Inc.
WHAT KIND OF EXPERIMENT?

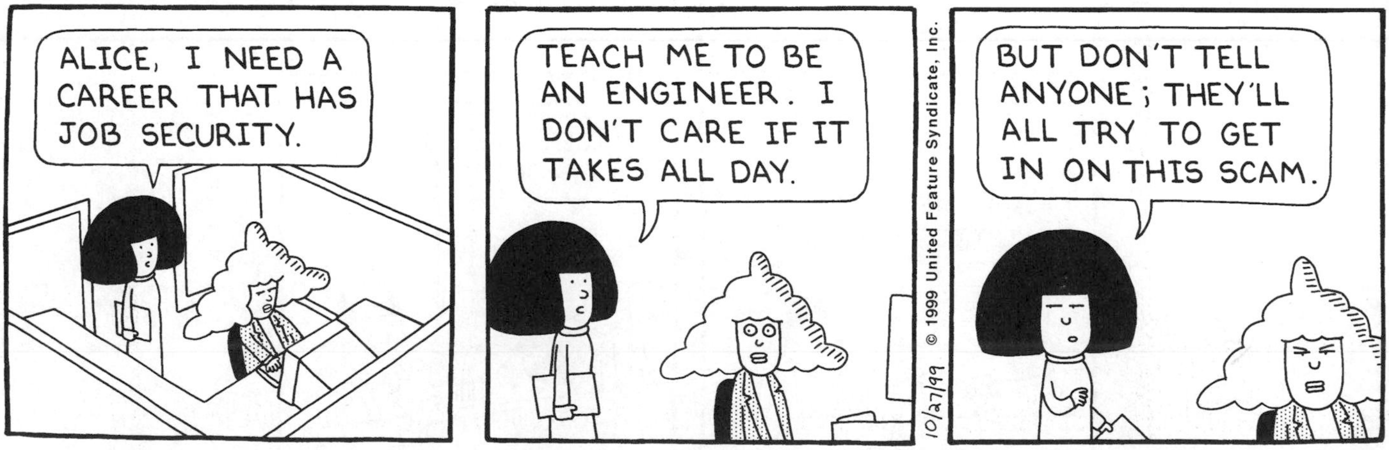
ALICE, I NEED A CAREER THAT HAS JOB SECURITY.
TEACH ME TO BE AN ENGINEER. I DON'T CARE IF IT TAKES ALL DAY.
10/27/99 © 1999 United Feature Syndicate, Inc.
BUT DON'T TELL ANYONE; THEY'LL ALL TRY TO GET IN ON THIS SCAM.

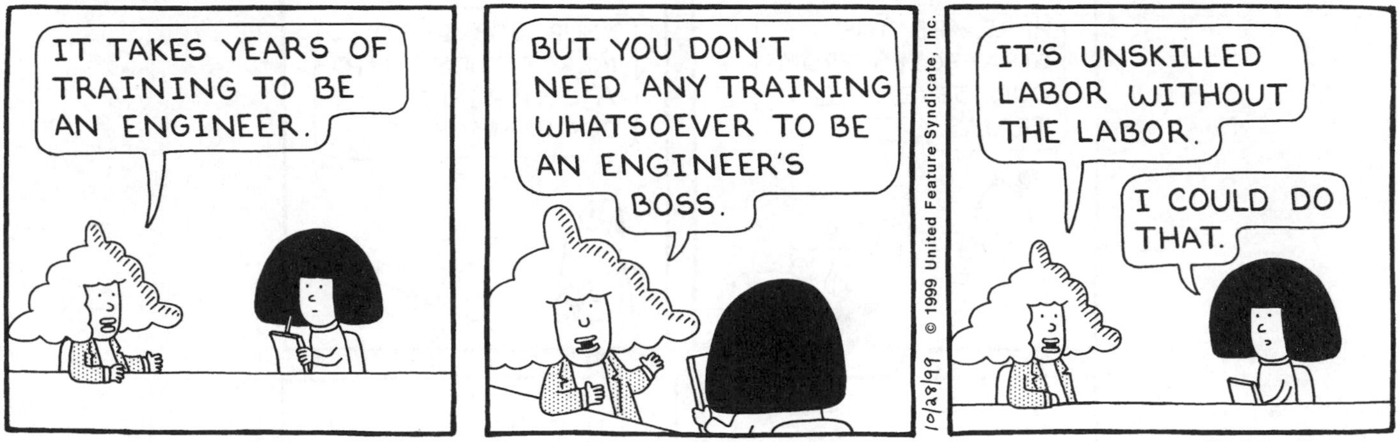
IT TAKES YEARS OF TRAINING TO BE AN ENGINEER.
BUT YOU DON'T NEED ANY TRAINING WHATSOEVER TO BE AN ENGINEER'S BOSS.
IT'S UNSKILLED LABOR WITHOUT THE LABOR.
I COULD DO THAT.
10/28/99

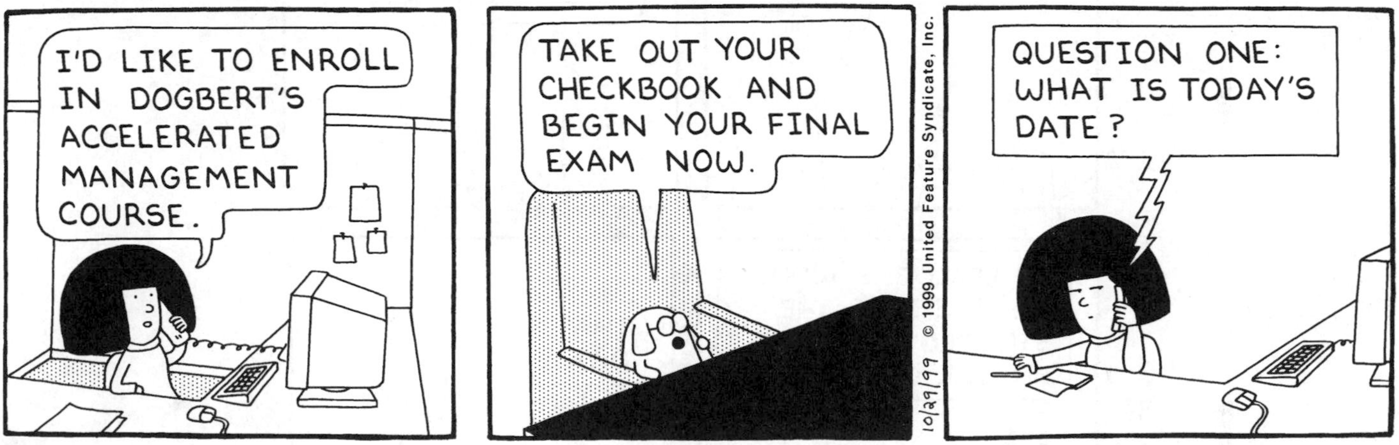
I'D LIKE TO ENROLL IN DOGBERT'S ACCELERATED MANAGEMENT COURSE.
TAKE OUT YOUR CHECKBOOK AND BEGIN YOUR FINAL EXAM NOW.
QUESTION ONE: WHAT IS TODAY'S DATE?
10/29/99

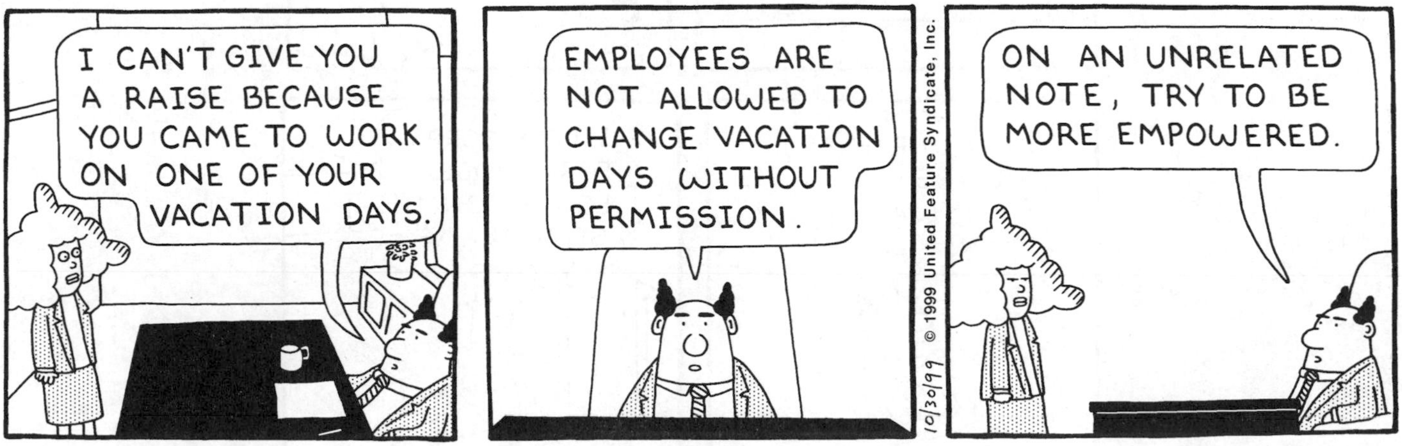
I CAN'T GIVE YOU A RAISE BECAUSE YOU CAME TO WORK ON ONE OF YOUR VACATION DAYS.
EMPLOYEES ARE NOT ALLOWED TO CHANGE VACATION DAYS WITHOUT PERMISSION.
ON AN UNRELATED NOTE, TRY TO BE MORE EMPOWERED.
10/30/99

HERE ARE THE STRATEGIES FROM OUR SEVEN SILO TEAMS.
YOUR JOB IS TO MERGE THEM INTO A COHERENT COMPANY PLAN.
THESE ARE ALL MUTUALLY EXCLUSIVE.
I'D HAVE TO TOTALLY CHANGE THEM TO MAKE THEM COHERENT.
IN EFFECT, I WOULD BE DECIDING THE STRATEGY FOR THE ENTIRE COMPANY.
© 1999 United Feature Syndicate, Inc.
10/31/99
THAT'S OKAY.
IT IS?
NO ONE EVER READS IT ANYWAY.
I FEEL SORRY FOR THOSE LOSERS ON THE SILO TEAMS.

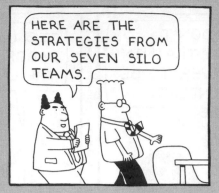

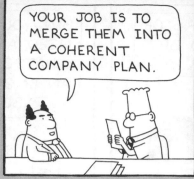

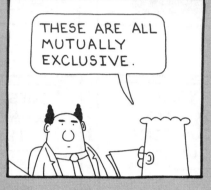

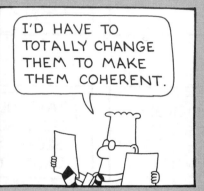

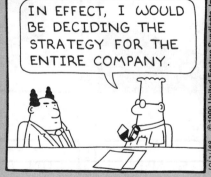

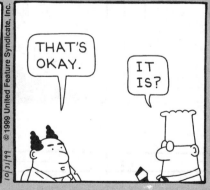

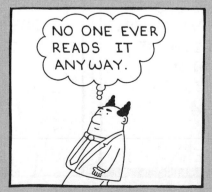

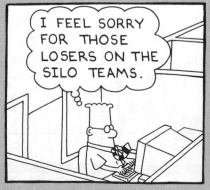

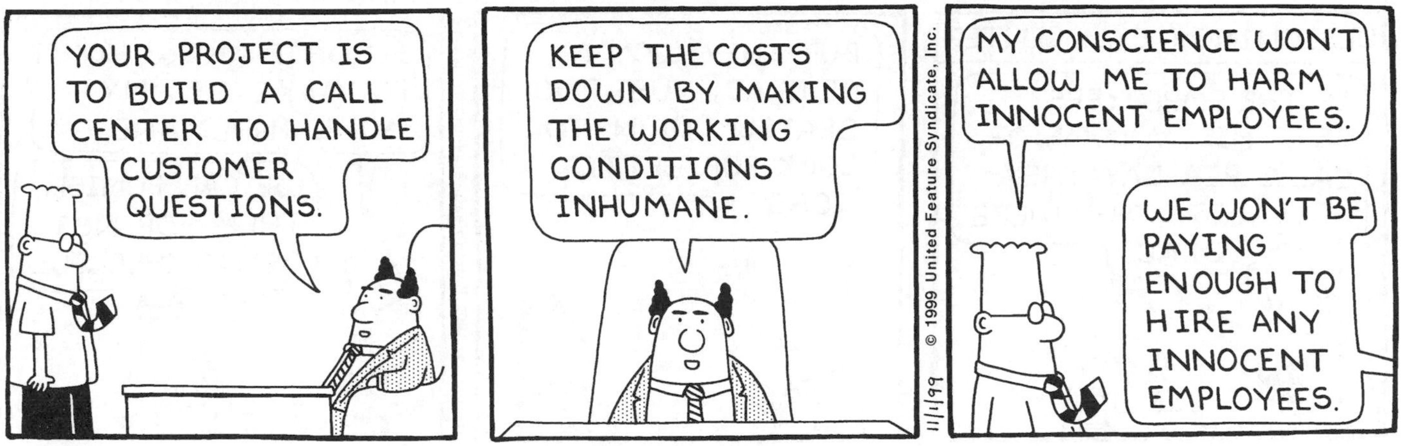
YOUR PROJECT IS TO BUILD A CALL CENTER TO HANDLE CUSTOMER QUESTIONS.
KEEP THE COSTS DOWN BY MAKING THE WORKING CONDITIONS INHUMANE.
11/1/99 © 1999 United Feature Syndicate, Inc.
MY CONSCIENCE WON'T ALLOW ME TO HARM INNOCENT EMPLOYEES.
WE WON'T BE PAYING ENOUGH TO HIRE ANY INNOCENT EMPLOYEES.

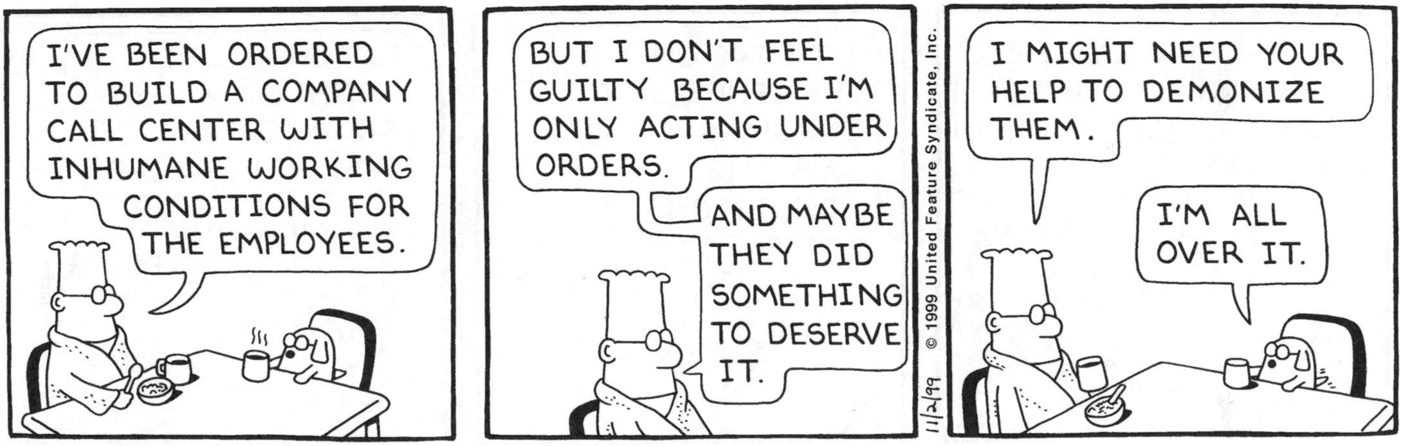
I'VE BEEN ORDERED TO BUILD A COMPANY CALL CENTER WITH INHUMANE WORKING CONDITIONS FOR THE EMPLOYEES.
BUT I DON'T FEEL GUILTY BECAUSE I'M ONLY ACTING UNDER ORDERS.
AND MAYBE THEY DID SOMETHING TO DESERVE IT.
11/2/99 © 1999 United Feature Syndicate, Inc.
I MIGHT NEED YOUR HELP TO DEMONIZE THEM.
I'M ALL OVER IT.

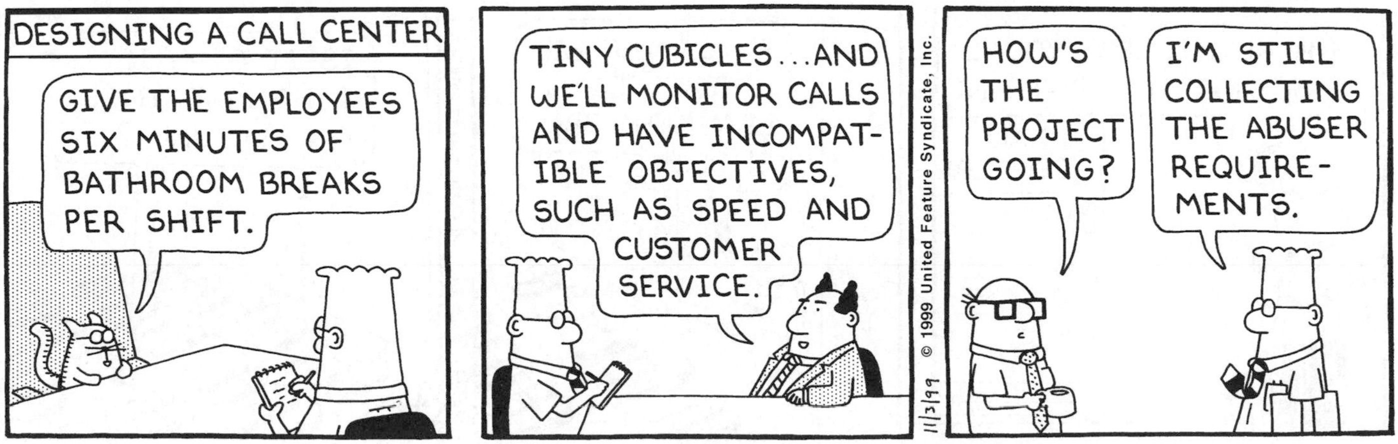
DESIGNING A CALL CENTER
GIVE THE EMPLOYEES SIX MINUTES OF BATHROOM BREAKS PER SHIFT.
TINY CUBICLES...AND WE'LL MONITOR CALLS AND HAVE INCOMPAT-IBLE OBJECTIVES, SUCH AS SPEED AND CUSTOMER SERVICE.
11/3/99 © 1999 United Feature Syndicate, Inc.
HOW'S THE PROJECT GOING?
I'M STILL COLLECTING THE ABUSER REQUIRE-MENTS.

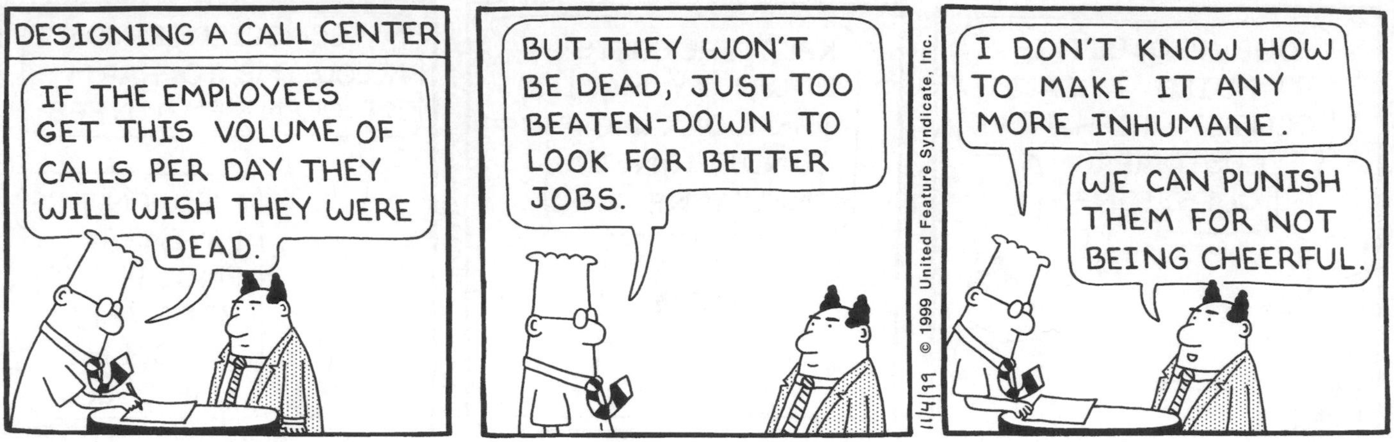
DESIGNING A CALL CENTER
IF THE EMPLOYEES GET THIS VOLUME OF CALLS PER DAY THEY WILL WISH THEY WERE DEAD.
BUT THEY WON'T BE DEAD, JUST TOO BEATEN-DOWN TO LOOK FOR BETTER JOBS.
11/4/99 © 1999 United Feature Syndicate, Inc.
I DON'T KNOW HOW TO MAKE IT ANY MORE INHUMANE.
WE CAN PUNISH THEM FOR NOT BEING CHEERFUL.

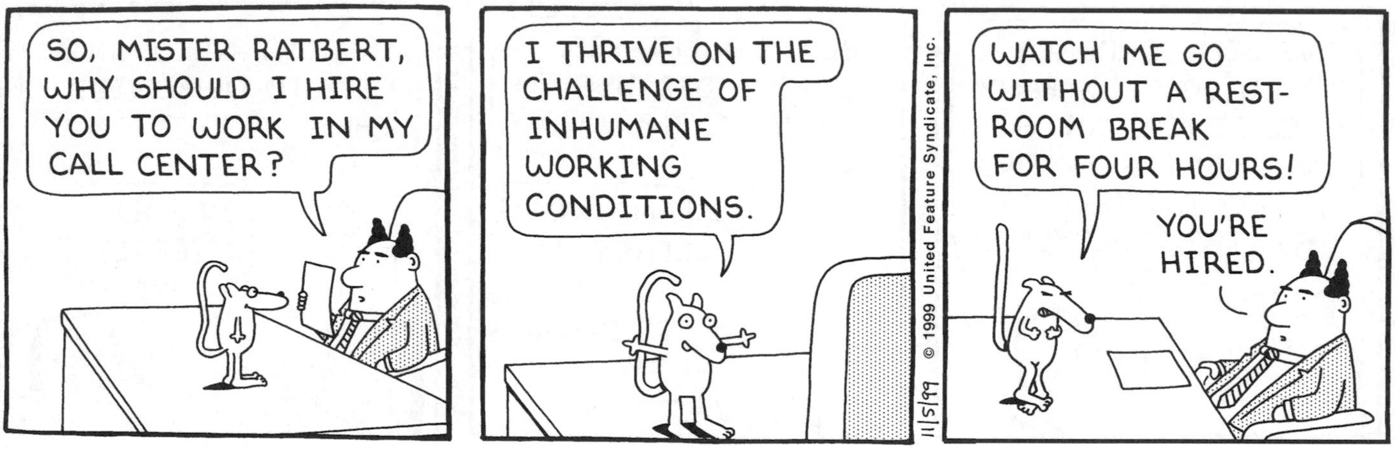
SO, MISTER RATBERT, WHY SHOULD I HIRE YOU TO WORK IN MY CALL CENTER?
I THRIVE ON THE CHALLENGE OF INHUMANE WORKING CONDITIONS.
11/5/99 © 1999 United Feature Syndicate, Inc.
WATCH ME GO WITHOUT A REST-ROOM BREAK FOR FOUR HOURS!
YOU'RE HIRED.

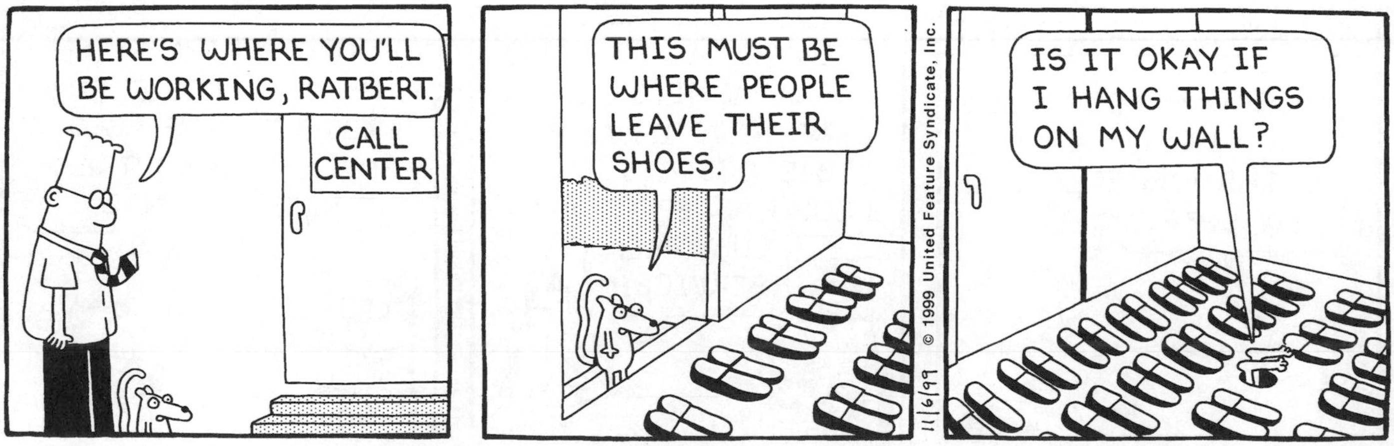
HERE'S WHERE YOU'LL BE WORKING, RATBERT.
CALL CENTER
THIS MUST BE WHERE PEOPLE LEAVE THEIR SHOES.
11/6/99 © 1999 United Feature Syndicate, Inc.
IS IT OKAY IF I HANG THINGS ON MY WALL?

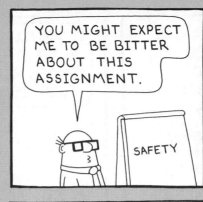

I'M THE NEWLY DESIGNATED FIRE WARDEN FOR THIS FLOOR.
SAFETY
YOU MIGHT EXPECT ME TO BE BITTER ABOUT THIS ASSIGNMENT.
SAFETY
GRANTED, IT TELLS THE WORLD I WASN'T PRODUCTIVE AT MY REGULAR JOB.
SAFETY
AND IF THE BUILDING BURNS, I'M EXPECTED TO BE THE LAST ONE OUT.
BUT MY ONLY CONCERN IS YOUR SAFETY.
SAFETY
IN THE EVENT OF A FIRE, DON'T BE TOO PROUD TO PANIC.
AAAGH!
IF THE WINDOWS WON'T OPEN, TRY FLUSHING YOURSELF TO SAFETY.
AND NEVER, EVER GET BETWEEN ME AND THE EXIT DOOR.
WALLY...
11/7/99
© 1999 United Feature Syndicate, Inc.

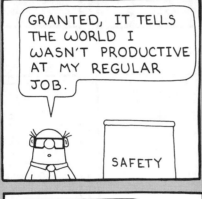

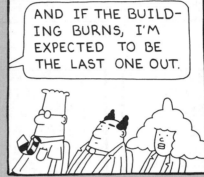

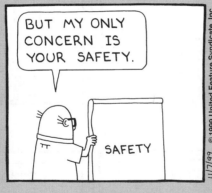

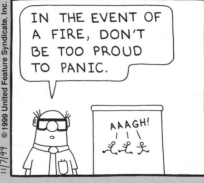

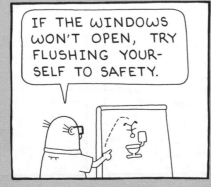

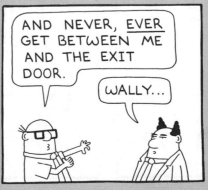

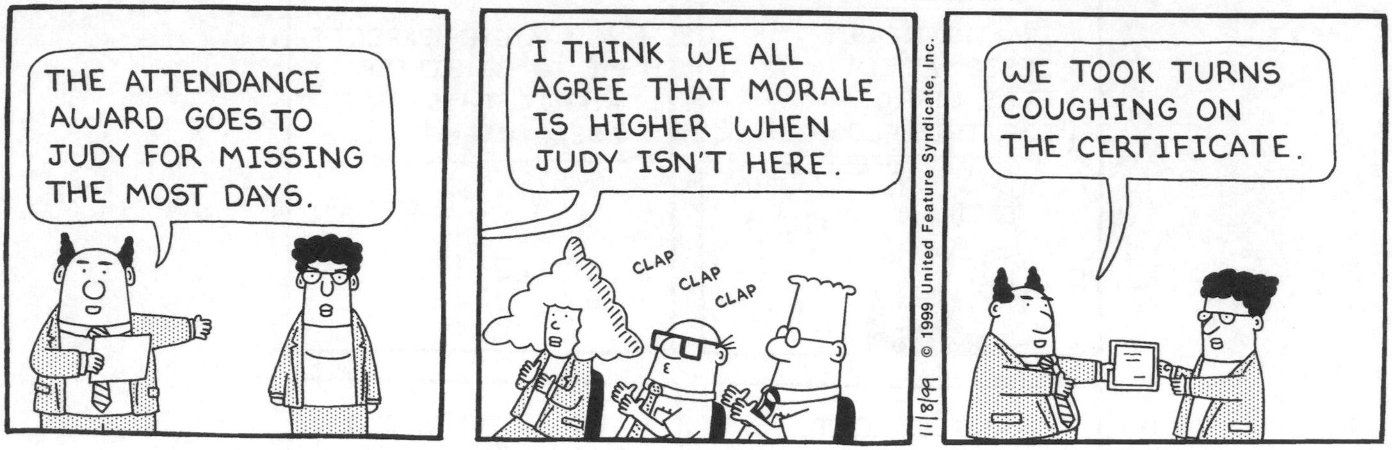
THE ATTENDANCE AWARD GOES TO JUDY FOR MISSING THE MOST DAYS.
I THINK WE ALL AGREE THAT MORALE IS HIGHER WHEN JUDY ISN'T HERE.
CLAP
CLAP
CLAP
11/8/99 © 1999 United Feature Syndicate, Inc.
WE TOOK TURNS COUGHING ON THE CERTIFICATE.

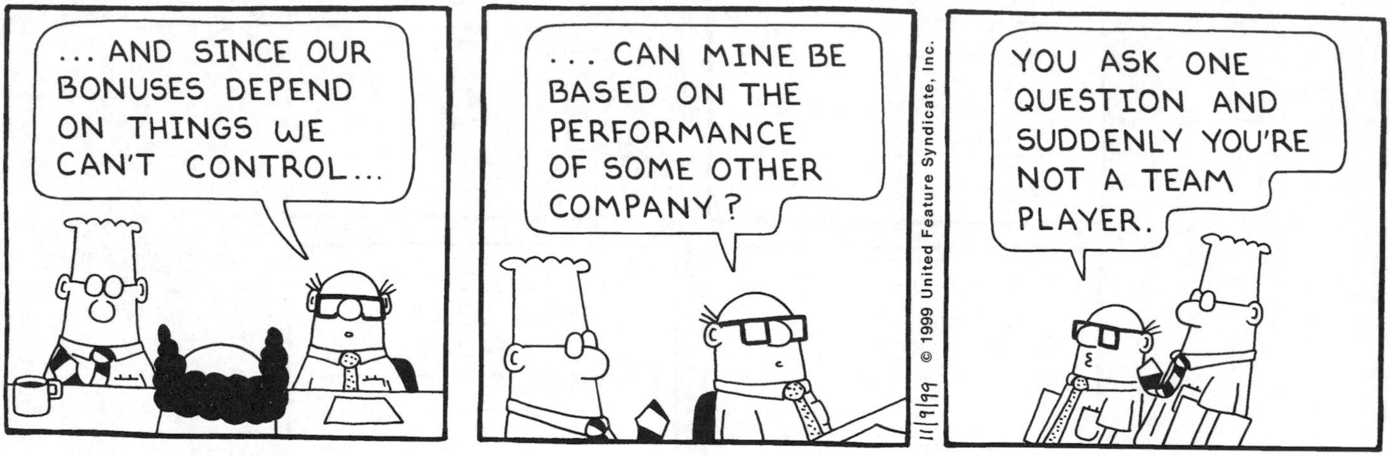
... AND SINCE OUR BONUSES DEPEND ON THINGS WE CAN'T CONTROL...
... CAN MINE BE BASED ON THE PERFORMANCE OF SOME OTHER COMPANY?
11/9/99 © 1999 United Feature Syndicate, Inc.
YOU ASK ONE QUESTION AND SUDDENLY YOU'RE NOT A TEAM PLAYER.

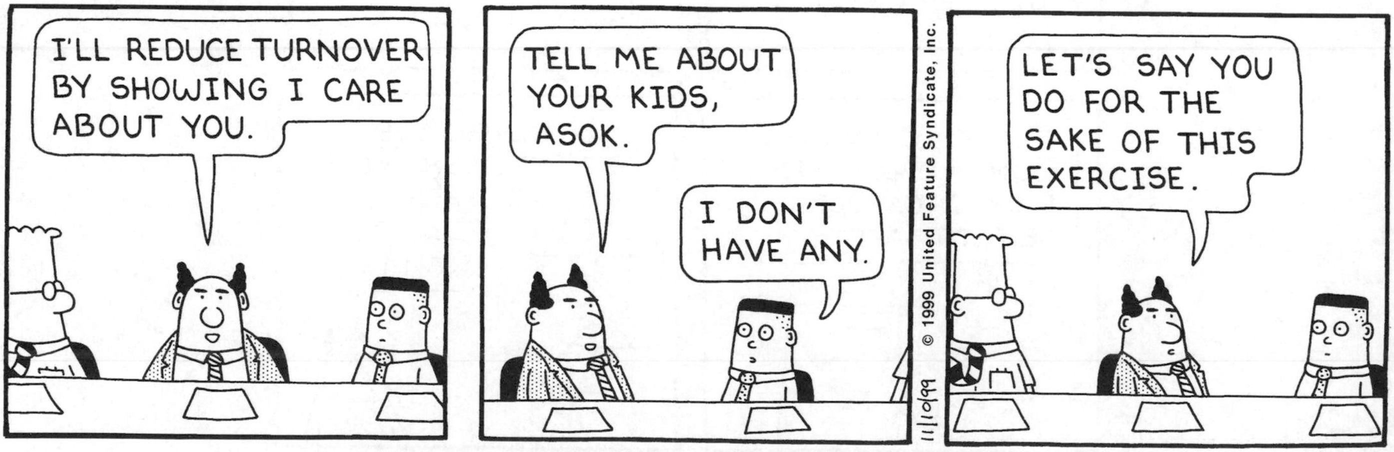
I'LL REDUCE TURNOVER BY SHOWING I CARE ABOUT YOU.
TELL ME ABOUT YOUR KIDS, ASOK.
I DON'T HAVE ANY.
11/10/99 © 1999 United Feature Syndicate, Inc.
LET'S SAY YOU DO FOR THE SAKE OF THIS EXERCISE.

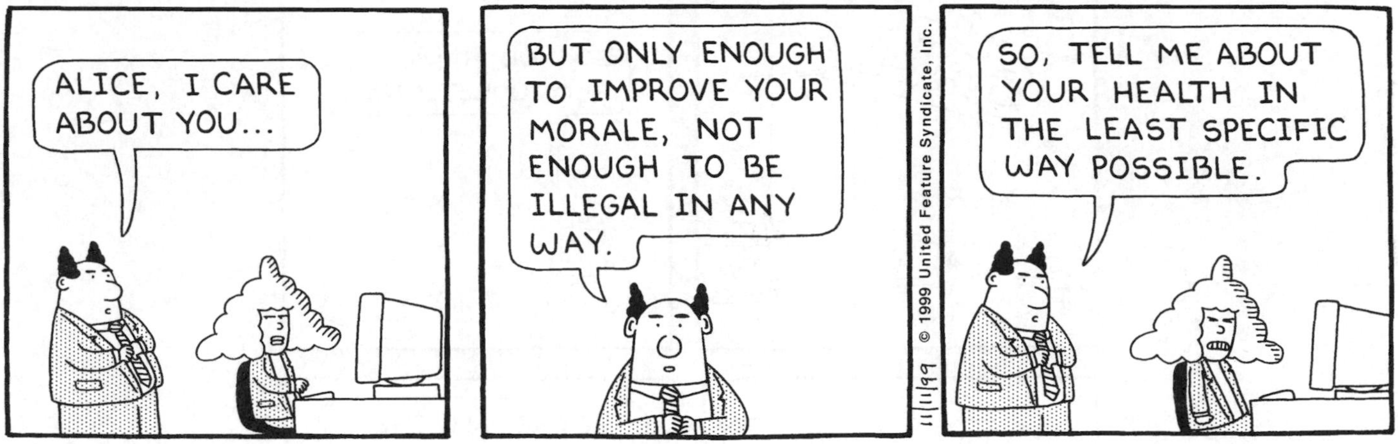
ALICE, I CARE ABOUT YOU...
BUT ONLY ENOUGH TO IMPROVE YOUR MORALE, NOT ENOUGH TO BE ILLEGAL IN ANY WAY.
11/11/99 © 1999 United Feature Syndicate, Inc.
SO, TELL ME ABOUT YOUR HEALTH IN THE LEAST SPECIFIC WAY POSSIBLE.

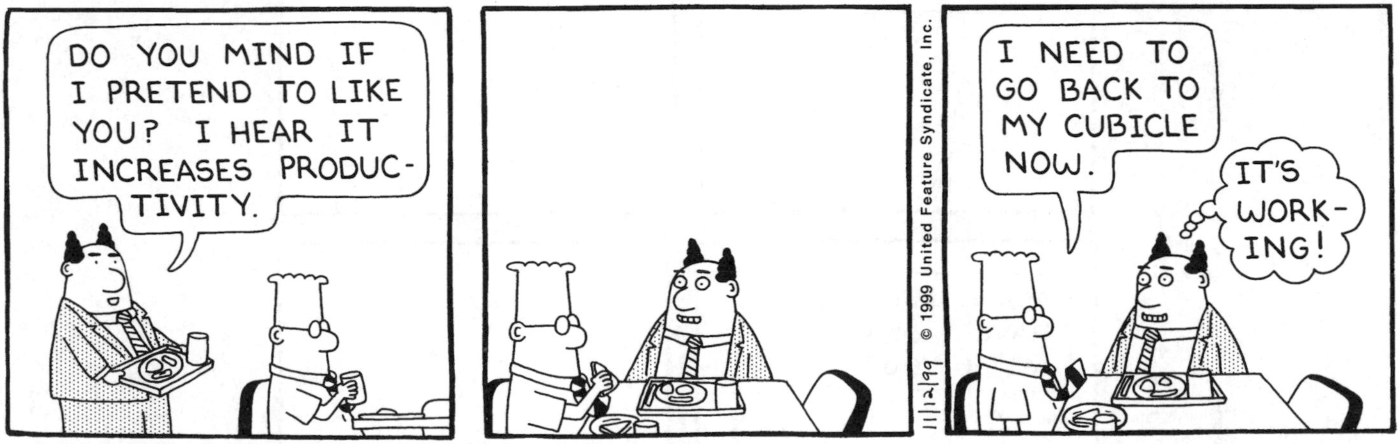
DO YOU MIND IF I PRETEND TO LIKE YOU? I HEAR IT INCREASES PRODUCTIVITY.
11/12/99 © 1999 United Feature Syndicate, Inc.
I NEED TO GO BACK TO MY CUBICLE NOW.
IT'S WORKING!

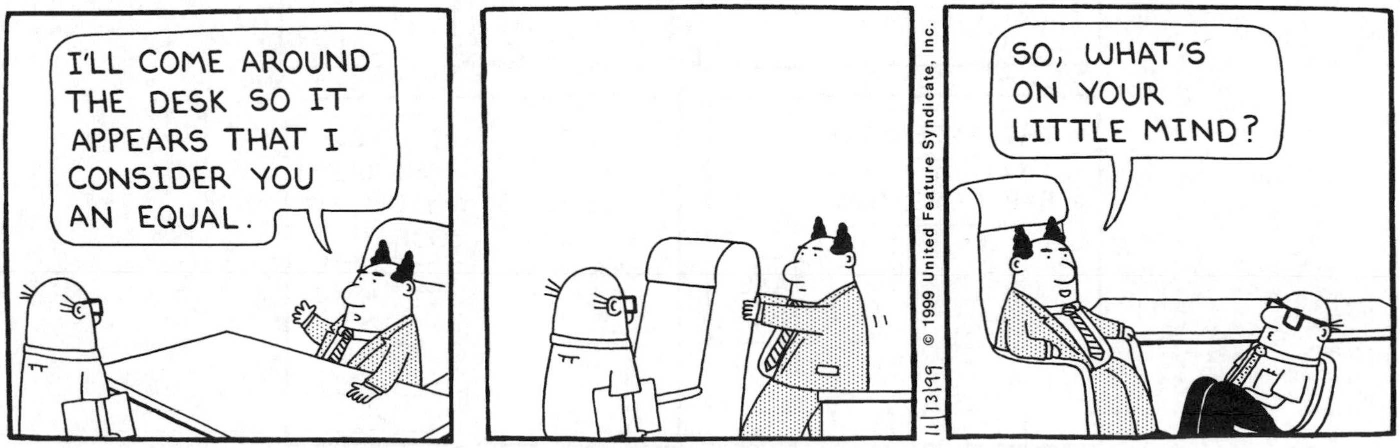
I'LL COME AROUND THE DESK SO IT APPEARS THAT I CONSIDER YOU AN EQUAL.
11/13/99 © 1999 United Feature Syndicate, Inc.
SO, WHAT'S ON YOUR LITTLE MIND?

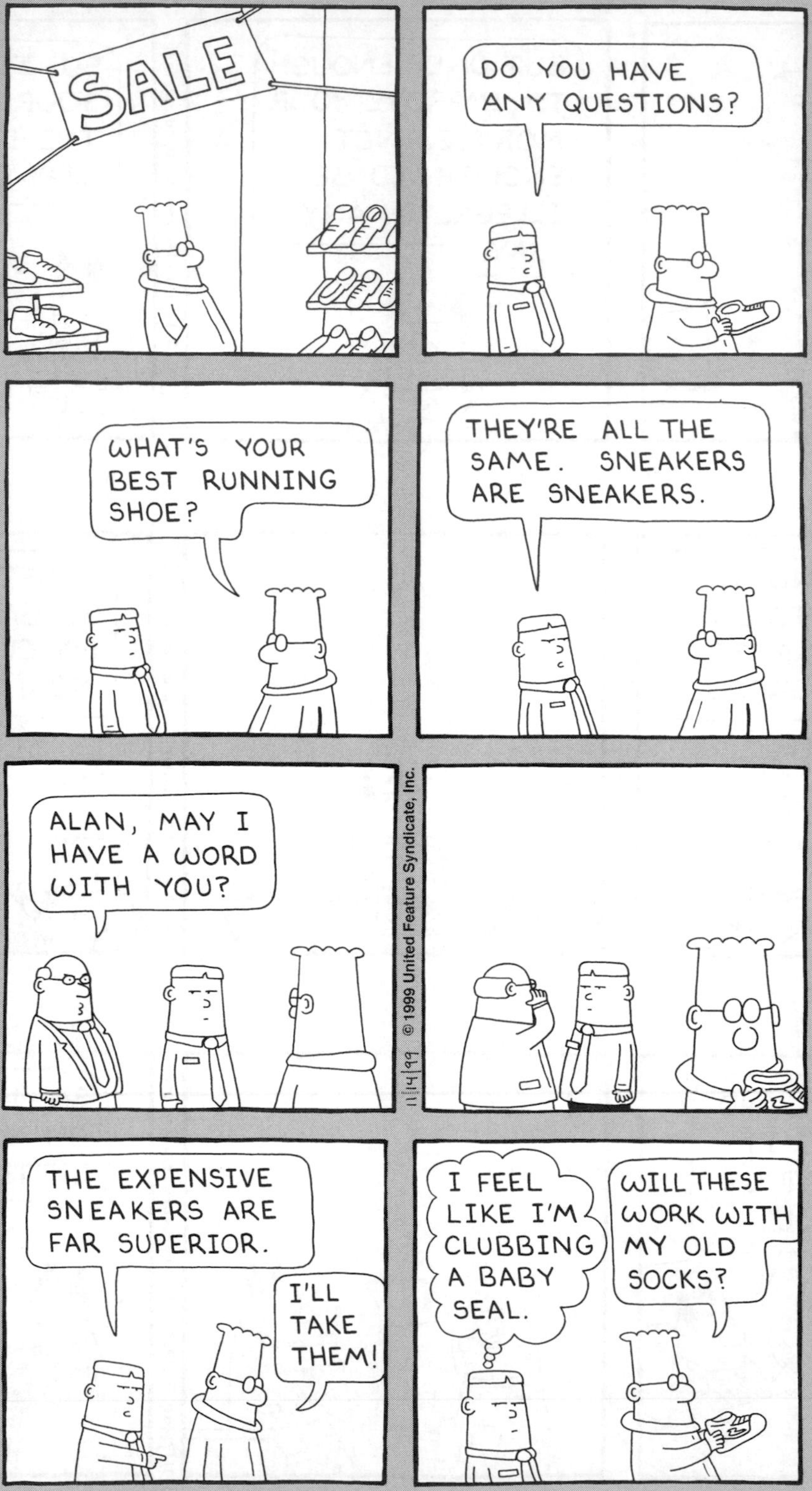
SALE
DO YOU HAVE ANY QUESTIONS?
WHAT'S YOUR BEST RUNNING SHOE?
THEY'RE ALL THE SAME. SNEAKERS ARE SNEAKERS.
ALAN, MAY I HAVE A WORD WITH YOU?
© 1999 United Feature Syndicate, Inc.
11/14/99
THE EXPENSIVE SNEAKERS ARE FAR SUPERIOR.
I'LL TAKE THEM!
I FEEL LIKE I'M CLUBBING A BABY SEAL.
WILL THESE WORK WITH MY OLD SOCKS?

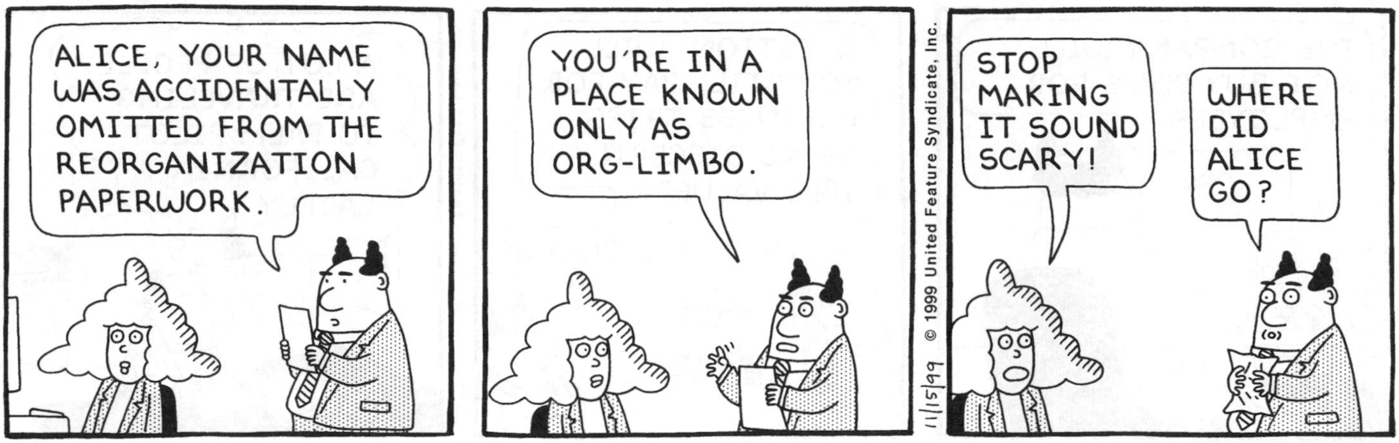
ALICE, YOUR NAME WAS ACCIDENTALLY OMITTED FROM THE REORGANIZATION PAPERWORK.
YOU'RE IN A PLACE KNOWN ONLY AS ORG-LIMBO.
11/15/99 © 1999 United Feature Syndicate, Inc.
STOP MAKING IT SOUND SCARY!
WHERE DID ALICE GO?

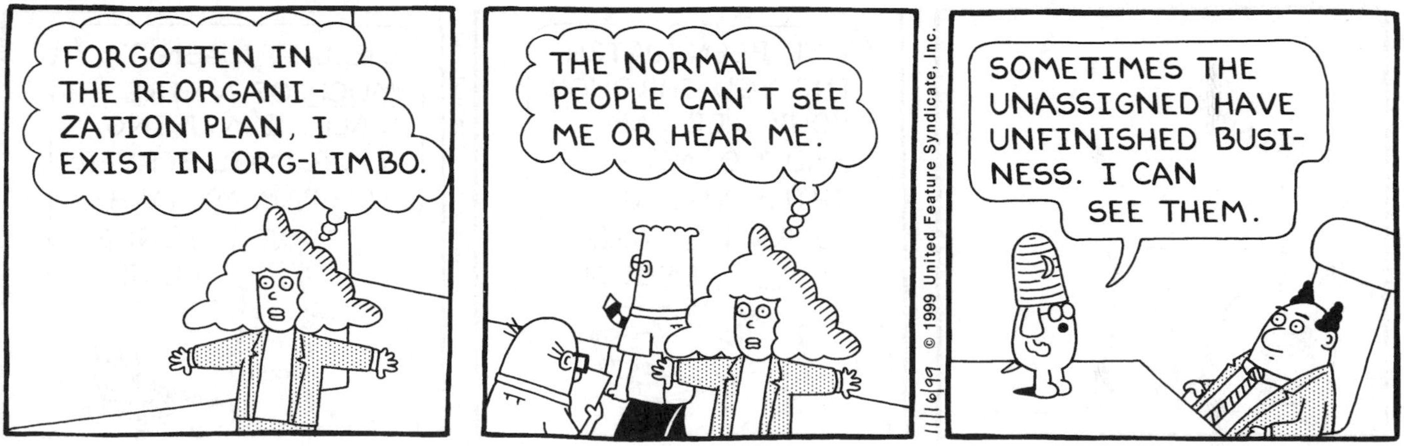
FORGOTTEN IN THE REORGANIZATION PLAN, I EXIST IN ORG-LIMBO.
THE NORMAL PEOPLE CAN'T SEE ME OR HEAR ME.
11/16/99 © 1999 United Feature Syndicate, Inc.
SOMETIMES THE UNASSIGNED HAVE UNFINISHED BUSINESS. I CAN SEE THEM.

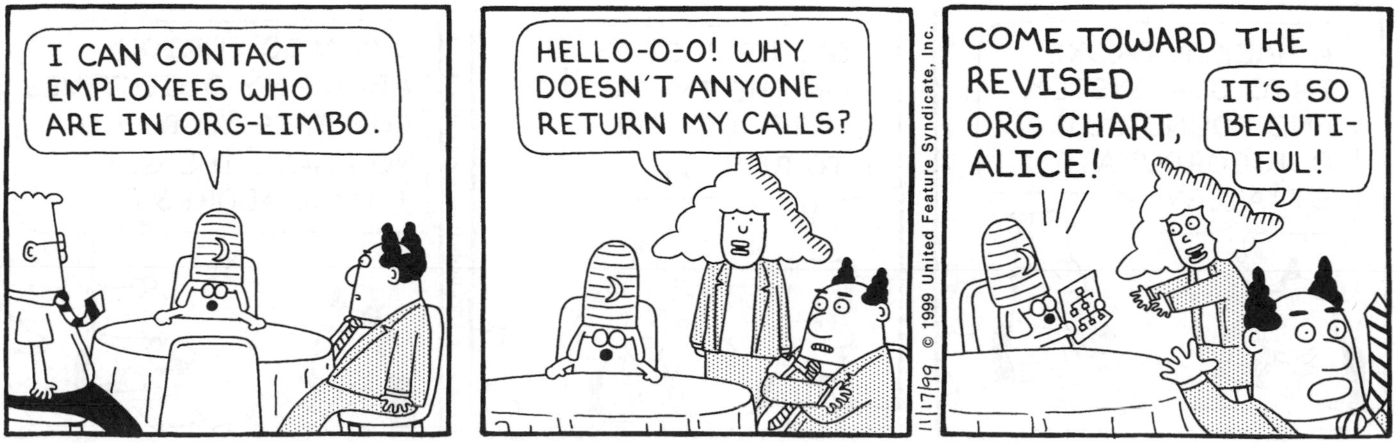
I CAN CONTACT EMPLOYEES WHO ARE IN ORG-LIMBO.
HELLO-O-O! WHY DOESN'T ANYONE RETURN MY CALLS?
11/17/99 © 1999 United Feature Syndicate, Inc.
COME TOWARD THE REVISED ORG CHART, ALICE!
IT'S SO BEAUTIFUL!

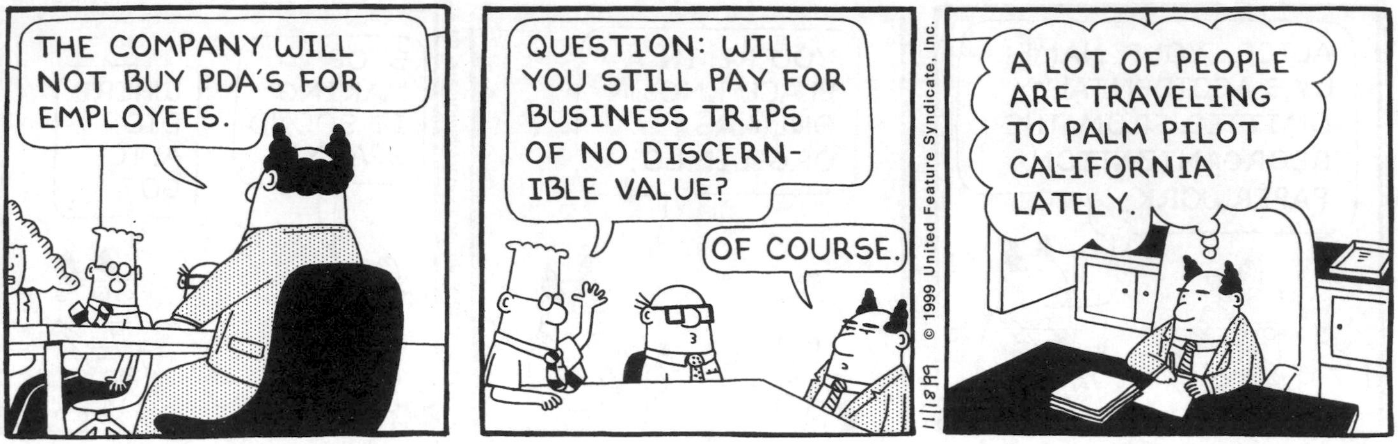
THE COMPANY WILL NOT BUY PDA'S FOR EMPLOYEES.
QUESTION: WILL YOU STILL PAY FOR BUSINESS TRIPS OF NO DISCERN-IBLE VALUE?
OF COURSE.
A LOT OF PEOPLE ARE TRAVELING TO PALM PILOT CALIFORNIA LATELY.
11/18/99
© 1999 United Feature Syndicate, Inc.

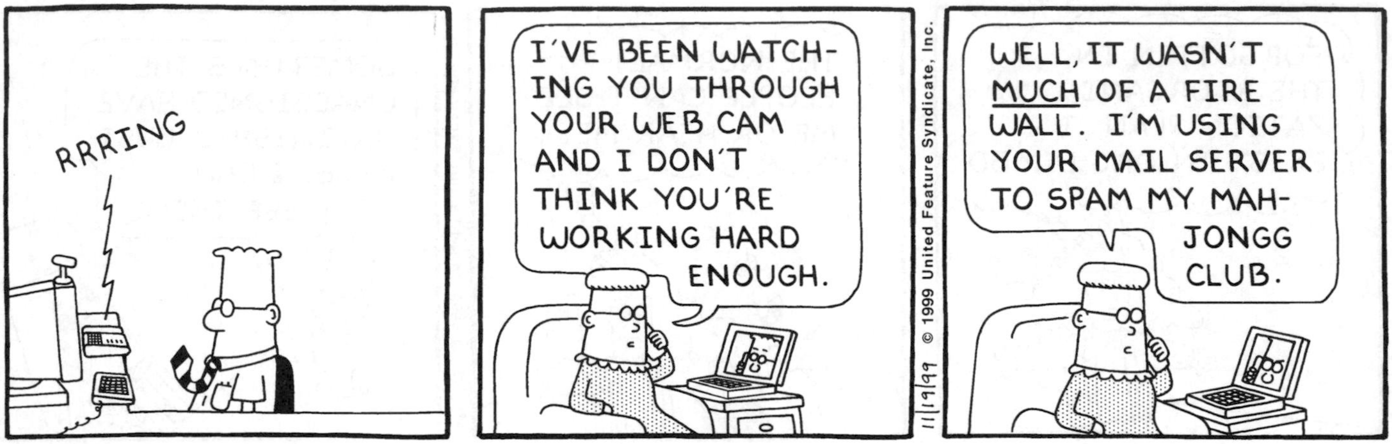
RRRING
I'VE BEEN WATCH-ING YOU THROUGH YOUR WEB CAM AND I DON'T THINK YOU'RE WORKING HARD ENOUGH.
WELL, IT WASN'T MUCH OF A FIRE WALL. I'M USING YOUR MAIL SERVER TO SPAM MY MAH-JONGG CLUB.
11/19/99
© 1999 United Feature Syndicate, Inc.

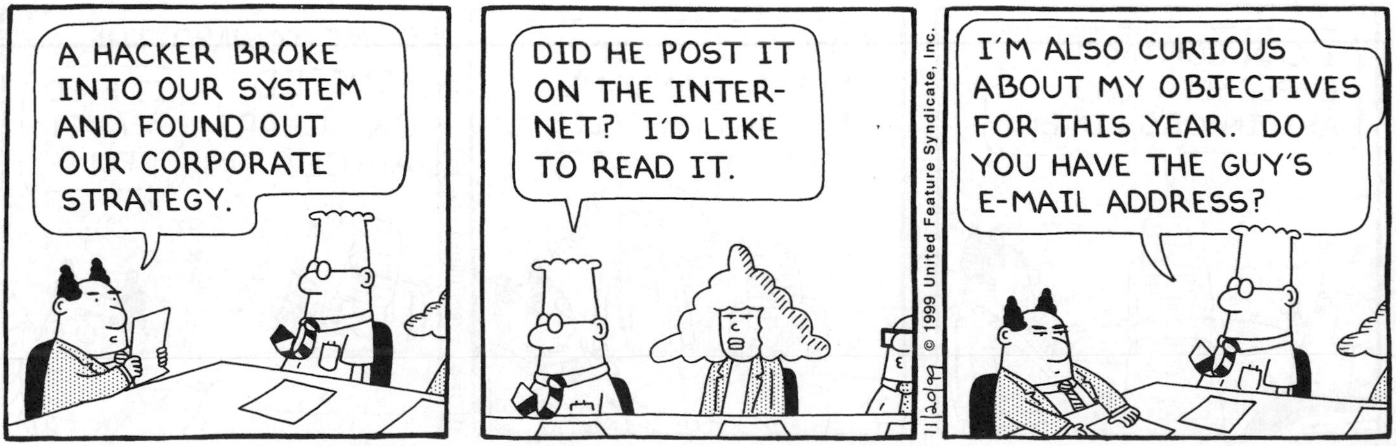
A HACKER BROKE INTO OUR SYSTEM AND FOUND OUT OUR CORPORATE STRATEGY.
DID HE POST IT ON THE INTER-NET? I'D LIKE TO READ IT.
I'M ALSO CURIOUS ABOUT MY OBJECTIVES FOR THIS YEAR. DO YOU HAVE THE GUY'S E-MAIL ADDRESS?
11/20/99
© 1999 United Feature Syndicate, Inc.

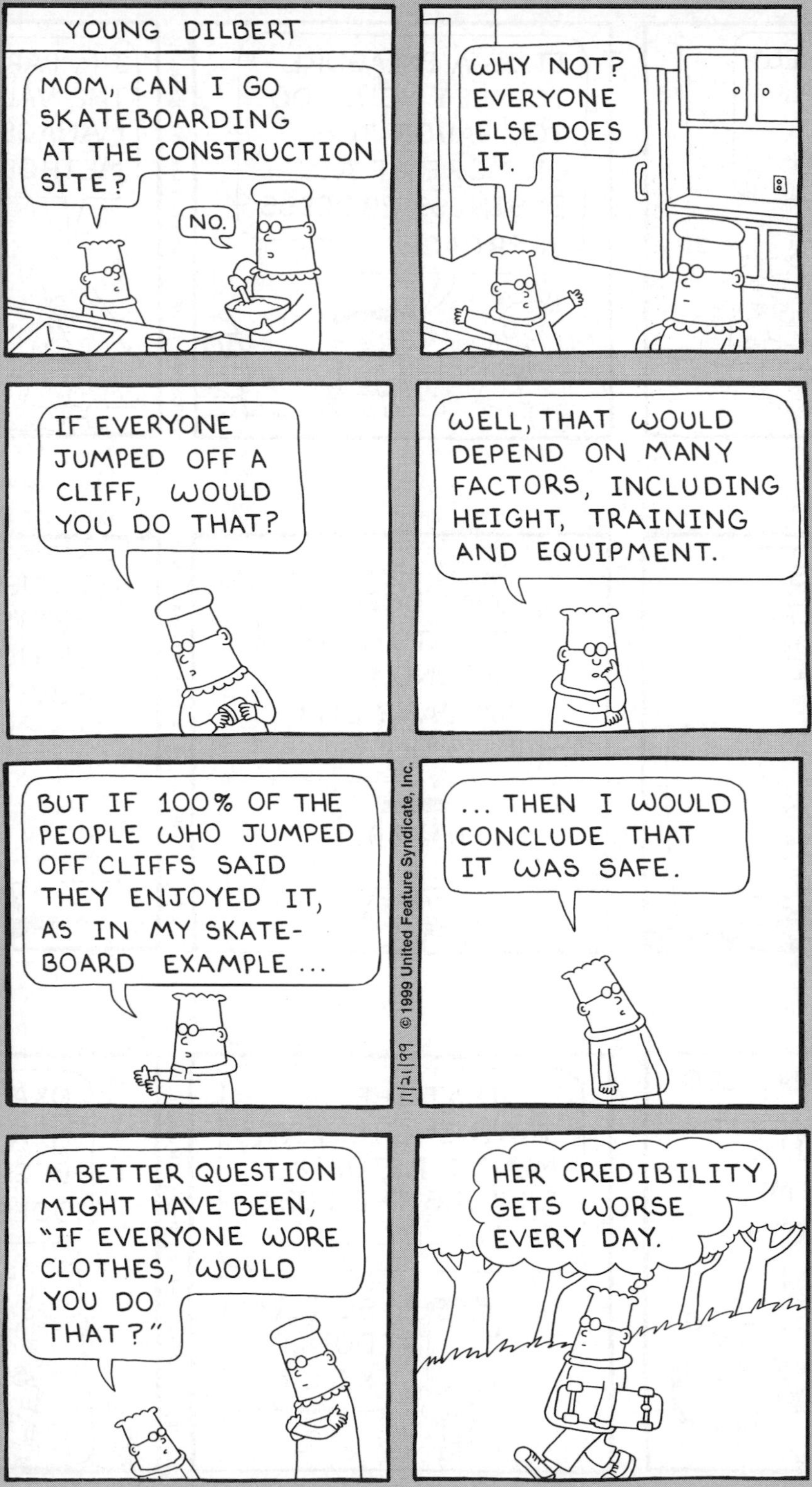
YOUNG DILBERT
MOM, CAN I GO SKATEBOARDING AT THE CONSTRUCTION SITE?
NO.
WHY NOT? EVERYONE ELSE DOES IT.
IF EVERYONE JUMPED OFF A CLIFF, WOULD YOU DO THAT?
WELL, THAT WOULD DEPEND ON MANY FACTORS, INCLUDING HEIGHT, TRAINING AND EQUIPMENT.
BUT IF 100% OF THE PEOPLE WHO JUMPED OFF CLIFFS SAID THEY ENJOYED IT, AS IN MY SKATE-BOARD EXAMPLE ...
... THEN I WOULD CONCLUDE THAT IT WAS SAFE.
A BETTER QUESTION MIGHT HAVE BEEN, "IF EVERYONE WORE CLOTHES, WOULD YOU DO THAT?"
HER CREDIBILITY GETS WORSE EVERY DAY.
© 1999 United Feature Syndicate, Inc.
11/21/99

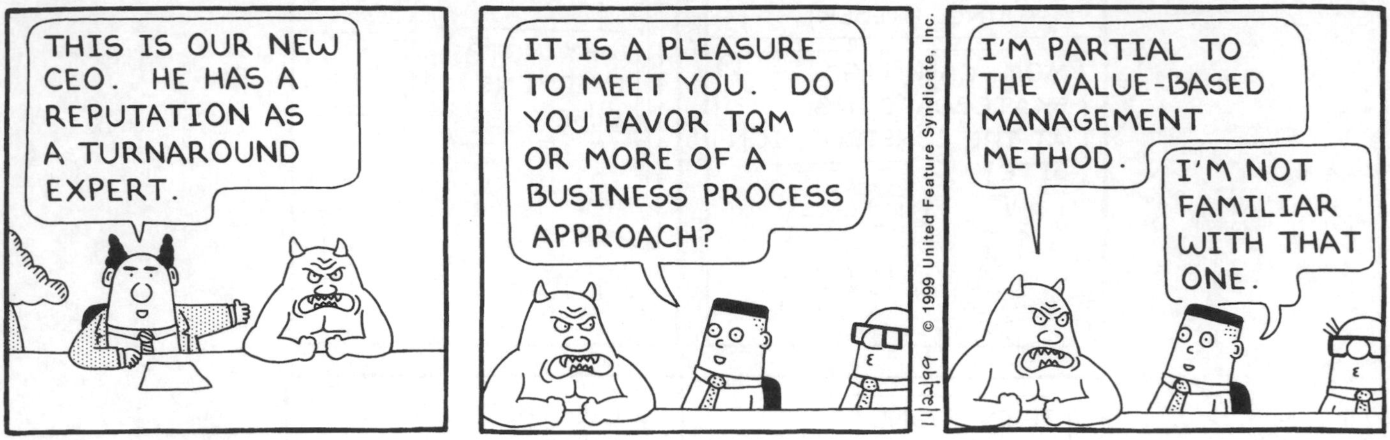
THIS IS OUR NEW CEO. HE HAS A REPUTATION AS A TURNAROUND EXPERT.
IT IS A PLEASURE TO MEET YOU. DO YOU FAVOR TQM OR MORE OF A BUSINESS PROCESS APPROACH?
11/22/99 © 1999 United Feature Syndicate, Inc.
I'M PARTIAL TO THE VALUE-BASED MANAGEMENT METHOD.
I'M NOT FAMILIAR WITH THAT ONE.

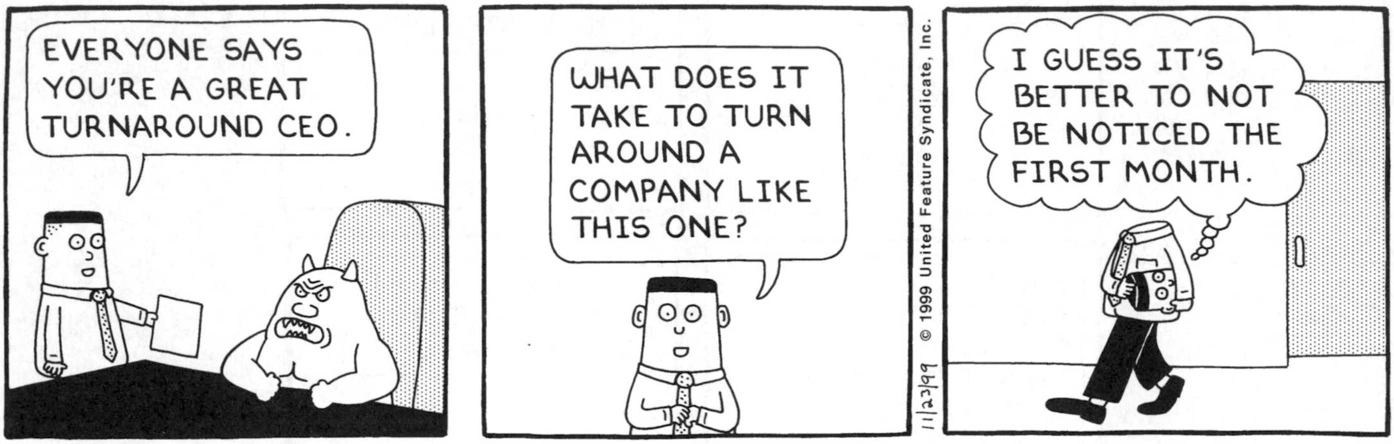
EVERYONE SAYS YOU'RE A GREAT TURNAROUND CEO.
WHAT DOES IT TAKE TO TURN AROUND A COMPANY LIKE THIS ONE?
11/23/99 © 1999 United Feature Syndicate, Inc.
I GUESS IT'S BETTER TO NOT BE NOTICED THE FIRST MONTH.

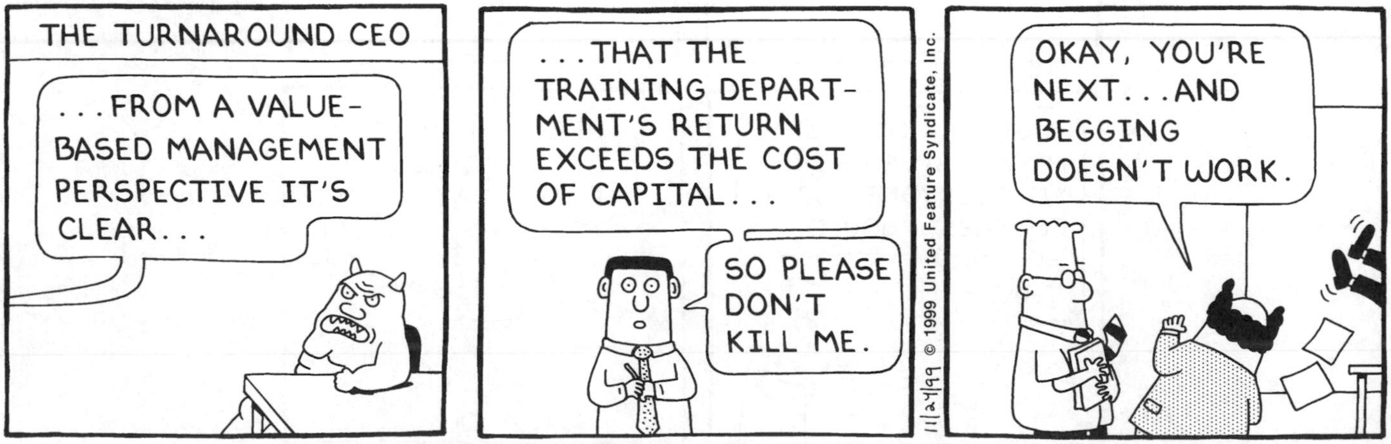
THE TURNAROUND CEO
...FROM A VALUE-BASED MANAGEMENT PERSPECTIVE IT'S CLEAR...
...THAT THE TRAINING DEPARTMENT'S RETURN EXCEEDS THE COST OF CAPITAL...
SO PLEASE DON'T KILL ME.
11/24/99 © 1999 United Feature Syndicate, Inc.
OKAY, YOU'RE NEXT...AND BEGGING DOESN'T WORK.

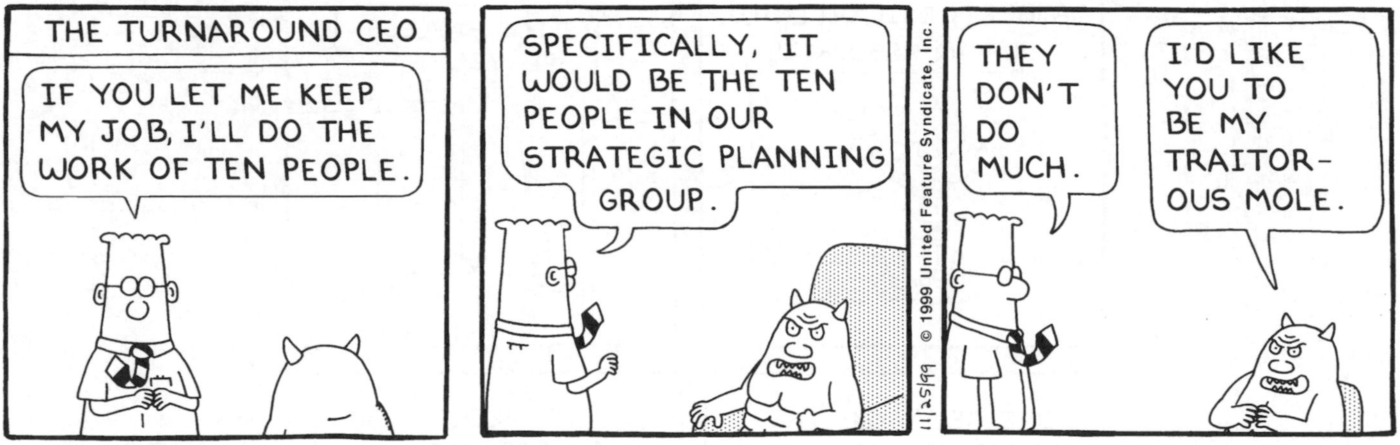
THE TURNAROUND CEO
IF YOU LET ME KEEP MY JOB, I'LL DO THE WORK OF TEN PEOPLE.
SPECIFICALLY, IT WOULD BE THE TEN PEOPLE IN OUR STRATEGIC PLANNING GROUP.
© 1999 United Feature Syndicate, Inc. 11/25/99
THEY DON'T DO MUCH.
I'D LIKE YOU TO BE MY TRAITOR-OUS MOLE.

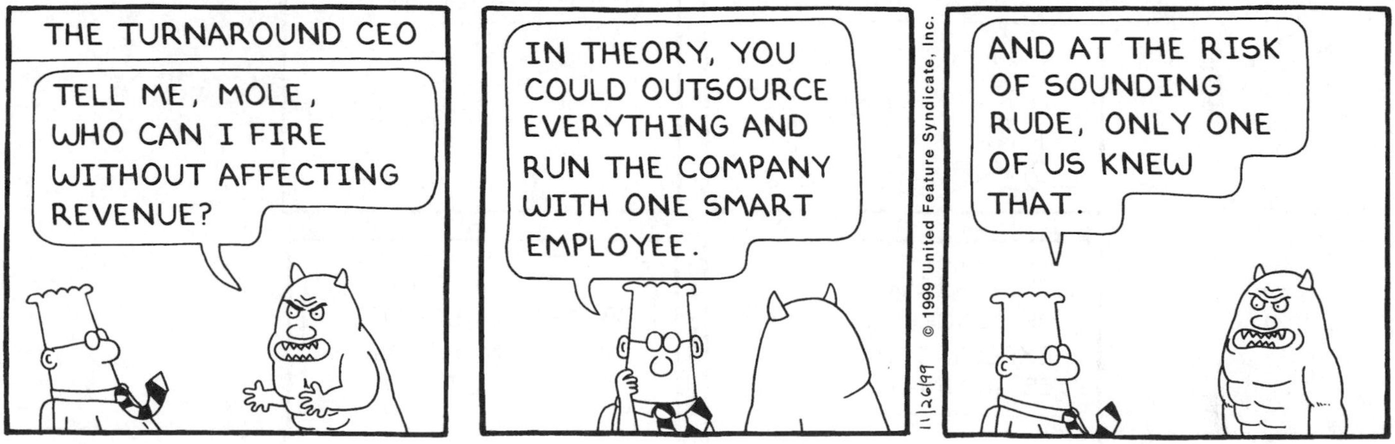
THE TURNAROUND CEO
TELL ME, MOLE, WHO CAN I FIRE WITHOUT AFFECTING REVENUE?
IN THEORY, YOU COULD OUTSOURCE EVERYTHING AND RUN THE COMPANY WITH ONE SMART EMPLOYEE.
© 1999 United Feature Syndicate, Inc. 11/26/99
AND AT THE RISK OF SOUNDING RUDE, ONLY ONE OF US KNEW THAT.

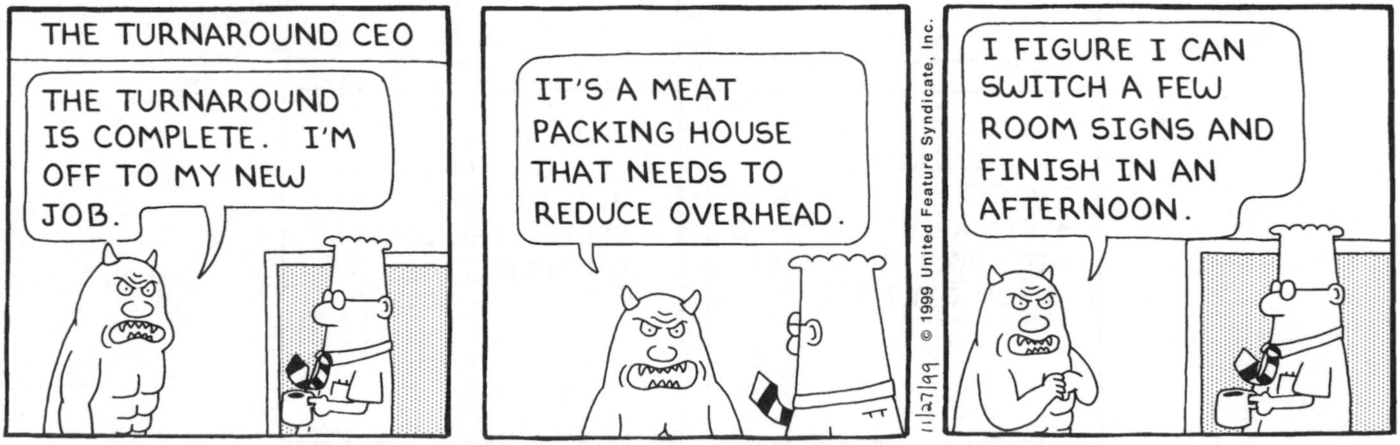
THE TURNAROUND CEO
THE TURNAROUND IS COMPLETE. I'M OFF TO MY NEW JOB.
IT'S A MEAT PACKING HOUSE THAT NEEDS TO REDUCE OVERHEAD.
© 1999 United Feature Syndicate, Inc. 11/27/99
I FIGURE I CAN SWITCH A FEW ROOM SIGNS AND FINISH IN AN AFTERNOON.

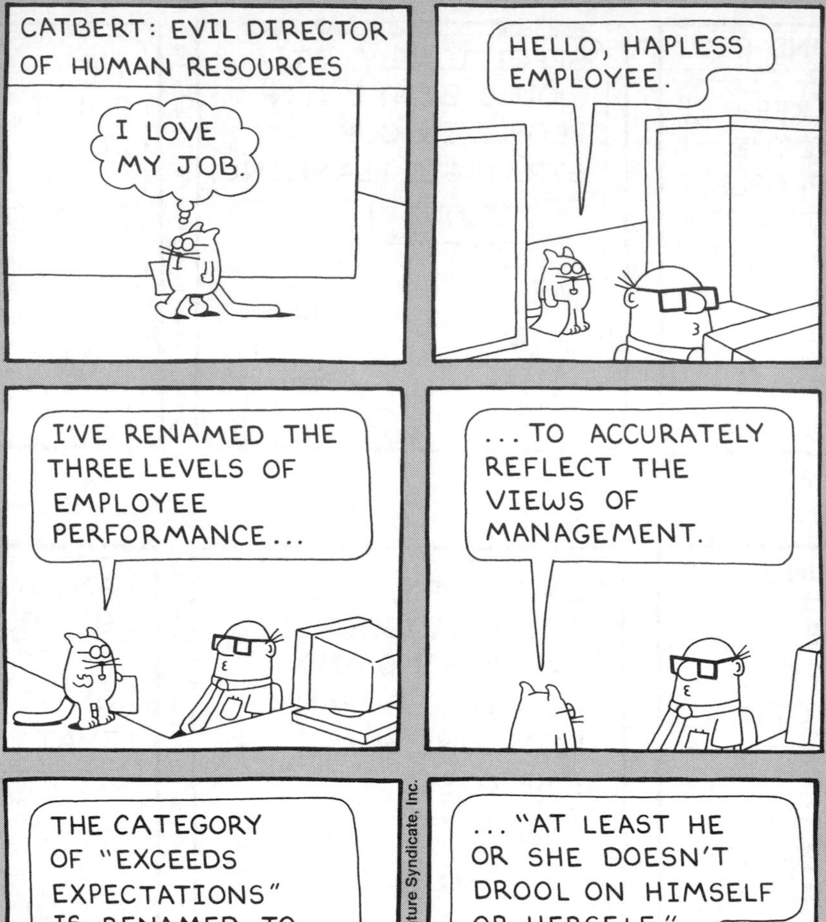
CATBERT: EVIL DIRECTOR OF HUMAN RESOURCES
I LOVE MY JOB.
HELLO, HAPLESS EMPLOYEE.
I'VE RENAMED THE THREE LEVELS OF EMPLOYEE PERFORMANCE...
...TO ACCURATELY REFLECT THE VIEWS OF MANAGEMENT.
THE CATEGORY OF "EXCEEDS EXPECTATIONS" IS RENAMED TO...
..."AT LEAST HE OR SHE DOESN'T DROOL ON HIMSELF OR HERSELF."
"MEETS EXPECTATIONS" WILL BE CALLED "LOSER". "DOES NOT MEET EXPECTATIONS" WILL NOW BE CALLED "DIE! DIE! DIE!"
I COULD SEND IT OUT BY E-MAIL BUT I ENJOY SEEING THE LOOKS ON THEIR FACES.
11/28/99

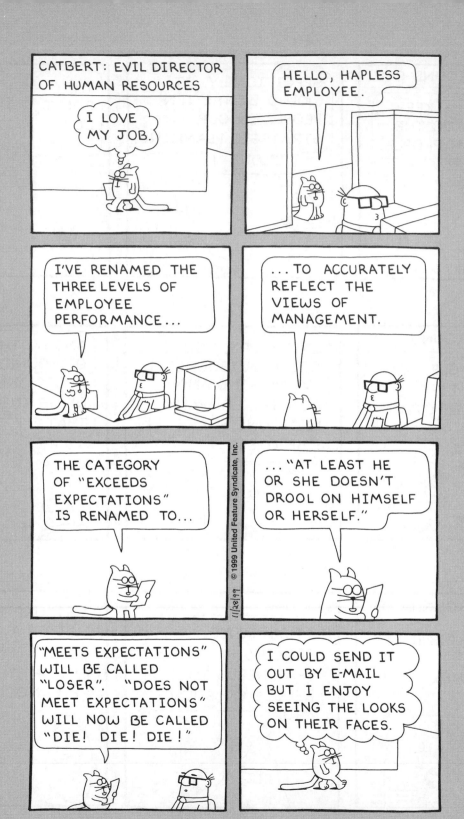

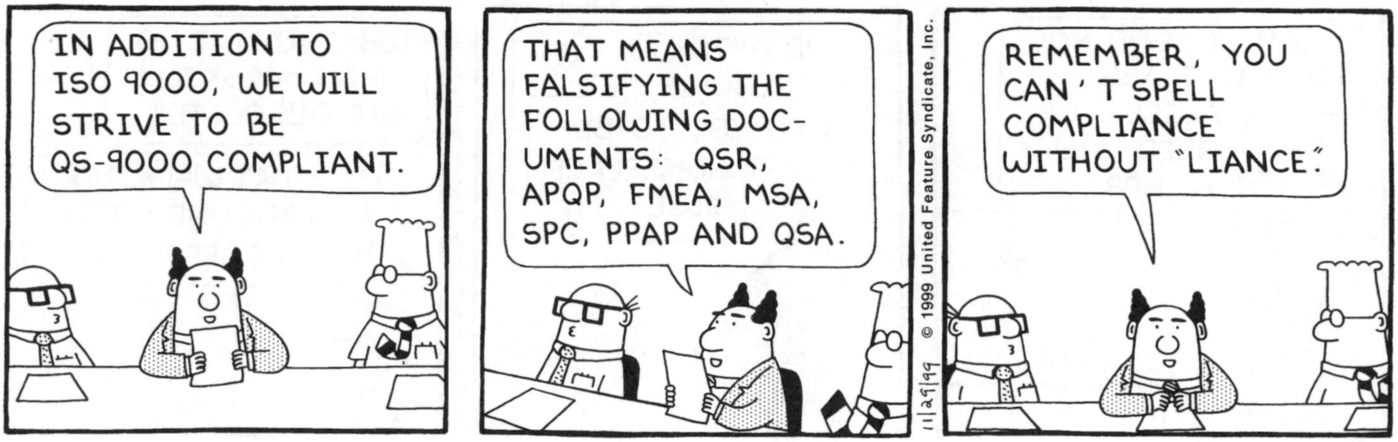
IN ADDITION TO ISO 9000, WE WILL STRIVE TO BE QS-9000 COMPLIANT.
THAT MEANS FALSIFYING THE FOLLOWING DOC-UMENTS: QSR, APQP, FMEA, MSA, SPC, PPAP AND QSA.
11/29/99 © 1999 United Feature Syndicate, Inc.
REMEMBER, YOU CAN'T SPELL COMPLIANCE WITHOUT "LIANCE."

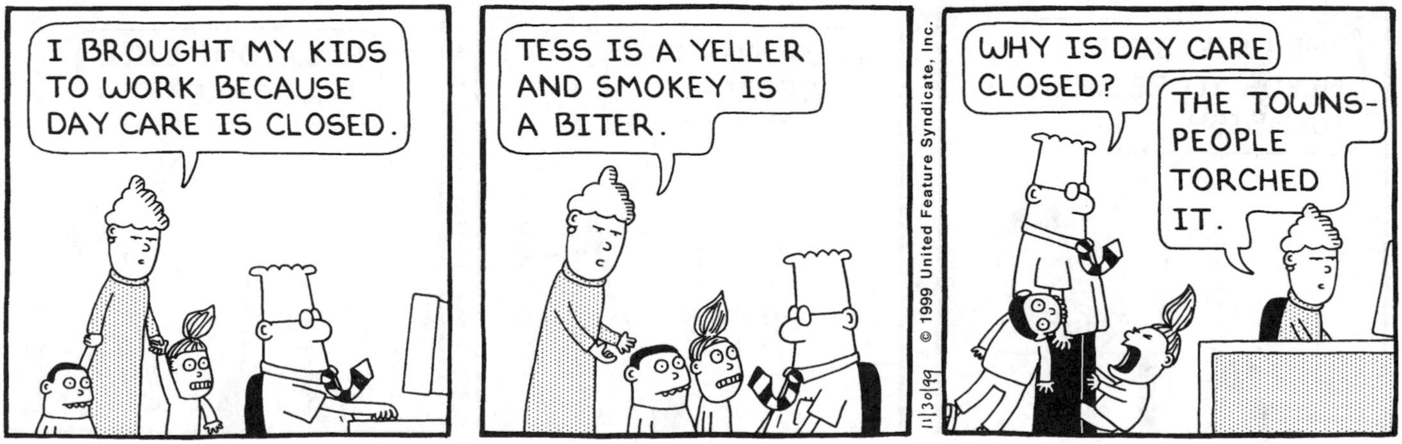
I BROUGHT MY KIDS TO WORK BECAUSE DAY CARE IS CLOSED.
TESS IS A YELLER AND SMOKEY IS A BITER.
11/30/99 © 1999 United Feature Syndicate, Inc.
WHY IS DAY CARE CLOSED?
THE TOWNS-PEOPLE TORCHED IT.

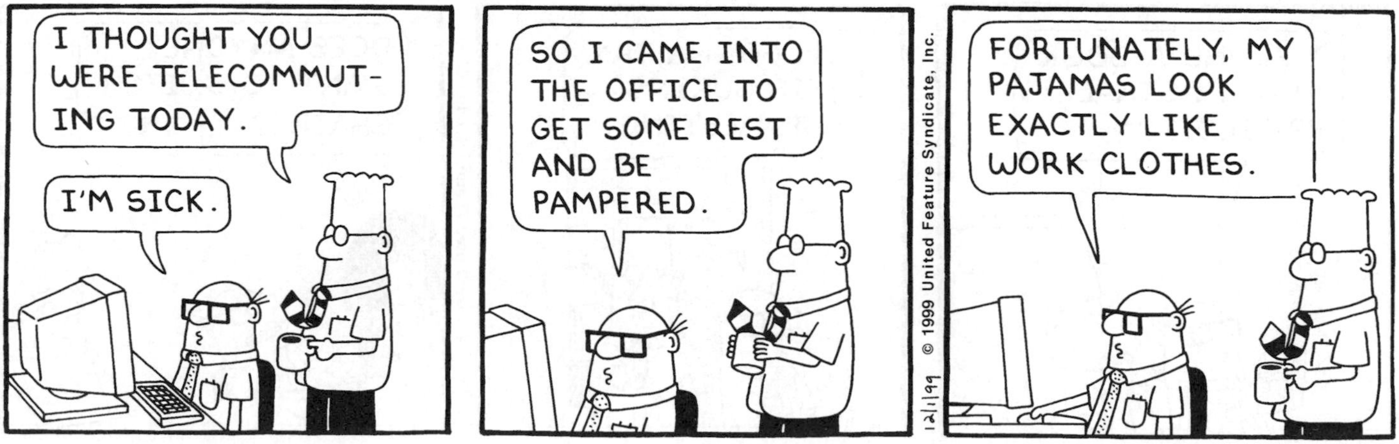
I THOUGHT YOU WERE TELECOMMUT-ING TODAY.
I'M SICK.
SO I CAME INTO THE OFFICE TO GET SOME REST AND BE PAMPERED.
12/1/99 © 1999 United Feature Syndicate, Inc.
FORTUNATELY, MY PAJAMAS LOOK EXACTLY LIKE WORK CLOTHES.

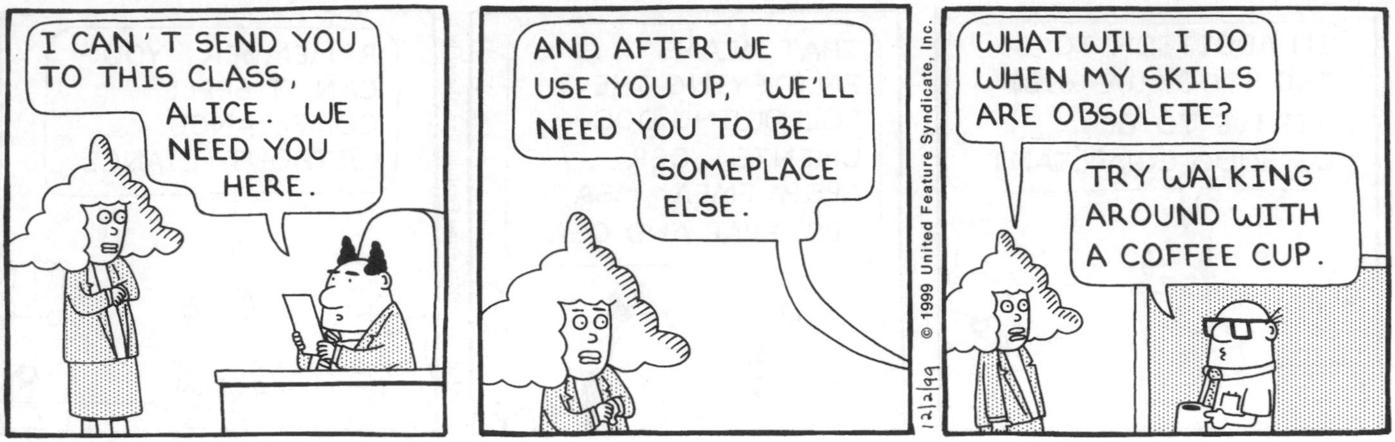
I CAN'T SEND YOU TO THIS CLASS, ALICE. WE NEED YOU HERE.
AND AFTER WE USE YOU UP, WE'LL NEED YOU TO BE SOMEPLACE ELSE.
WHAT WILL I DO WHEN MY SKILLS ARE OBSOLETE?
TRY WALKING AROUND WITH A COFFEE CUP.
12/2/99 © 1999 United Feature Syndicate, Inc.

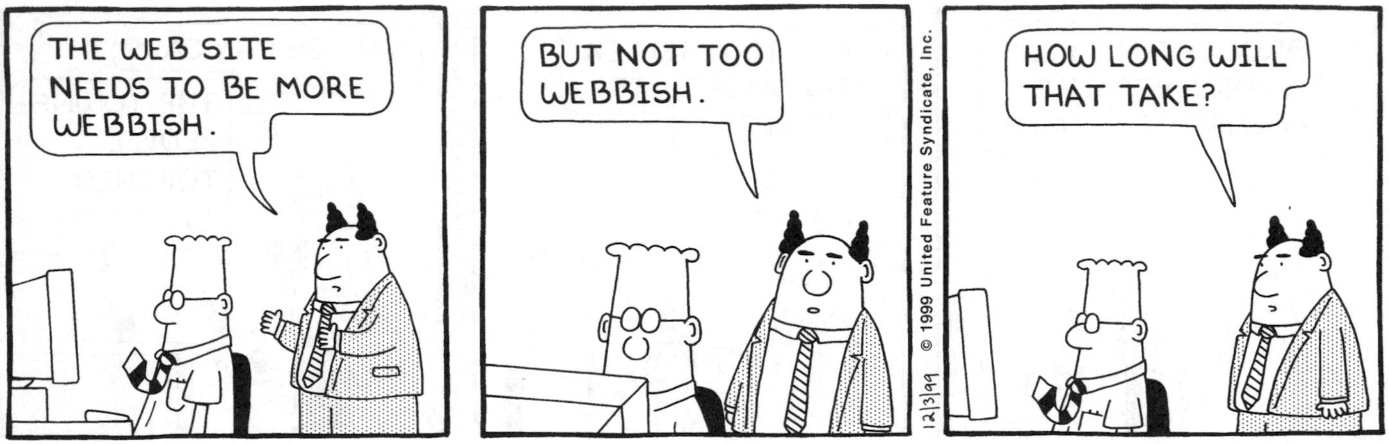
THE WEB SITE NEEDS TO BE MORE WEBBISH.
BUT NOT TOO WEBBISH.
HOW LONG WILL THAT TAKE?
12/3/99 © 1999 United Feature Syndicate, Inc.

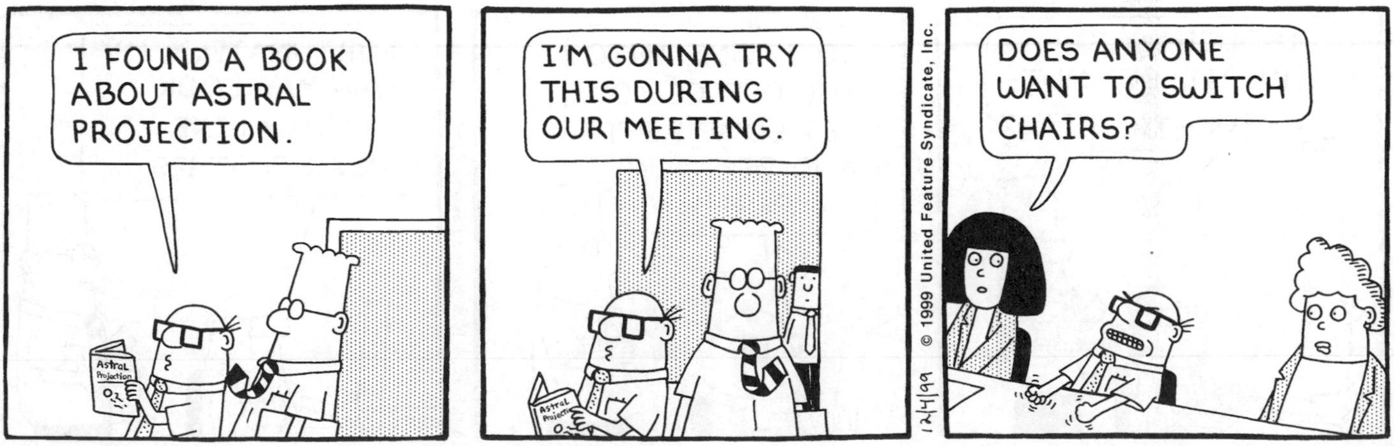
I FOUND A BOOK ABOUT ASTRAL PROJECTION.
Astral Projection
I'M GONNA TRY THIS DURING OUR MEETING.
DOES ANYONE WANT TO SWITCH CHAIRS?
12/4/99 © 1999 United Feature Syndicate, Inc.

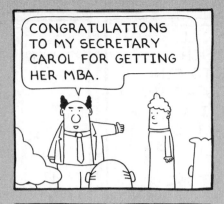

CONGRATULATIONS TO MY SECRETARY CAROL FOR GETTING HER MBA.
AT THIS COMPANY WE BELIEVE HARD WORK SHOULD BE REWARDED.
THE NEXT TIME YOU FETCH MY COFFEE, GET SOME COFFEE FOR YOURSELF TOO!
YOU SHOULD BE PROMOTING ME, YOU POMPOUS BABOON!
HOW CAN I EXPLAIN THIS IN THE MOST SENSITIVE WAY?
THE SECRETARIAL STIGMA WILL COVER YOU LIKE A MOUNTAIN OF WET CARPETS UNTIL THE DAY YOU DIE.
I'M GLAD WE HAD THIS TALK. I THINK IT HELPED.
THE NEXT TIME YOU ASK FOR COFFEE, WE'D LIKE TO WATCH.
12/5/99 © 1999 United Feature Syndicate, Inc.

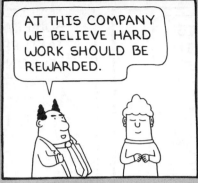

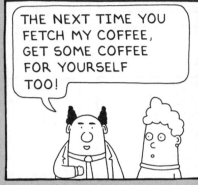

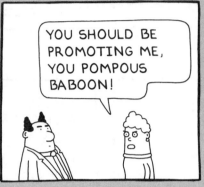

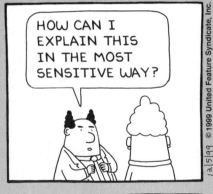

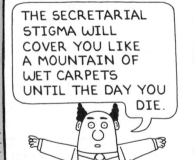

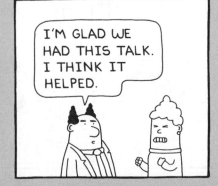

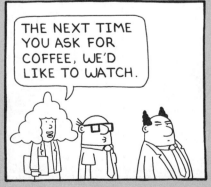

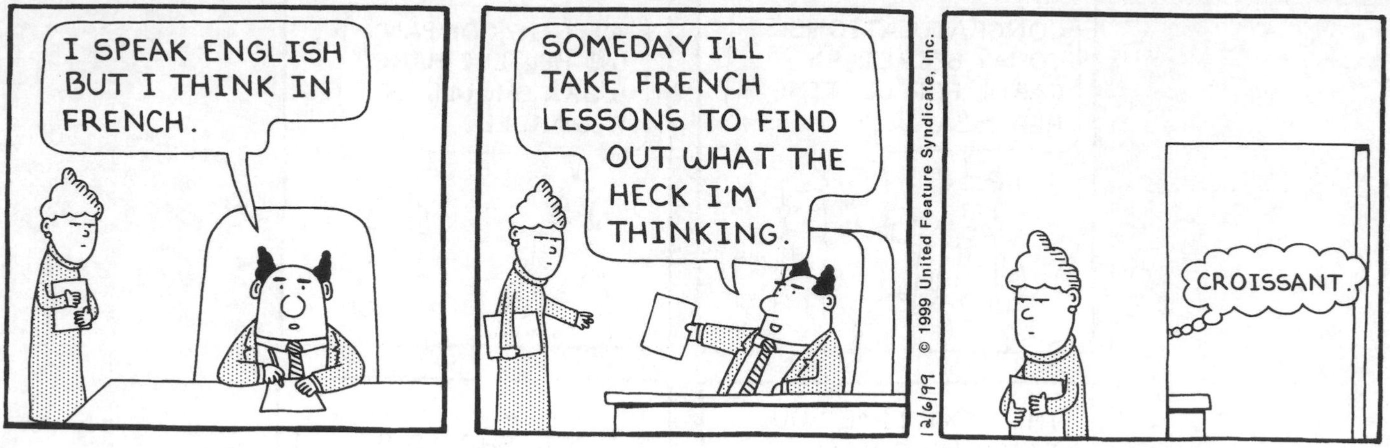
I SPEAK ENGLISH BUT I THINK IN FRENCH.
SOMEDAY I'LL TAKE FRENCH LESSONS TO FIND OUT WHAT THE HECK I'M THINKING.
CROISSANT.

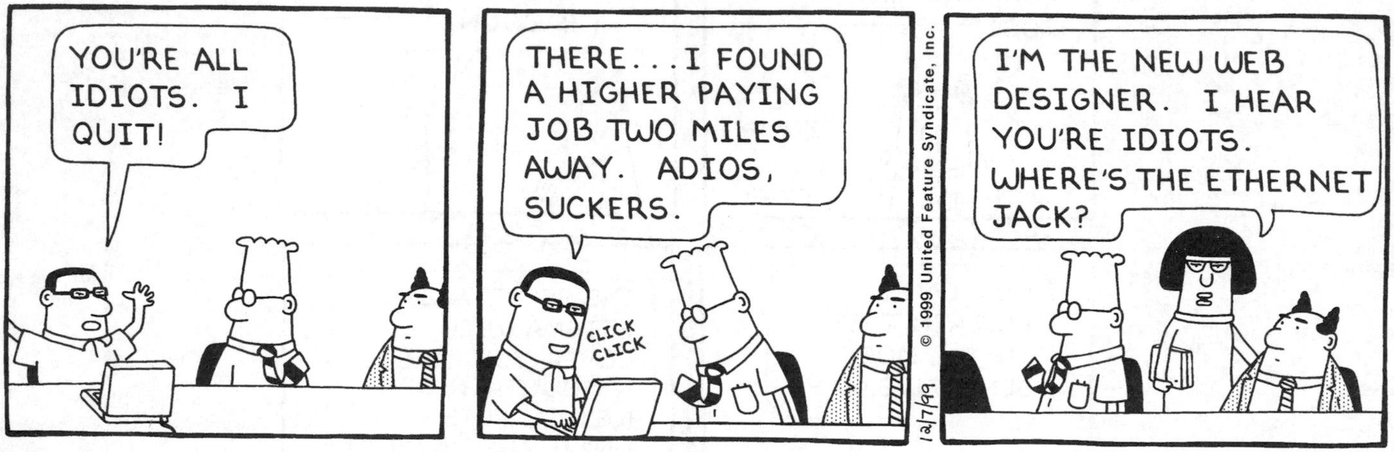
YOU'RE ALL IDIOTS. I QUIT!
THERE... I FOUND A HIGHER PAYING JOB TWO MILES AWAY. ADIOS, SUCKERS.
CLICK CLICK
I'M THE NEW WEB DESIGNER. I HEAR YOU'RE IDIOTS. WHERE'S THE ETHERNET JACK?

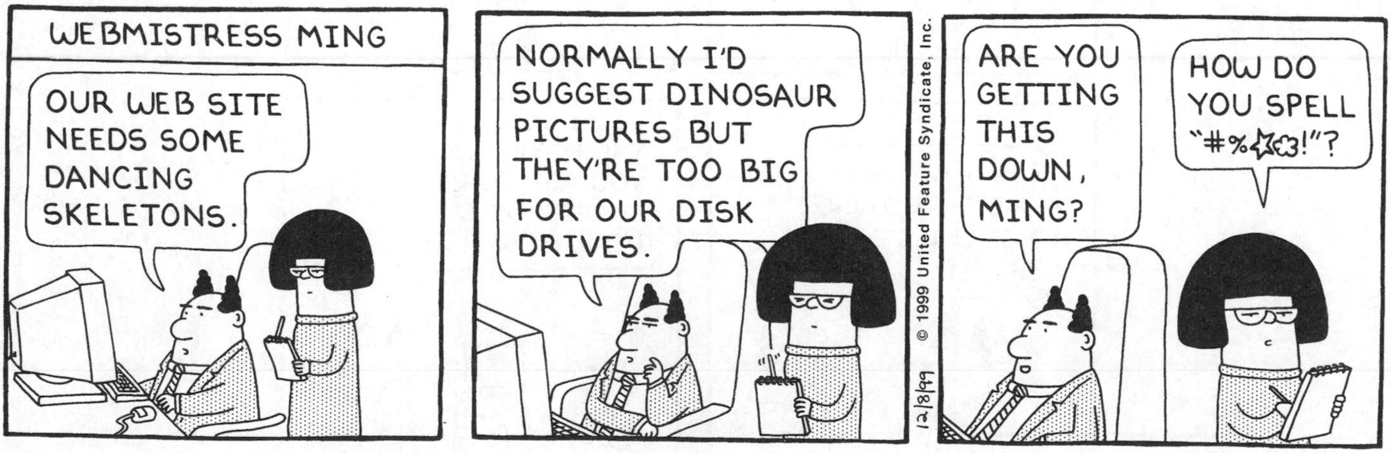
WEBMISTRESS MING
OUR WEB SITE NEEDS SOME DANCING SKELETONS.
NORMALLY I'D SUGGEST DINOSAUR PICTURES BUT THEY'RE TOO BIG FOR OUR DISK DRIVES.
ARE YOU GETTING THIS DOWN, MING?
HOW DO YOU SPELL "#%☆✿!"?

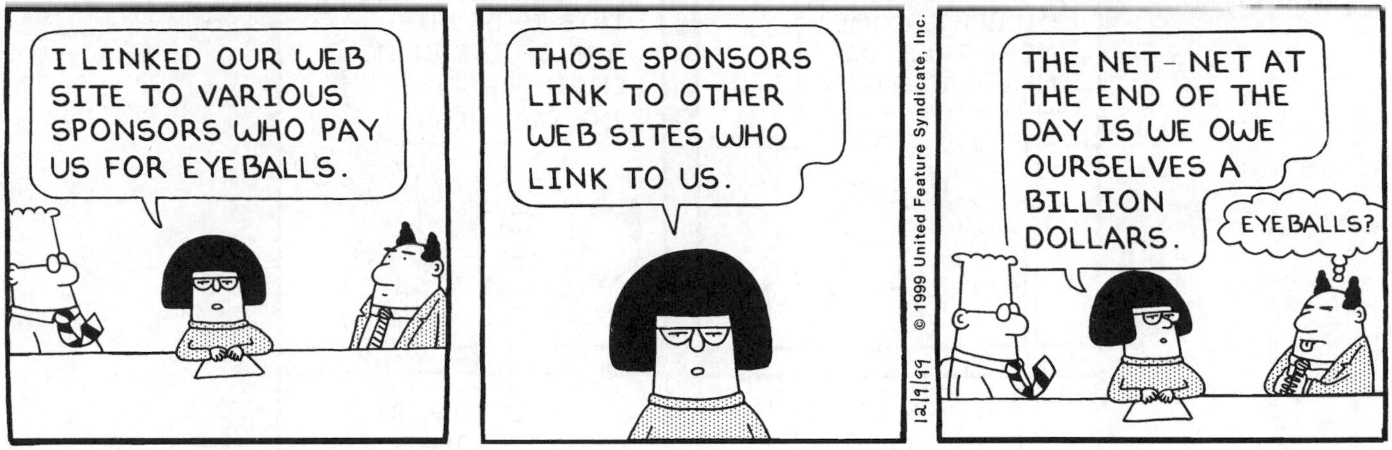
I LINKED OUR WEB SITE TO VARIOUS SPONSORS WHO PAY US FOR EYEBALLS.
THOSE SPONSORS LINK TO OTHER WEB SITES WHO LINK TO US.
12/9/99 © 1999 United Feature Syndicate, Inc.
THE NET-NET AT THE END OF THE DAY IS WE OWE OURSELVES A BILLION DOLLARS.
EYEBALLS?

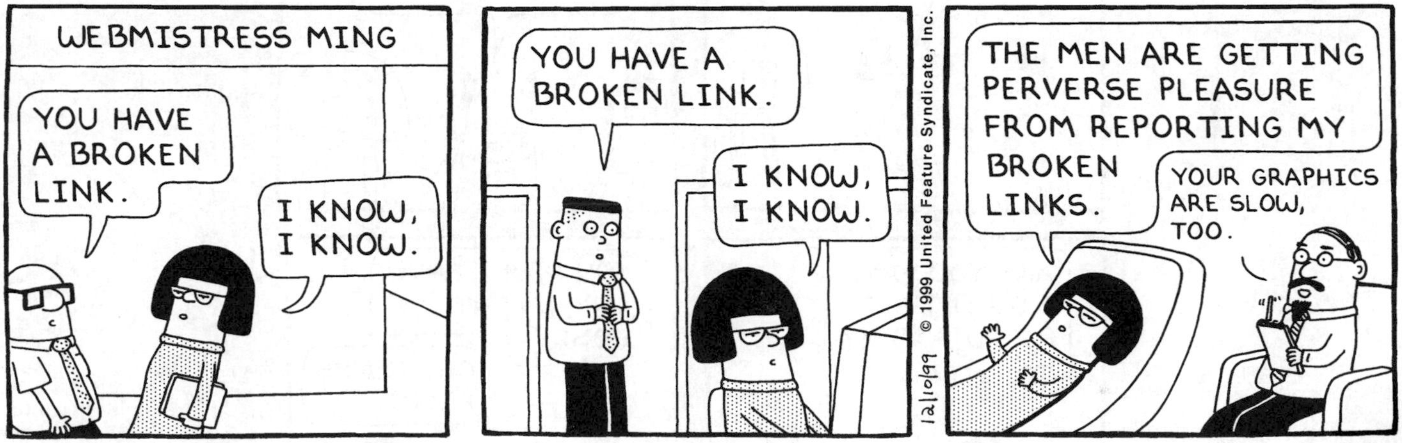
WEBMISTRESS MING
YOU HAVE A BROKEN LINK.
I KNOW, I KNOW.
YOU HAVE A BROKEN LINK.
I KNOW, I KNOW.
12/10/99 © 1999 United Feature Syndicate, Inc.
THE MEN ARE GETTING PERVERSE PLEASURE FROM REPORTING MY BROKEN LINKS.
YOUR GRAPHICS ARE SLOW, TOO.

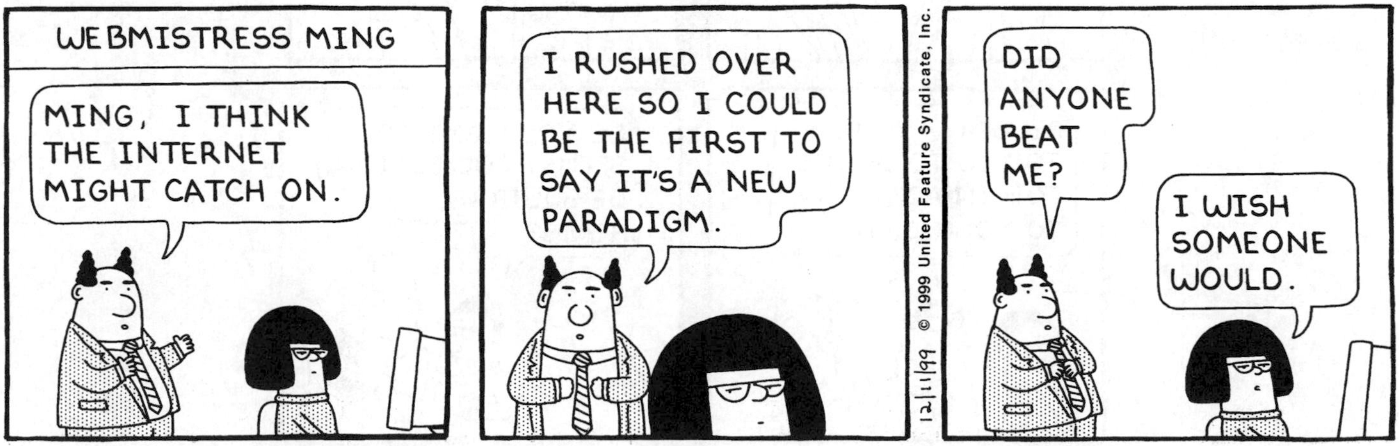
WEBMISTRESS MING
MING, I THINK THE INTERNET MIGHT CATCH ON.
I RUSHED OVER HERE SO I COULD BE THE FIRST TO SAY IT'S A NEW PARADIGM.
12/11/99 © 1999 United Feature Syndicate, Inc.
DID ANYONE BEAT ME?
I WISH SOMEONE WOULD.

DILBERT, COME MEET THE TWO NEW EMPLOYEES.
THIS IS SOPHIE, ONE OF THE BEST ENGINEERS IN THE BUSINESS.
THE OTHER ONE IS HER INCOMPETENT HUSBAND.
WE HAD TO HIRE HIM SO SOPHIE WOULD AGREE TO RELOCATE.
ARE YOU SAYING I DIDN'T GET HIRED FOR MY TALENT?
YOU DON'T HAVE ANY TALENT, HONEY.
OH, THAT'S RIGHT.
DILBERT, YOUR JOB IS TO DO HIS JOB IN ADDITION TO YOUR OWN.
DO YOU WANT TO SEE MY COLLECTION OF SQUIRREL HEADS?
12/12/99 © 1999 United Feature Syndicate, Inc.

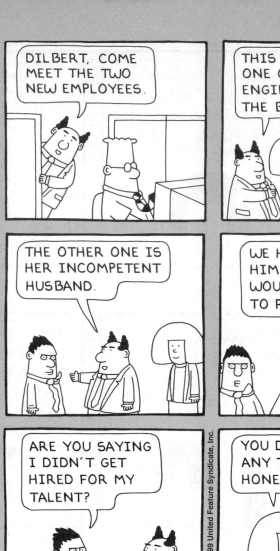

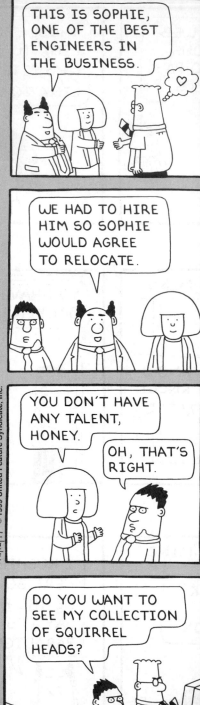

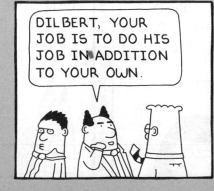

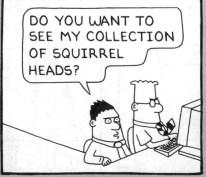

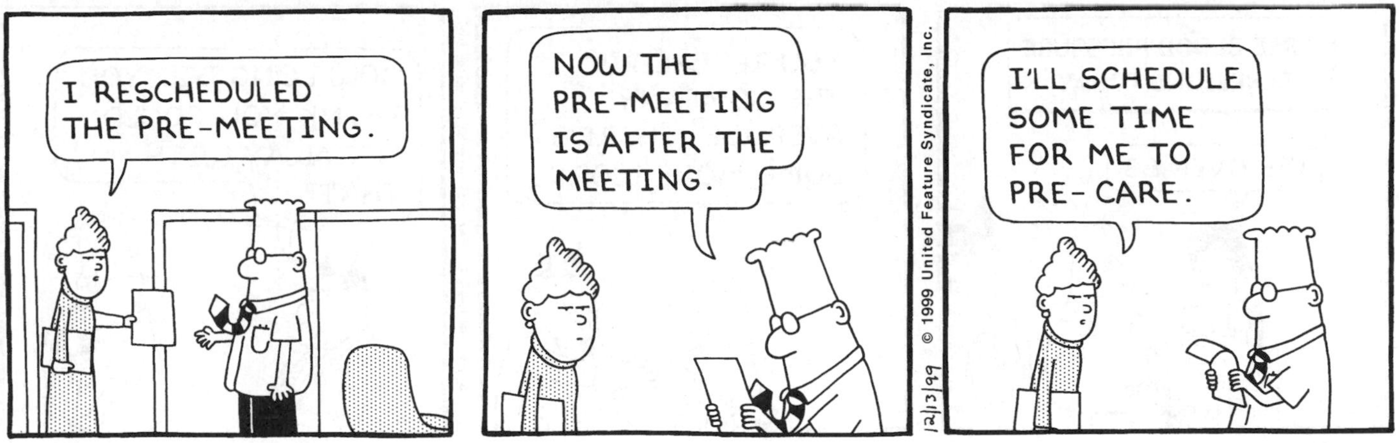
I RESCHEDULED THE PRE-MEETING.
NOW THE PRE-MEETING IS AFTER THE MEETING.
12/13/99 © 1999 United Feature Syndicate, Inc.
I'LL SCHEDULE SOME TIME FOR ME TO PRE-CARE.

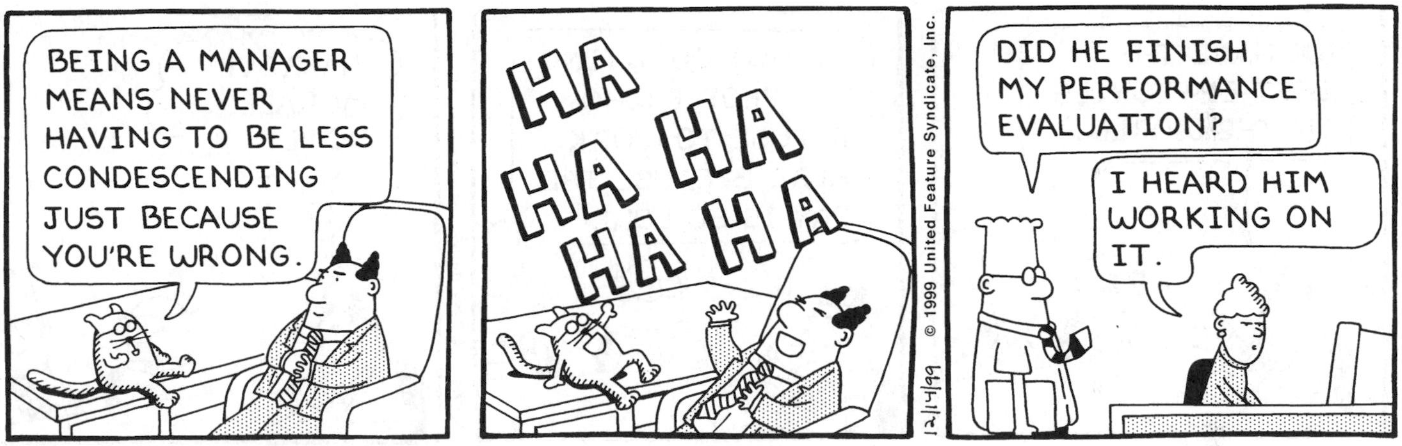
BEING A MANAGER MEANS NEVER HAVING TO BE LESS CONDESCENDING JUST BECAUSE YOU'RE WRONG.
HA HA HA HA HA HA
12/14/99 © 1999 United Feature Syndicate, Inc.
DID HE FINISH MY PERFORMANCE EVALUATION?
I HEARD HIM WORKING ON IT.

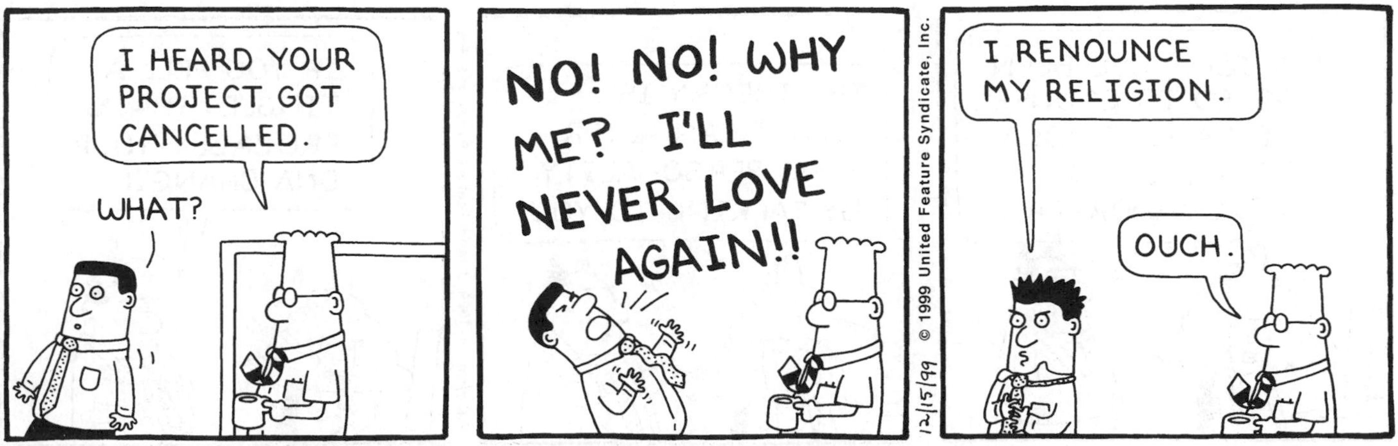
I HEARD YOUR PROJECT GOT CANCELLED.
WHAT?
NO! NO! WHY ME? I'LL NEVER LOVE AGAIN!!
12/15/99 © 1999 United Feature Syndicate, Inc.
I RENOUNCE MY RELIGION.
OUCH.

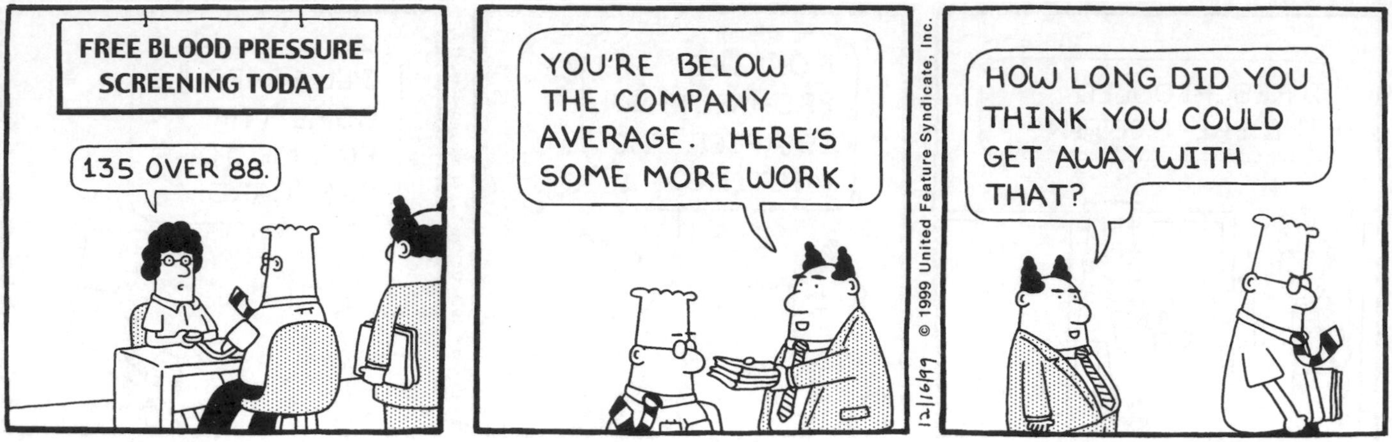
FREE BLOOD PRESSURE SCREENING TODAY
135 OVER 88.
YOU'RE BELOW THE COMPANY AVERAGE. HERE'S SOME MORE WORK.
12/16/99 © 1999 United Feature Syndicate, Inc.
HOW LONG DID YOU THINK YOU COULD GET AWAY WITH THAT?

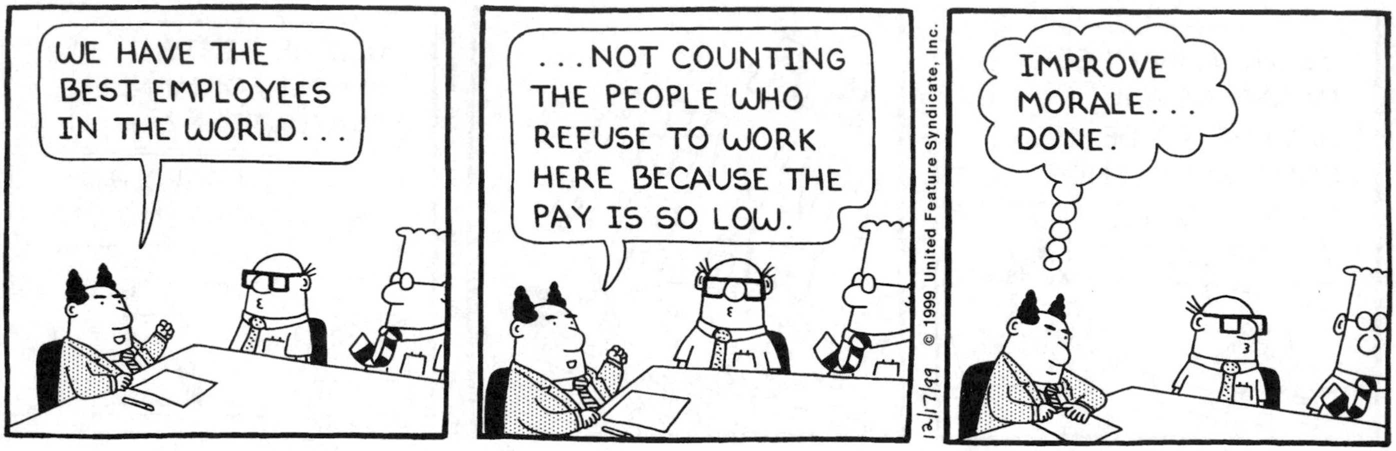
WE HAVE THE BEST EMPLOYEES IN THE WORLD...
...NOT COUNTING THE PEOPLE WHO REFUSE TO WORK HERE BECAUSE THE PAY IS SO LOW.
12/17/99 © 1999 United Feature Syndicate, Inc.
IMPROVE MORALE... DONE.

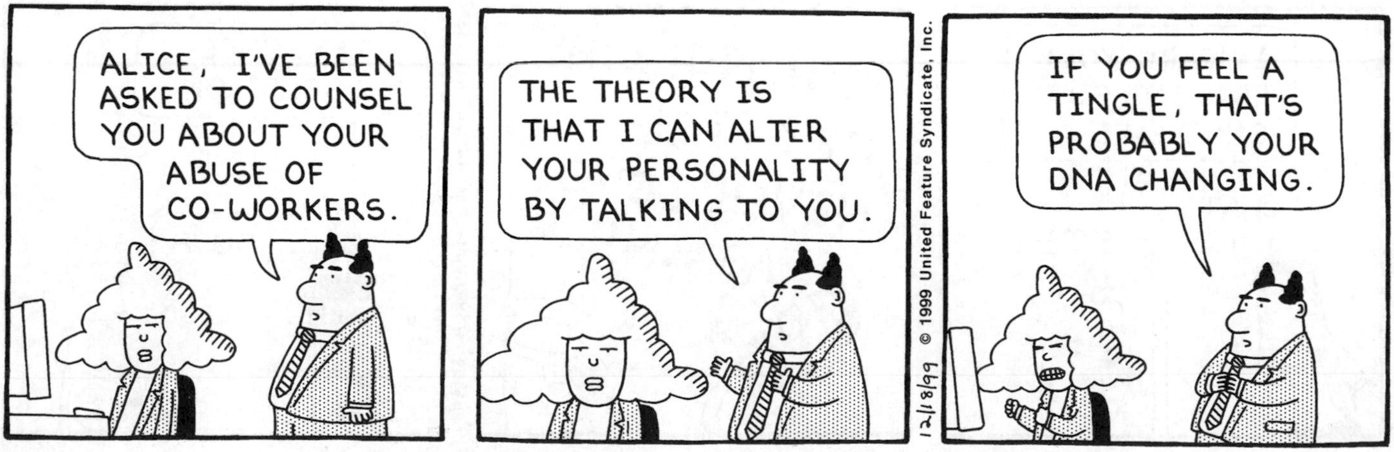
ALICE, I'VE BEEN ASKED TO COUNSEL YOU ABOUT YOUR ABUSE OF CO-WORKERS.
THE THEORY IS THAT I CAN ALTER YOUR PERSONALITY BY TALKING TO YOU.
12/18/99 © 1999 United Feature Syndicate, Inc.
IF YOU FEEL A TINGLE, THAT'S PROBABLY YOUR DNA CHANGING.

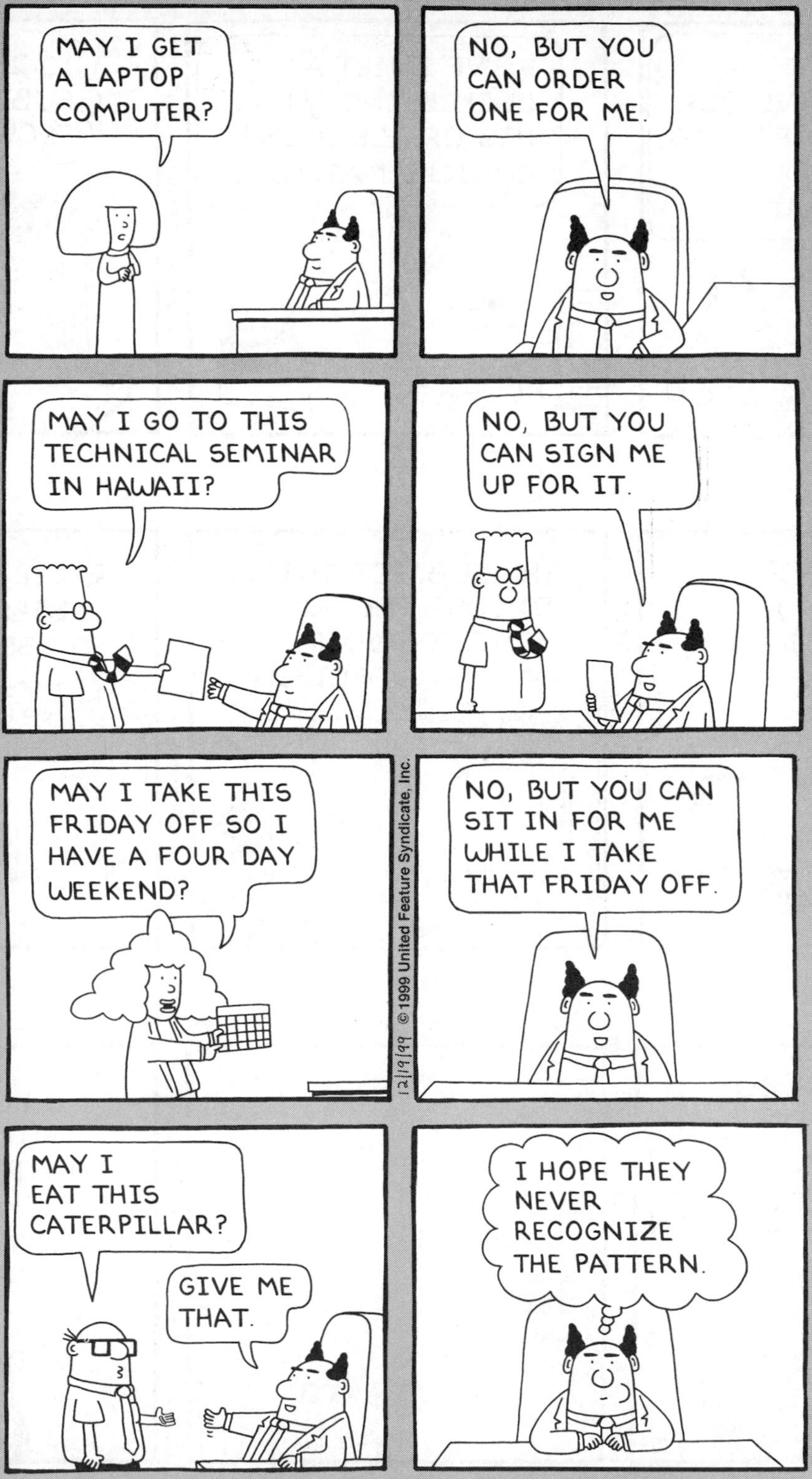
MAY I GET A LAPTOP COMPUTER?
NO, BUT YOU CAN ORDER ONE FOR ME.
MAY I GO TO THIS TECHNICAL SEMINAR IN HAWAII?
NO, BUT YOU CAN SIGN ME UP FOR IT.
MAY I TAKE THIS FRIDAY OFF SO I HAVE A FOUR DAY WEEKEND?
NO, BUT YOU CAN SIT IN FOR ME WHILE I TAKE THAT FRIDAY OFF.
MAY I EAT THIS CATERPILLAR?
GIVE ME THAT.
I HOPE THEY NEVER RECOGNIZE THE PATTERN.
12/19/99 © 1999 United Feature Syndicate, Inc.

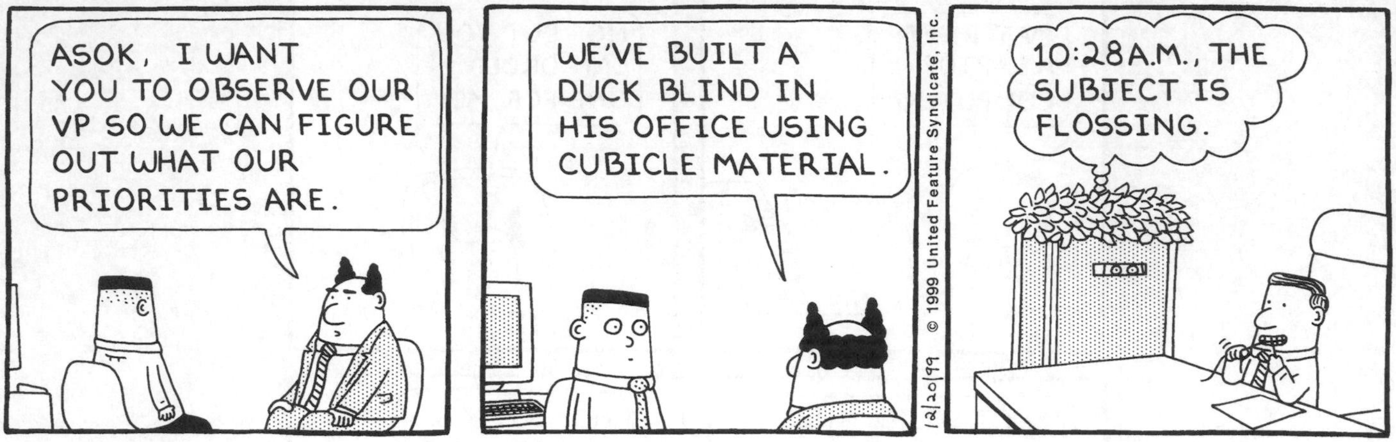
ASOK, I WANT YOU TO OBSERVE OUR VP SO WE CAN FIGURE OUT WHAT OUR PRIORITIES ARE.
WE'VE BUILT A DUCK BLIND IN HIS OFFICE USING CUBICLE MATERIAL.
12/20/99 © 1999 United Feature Syndicate, Inc.
10:28 A.M., THE SUBJECT IS FLOSSING.

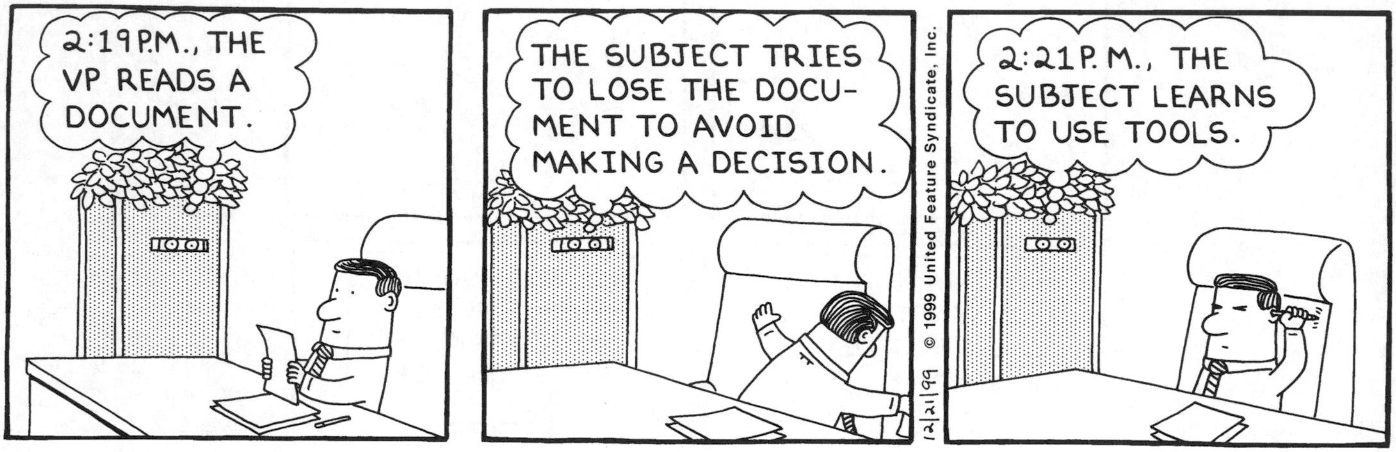
2:19 P.M., THE VP READS A DOCUMENT.
THE SUBJECT TRIES TO LOSE THE DOCU-MENT TO AVOID MAKING A DECISION.
12/21/99 © 1999 United Feature Syndicate, Inc.
2:21 P. M., THE SUBJECT LEARNS TO USE TOOLS.

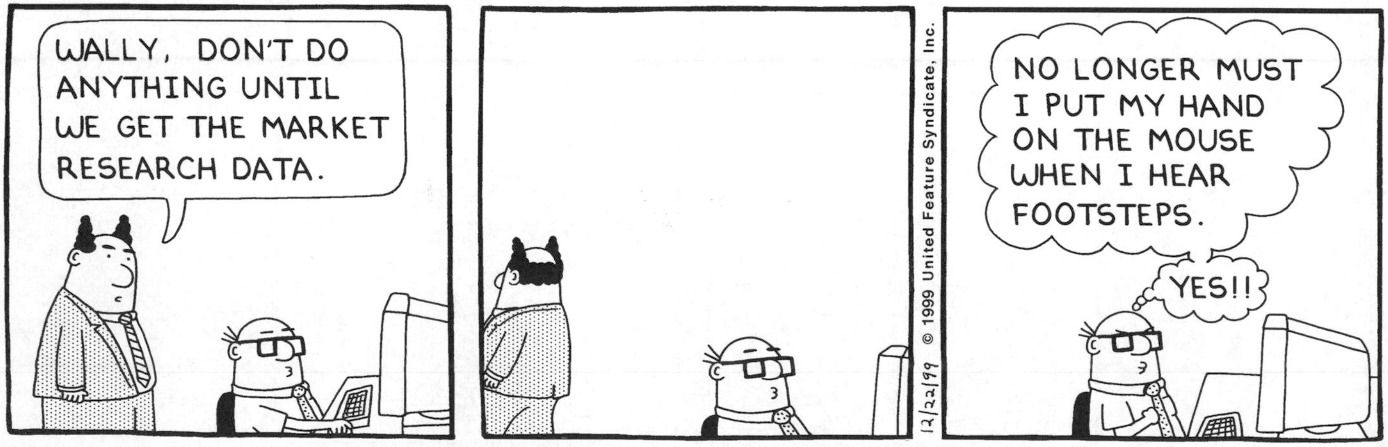
WALLY, DON'T DO ANYTHING UNTIL WE GET THE MARKET RESEARCH DATA.
12/22/99 © 1999 United Feature Syndicate, Inc.
NO LONGER MUST I PUT MY HAND ON THE MOUSE WHEN I HEAR FOOTSTEPS.
YES!!

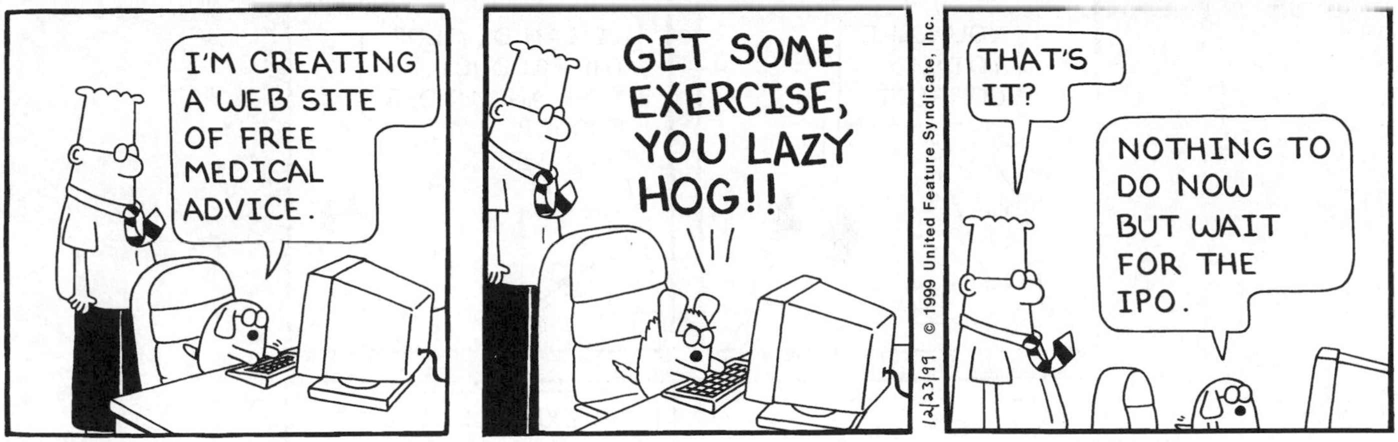
I'M CREATING A WEB SITE OF FREE MEDICAL ADVICE.
GET SOME EXERCISE, YOU LAZY HOG!!
12/23/99 © 1999 United Feature Syndicate, Inc.
THAT'S IT?
NOTHING TO DO NOW BUT WAIT FOR THE IPO.

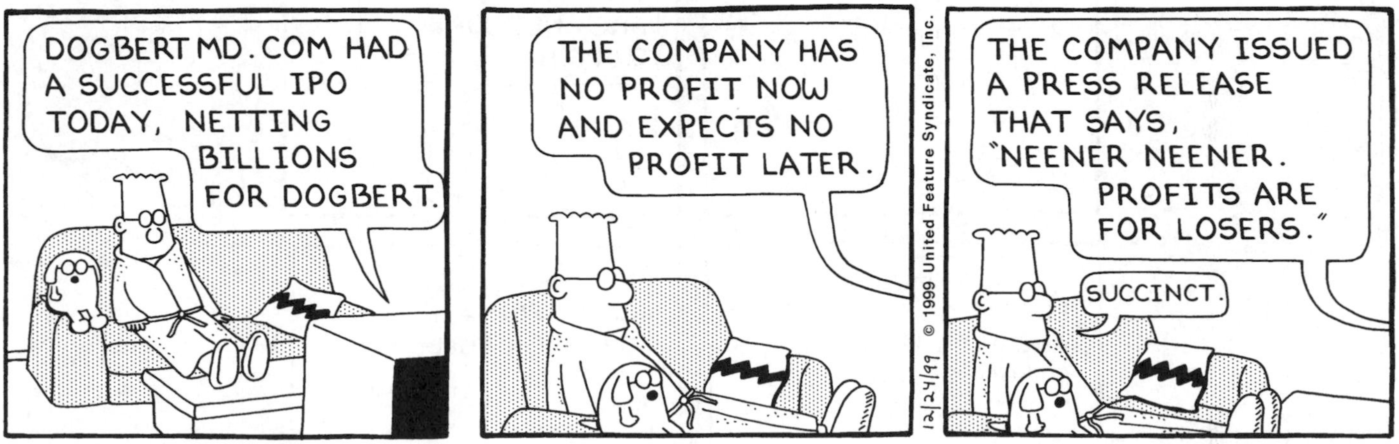
DOGBERTMD.COM HAD A SUCCESSFUL IPO TODAY, NETTING BILLIONS FOR DOGBERT.
THE COMPANY HAS NO PROFIT NOW AND EXPECTS NO PROFIT LATER.
12/24/99 © 1999 United Feature Syndicate, Inc.
THE COMPANY ISSUED A PRESS RELEASE THAT SAYS, "NEENER NEENER. PROFITS ARE FOR LOSERS."
SUCCINCT.

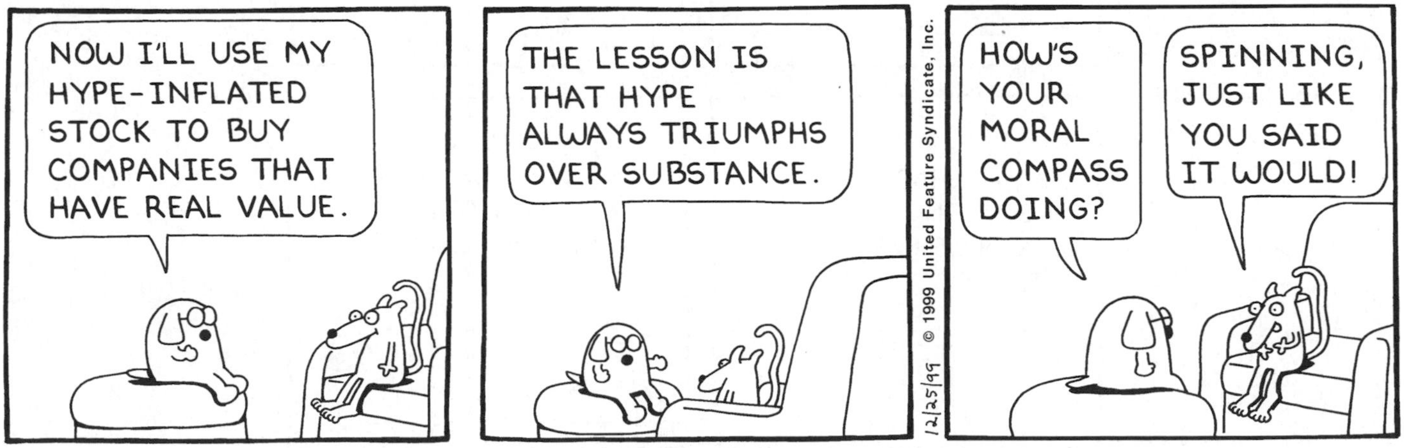
NOW I'LL USE MY HYPE-INFLATED STOCK TO BUY COMPANIES THAT HAVE REAL VALUE.
THE LESSON IS THAT HYPE ALWAYS TRIUMPHS OVER SUBSTANCE.
12/25/99 © 1999 United Feature Syndicate, Inc.
HOW'S YOUR MORAL COMPASS DOING?
SPINNING, JUST LIKE YOU SAID IT WOULD!

YOU WERE TOTALLY CORRECT.
WE CAN DEVELOP THE PRODUCT ON TIME AND UNDER BUDGET.
ALL WE HAVE TO DO IS GIVE UP SOME FEATURES.
FOR EXAMPLE, THE ORIGINAL DESIGN CALLED FOR A SCALABLE WIDE AREA NETWORK SWITCH...
...WITH MULTI-PROTOCOL SUPPORT AND FULL NETWORK DIAGNOSTICS.
THE NEW DESIGN CALLS FOR A SHOEBOX FULL OF YARN.
SO WE'RE IN GOOD SHAPE.. ASSUMING YARN IS FREE.
YOU'RE A SERIOUS THREAT TO MY OPEN DOOR POLICY.
12/26/99 © 1999 United Feature Syndicate, Inc.

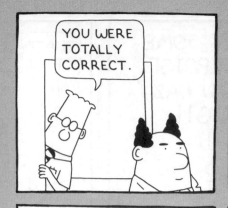

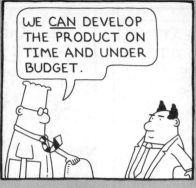

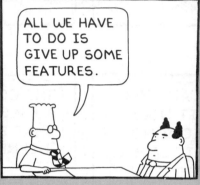

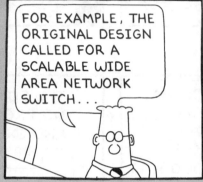

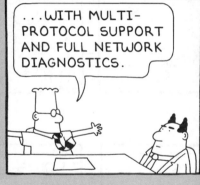

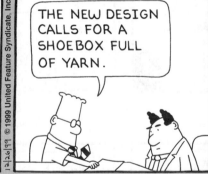

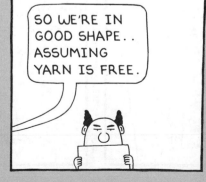

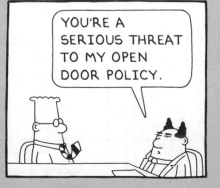

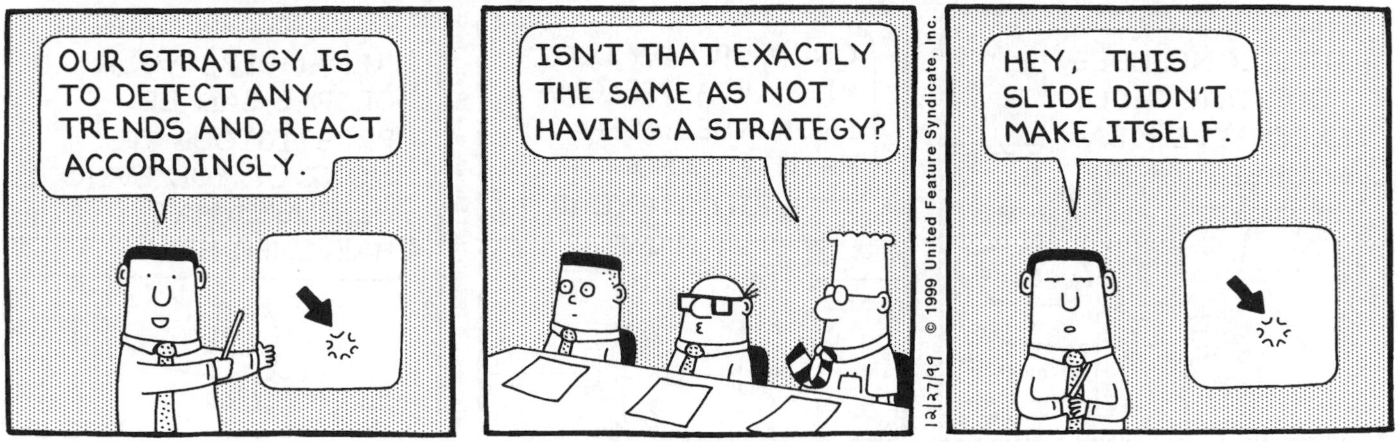
OUR STRATEGY IS TO DETECT ANY TRENDS AND REACT ACCORDINGLY.
ISN'T THAT EXACTLY THE SAME AS NOT HAVING A STRATEGY?
HEY, THIS SLIDE DIDN'T MAKE ITSELF.
12/27/99 © 1999 United Feature Syndicate, Inc.

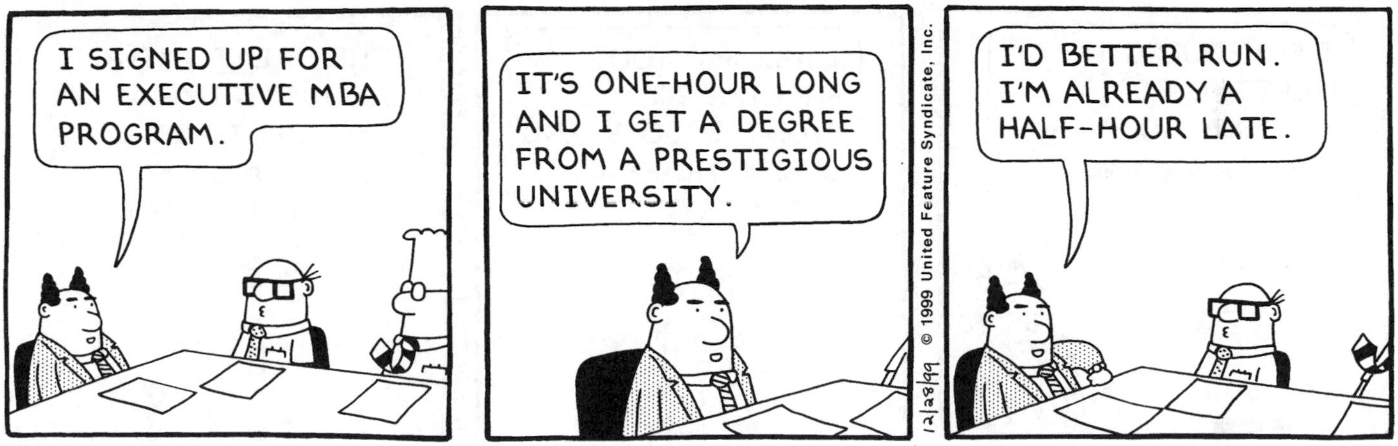
I SIGNED UP FOR AN EXECUTIVE MBA PROGRAM.
IT'S ONE-HOUR LONG AND I GET A DEGREE FROM A PRESTIGIOUS UNIVERSITY.
I'D BETTER RUN. I'M ALREADY A HALF-HOUR LATE.
12/28/99 © 1999 United Feature Syndicate, Inc.

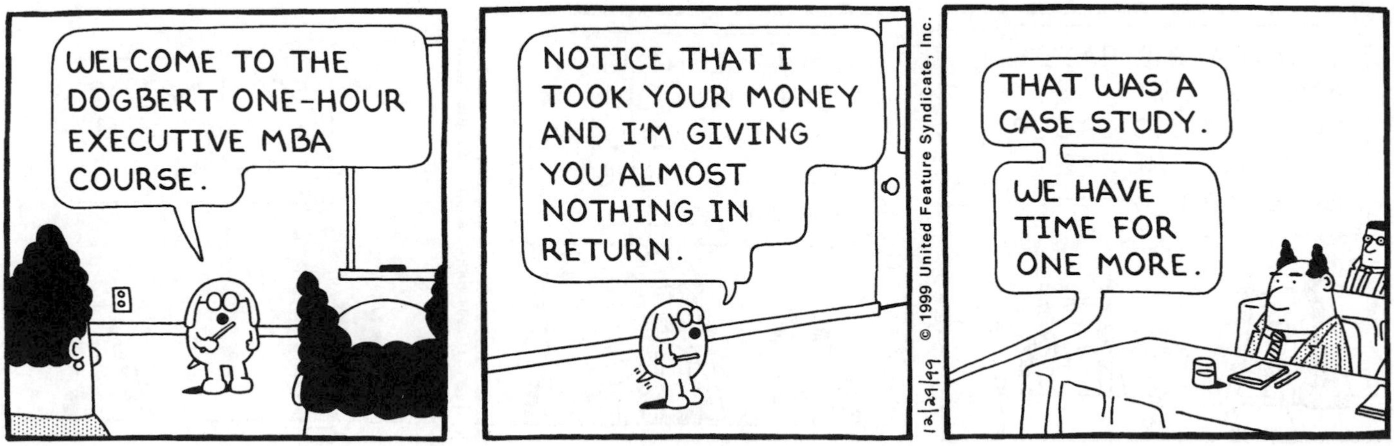
WELCOME TO THE DOGBERT ONE-HOUR EXECUTIVE MBA COURSE.
NOTICE THAT I TOOK YOUR MONEY AND I'M GIVING YOU ALMOST NOTHING IN RETURN.
THAT WAS A CASE STUDY.
WE HAVE TIME FOR ONE MORE.
12/29/99 © 1999 United Feature Syndicate, Inc.

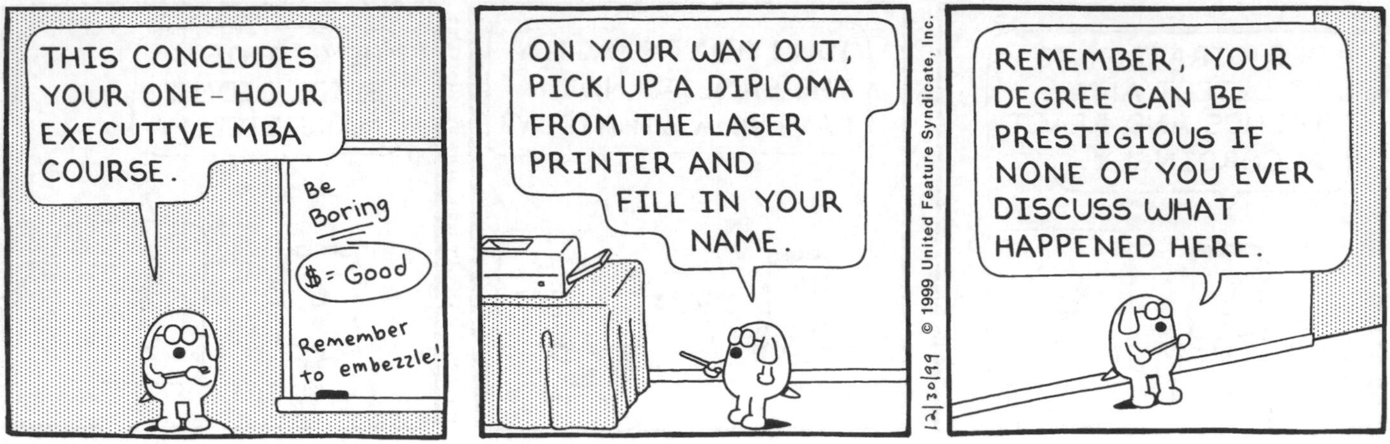
THIS CONCLUDES YOUR ONE-HOUR EXECUTIVE MBA COURSE.
Be Boring
$ = Good
Remember to embezzle!
ON YOUR WAY OUT, PICK UP A DIPLOMA FROM THE LASER PRINTER AND FILL IN YOUR NAME.
12/30/99 © 1999 United Feature Syndicate, Inc.
REMEMBER, YOUR DEGREE CAN BE PRESTIGIOUS IF NONE OF YOU EVER DISCUSS WHAT HAPPENED HERE.

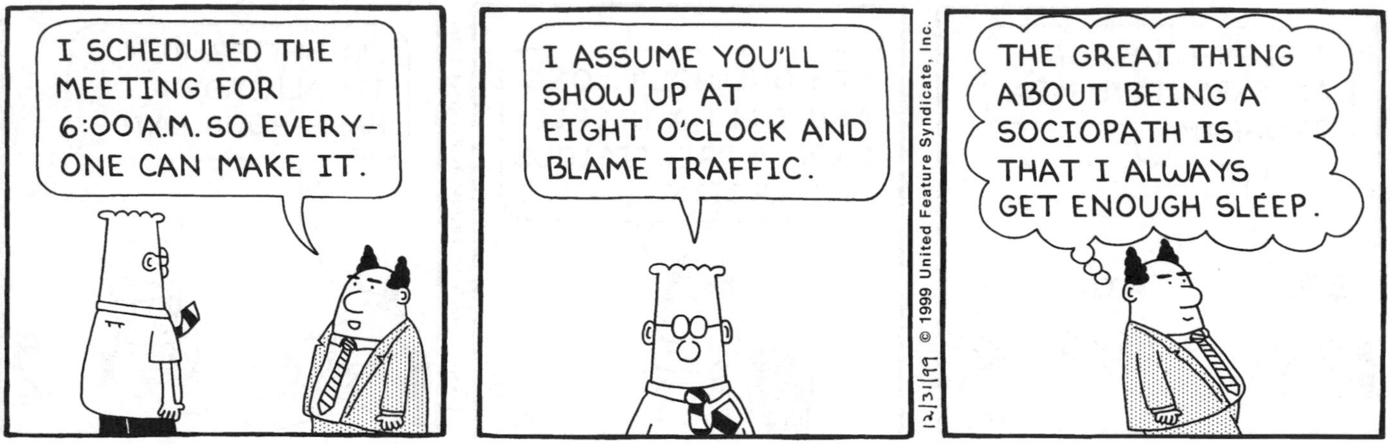
I SCHEDULED THE MEETING FOR 6:00 A.M. SO EVERYONE CAN MAKE IT.
I ASSUME YOU'LL SHOW UP AT EIGHT O'CLOCK AND BLAME TRAFFIC.
12/31/99 © 1999 United Feature Syndicate, Inc.
THE GREAT THING ABOUT BEING A SOCIOPATH IS THAT I ALWAYS GET ENOUGH SLEEP.

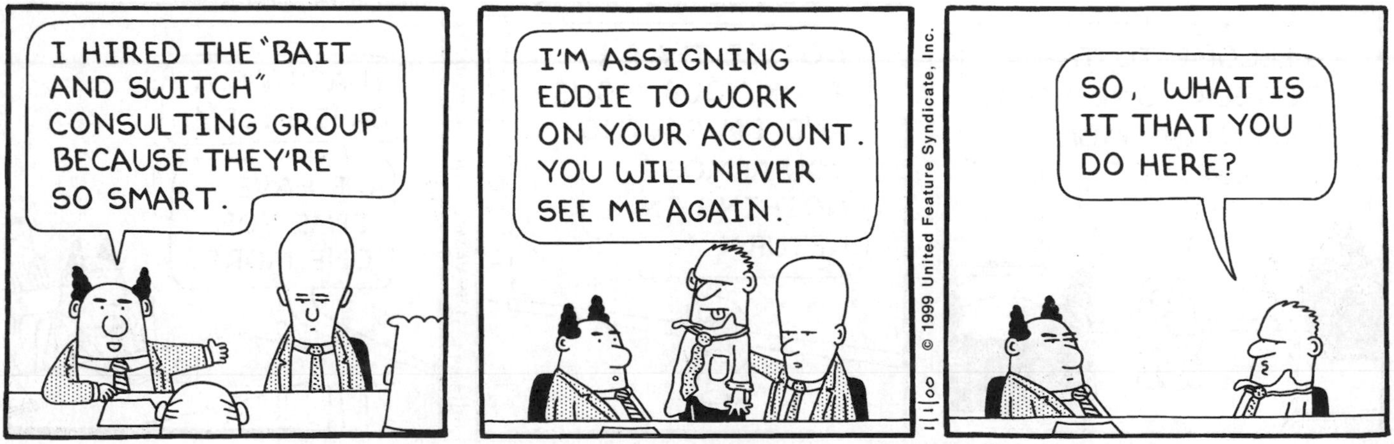
I HIRED THE "BAIT AND SWITCH" CONSULTING GROUP BECAUSE THEY'RE SO SMART.
I'M ASSIGNING EDDIE TO WORK ON YOUR ACCOUNT. YOU WILL NEVER SEE ME AGAIN.
1/1/00 © 1999 United Feature Syndicate, Inc.
SO, WHAT IS IT THAT YOU DO HERE?

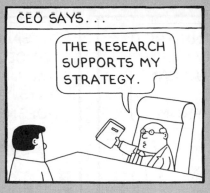

CEO SAYS...
THE RESEARCH SUPPORTS MY STRATEGY.
YOU CAN READ THE RESEARCH BUT DON'T MAKE COPIES.
SENIOR VP SAYS...
I CAN TELL YOU ABOUT IT BUT YOU CAN'T READ IT.
VP SAYS...
I DON'T REMEMBER THE REASON BUT I'M SURE THERE IS ONE.
ASSISTANT VP SAYS...
THERE'S NO REASON.
© 1999 United Feature Syndicate, Inc.
1/2/00
OUR STRATEGY IS A HUGE MISTAKE BUT WE HAVE TO DO IT ANYWAY.
AFTER I FALL ASLEEP TONIGHT, PLEASE SMOTHER ME WITH A PILLOW.
MY PEOPLE LOVE ME BECAUSE I MANAGE WITH DATA.

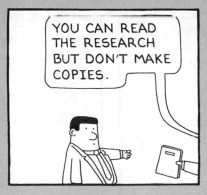

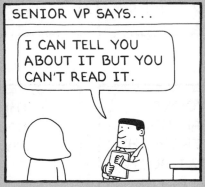

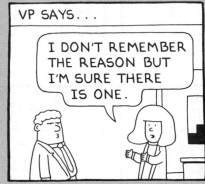

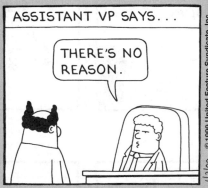

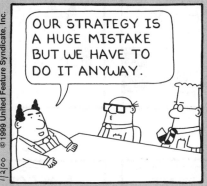

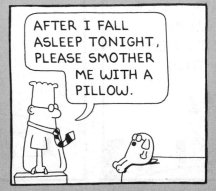

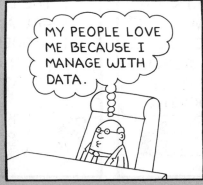

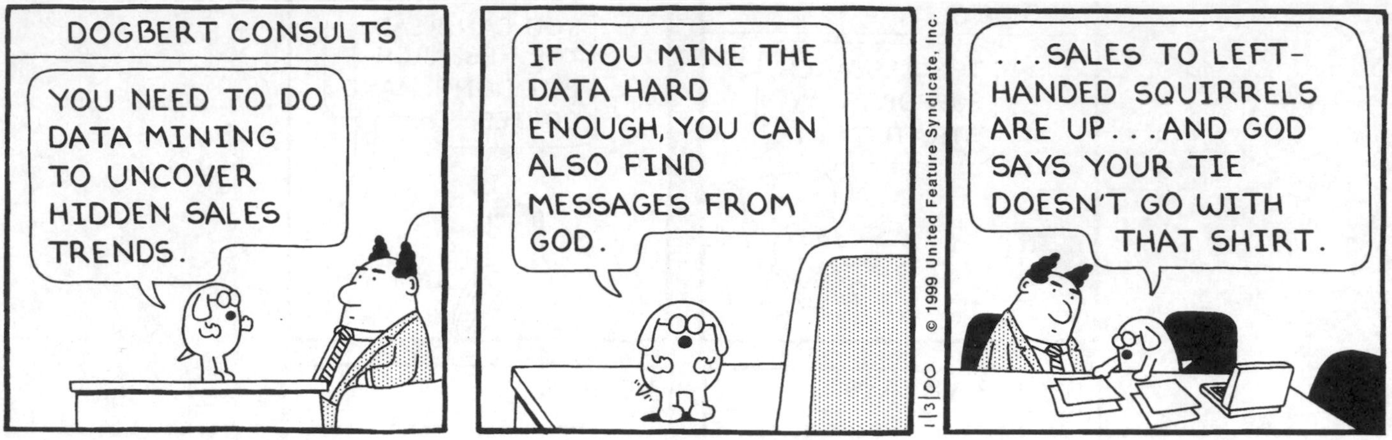
DOGBERT CONSULTS
YOU NEED TO DO DATA MINING TO UNCOVER HIDDEN SALES TRENDS.
IF YOU MINE THE DATA HARD ENOUGH, YOU CAN ALSO FIND MESSAGES FROM GOD.
1/3/00 © 1999 United Feature Syndicate, Inc.
. . .SALES TO LEFT-HANDED SQUIRRELS ARE UP. . .AND GOD SAYS YOUR TIE DOESN'T GO WITH THAT SHIRT.

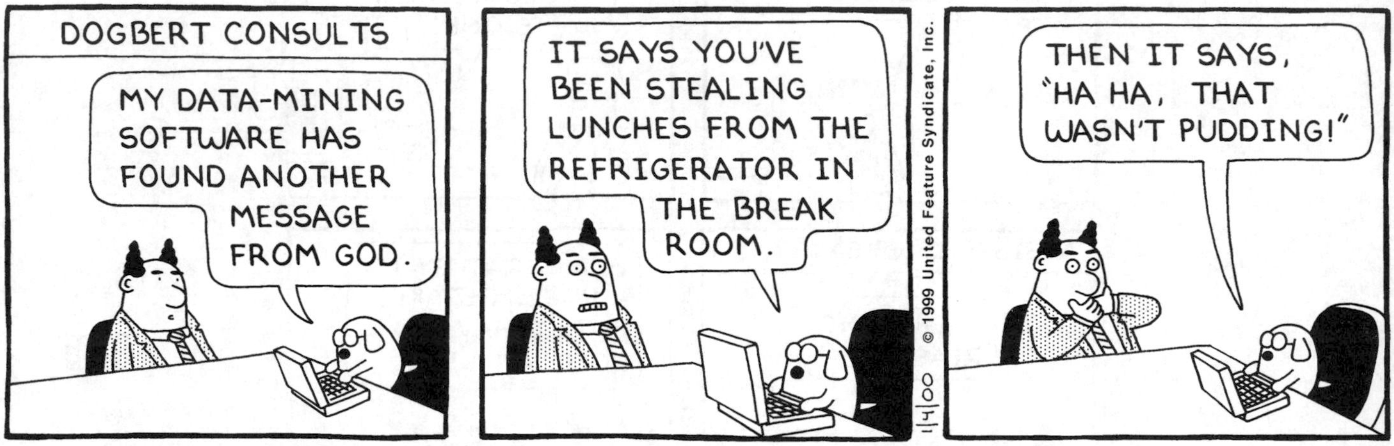
DOGBERT CONSULTS
MY DATA-MINING SOFTWARE HAS FOUND ANOTHER MESSAGE FROM GOD.
IT SAYS YOU'VE BEEN STEALING LUNCHES FROM THE REFRIGERATOR IN THE BREAK ROOM.
1/4/00 © 1999 United Feature Syndicate, Inc.
THEN IT SAYS, "HA HA, THAT WASN'T PUDDING!"

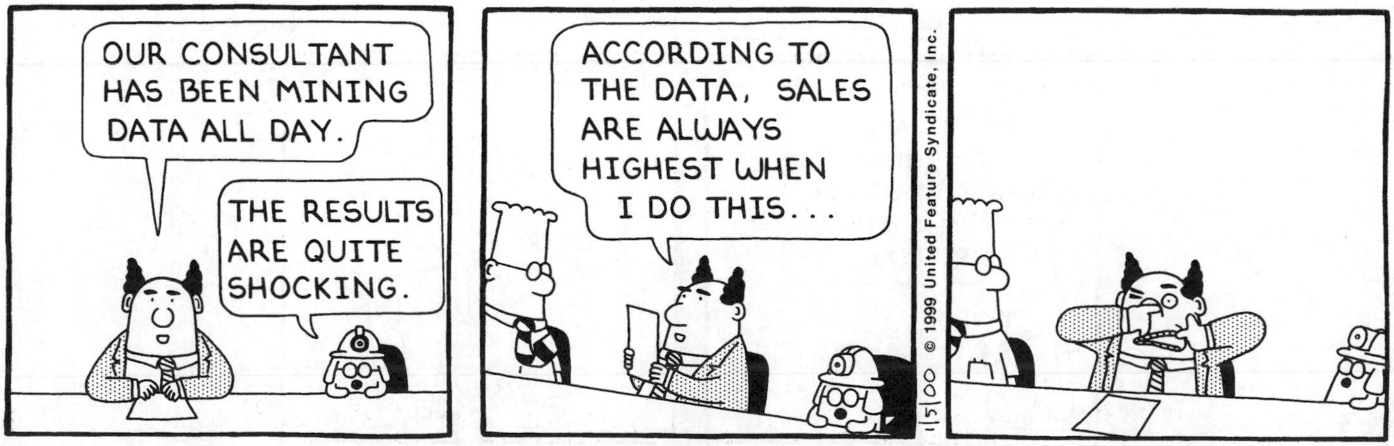
OUR CONSULTANT HAS BEEN MINING DATA ALL DAY.
THE RESULTS ARE QUITE SHOCKING.
ACCORDING TO THE DATA, SALES ARE ALWAYS HIGHEST WHEN I DO THIS. . .
1/5/00 © 1999 United Feature Syndicate, Inc.

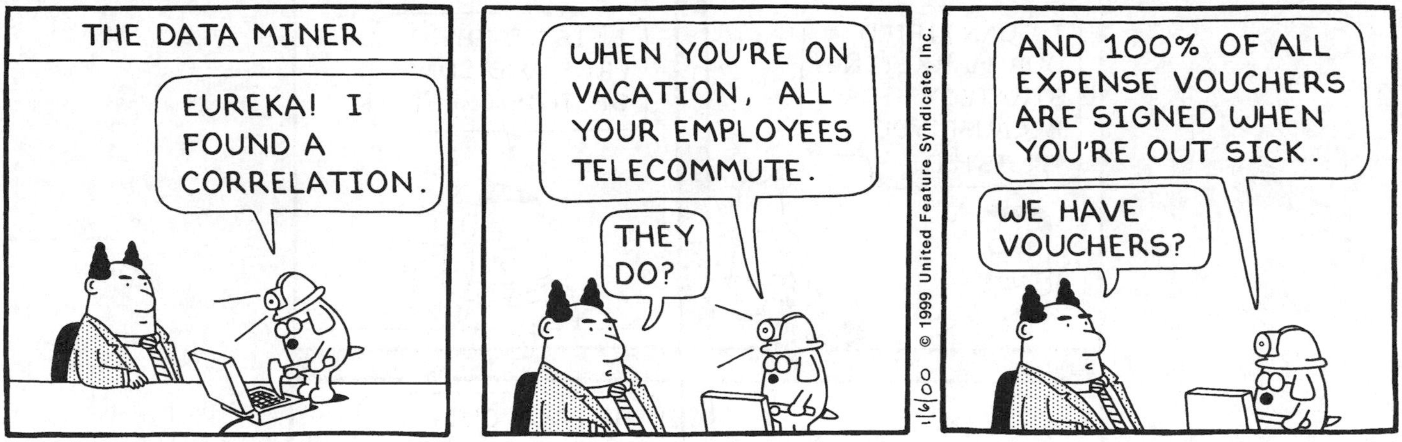
THE DATA MINER
EUREKA! I FOUND A CORRELATION.
WHEN YOU'RE ON VACATION, ALL YOUR EMPLOYEES TELECOMMUTE.
THEY DO?
AND 100% OF ALL EXPENSE VOUCHERS ARE SIGNED WHEN YOU'RE OUT SICK.
WE HAVE VOUCHERS?
1/6/00 © 1999 United Feature Syndicate, Inc.

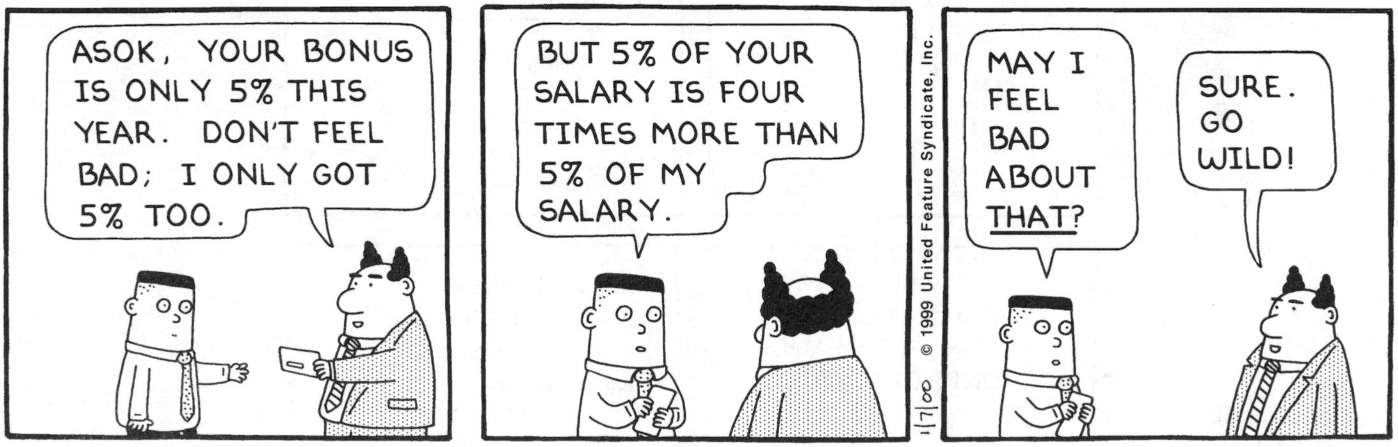
ASOK, YOUR BONUS IS ONLY 5% THIS YEAR. DON'T FEEL BAD; I ONLY GOT 5% TOO.
BUT 5% OF YOUR SALARY IS FOUR TIMES MORE THAN 5% OF MY SALARY.
MAY I FEEL BAD ABOUT THAT?
SURE. GO WILD!
1/7/00 © 1999 United Feature Syndicate, Inc.

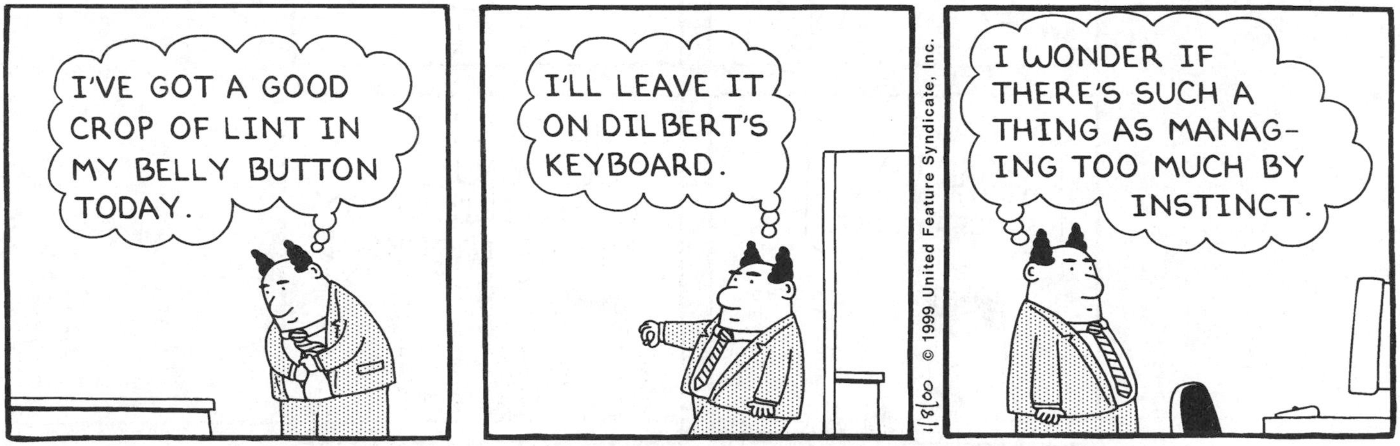
I'VE GOT A GOOD CROP OF LINT IN MY BELLY BUTTON TODAY.
I'LL LEAVE IT ON DILBERT'S KEYBOARD.
I WONDER IF THERE'S SUCH A THING AS MANAGING TOO MUCH BY INSTINCT.
1/8/00 © 1999 United Feature Syndicate, Inc.

I QUANTIFIED OUR MARKETING STRATEGY BECAUSE YOU INSISTED.
I LISTED THE PROS AND CONS ON THIS SHEET.
THEN I ADDED UP THE COLUMNS.
THE PROS OUT-NUMBER THE CONS, SO WE'RE GOING FORWARD.
LET'S SEE. YOUR CONS INCLUDE... UNHEALTHY AND UNPROFITABLE.
1/9/00 © 2000 United Feature Syndicate, Inc.
YOUR PROS ARE.. WAFFLES, EGGS, BANANAS AND MILK.
OOPS. THAT MIGHT BE MY GROCERY LIST.
YOU FOOL! I TOLD YOU QUANTIFICATION NEVER WORKS!!

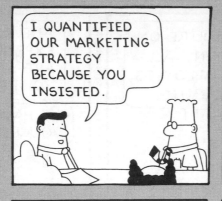

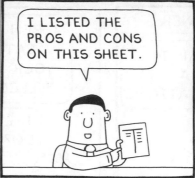

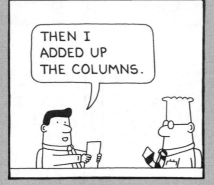

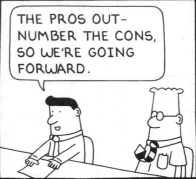

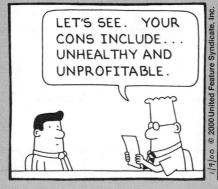

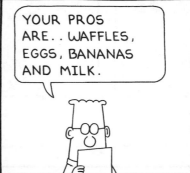

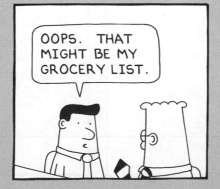

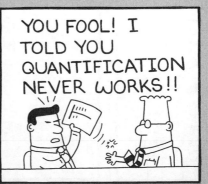

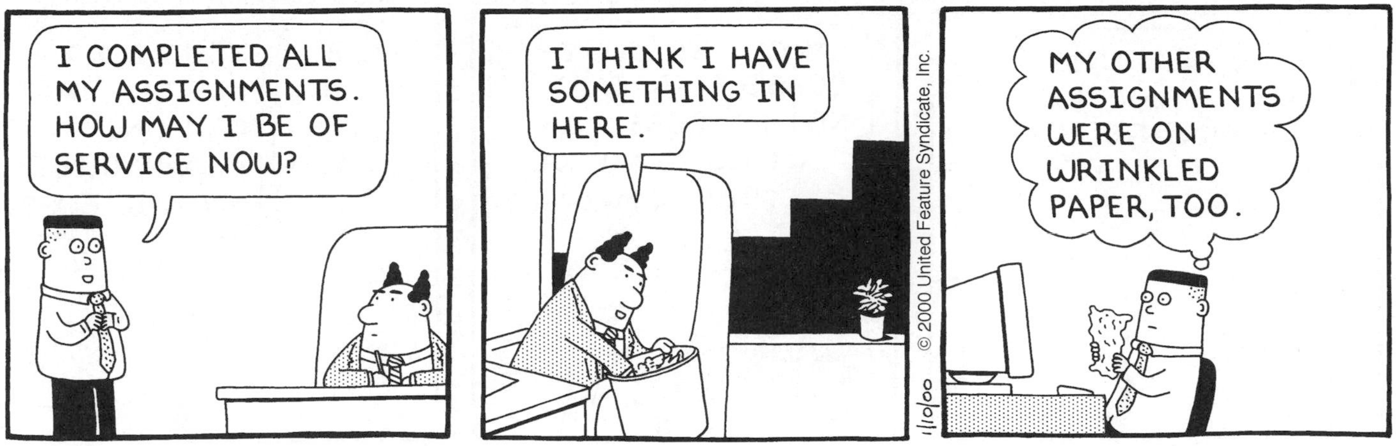
I COMPLETED ALL MY ASSIGNMENTS. HOW MAY I BE OF SERVICE NOW?
I THINK I HAVE SOMETHING IN HERE.
1/10/00 © 2000 United Feature Syndicate, Inc.
MY OTHER ASSIGNMENTS WERE ON WRINKLED PAPER, TOO.

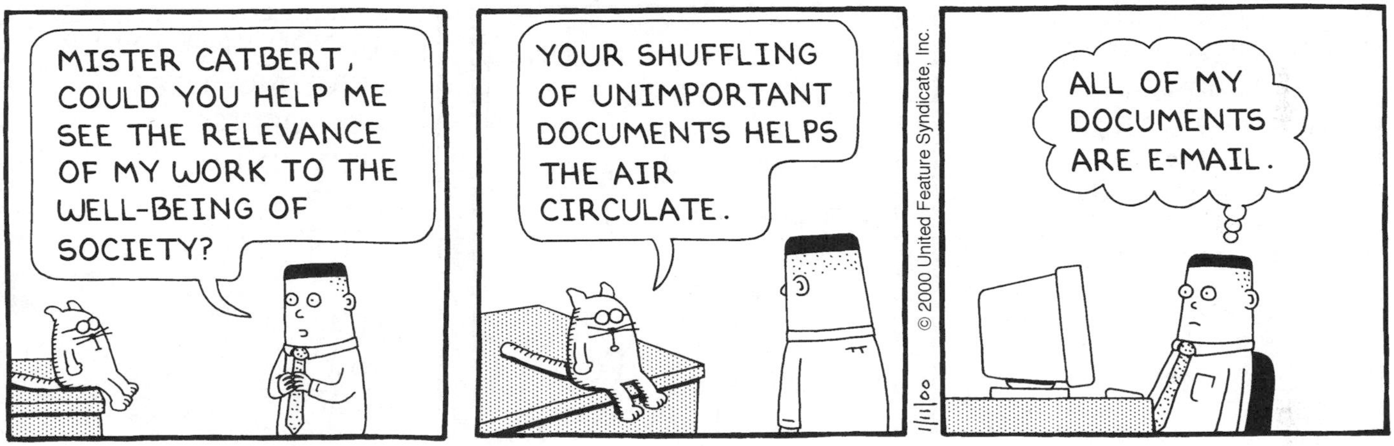
MISTER CATBERT, COULD YOU HELP ME SEE THE RELEVANCE OF MY WORK TO THE WELL-BEING OF SOCIETY?
YOUR SHUFFLING OF UNIMPORTANT DOCUMENTS HELPS THE AIR CIRCULATE.
1/11/00 © 2000 United Feature Syndicate, Inc.
ALL OF MY DOCUMENTS ARE E-MAIL.

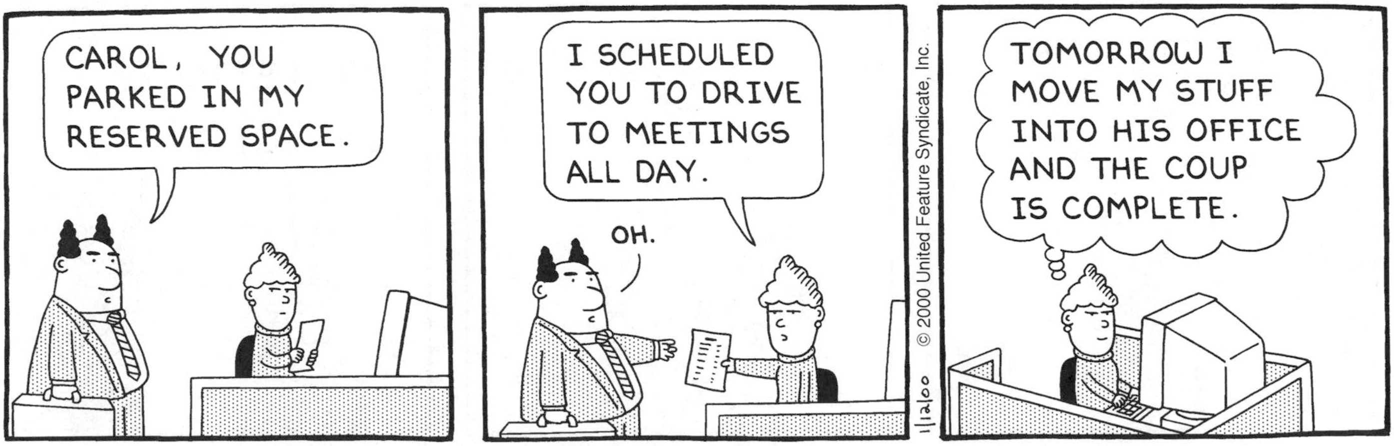
CAROL, YOU PARKED IN MY RESERVED SPACE.
I SCHEDULED YOU TO DRIVE TO MEETINGS ALL DAY.
OH.
1/12/00 © 2000 United Feature Syndicate, Inc.
TOMORROW I MOVE MY STUFF INTO HIS OFFICE AND THE COUP IS COMPLETE.

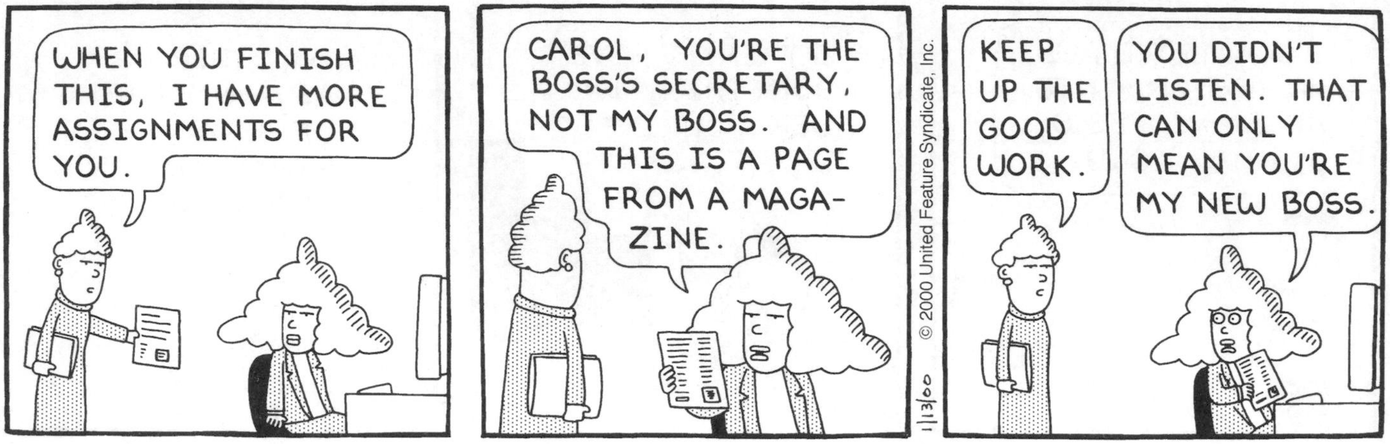
WHEN YOU FINISH THIS, I HAVE MORE ASSIGNMENTS FOR YOU.
CAROL, YOU'RE THE BOSS'S SECRETARY, NOT MY BOSS. AND THIS IS A PAGE FROM A MAGAZINE.
KEEP UP THE GOOD WORK.
YOU DIDN'T LISTEN. THAT CAN ONLY MEAN YOU'RE MY NEW BOSS.
© 2000 United Feature Syndicate, Inc.
1/13/00

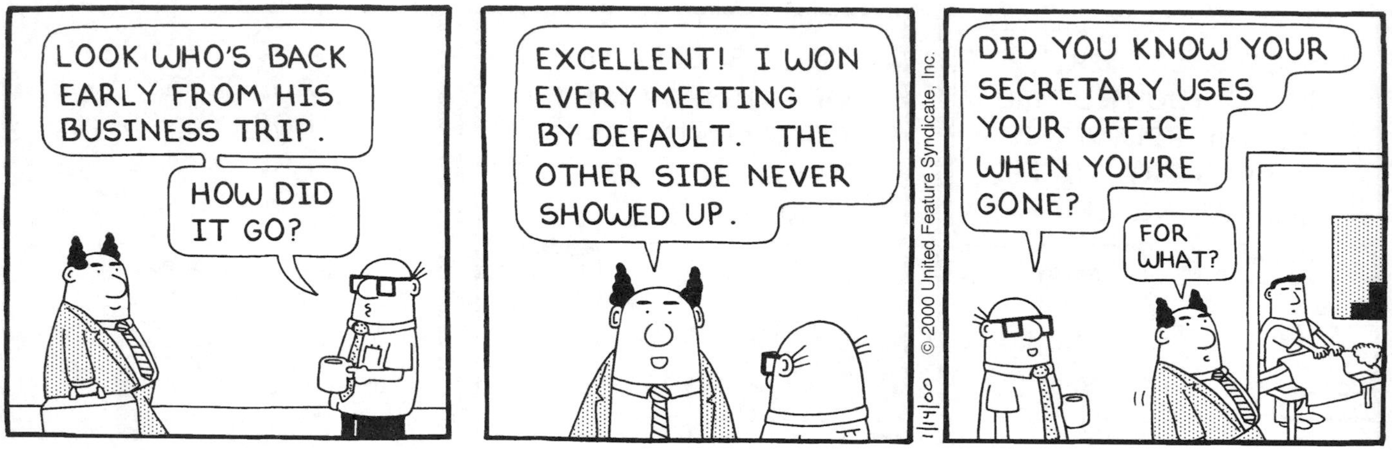
LOOK WHO'S BACK EARLY FROM HIS BUSINESS TRIP.
HOW DID IT GO?
EXCELLENT! I WON EVERY MEETING BY DEFAULT. THE OTHER SIDE NEVER SHOWED UP.
DID YOU KNOW YOUR SECRETARY USES YOUR OFFICE WHEN YOU'RE GONE?
FOR WHAT?
© 2000 United Feature Syndicate, Inc.
1/14/00

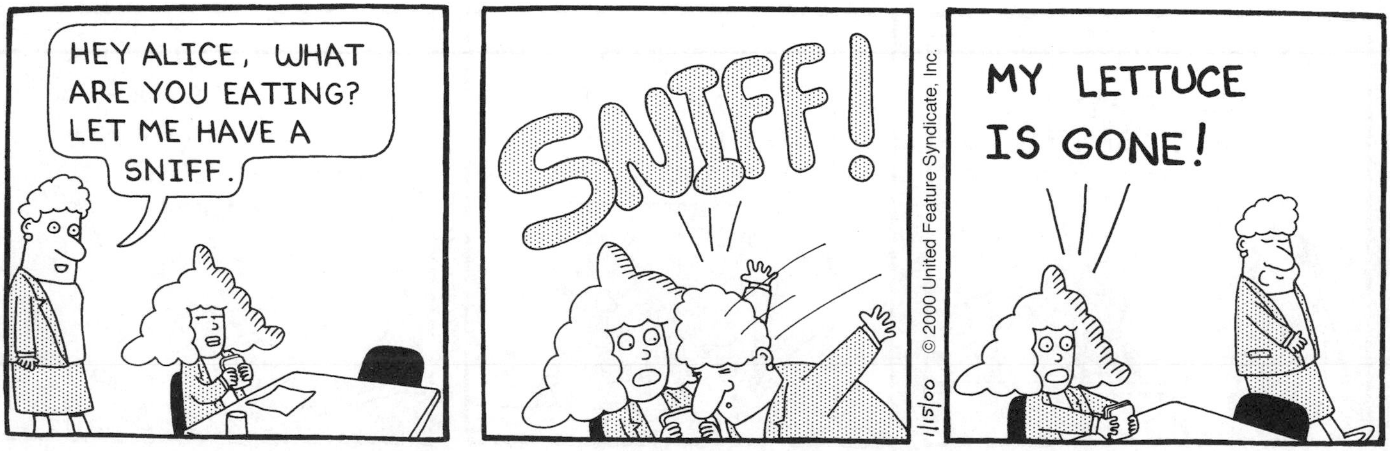
HEY ALICE, WHAT ARE YOU EATING? LET ME HAVE A SNIFF.
SNIFF!
MY LETTUCE IS GONE!
© 2000 United Feature Syndicate, Inc.
1/15/00

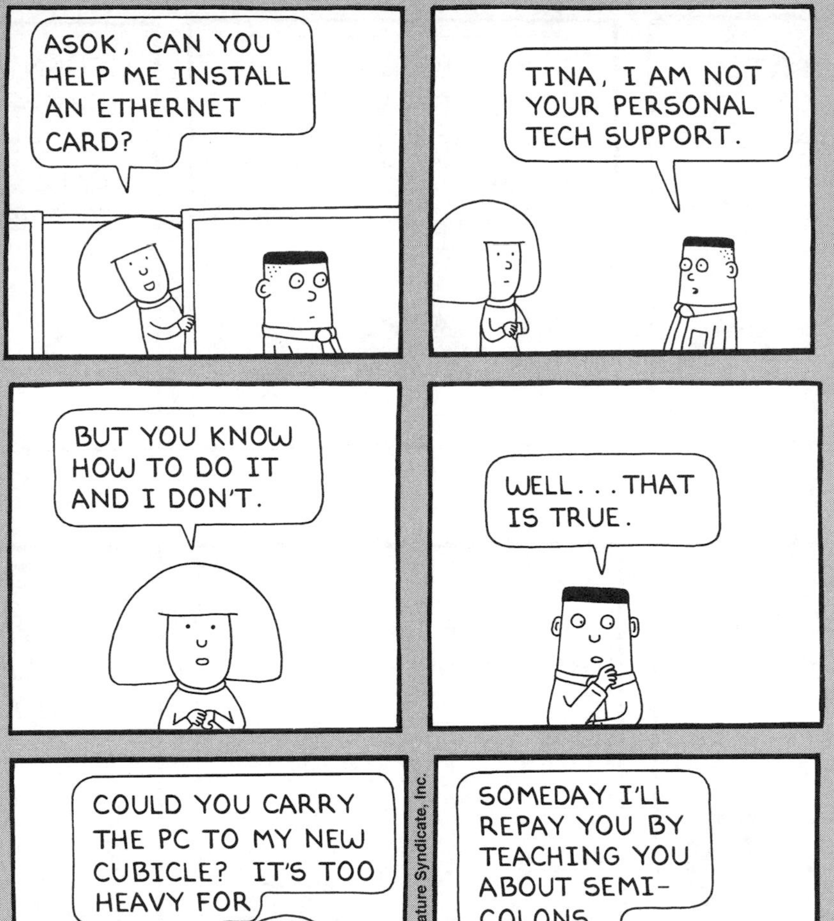
ASOK, CAN YOU HELP ME INSTALL AN ETHERNET CARD?
TINA, I AM NOT YOUR PERSONAL TECH SUPPORT.
BUT YOU KNOW HOW TO DO IT AND I DON'T.
WELL... THAT IS TRUE.
COULD YOU CARRY THE PC TO MY NEW CUBICLE? IT'S TOO HEAVY FOR ME.
SOMEDAY I'LL REPAY YOU BY TEACHING YOU ABOUT SEMI-COLONS.
HOW COME I HAVE MANY USEFUL SKILLS AND YOU HAVE NONE?
I GUESS I'M JUST LUCKY.
© 2000 United Feature Syndicate, Inc.
1/16/00

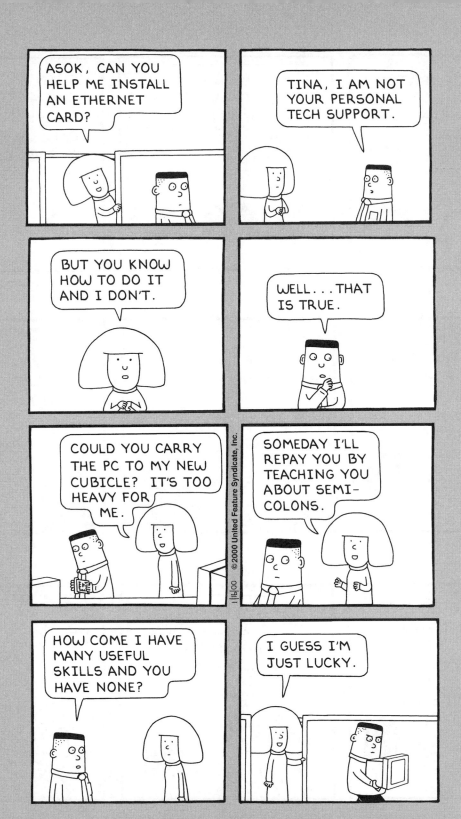

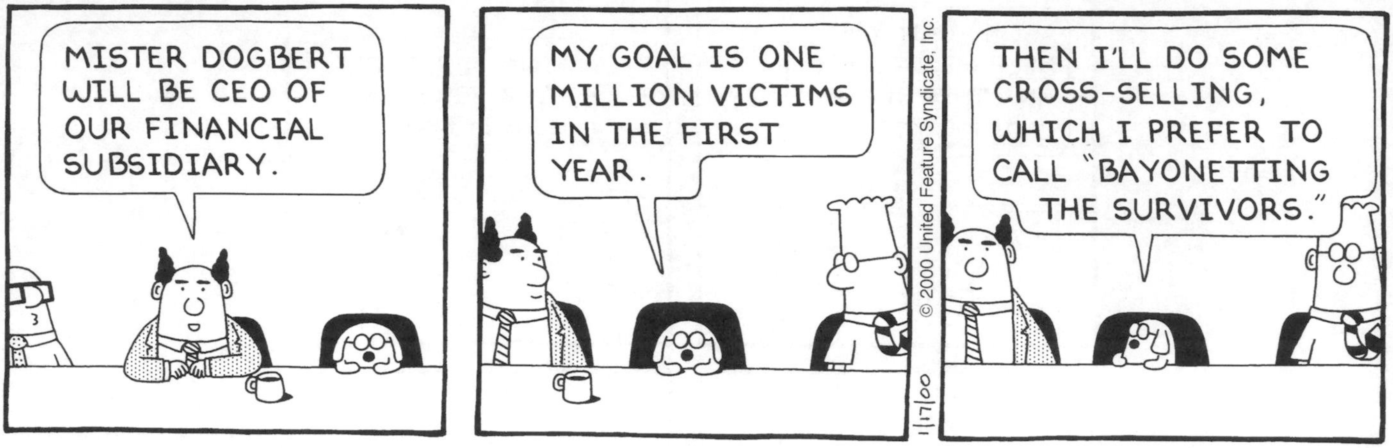
MISTER DOGBERT WILL BE CEO OF OUR FINANCIAL SUBSIDIARY.
MY GOAL IS ONE MILLION VICTIMS IN THE FIRST YEAR.
THEN I'LL DO SOME CROSS-SELLING, WHICH I PREFER TO CALL "BAYONETTING THE SURVIVORS."
© 2000 United Feature Syndicate, Inc.
1/17/00

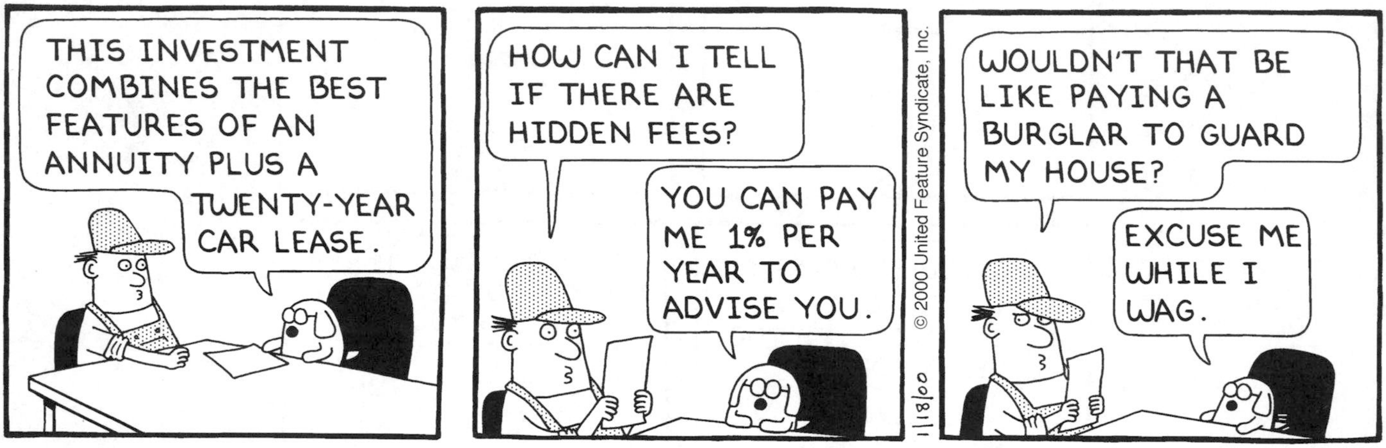
THIS INVESTMENT COMBINES THE BEST FEATURES OF AN ANNUITY PLUS A TWENTY-YEAR CAR LEASE.
HOW CAN I TELL IF THERE ARE HIDDEN FEES?
YOU CAN PAY ME 1% PER YEAR TO ADVISE YOU.
WOULDN'T THAT BE LIKE PAYING A BURGLAR TO GUARD MY HOUSE?
EXCUSE ME WHILE I WAG.
© 2000 United Feature Syndicate, Inc.
1/18/00

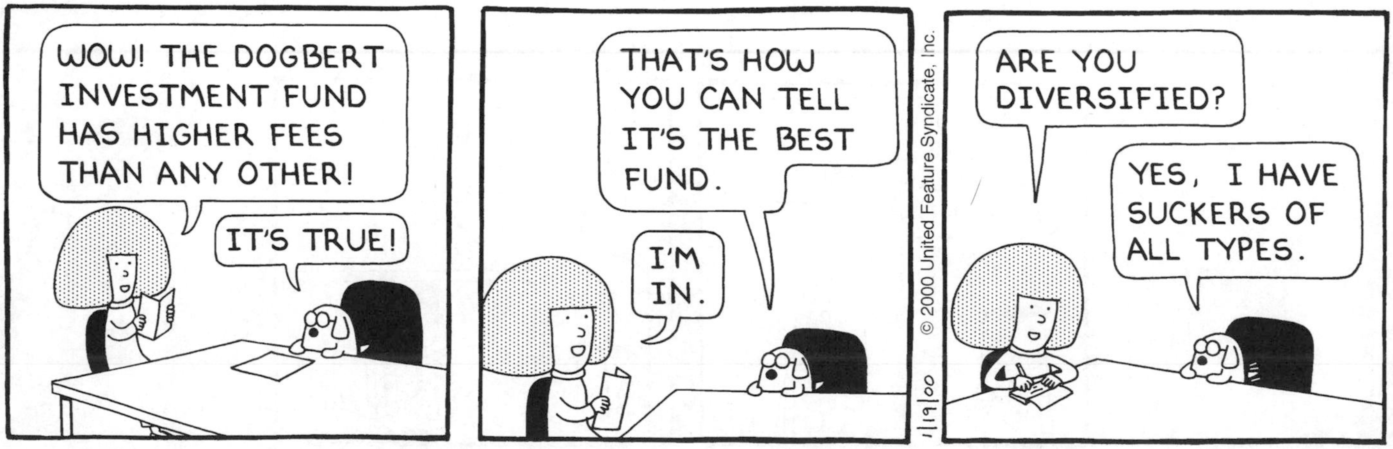
WOW! THE DOGBERT INVESTMENT FUND HAS HIGHER FEES THAN ANY OTHER!
IT'S TRUE!
THAT'S HOW YOU CAN TELL IT'S THE BEST FUND.
I'M IN.
ARE YOU DIVERSIFIED?
YES, I HAVE SUCKERS OF ALL TYPES.
© 2000 United Feature Syndicate, Inc.
1/19/00

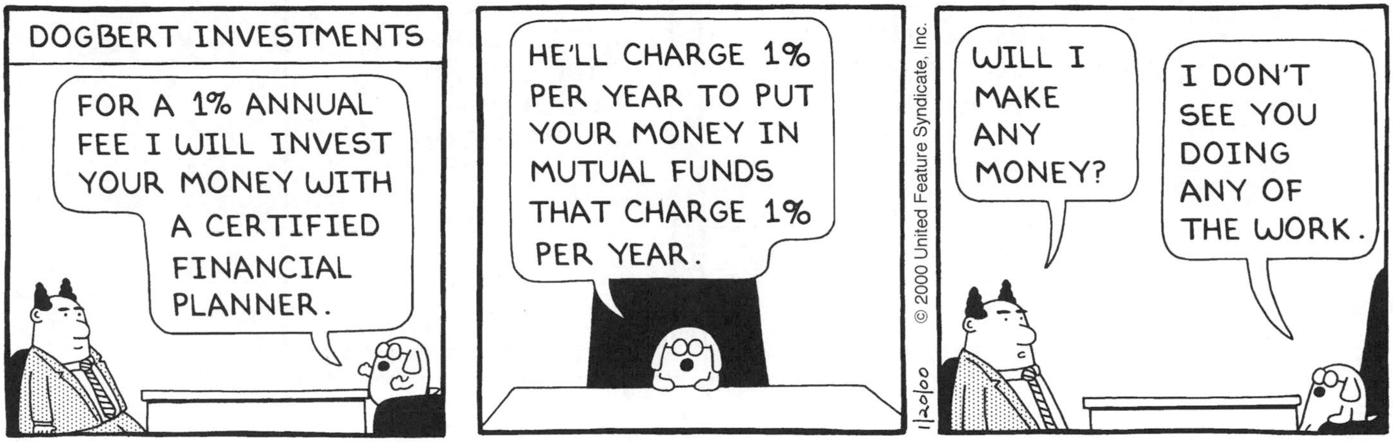
DOGBERT INVESTMENTS
FOR A 1% ANNUAL FEE I WILL INVEST YOUR MONEY WITH A CERTIFIED FINANCIAL PLANNER.
HE'LL CHARGE 1% PER YEAR TO PUT YOUR MONEY IN MUTUAL FUNDS THAT CHARGE 1% PER YEAR.
© 2000 United Feature Syndicate, Inc.
1/20/00
WILL I MAKE ANY MONEY?
I DON'T SEE YOU DOING ANY OF THE WORK.

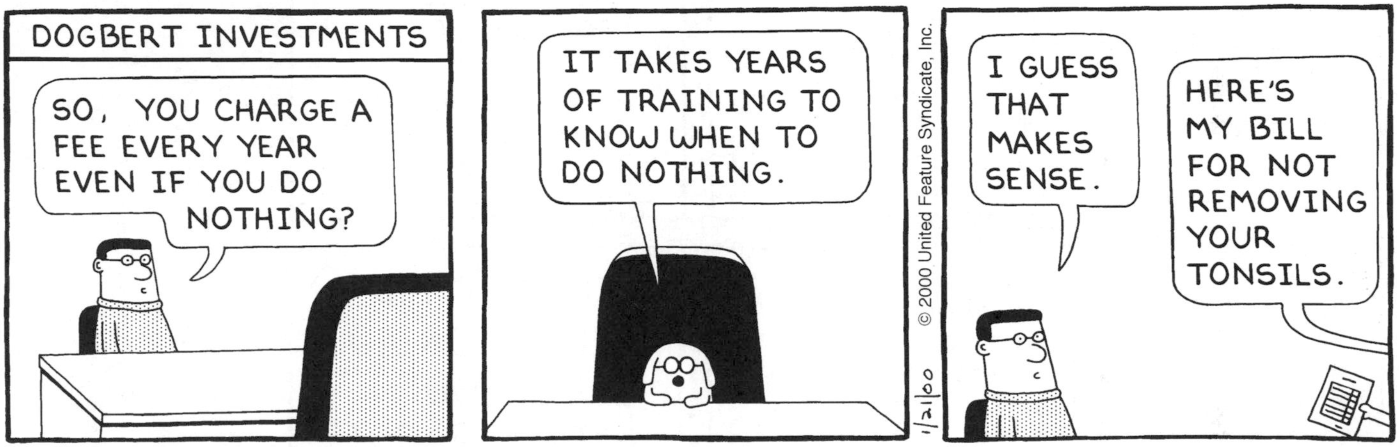
DOGBERT INVESTMENTS
SO, YOU CHARGE A FEE EVERY YEAR EVEN IF YOU DO NOTHING?
IT TAKES YEARS OF TRAINING TO KNOW WHEN TO DO NOTHING.
© 2000 United Feature Syndicate, Inc.
1/21/00
I GUESS THAT MAKES SENSE.
HERE'S MY BILL FOR NOT REMOVING YOUR TONSILS.

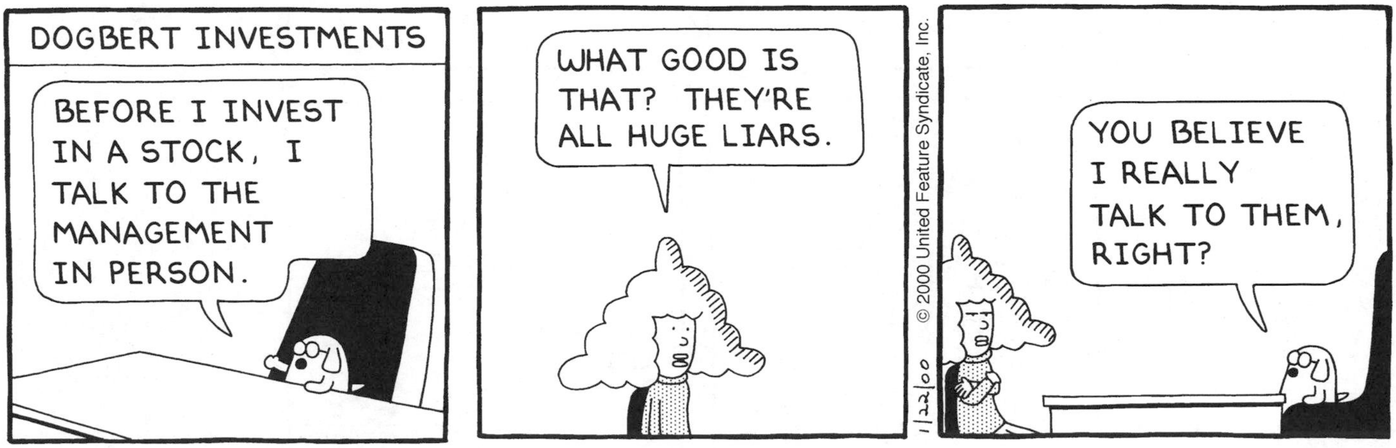
DOGBERT INVESTMENTS
BEFORE I INVEST IN A STOCK, I TALK TO THE MANAGEMENT IN PERSON.
WHAT GOOD IS THAT? THEY'RE ALL HUGE LIARS.
© 2000 United Feature Syndicate, Inc.
1/22/00
YOU BELIEVE I REALLY TALK TO THEM, RIGHT?

WE'RE CHANGING TO A CASH BALANCE PENSION PLAN.
IT WILL MAKE THE COMPANY MUCH MORE COMPETITIVE.
YIPPEE!!! A CASH BALANCE PLAN IS GOOD FOR YOUNG EMPLOYEES!
OH, YEAH? WELL IT'S NOT SO GOOD FOR ME!
I DEMAND THAT YOU CHANGE IT BACK!
NO!
I'LL SNAP YOU LIKE A DRIED TWIG, YOU LITTLE ZYGOTE!
OUCH! STOP CLUBBING ME WITH YOUR ARTIFICIAL HIP!!
ON THE PLUS SIDE, THEY DO SEEM MORE COMPETITIVE.
1/23/00
© 2000 United Feature Syndicate, Inc.

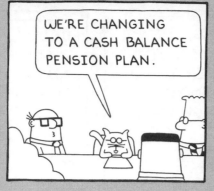

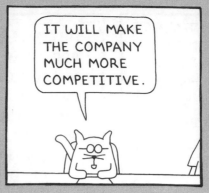

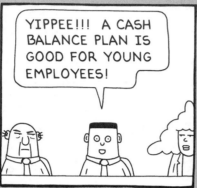

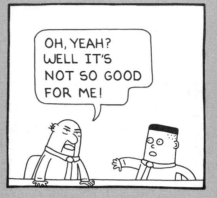

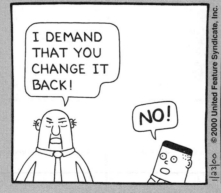

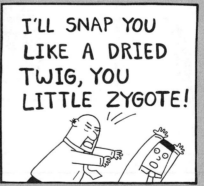

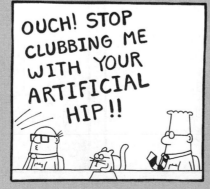

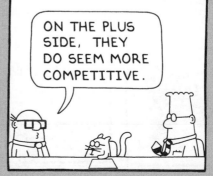

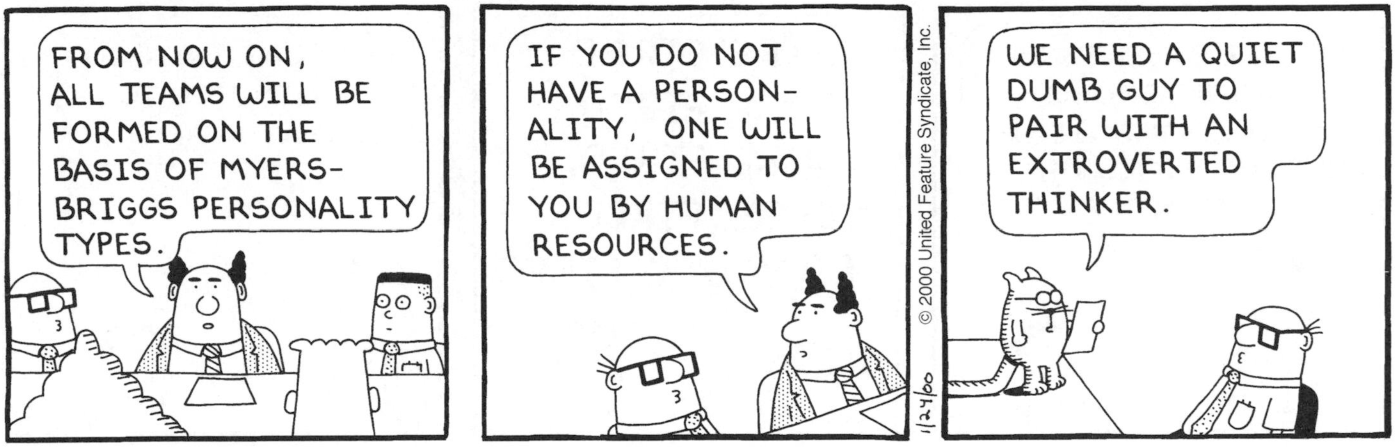
FROM NOW ON, ALL TEAMS WILL BE FORMED ON THE BASIS OF MYERS-BRIGGS PERSONALITY TYPES.
IF YOU DO NOT HAVE A PERSON-ALITY, ONE WILL BE ASSIGNED TO YOU BY HUMAN RESOURCES.
1/24/00 © 2000 United Feature Syndicate, Inc.
WE NEED A QUIET DUMB GUY TO PAIR WITH AN EXTROVERTED THINKER.

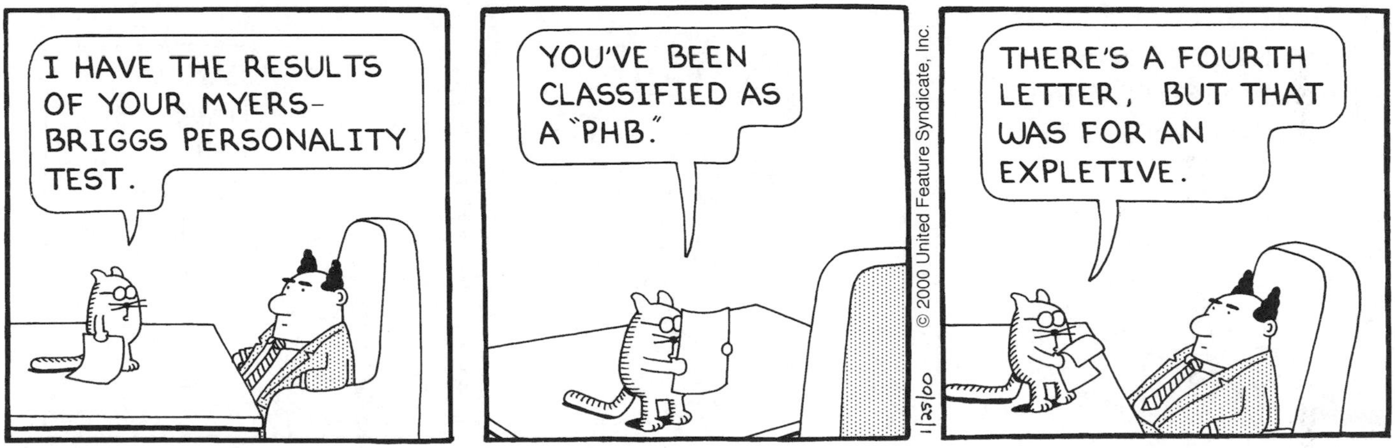
I HAVE THE RESULTS OF YOUR MYERS-BRIGGS PERSONALITY TEST.
YOU'VE BEEN CLASSIFIED AS A "PHB."
1/25/00 © 2000 United Feature Syndicate, Inc.
THERE'S A FOURTH LETTER, BUT THAT WAS FOR AN EXPLETIVE.

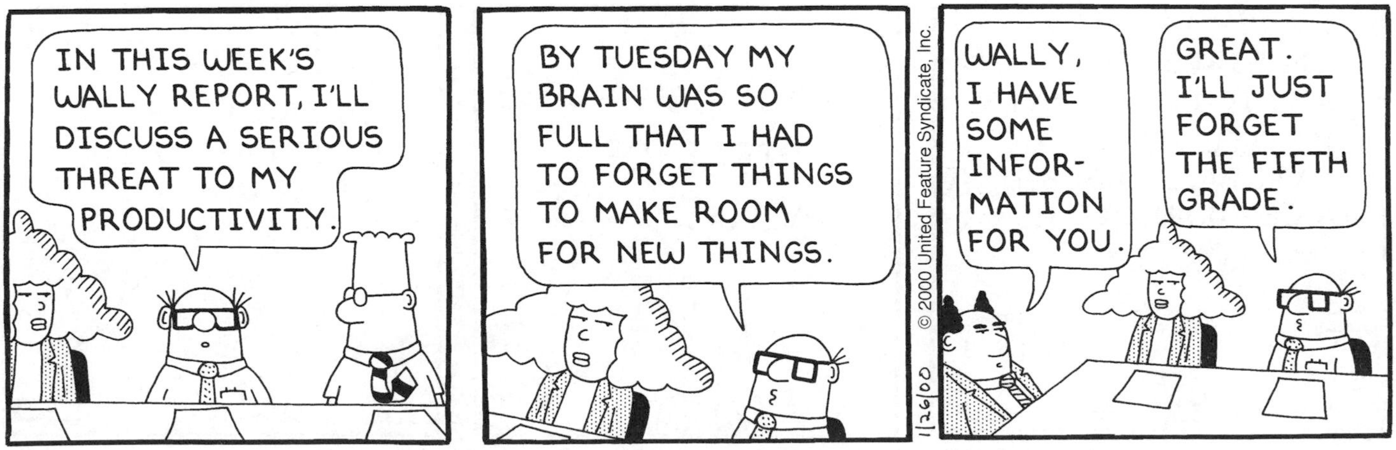
IN THIS WEEK'S WALLY REPORT, I'LL DISCUSS A SERIOUS THREAT TO MY PRODUCTIVITY.
BY TUESDAY MY BRAIN WAS SO FULL THAT I HAD TO FORGET THINGS TO MAKE ROOM FOR NEW THINGS.
1/26/00 © 2000 United Feature Syndicate, Inc.
WALLY, I HAVE SOME INFOR-MATION FOR YOU.
GREAT. I'LL JUST FORGET THE FIFTH GRADE.

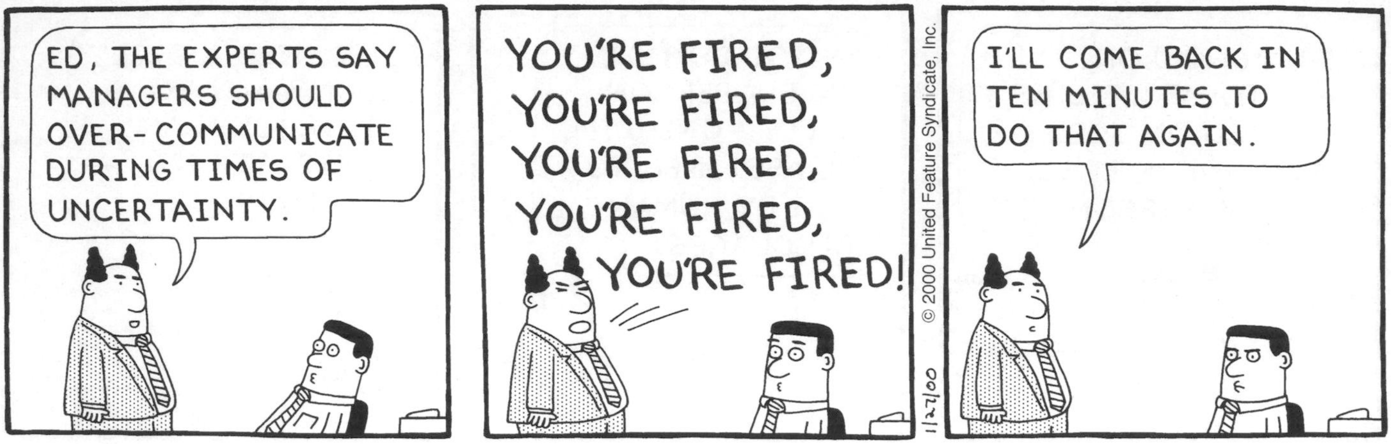
ED, THE EXPERTS SAY MANAGERS SHOULD OVER-COMMUNICATE DURING TIMES OF UNCERTAINTY.
YOU'RE FIRED, YOU'RE FIRED, YOU'RE FIRED, YOU'RE FIRED, YOU'RE FIRED!
© 2000 United Feature Syndicate, Inc.
1/27/00
I'LL COME BACK IN TEN MINUTES TO DO THAT AGAIN.

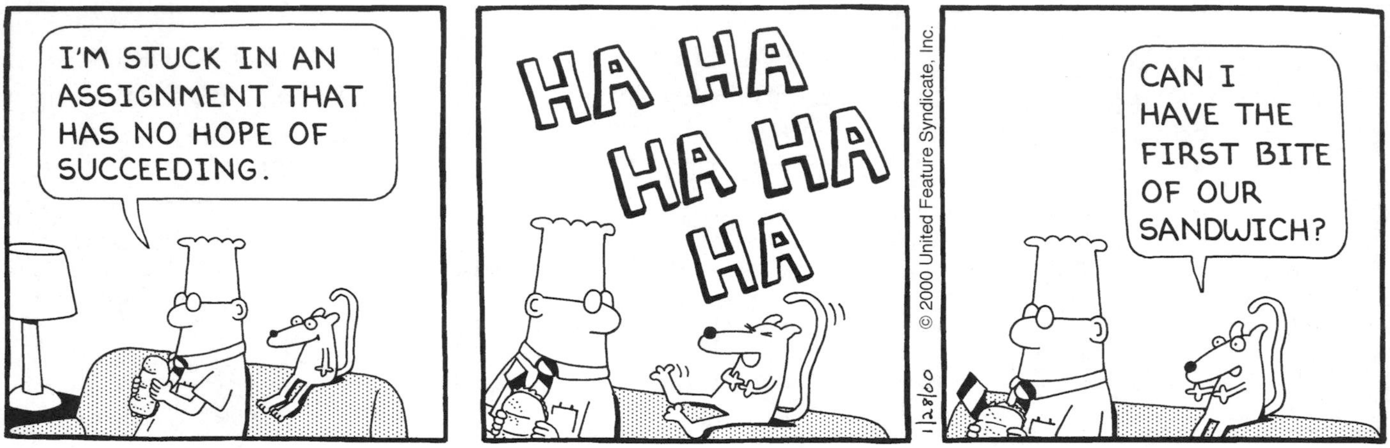
I'M STUCK IN AN ASSIGNMENT THAT HAS NO HOPE OF SUCCEEDING.
HA HA HA HA HA
© 2000 United Feature Syndicate, Inc.
1/28/00
CAN I HAVE THE FIRST BITE OF OUR SANDWICH?

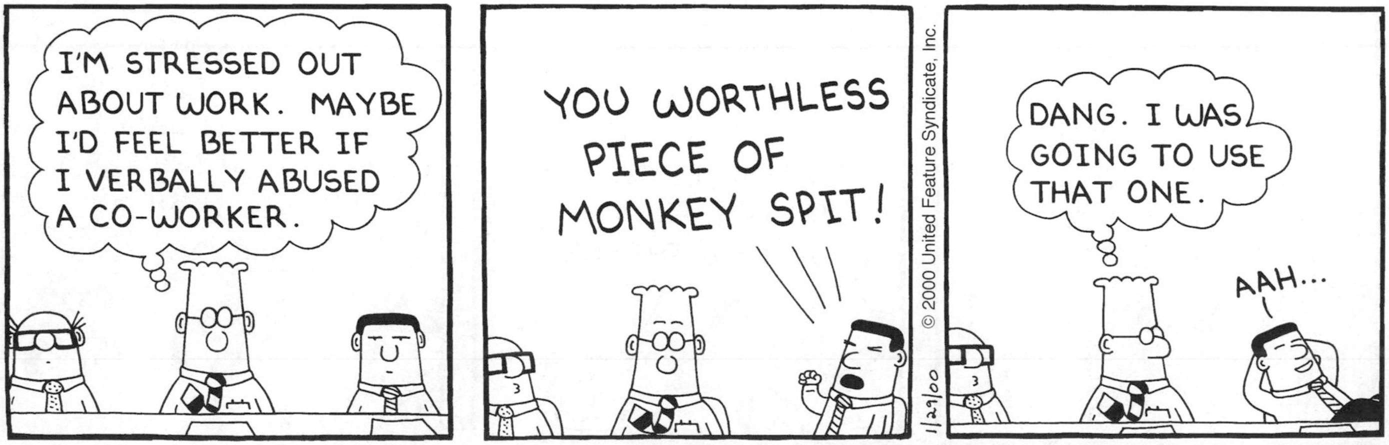
I'M STRESSED OUT ABOUT WORK. MAYBE I'D FEEL BETTER IF I VERBALLY ABUSED A CO-WORKER.
YOU WORTHLESS PIECE OF MONKEY SPIT!
© 2000 United Feature Syndicate, Inc.
1/29/00
DANG. I WAS GOING TO USE THAT ONE.
AAH...

MY ANTI- SPAM SOFTWARE IS COMPLETE.
IT CHECKS MY INCOMING E-MAIL FOR KEY WORDS.
THEN IT DELETES ANYTHING THAT LOOKS LIKE AN ADVERTISEMENT.
SUPPOSE A BEAUTIFUL WOMAN SENDS YOU A MESSAGE SAYING...
"I AM A MODEL FOR VICTORIA'S SECRET. I WANT TO DATE YOU ON MY SAILBOAT."
1/30/00 © 2000 United Feature Syndicate, Inc.
BUT SHE SPELLS SAIL S-A-L-E.
WHAT THEN?
WHAT'S SHE WEARING?

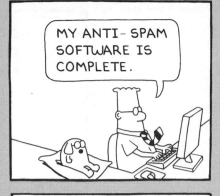

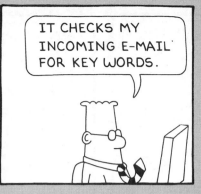

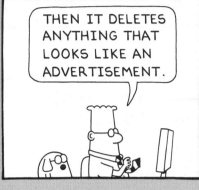

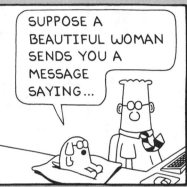

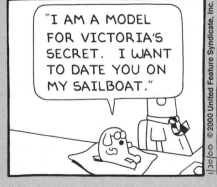

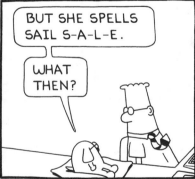

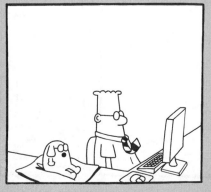

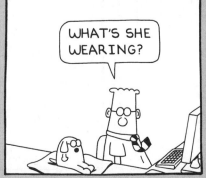

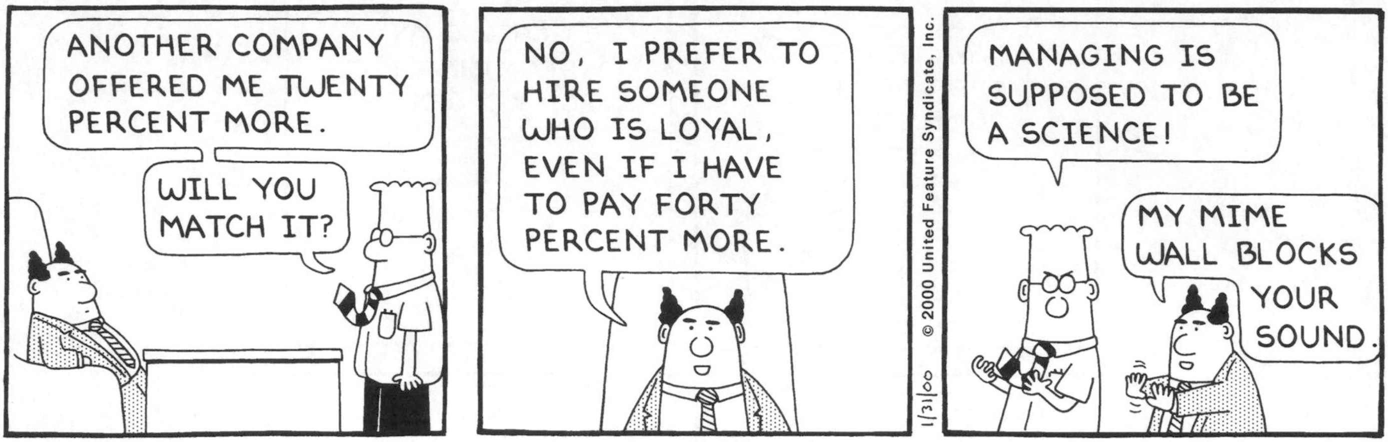
ANOTHER COMPANY OFFERED ME TWENTY PERCENT MORE.
WILL YOU MATCH IT?
NO, I PREFER TO HIRE SOMEONE WHO IS LOYAL, EVEN IF I HAVE TO PAY FORTY PERCENT MORE.
1/31/00
MANAGING IS SUPPOSED TO BE A SCIENCE!
MY MIME WALL BLOCKS YOUR SOUND.

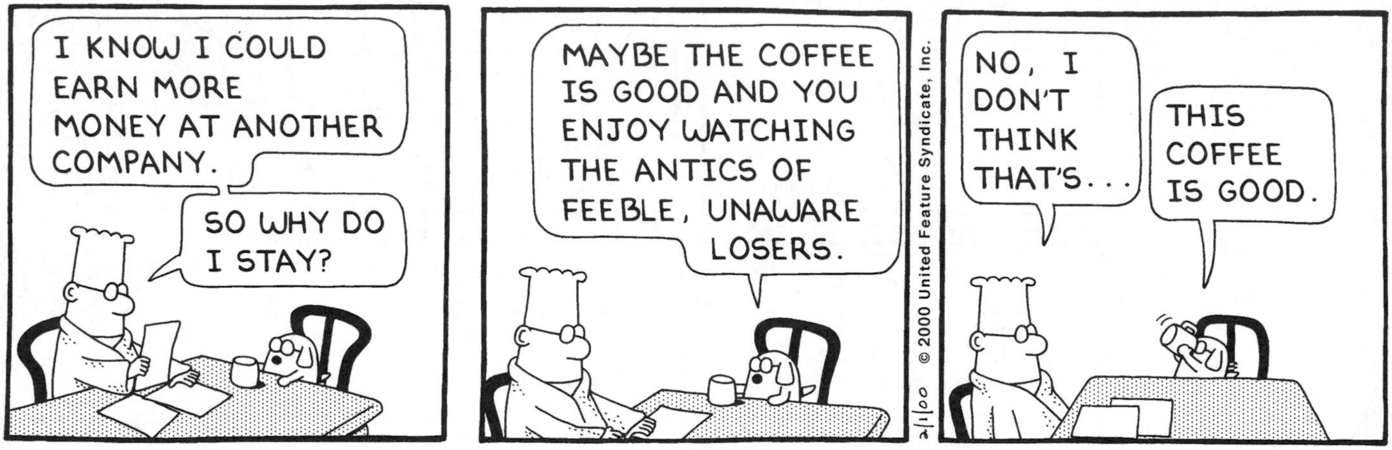
I KNOW I COULD EARN MORE MONEY AT ANOTHER COMPANY.
SO WHY DO I STAY?
MAYBE THE COFFEE IS GOOD AND YOU ENJOY WATCHING THE ANTICS OF FEEBLE, UNAWARE LOSERS.
2/1/00
NO, I DON'T THINK THAT'S. . .
THIS COFFEE IS GOOD.

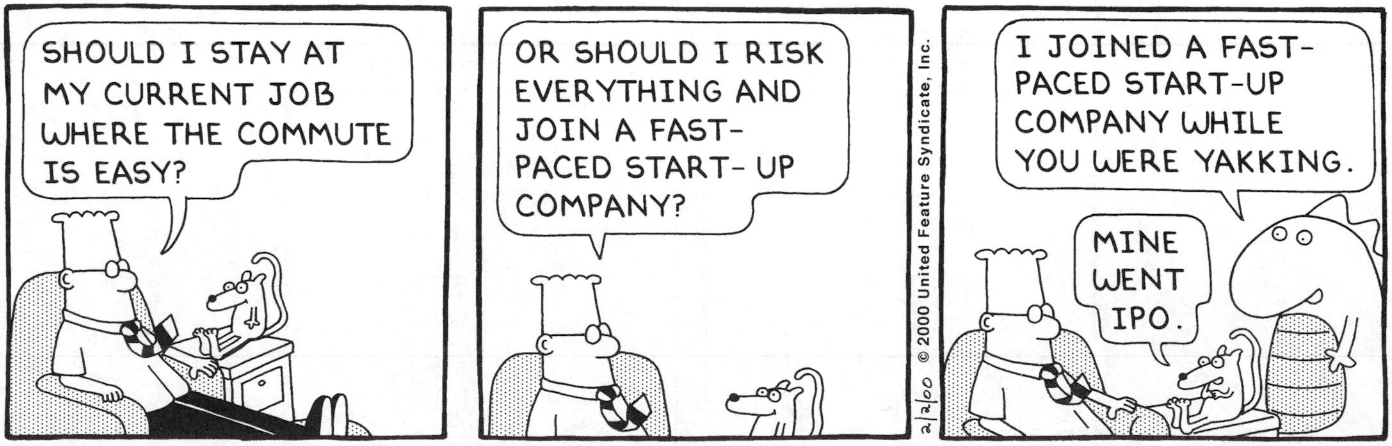
SHOULD I STAY AT MY CURRENT JOB WHERE THE COMMUTE IS EASY?
OR SHOULD I RISK EVERYTHING AND JOIN A FAST-PACED START-UP COMPANY?
2/2/00
I JOINED A FAST-PACED START-UP COMPANY WHILE YOU WERE YAKKING.
MINE WENT IPO.

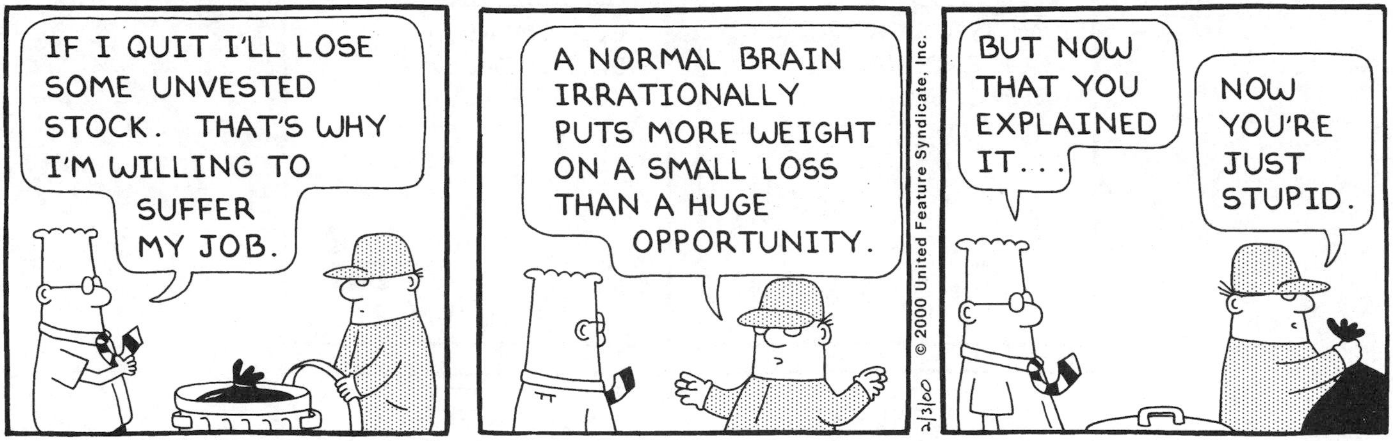
IF I QUIT I'LL LOSE SOME UNVESTED STOCK. THAT'S WHY I'M WILLING TO SUFFER MY JOB.
A NORMAL BRAIN IRRATIONALLY PUTS MORE WEIGHT ON A SMALL LOSS THAN A HUGE OPPORTUNITY.
BUT NOW THAT YOU EXPLAINED IT...
NOW YOU'RE JUST STUPID.
2/3/00

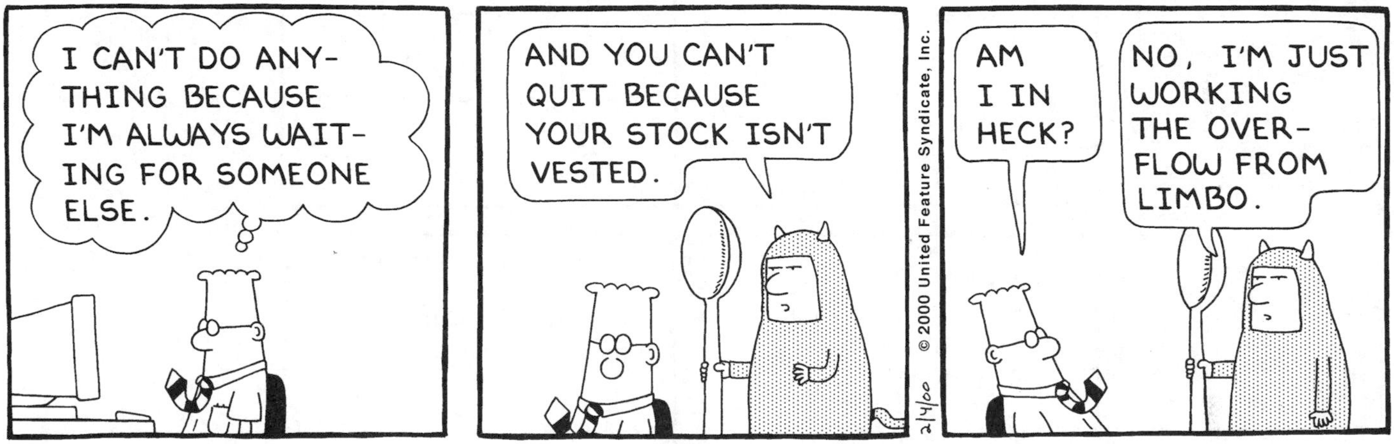
I CAN'T DO ANYTHING BECAUSE I'M ALWAYS WAITING FOR SOMEONE ELSE.
AND YOU CAN'T QUIT BECAUSE YOUR STOCK ISN'T VESTED.
AM I IN HECK?
NO, I'M JUST WORKING THE OVERFLOW FROM LIMBO.
2/4/00

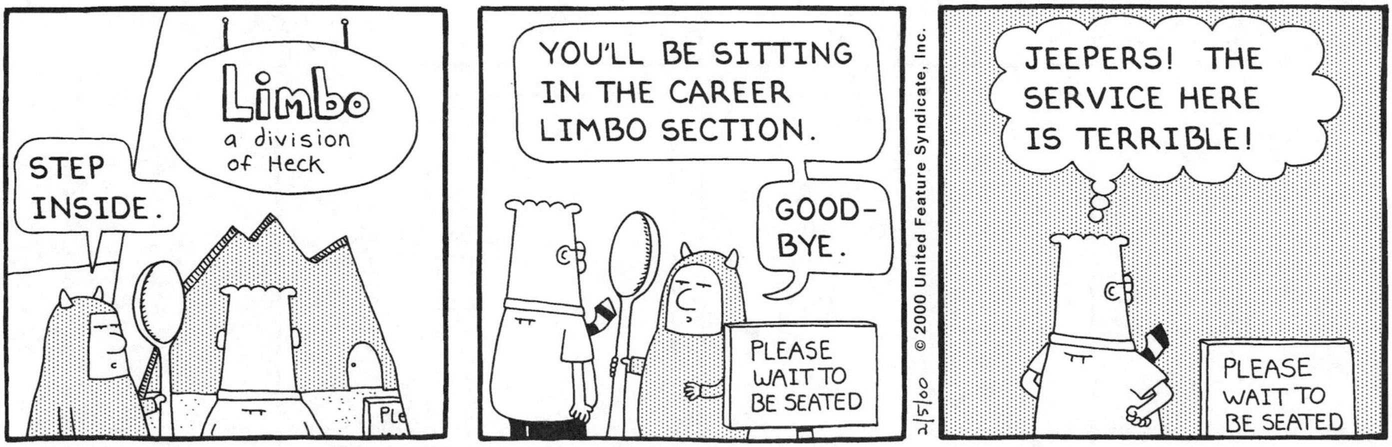
Limbo
a division of Heck
STEP INSIDE.
YOU'LL BE SITTING IN THE CAREER LIMBO SECTION.
GOOD-BYE.
PLEASE WAIT TO BE SEATED
JEEPERS! THE SERVICE HERE IS TERRIBLE!
PLEASE WAIT TO BE SEATED
2/5/00

MY TESTS PROVE OUR PRODUCT IS DEFECTIVE.

CUSTOMERS EXPECT DELIVERY TOMORROW.

OUR CORPORATE PHILOSOPHY IS "QUALITY IS OUR PRIMARY GOAL."

SO . . . YOU WANT ME TO DELAY SHIPMENT UNTIL WE FIX THE PROBLEMS?

NO.

I WANT YOU TO SHIP NOW SO WE CAN BOOK THE REVENUE.

GAAA! THAT'S THE OPPOSITE OF OUR PHILOSOPHY!!!

© 2000 United Feature Syndicate, Inc.

NOW YOU KNOW WHY THERE AREN'T ANY RICH PHILOSOPHERS.

THERE USED TO BE ONE, BUT HE BELIEVED I WAS A SWISS BANK.

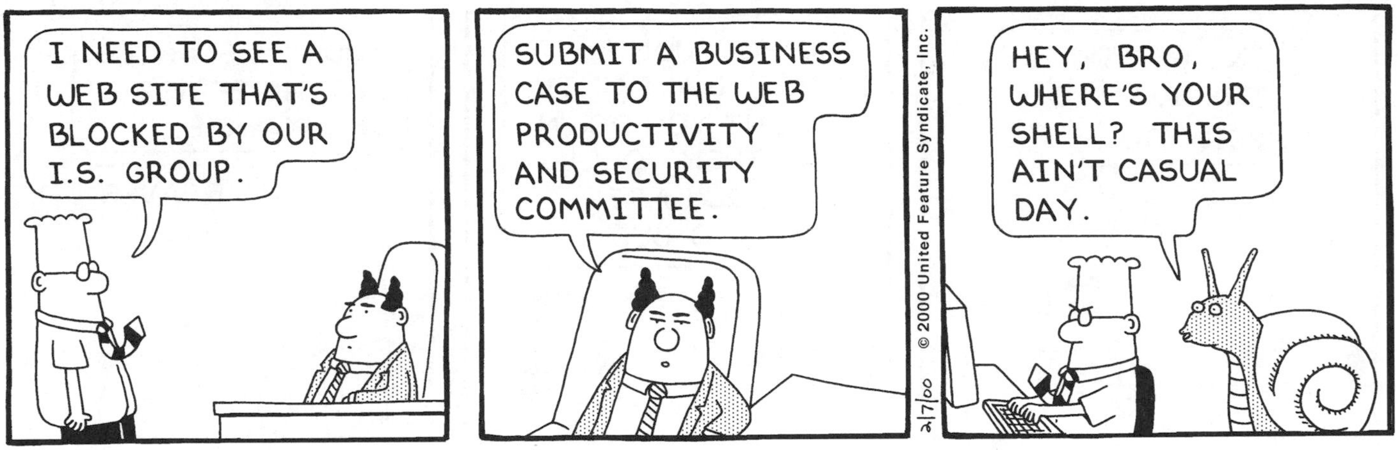
I NEED TO SEE A WEB SITE THAT'S BLOCKED BY OUR I.S. GROUP.
SUBMIT A BUSINESS CASE TO THE WEB PRODUCTIVITY AND SECURITY COMMITTEE.
2/7/00 © 2000 United Feature Syndicate, Inc.
HEY, BRO, WHERE'S YOUR SHELL? THIS AIN'T CASUAL DAY.

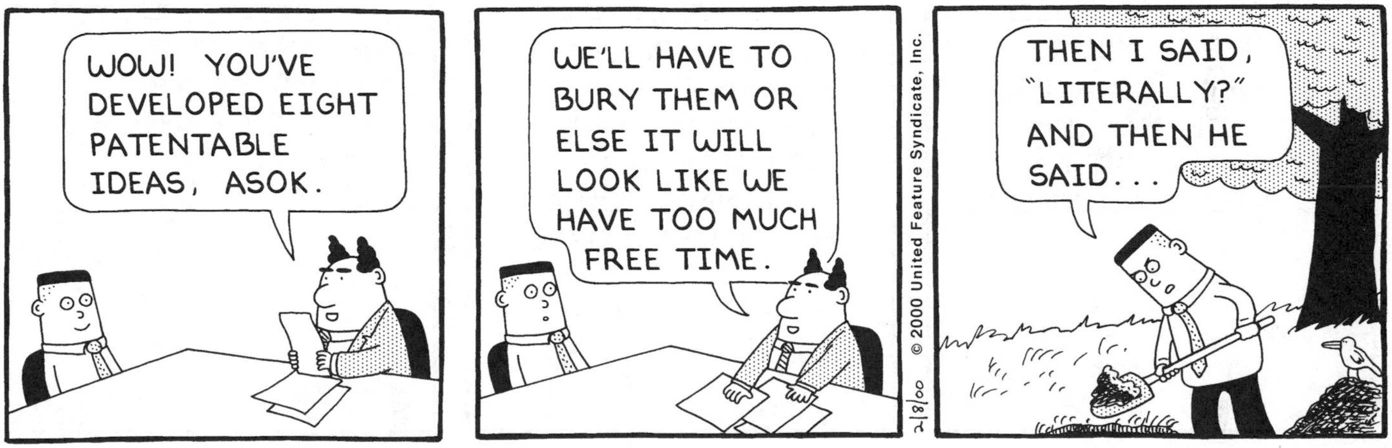
WOW! YOU'VE DEVELOPED EIGHT PATENTABLE IDEAS, ASOK.
WE'LL HAVE TO BURY THEM OR ELSE IT WILL LOOK LIKE WE HAVE TOO MUCH FREE TIME.
2/8/00 © 2000 United Feature Syndicate, Inc.
THEN I SAID, "LITERALLY?" AND THEN HE SAID...

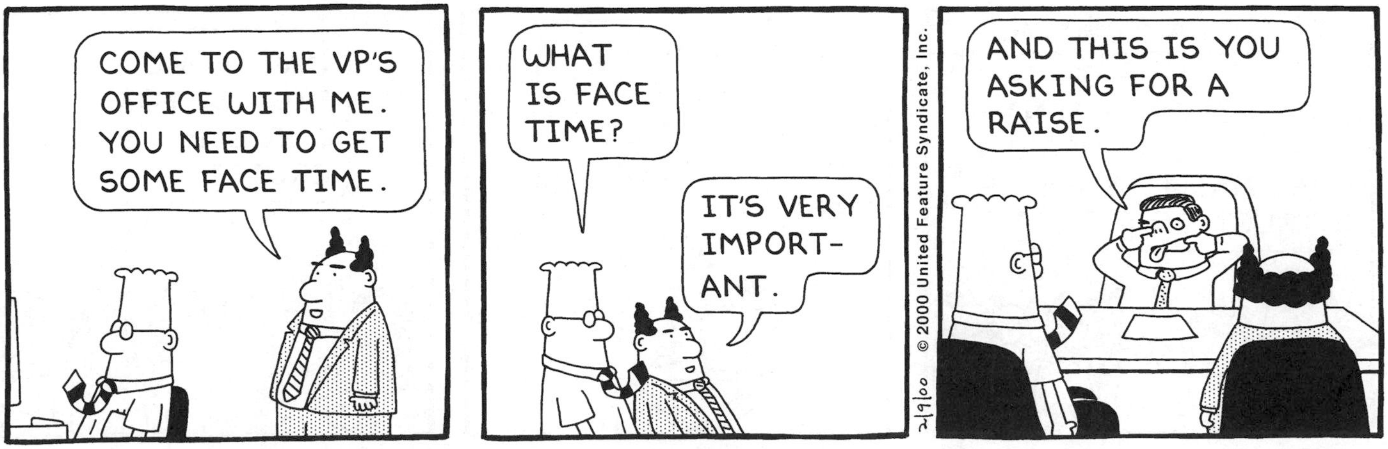
COME TO THE VP'S OFFICE WITH ME. YOU NEED TO GET SOME FACE TIME.
WHAT IS FACE TIME?
IT'S VERY IMPORT-ANT.
2/9/00 © 2000 United Feature Syndicate, Inc.
AND THIS IS YOU ASKING FOR A RAISE.

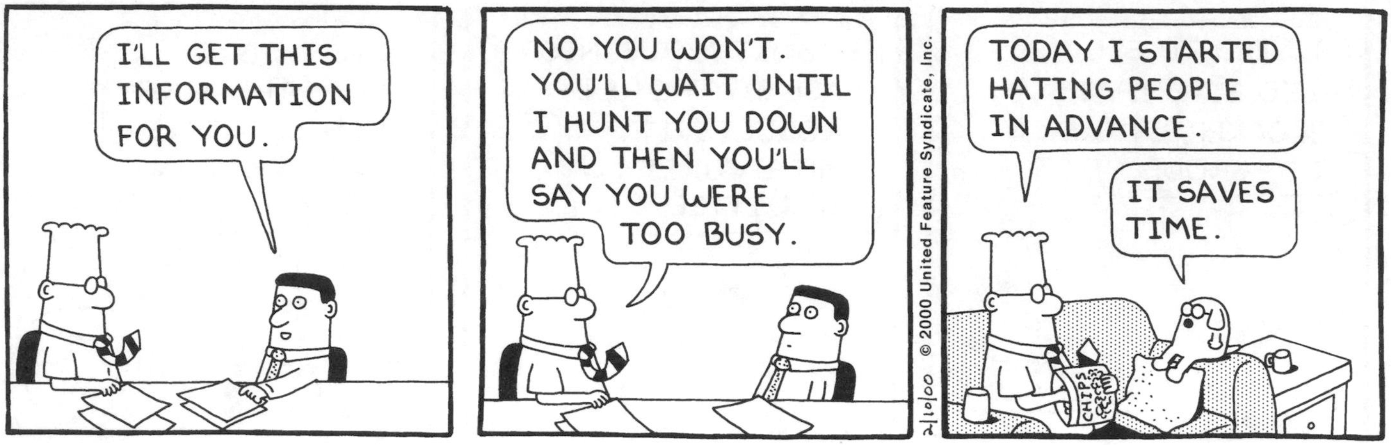
I'LL GET THIS INFORMATION FOR YOU.
NO YOU WON'T. YOU'LL WAIT UNTIL I HUNT YOU DOWN AND THEN YOU'LL SAY YOU WERE TOO BUSY.
2/10/00 © 2000 United Feature Syndicate, Inc.
TODAY I STARTED HATING PEOPLE IN ADVANCE.
IT SAVES TIME.
CHIPS

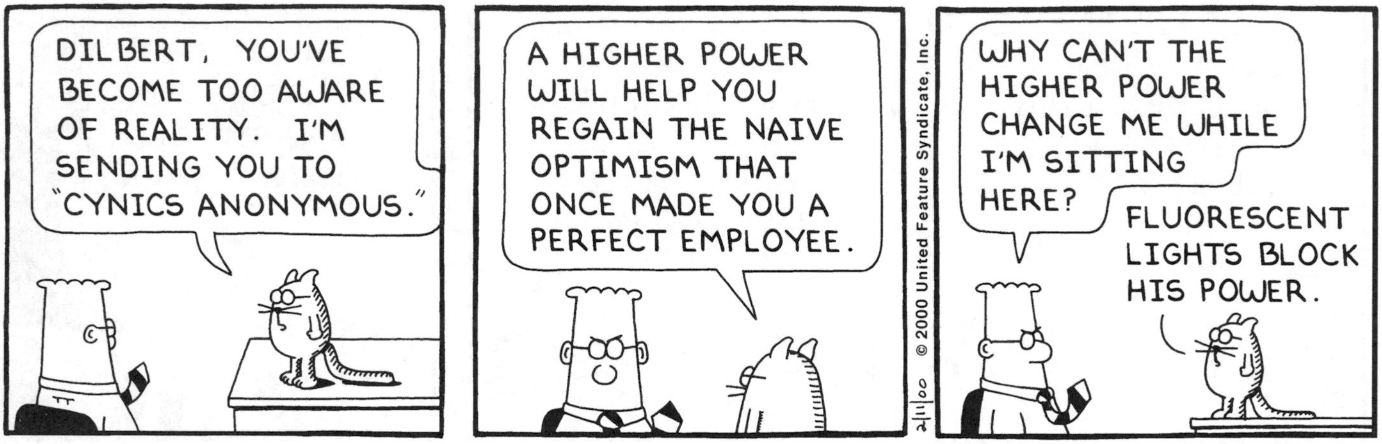
DILBERT, YOU'VE BECOME TOO AWARE OF REALITY. I'M SENDING YOU TO "CYNICS ANONYMOUS."
A HIGHER POWER WILL HELP YOU REGAIN THE NAIVE OPTIMISM THAT ONCE MADE YOU A PERFECT EMPLOYEE.
2/11/00 © 2000 United Feature Syndicate, Inc.
WHY CAN'T THE HIGHER POWER CHANGE ME WHILE I'M SITTING HERE?
FLUORESCENT LIGHTS BLOCK HIS POWER.

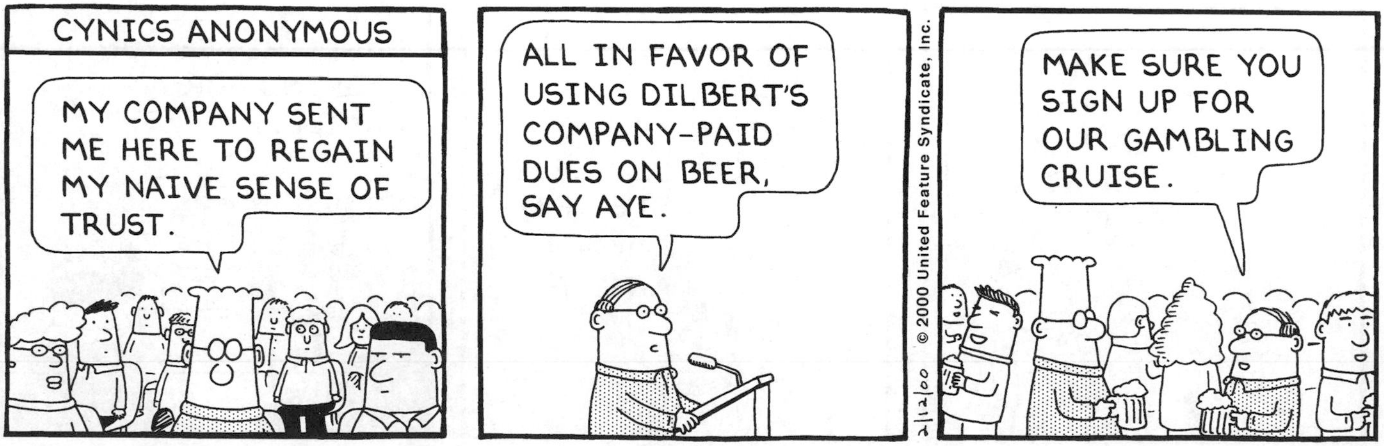
CYNICS ANONYMOUS
MY COMPANY SENT ME HERE TO REGAIN MY NAIVE SENSE OF TRUST.
ALL IN FAVOR OF USING DILBERT'S COMPANY-PAID DUES ON BEER, SAY AYE.
2/12/00 © 2000 United Feature Syndicate, Inc.
MAKE SURE YOU SIGN UP FOR OUR GAMBLING CRUISE.

DON'T INVITE MARKETING TO THE PLANNING MEETING.
IF I DON'T, THEY'LL SABOTAGE THE IMPLEMENTATION.
YES, BUT IF YOU DO INCLUDE THEM IN THE PLANNING...
...THEY'LL HOSE THE PLAN?
EXACTLY.
AND THEY'LL STILL BOTCH THE IMPLEMENTATION.
IF WE KNOW IT'S DOOMED, WHY DO WE BOTHER?
IT'S THE SAME REASON I HAD KIDS.
AT LEAST THERE'S A REASON.
2/13/00
©2000 United Feature Syndicate, Inc.

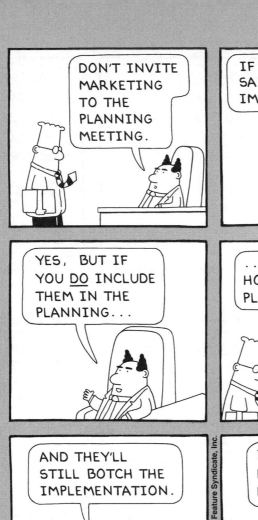

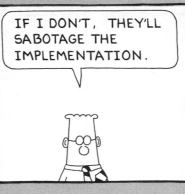

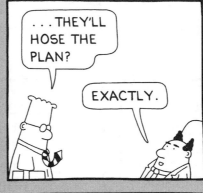

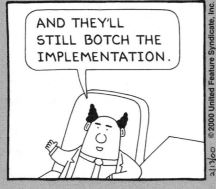

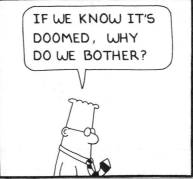

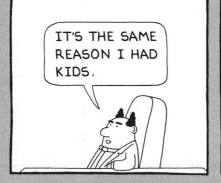

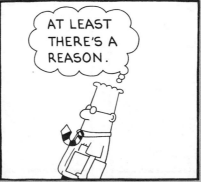

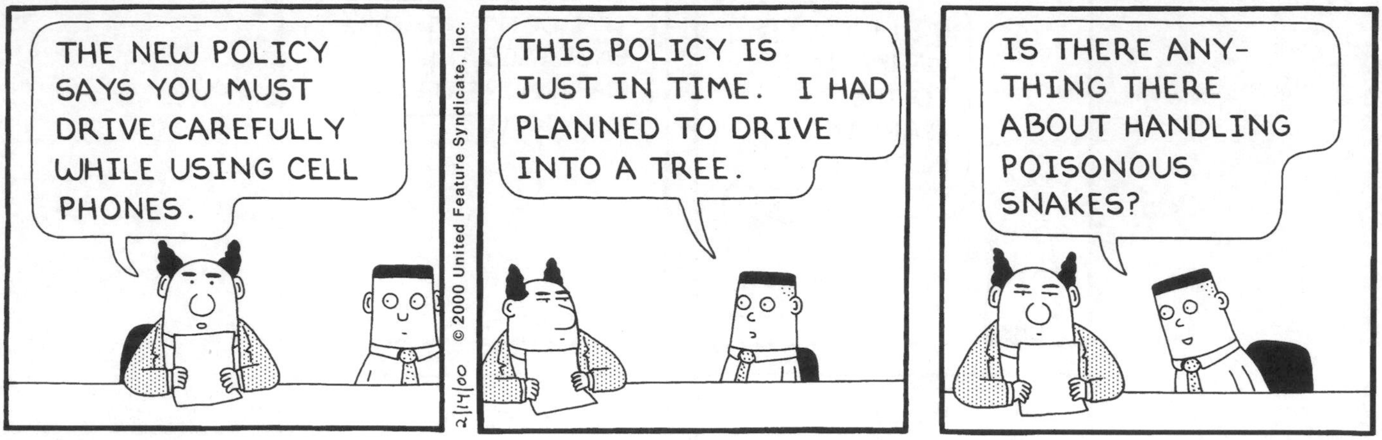
THE NEW POLICY SAYS YOU MUST DRIVE CAREFULLY WHILE USING CELL PHONES.
THIS POLICY IS JUST IN TIME. I HAD PLANNED TO DRIVE INTO A TREE.
IS THERE ANYTHING THERE ABOUT HANDLING POISONOUS SNAKES?
2/14/00 © 2000 United Feature Syndicate, Inc.

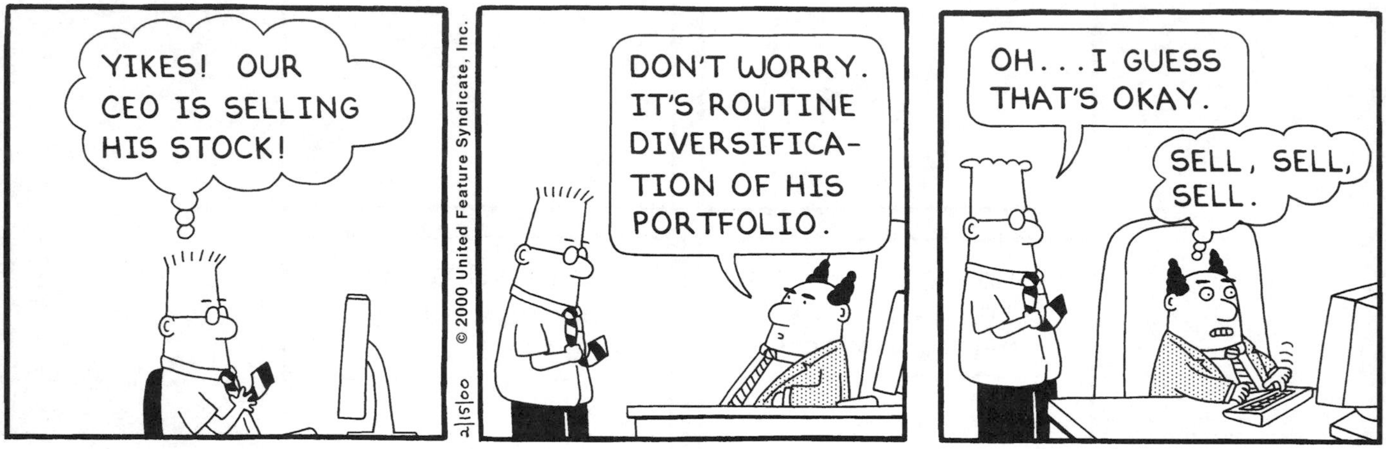
YIKES! OUR CEO IS SELLING HIS STOCK!
DON'T WORRY. IT'S ROUTINE DIVERSIFICATION OF HIS PORTFOLIO.
OH . . . I GUESS THAT'S OKAY.
SELL, SELL, SELL.
2/15/00 © 2000 United Feature Syndicate, Inc.

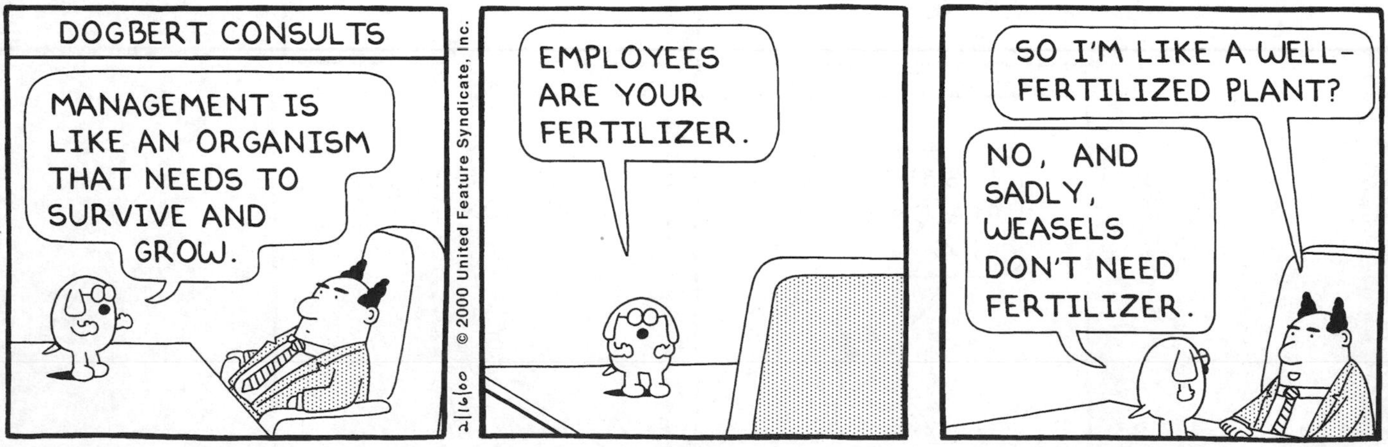
DOGBERT CONSULTS
MANAGEMENT IS LIKE AN ORGANISM THAT NEEDS TO SURVIVE AND GROW.
EMPLOYEES ARE YOUR FERTILIZER.
SO I'M LIKE A WELL-FERTILIZED PLANT?
NO, AND SADLY, WEASELS DON'T NEED FERTILIZER.
2/16/00 © 2000 United Feature Syndicate, Inc.

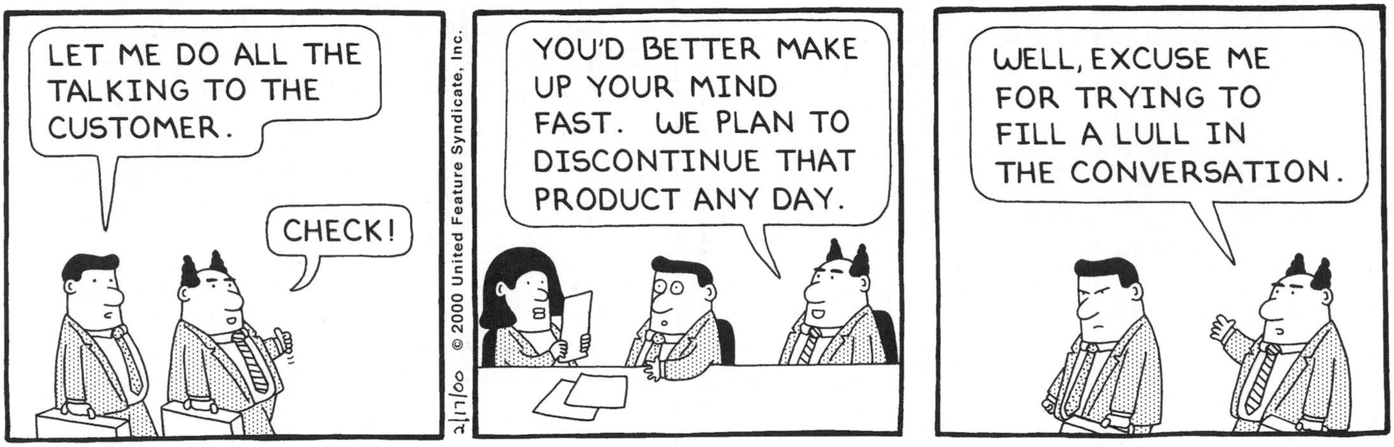
LET ME DO ALL THE TALKING TO THE CUSTOMER.
CHECK!
2/17/00 © 2000 United Feature Syndicate, Inc.
YOU'D BETTER MAKE UP YOUR MIND FAST. WE PLAN TO DISCONTINUE THAT PRODUCT ANY DAY.
WELL, EXCUSE ME FOR TRYING TO FILL A LULL IN THE CONVERSATION.

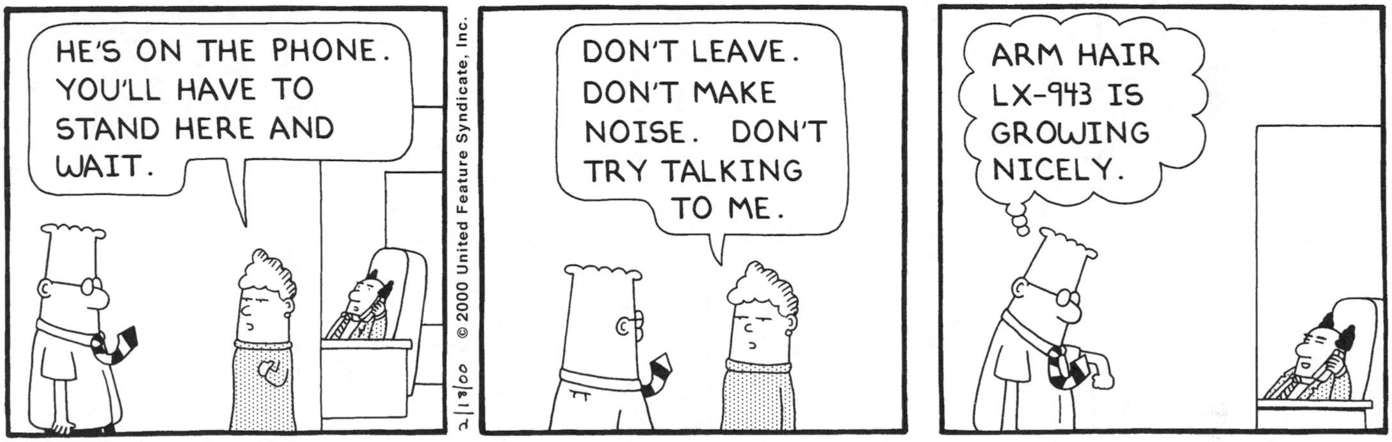
HE'S ON THE PHONE. YOU'LL HAVE TO STAND HERE AND WAIT.
2/18/00 © 2000 United Feature Syndicate, Inc.
DON'T LEAVE. DON'T MAKE NOISE. DON'T TRY TALKING TO ME.
ARM HAIR LX-943 IS GROWING NICELY.

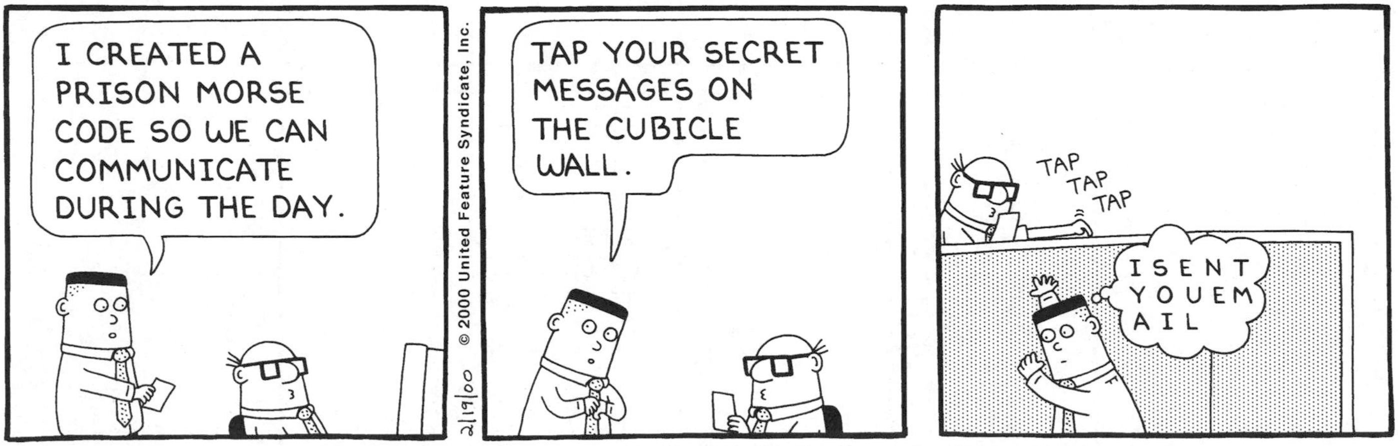
I CREATED A PRISON MORSE CODE SO WE CAN COMMUNICATE DURING THE DAY.
2/19/00 © 2000 United Feature Syndicate, Inc.
TAP YOUR SECRET MESSAGES ON THE CUBICLE WALL.
TAP TAP TAP
I S E N T
Y O U E M
A I L

OUR DIVISION IS UNUSUALLY PROFITABLE THIS YEAR.
THAT MEANS OUR TARGETS FOR NEXT YEAR WILL BE SET IMPOSSIBLY HIGH.
OUR ONLY HOPE OF REACHING OUR PROFIT TARGET NEXT YEAR . . .
. . . IS TO SABOTAGE PROFITS FOR THE REST OF THIS YEAR.
IT'S TOO LATE TO STOP CUSTOMERS FROM BUYING OUR PRODUCTS.
SO WE'LL FOCUS ON INCREASING OUR WASTEFUL SPENDING.
2/20/00
WALLY, I'M SENDING YOU TO A LEADER-SHIP TRAINING CLASS.
DID YOU EVER STICK OUT YOUR COFFEE MUG AND JUST FOLLOW WHERE IT TOOK YOU?

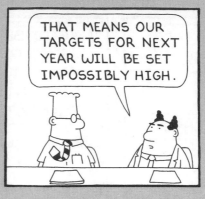

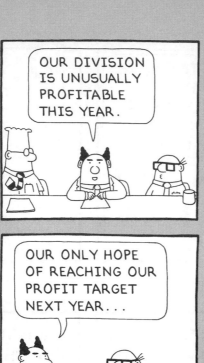

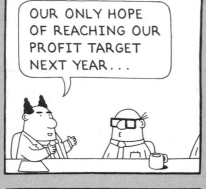

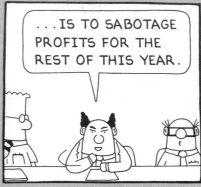

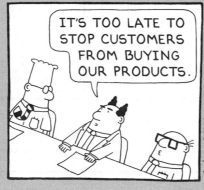

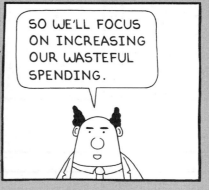

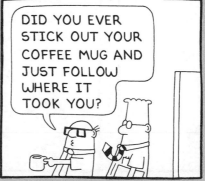

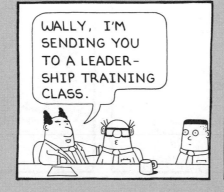

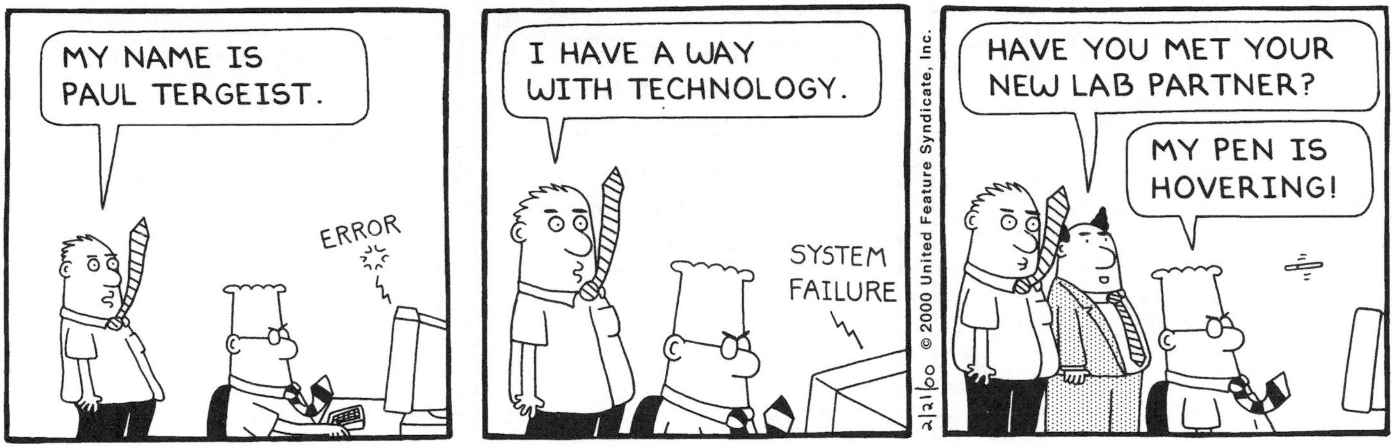
MY NAME IS PAUL TERGEIST.
ERROR
I HAVE A WAY WITH TECHNOLOGY.
SYSTEM FAILURE
2/21/00 © 2000 United Feature Syndicate, Inc.
HAVE YOU MET YOUR NEW LAB PARTNER?
MY PEN IS HOVERING!

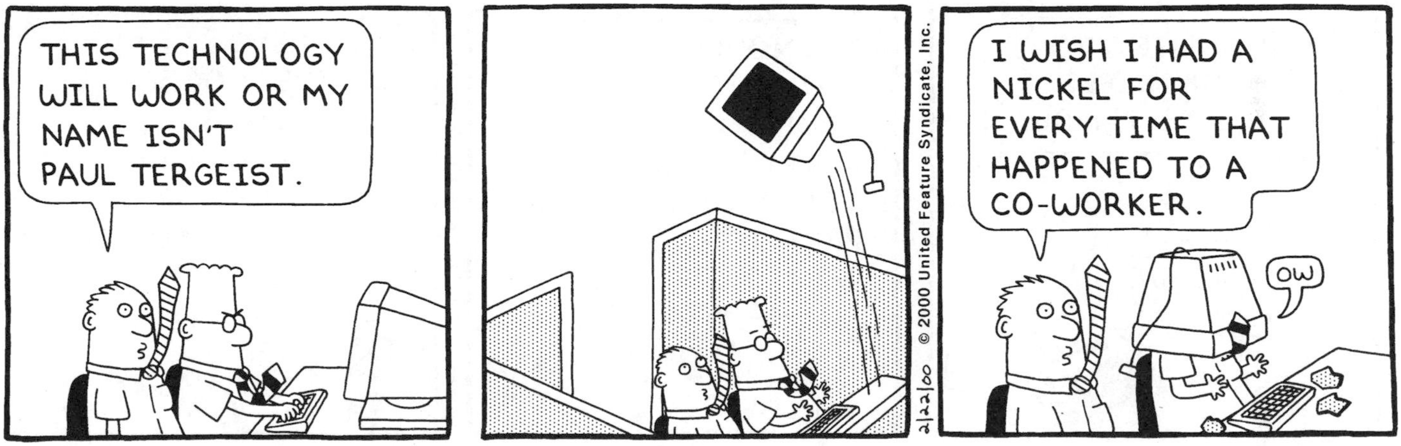
THIS TECHNOLOGY WILL WORK OR MY NAME ISN'T PAUL TERGEIST.
2/22/00 © 2000 United Feature Syndicate, Inc.
I WISH I HAD A NICKEL FOR EVERY TIME THAT HAPPENED TO A CO-WORKER.
OW

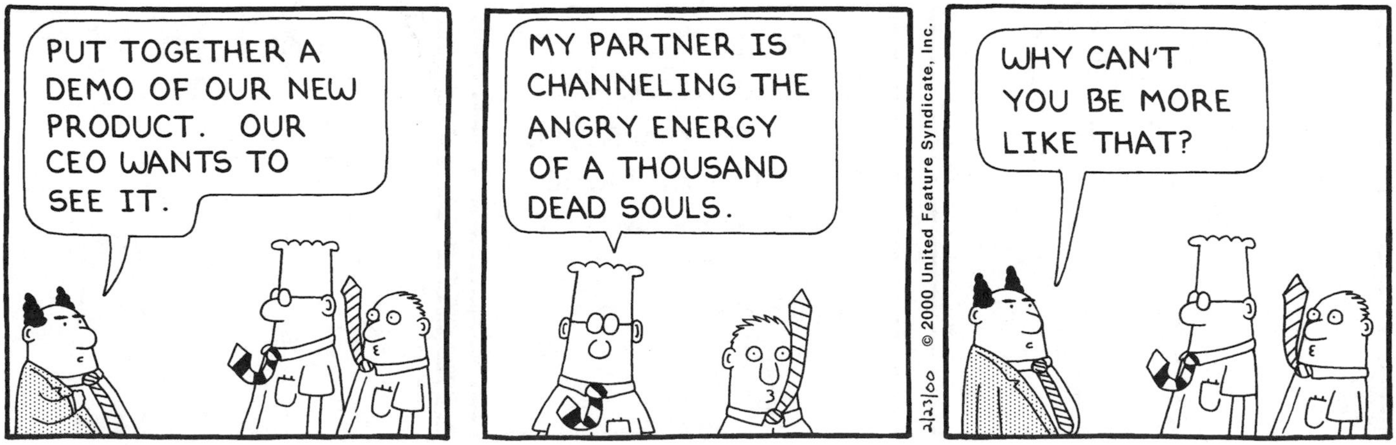
PUT TOGETHER A DEMO OF OUR NEW PRODUCT. OUR CEO WANTS TO SEE IT.
MY PARTNER IS CHANNELING THE ANGRY ENERGY OF A THOUSAND DEAD SOULS.
2/23/00 © 2000 United Feature Syndicate, Inc.
WHY CAN'T YOU BE MORE LIKE THAT?

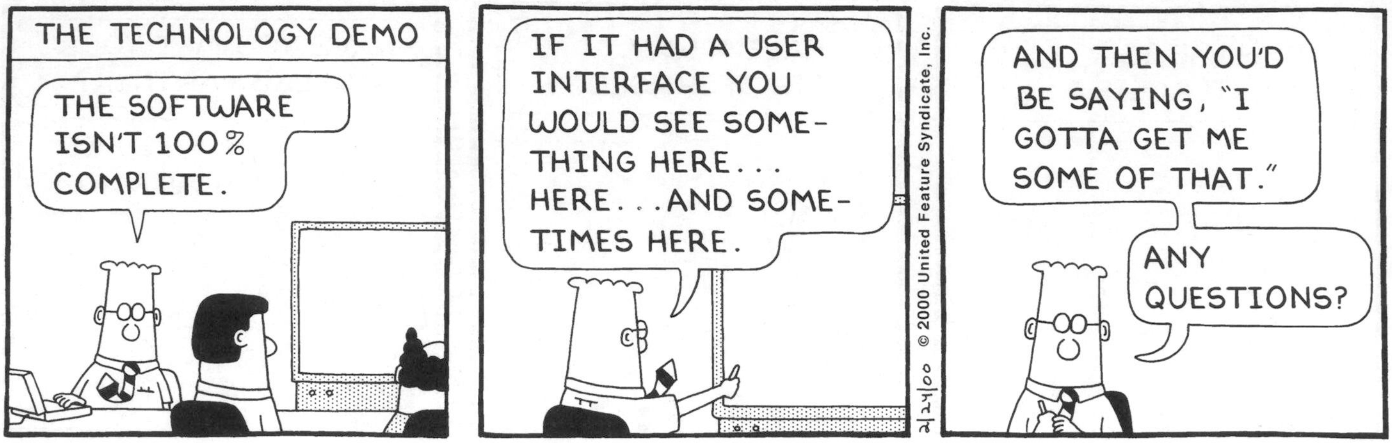
THE TECHNOLOGY DEMO
THE SOFTWARE ISN'T 100% COMPLETE.
IF IT HAD A USER INTERFACE YOU WOULD SEE SOMETHING HERE... HERE...AND SOMETIMES HERE.
© 2000 United Feature Syndicate, Inc.
2/24/00
AND THEN YOU'D BE SAYING, "I GOTTA GET ME SOME OF THAT."
ANY QUESTIONS?

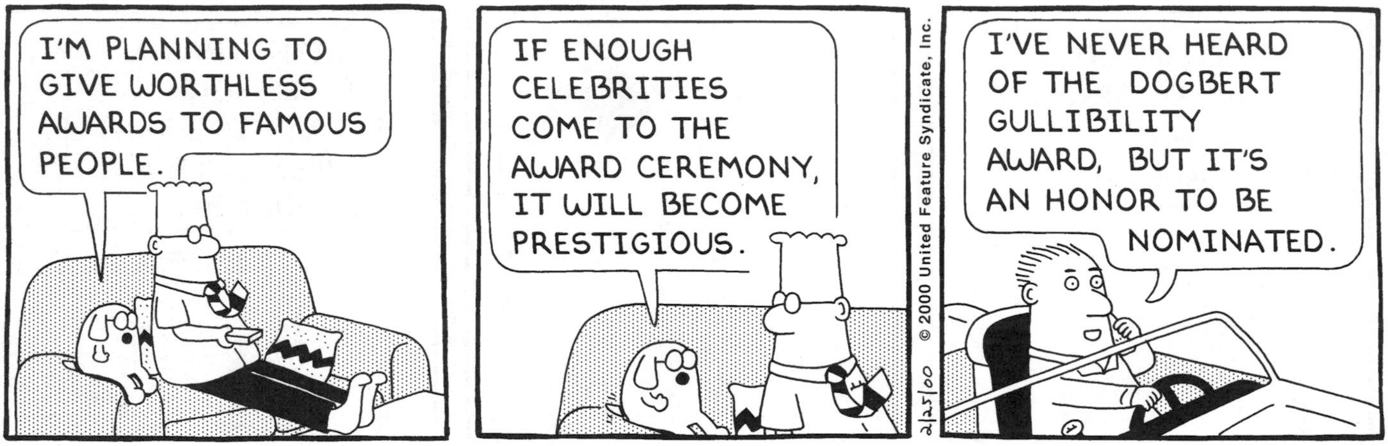
I'M PLANNING TO GIVE WORTHLESS AWARDS TO FAMOUS PEOPLE.
IF ENOUGH CELEBRITIES COME TO THE AWARD CEREMONY, IT WILL BECOME PRESTIGIOUS.
© 2000 United Feature Syndicate, Inc.
2/25/00
I'VE NEVER HEARD OF THE DOGBERT GULLIBILITY AWARD, BUT IT'S AN HONOR TO BE NOMINATED.

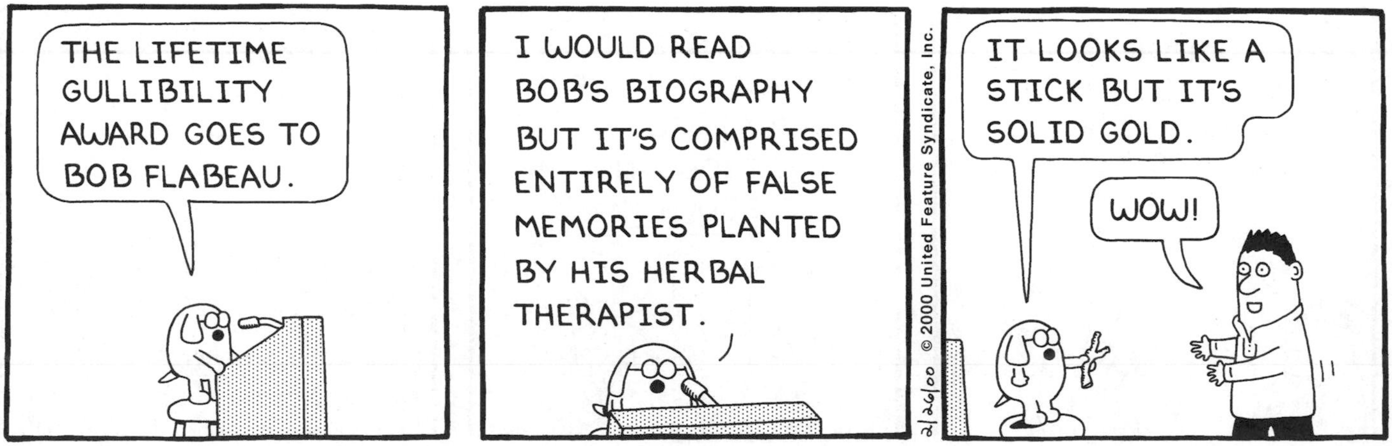
THE LIFETIME GULLIBILITY AWARD GOES TO BOB FLABEAU.
I WOULD READ BOB'S BIOGRAPHY BUT IT'S COMPRISED ENTIRELY OF FALSE MEMORIES PLANTED BY HIS HERBAL THERAPIST.
© 2000 United Feature Syndicate, Inc.
2/26/00
IT LOOKS LIKE A STICK BUT IT'S SOLID GOLD.
WOW!

I'D LIKE TO START WITH A DIAGRAM.
2/27/00
IT'S A BUNCH OF SHAPES CONNECTED BY LINES.
NOW I WILL SAY SOME IMPRESSIVE WORDS.
SYNCHRONIZED INCREMENTAL DIGITAL INTEGRATED DYNAMIC E-COMMERCE SPACE.

ANY QUESTIONS?
©2000 United Feature Syndicate, Inc.
MAY I HAVE A COPY OF YOUR PRESENTATION?
THE RESULTS OF MY EXPERIMENT ARE DISTURBING.

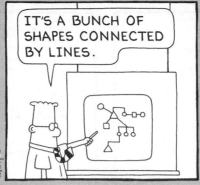

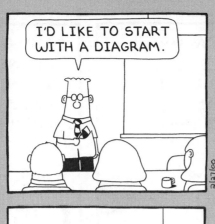

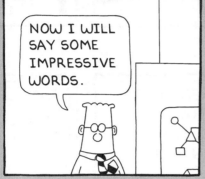

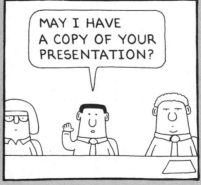

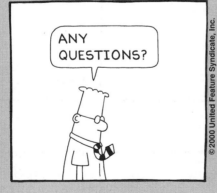

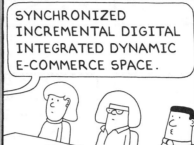

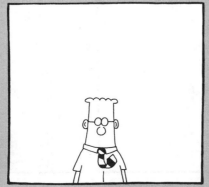

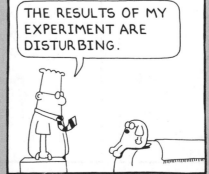

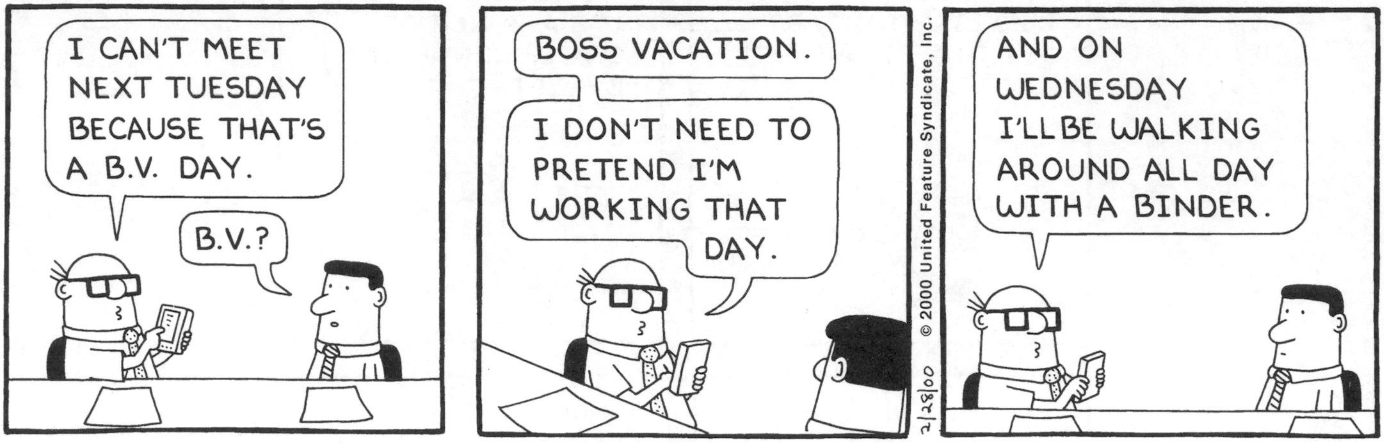
I CAN'T MEET NEXT TUESDAY BECAUSE THAT'S A B.V. DAY.
B.V.?
BOSS VACATION.
I DON'T NEED TO PRETEND I'M WORKING THAT DAY.
AND ON WEDNESDAY I'LLBE WALKING AROUND ALL DAY WITH A BINDER.
2/28/00 © 2000 United Feature Syndicate, Inc.

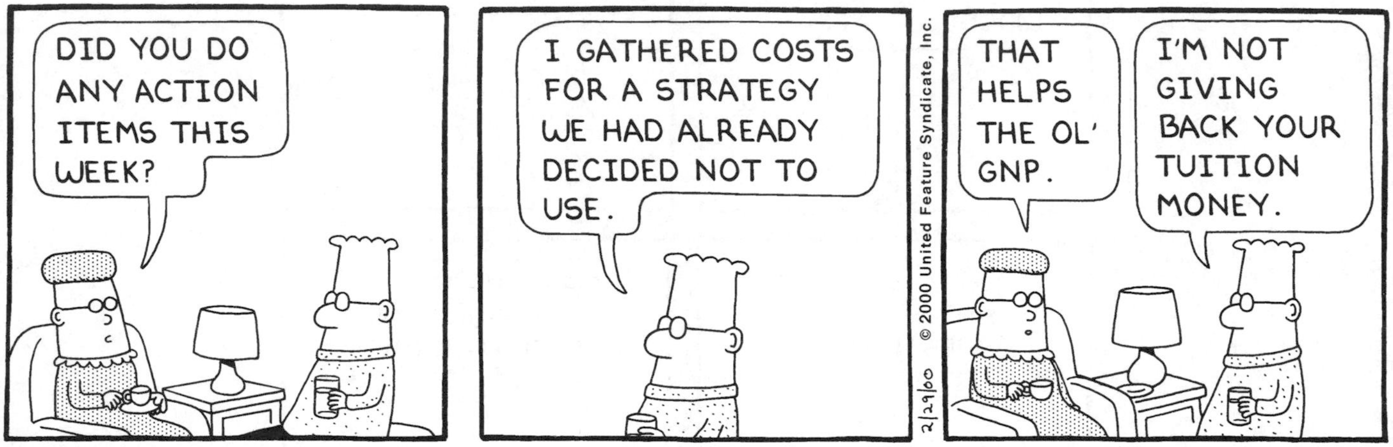
DID YOU DO ANY ACTION ITEMS THIS WEEK?
I GATHERED COSTS FOR A STRATEGY WE HAD ALREADY DECIDED NOT TO USE.
THAT HELPS THE OL' GNP.
I'M NOT GIVING BACK YOUR TUITION MONEY.
2/29/00 © 2000 United Feature Syndicate, Inc.

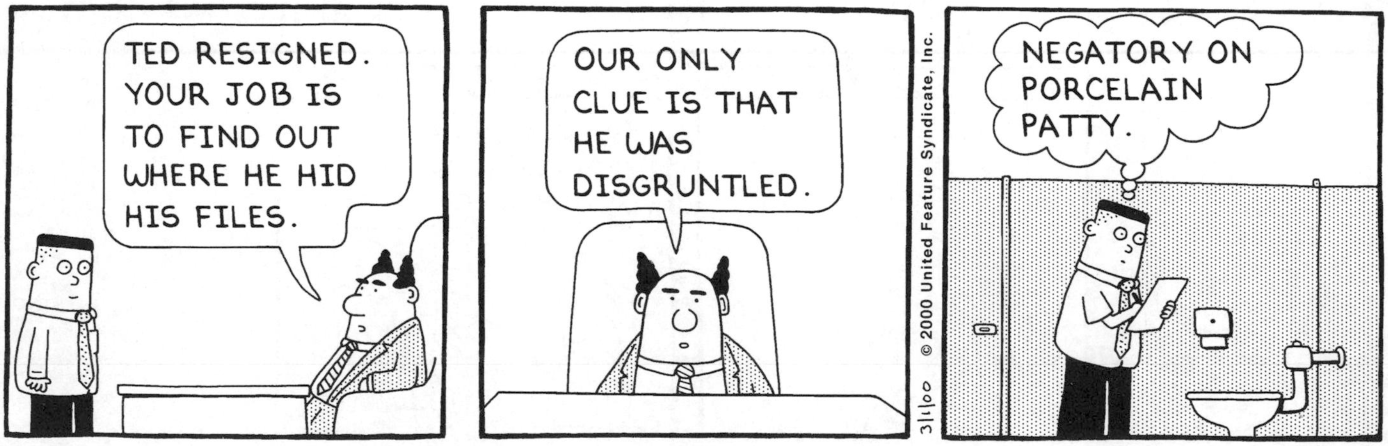
TED RESIGNED. YOUR JOB IS TO FIND OUT WHERE HE HID HIS FILES.
OUR ONLY CLUE IS THAT HE WAS DISGRUNTLED.
NEGATORY ON PORCELAIN PATTY.
3/1/00 © 2000 United Feature Syndicate, Inc.

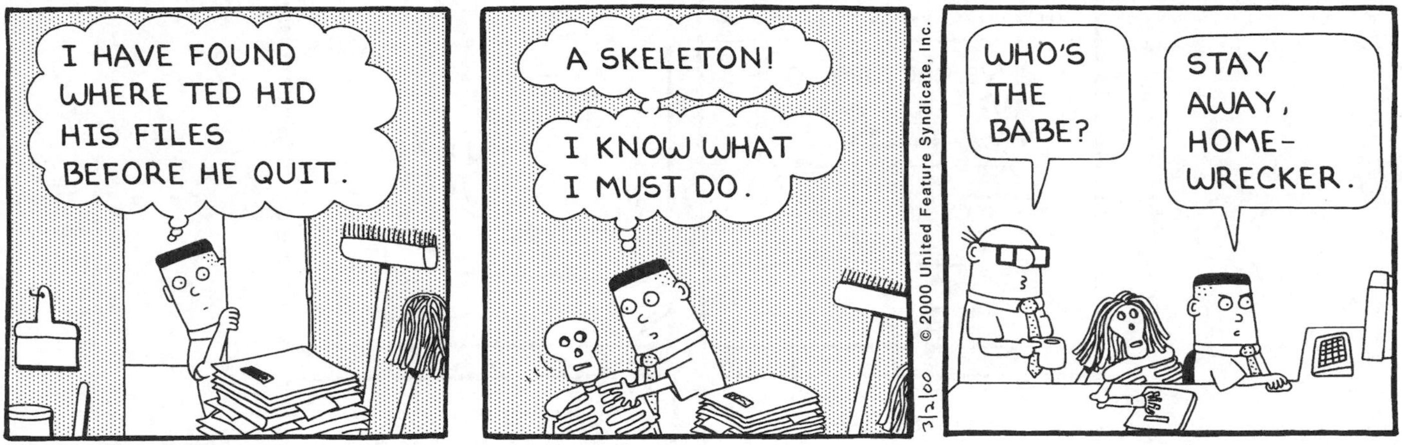
I HAVE FOUND WHERE TED HID HIS FILES BEFORE HE QUIT.
A SKELETON!
I KNOW WHAT I MUST DO.
3/2/00 © 2000 United Feature Syndicate, Inc.
WHO'S THE BABE?
STAY AWAY, HOME-WRECKER.

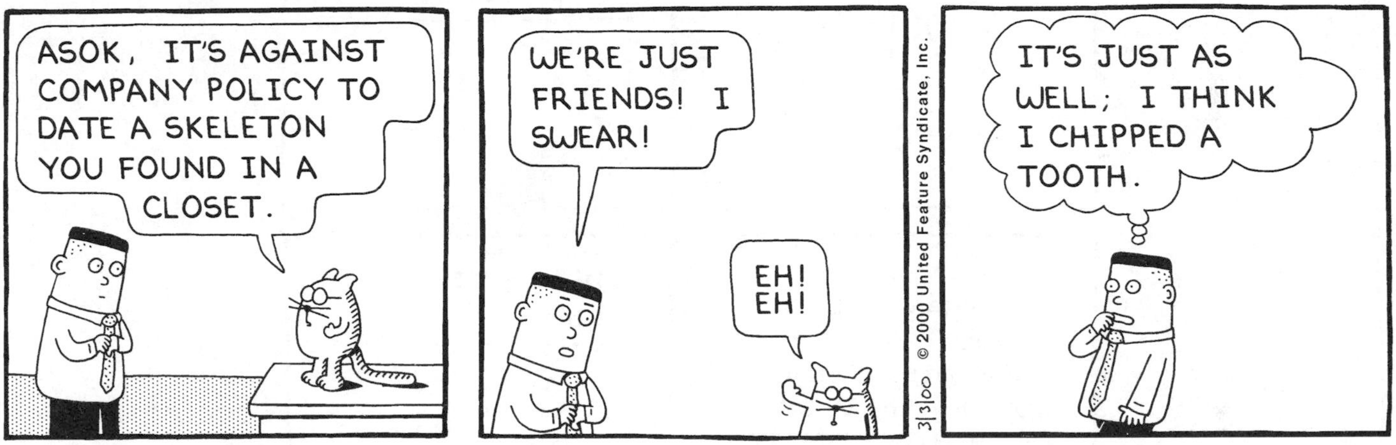
ASOK, IT'S AGAINST COMPANY POLICY TO DATE A SKELETON YOU FOUND IN A CLOSET.
WE'RE JUST FRIENDS! I SWEAR!
EH! EH!
3/3/00 © 2000 United Feature Syndicate, Inc.
IT'S JUST AS WELL; I THINK I CHIPPED A TOOTH.

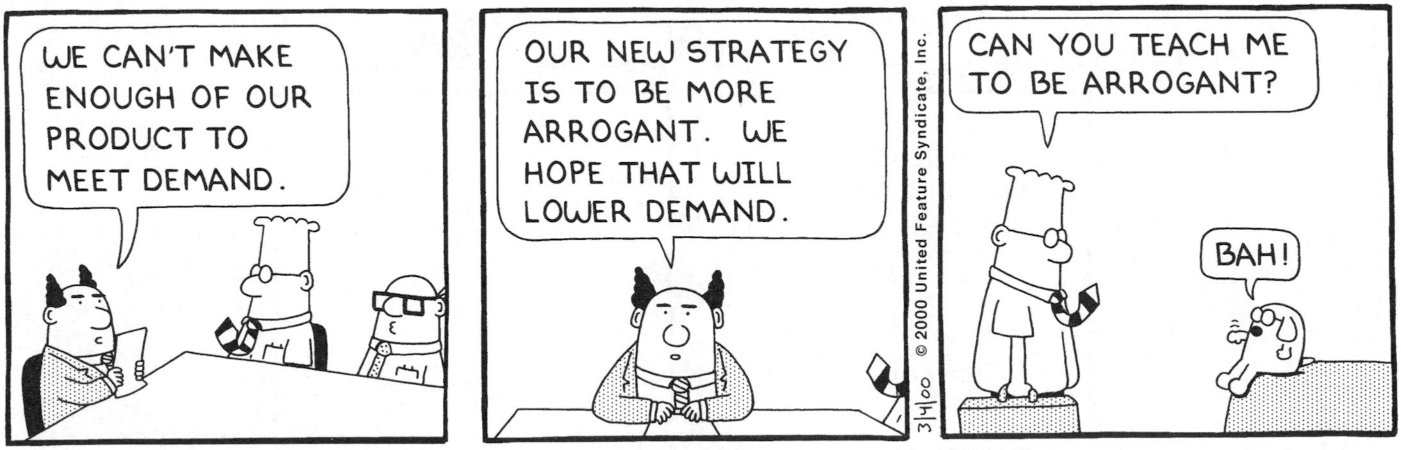
WE CAN'T MAKE ENOUGH OF OUR PRODUCT TO MEET DEMAND.
OUR NEW STRATEGY IS TO BE MORE ARROGANT. WE HOPE THAT WILL LOWER DEMAND.
3/4/00 © 2000 United Feature Syndicate, Inc.
CAN YOU TEACH ME TO BE ARROGANT?
BAH!

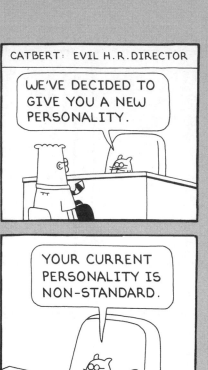

CATBERT: EVIL H.R. DIRECTOR
WE'VE DECIDED TO GIVE YOU A NEW PERSONALITY.
WHAT?
WHY?
YOUR CURRENT PERSONALITY IS NON-STANDARD.
YOU MUST CHOOSE ONE OF THE APPROVED CORPORATE PERSONALITIES.
THE CHOICES ARE SYCOPHANT, GLAD-HANDER, SADIST, QUANTOID, PRIMA DONNA, EMPTY SUIT OR WHINING MISFIT.
EMPTY SUIT SOUNDS INTERESTING.
EXCELLENT CHOICE. HERE'S THE SPEC SHEET.
HOW DID IT GO?
SAME OL' SAME OL'. YOU GOT THAT RIGHT.
©2000 United Feature Syndicate, Inc.
3/5/00

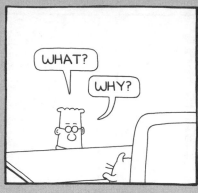

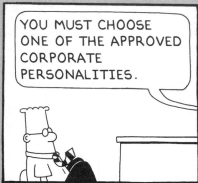

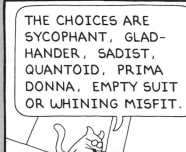

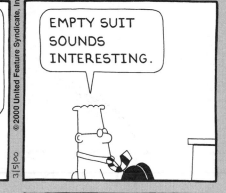

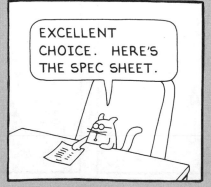

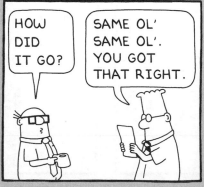

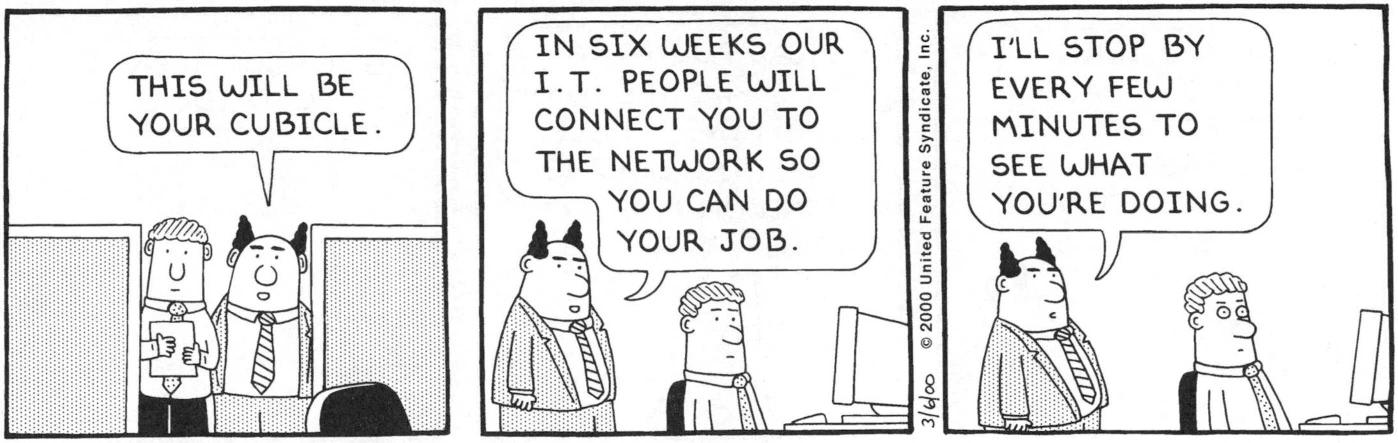
THIS WILL BE YOUR CUBICLE.
IN SIX WEEKS OUR I.T. PEOPLE WILL CONNECT YOU TO THE NETWORK SO YOU CAN DO YOUR JOB.
I'LL STOP BY EVERY FEW MINUTES TO SEE WHAT YOU'RE DOING.
3/6/00

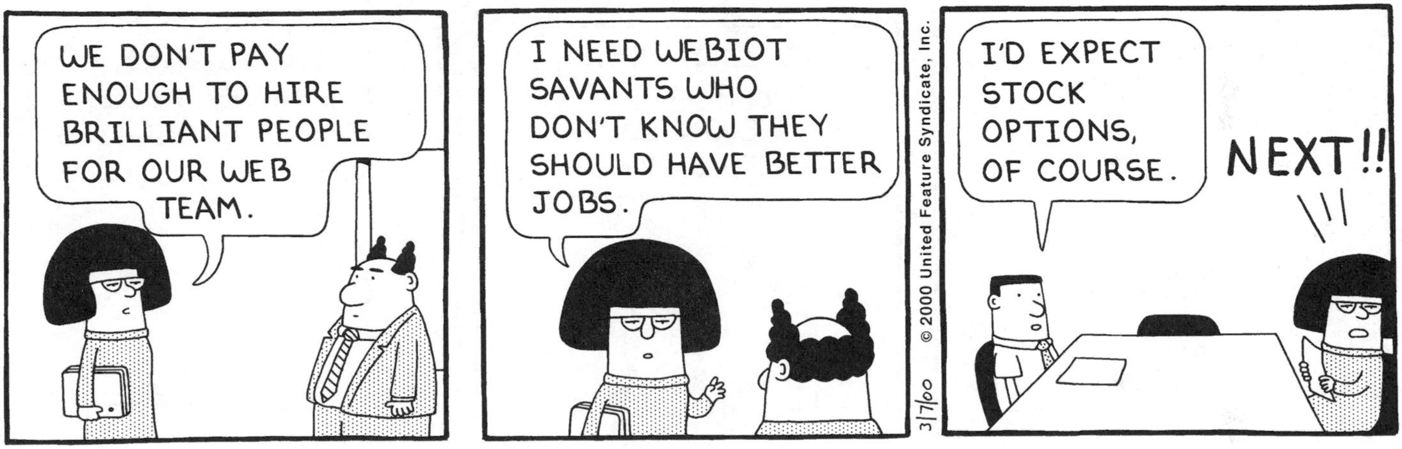
WE DON'T PAY ENOUGH TO HIRE BRILLIANT PEOPLE FOR OUR WEB TEAM.
I NEED WEBIOT SAVANTS WHO DON'T KNOW THEY SHOULD HAVE BETTER JOBS.
I'D EXPECT STOCK OPTIONS, OF COURSE.
NEXT!!
3/7/00

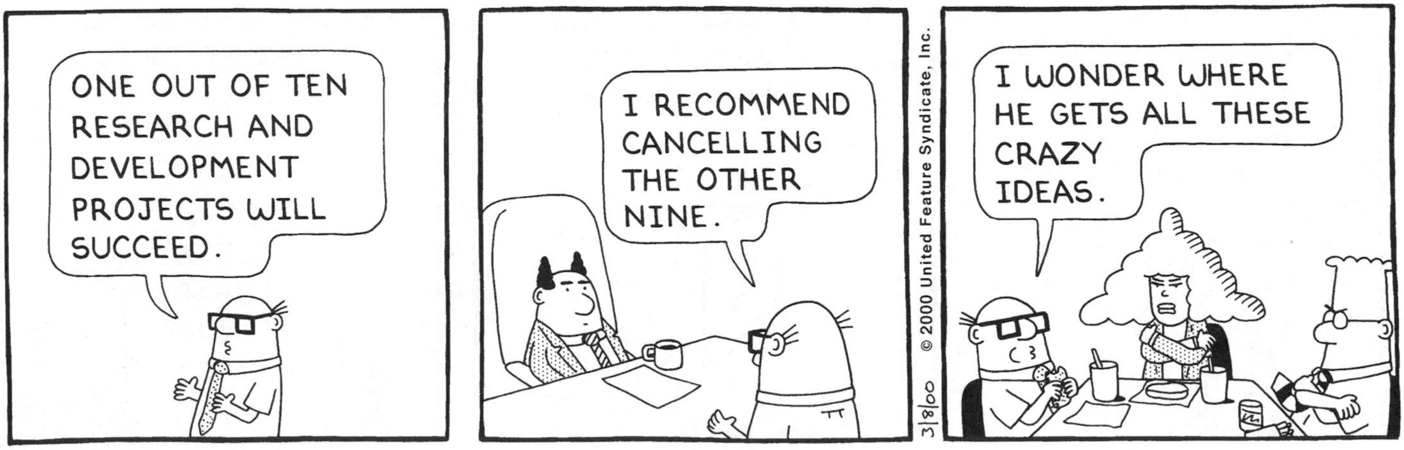
ONE OUT OF TEN RESEARCH AND DEVELOPMENT PROJECTS WILL SUCCEED.
I RECOMMEND CANCELLING THE OTHER NINE.
I WONDER WHERE HE GETS ALL THESE CRAZY IDEAS.
3/8/00

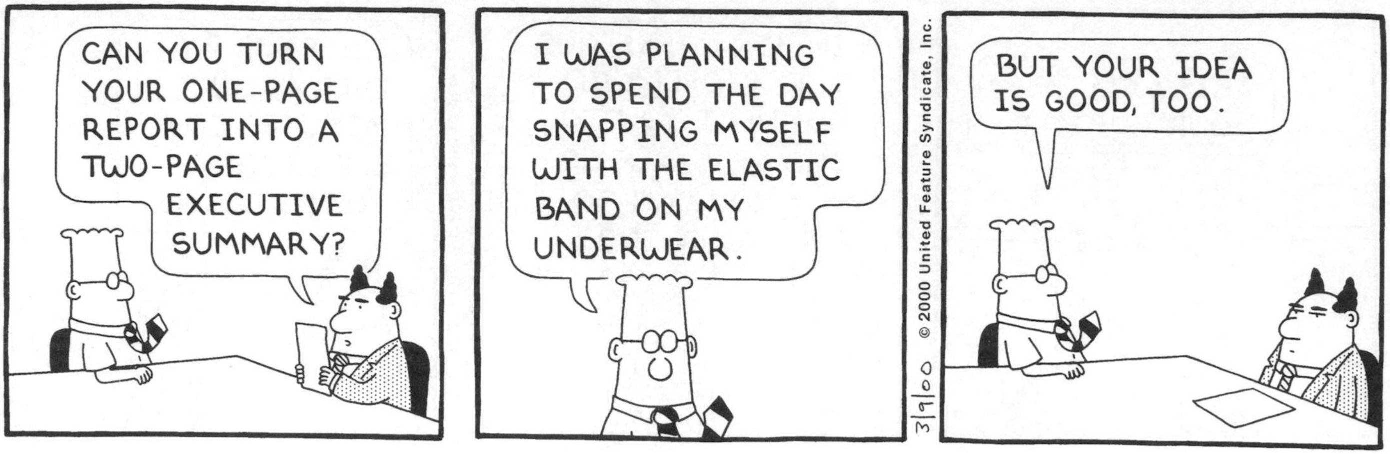
CAN YOU TURN YOUR ONE-PAGE REPORT INTO A TWO-PAGE EXECUTIVE SUMMARY?
I WAS PLANNING TO SPEND THE DAY SNAPPING MYSELF WITH THE ELASTIC BAND ON MY UNDERWEAR.
3/9/00 © 2000 United Feature Syndicate, Inc.
BUT YOUR IDEA IS GOOD, TOO.

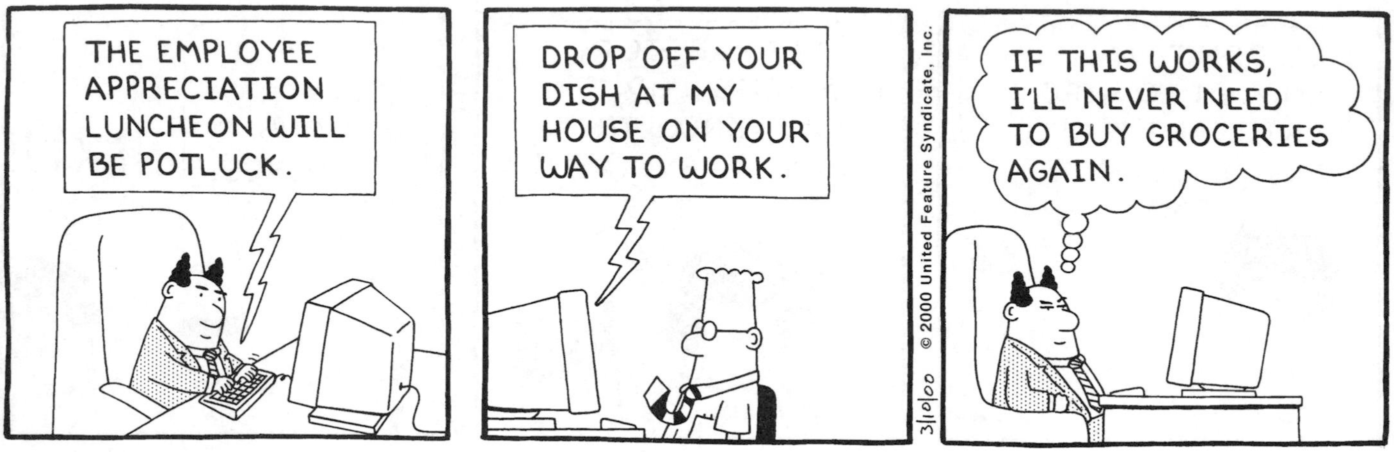
THE EMPLOYEE APPRECIATION LUNCHEON WILL BE POTLUCK.
DROP OFF YOUR DISH AT MY HOUSE ON YOUR WAY TO WORK.
3/10/00 © 2000 United Feature Syndicate, Inc.
IF THIS WORKS, I'LL NEVER NEED TO BUY GROCERIES AGAIN.

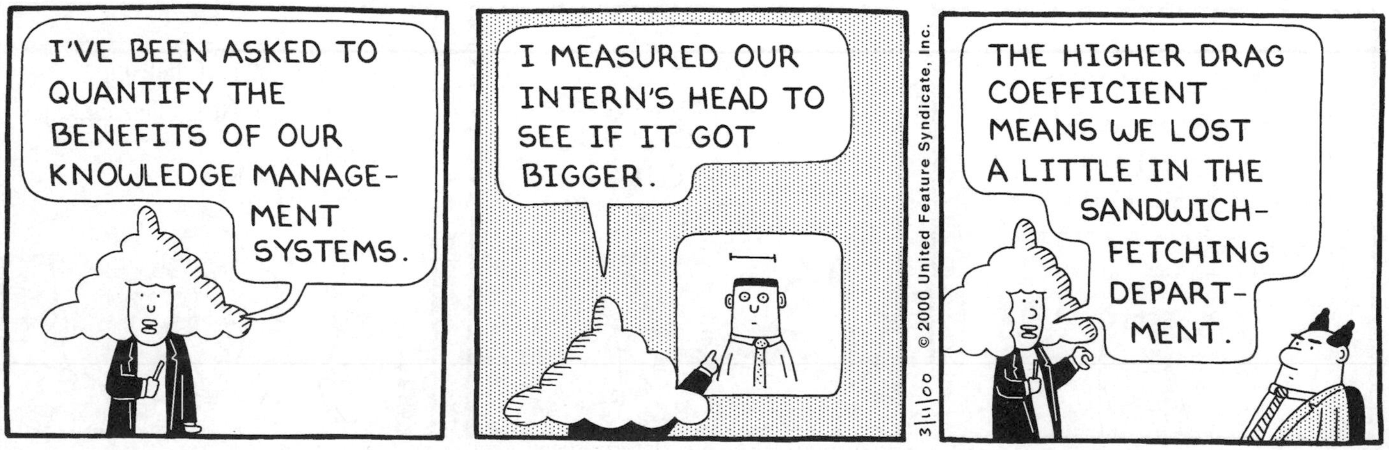
I'VE BEEN ASKED TO QUANTIFY THE BENEFITS OF OUR KNOWLEDGE MANAGE-MENT SYSTEMS.
I MEASURED OUR INTERN'S HEAD TO SEE IF IT GOT BIGGER.
3/11/00 © 2000 United Feature Syndicate, Inc.
THE HIGHER DRAG COEFFICIENT MEANS WE LOST A LITTLE IN THE SANDWICH-FETCHING DEPART-MENT.

ALICE
STIRRUP PANTS ARE NOT PROFESSIONAL ATTIRE.
I JUST FILED A PATENT THAT WILL EARN FIFTY MILLION IN LICENSE FEES FOR THE COMPANY.
REALLY?
WOW.
BUT IT'S NO EXCUSE FOR BAD PANTS.
© 2000 United Feature Syndicate, Inc.
3/12/00
WHATEVER.
DID YOU SIGN THE BUDGET REQUEST I GAVE YOU LAST WEEK?
NO... I'VE BEEN BUSY WITH VARIOUS PANT-RELATED CRISES.
HERE'S ANOTHER.

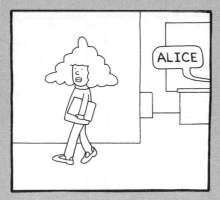

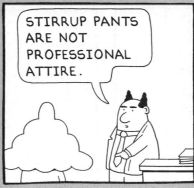

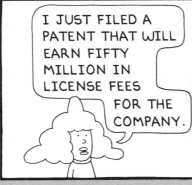

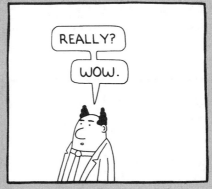

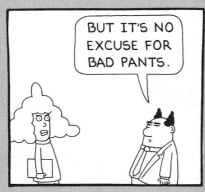

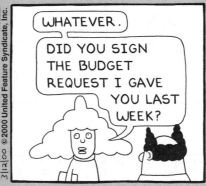

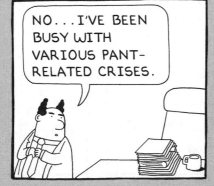

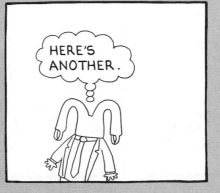

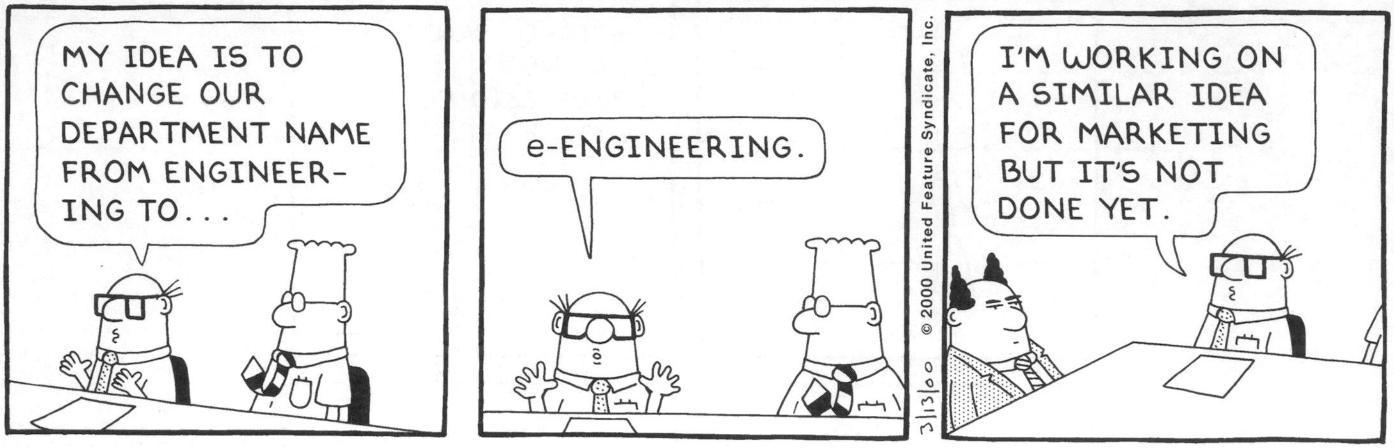
MY IDEA IS TO CHANGE OUR DEPARTMENT NAME FROM ENGINEER-ING TO . . .
e-ENGINEERING.
3/13/00 © 2000 United Feature Syndicate, Inc.
I'M WORKING ON A SIMILAR IDEA FOR MARKETING BUT IT'S NOT DONE YET.

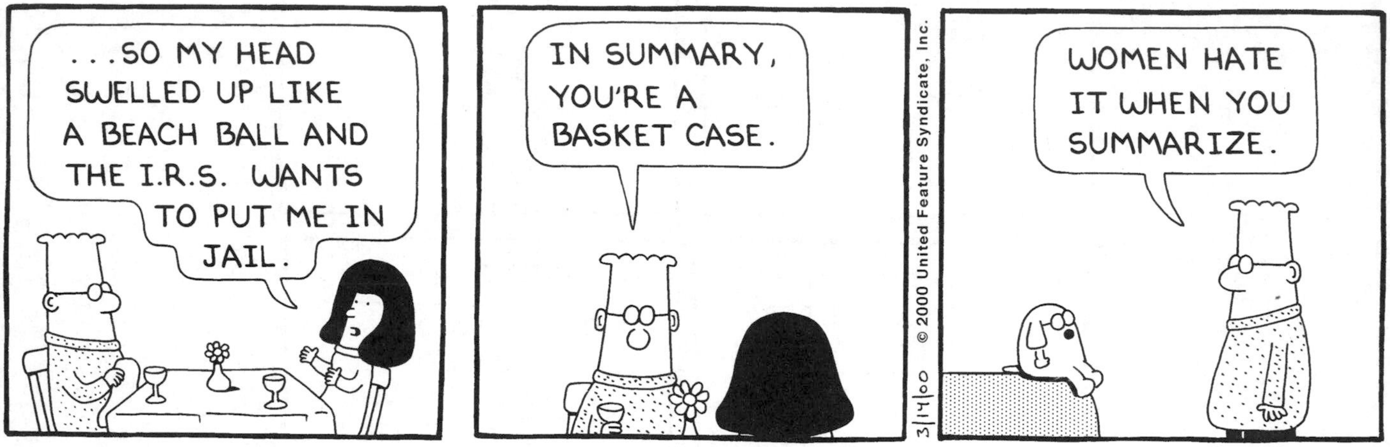
. . . SO MY HEAD SWELLED UP LIKE A BEACH BALL AND THE I.R.S. WANTS TO PUT ME IN JAIL.
IN SUMMARY, YOU'RE A BASKET CASE.
3/14/00 © 2000 United Feature Syndicate, Inc.
WOMEN HATE IT WHEN YOU SUMMARIZE.

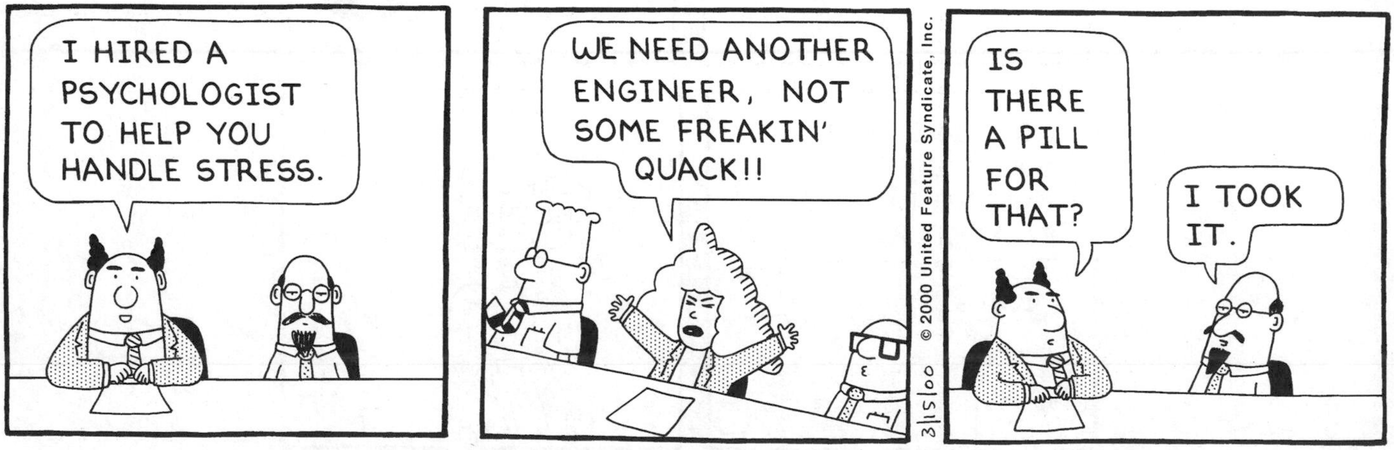
I HIRED A PSYCHOLOGIST TO HELP YOU HANDLE STRESS.
WE NEED ANOTHER ENGINEER, NOT SOME FREAKIN' QUACK!!
3/15/00 © 2000 United Feature Syndicate, Inc.
IS THERE A PILL FOR THAT?
I TOOK IT.

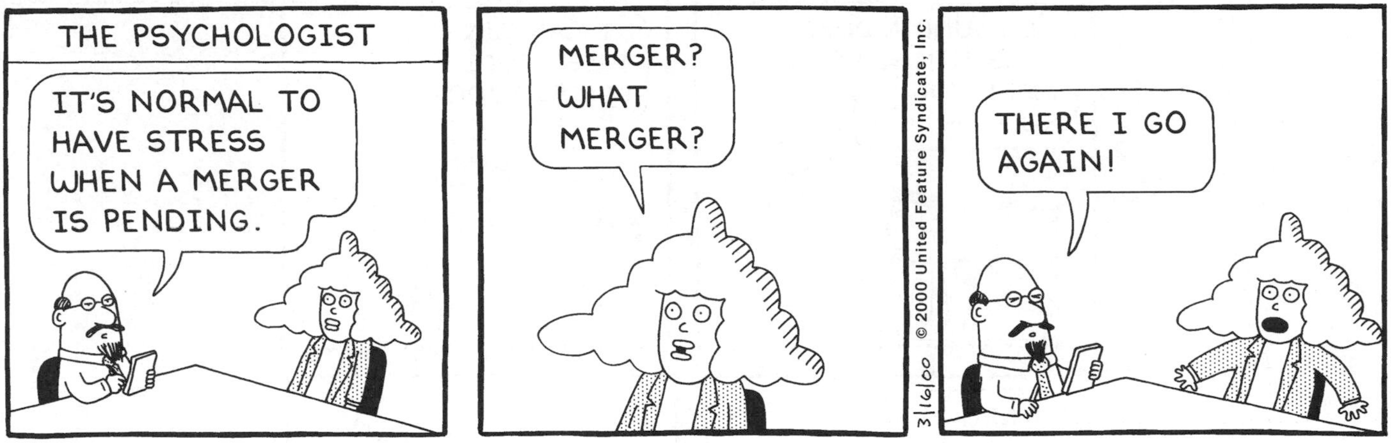
THE PSYCHOLOGIST
IT'S NORMAL TO HAVE STRESS WHEN A MERGER IS PENDING.
MERGER? WHAT MERGER?
THERE I GO AGAIN!
3/16/00 © 2000 United Feature Syndicate, Inc.

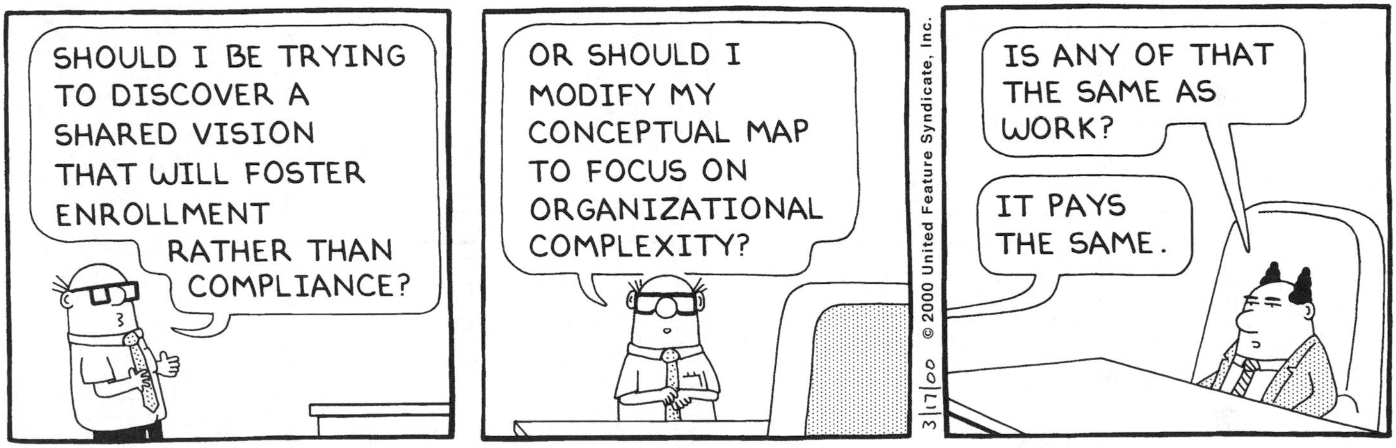
SHOULD I BE TRYING TO DISCOVER A SHARED VISION THAT WILL FOSTER ENROLLMENT RATHER THAN COMPLIANCE?
OR SHOULD I MODIFY MY CONCEPTUAL MAP TO FOCUS ON ORGANIZATIONAL COMPLEXITY?
IS ANY OF THAT THE SAME AS WORK?
IT PAYS THE SAME.
3/17/00 © 2000 United Feature Syndicate, Inc.

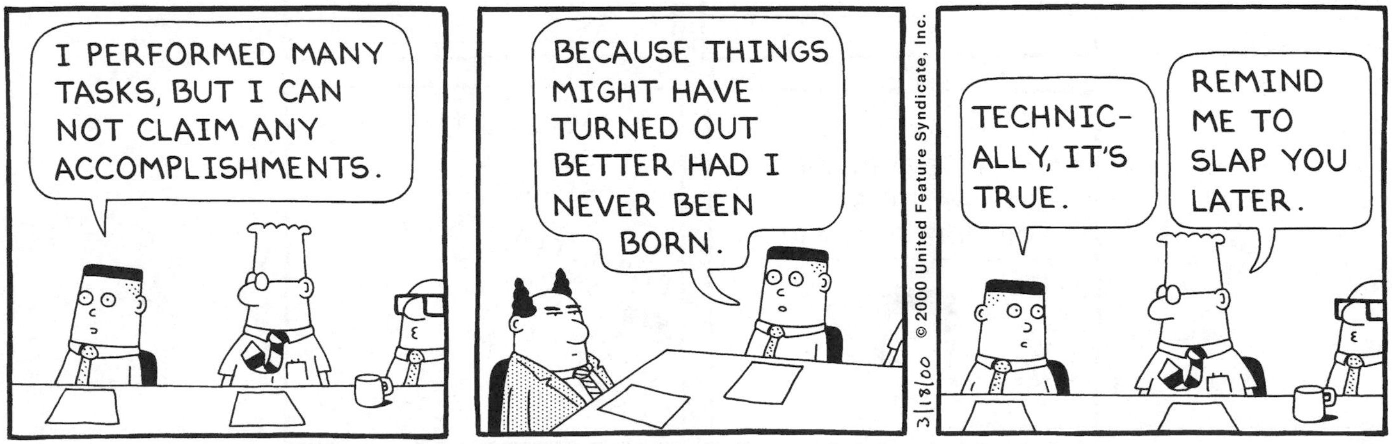
I PERFORMED MANY TASKS, BUT I CAN NOT CLAIM ANY ACCOMPLISHMENTS.
BECAUSE THINGS MIGHT HAVE TURNED OUT BETTER HAD I NEVER BEEN BORN.
TECHNIC-ALLY, IT'S TRUE.
REMIND ME TO SLAP YOU LATER.
3/18/00 © 2000 United Feature Syndicate, Inc.

WE FOUND A DOZEN BUGS IN THE SOFT-WARE YOU SOLD US.
WE CAN FIX THESE BUGS FOR $20,000.
WHAT?!
YOU CAN'T CHARGE US TO FIX YOUR OWN DEFECTIVE PRODUCT!
BUWAHAHA!!
SORRY. . . I WAS OVERCOME BY AN EVIL EUPHORIA.
3/19/00 ©2000 United Feature Syndicate, Inc.
I GUESS WE HAVE TO PAY. WE HAVE NO CHOICE!
EXCUSE ME.
PUT MORE BUGS IN THE SOFTWARE! I'M MAKING A FORTUNE OUT HERE!
PHBLLLT!
I'M STARTING TO QUESTION OUR SINGLE SOURCE STRATEGY.

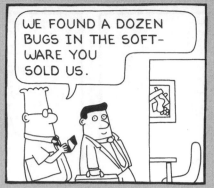

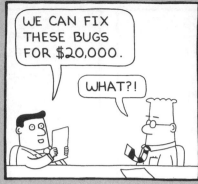

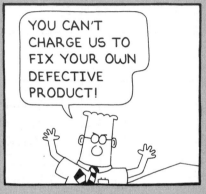

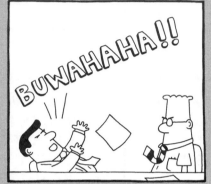

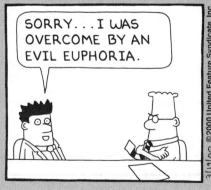

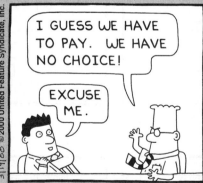

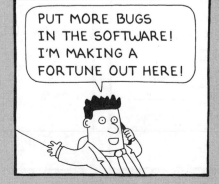

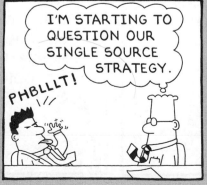

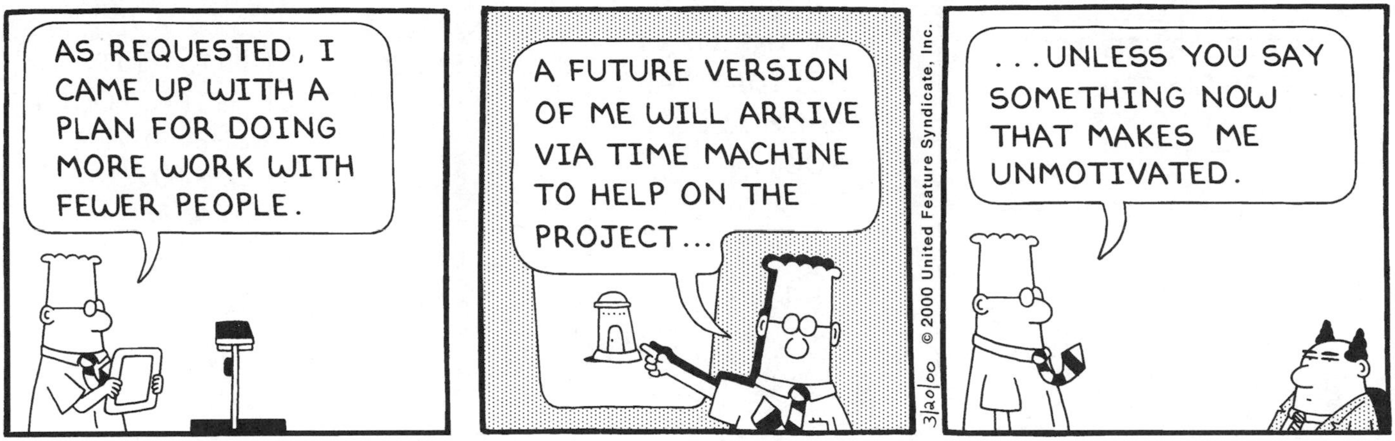
AS REQUESTED, I CAME UP WITH A PLAN FOR DOING MORE WORK WITH FEWER PEOPLE.
A FUTURE VERSION OF ME WILL ARRIVE VIA TIME MACHINE TO HELP ON THE PROJECT...
3/20/00 © 2000 United Feature Syndicate, Inc.
...UNLESS YOU SAY SOMETHING NOW THAT MAKES ME UNMOTIVATED.

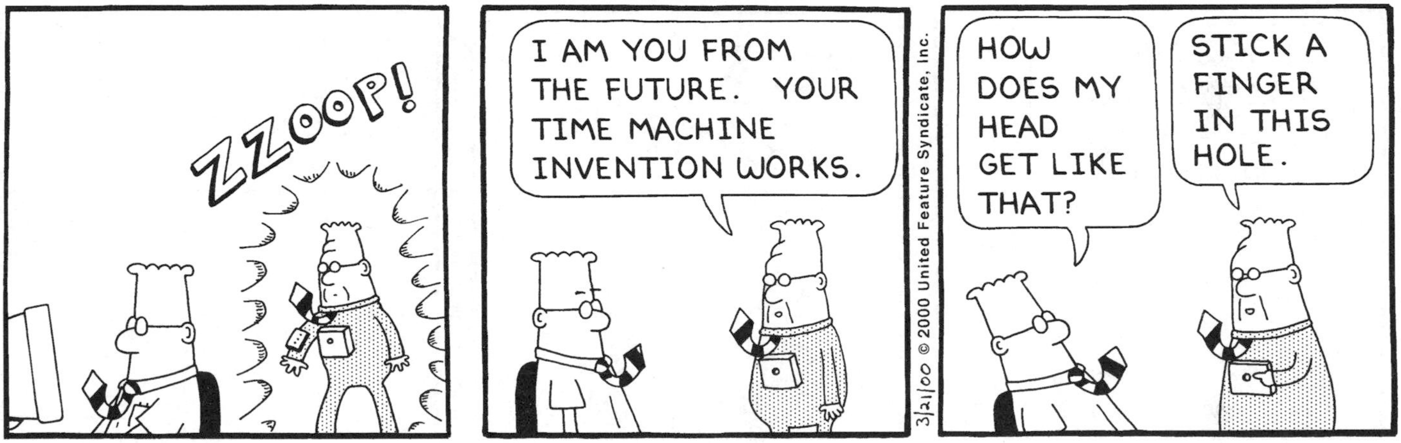
ZZOOP!
I AM YOU FROM THE FUTURE. YOUR TIME MACHINE INVENTION WORKS.
3/21/00 © 2000 United Feature Syndicate, Inc.
HOW DOES MY HEAD GET LIKE THAT?
STICK A FINGER IN THIS HOLE.

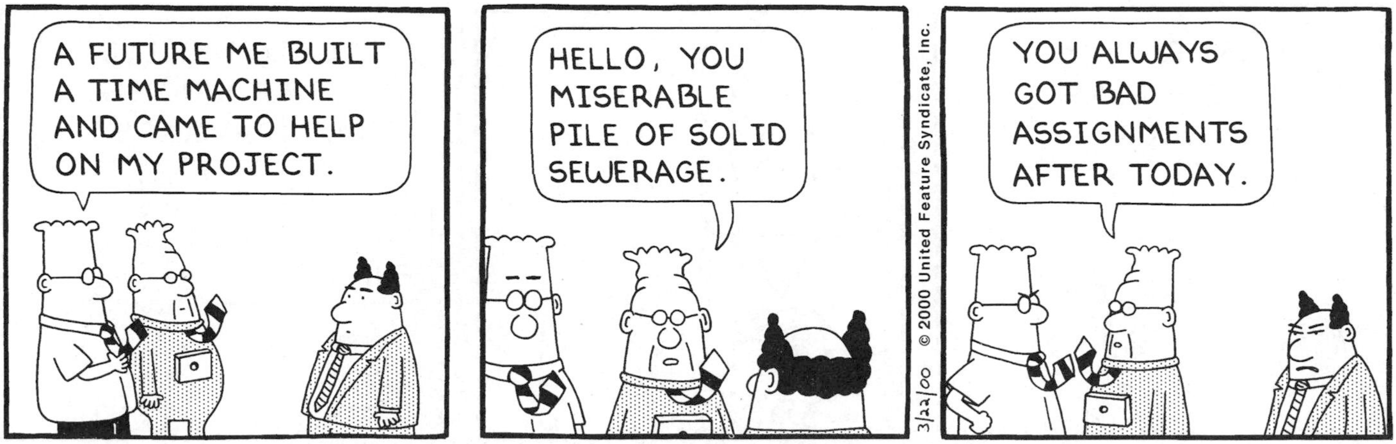
A FUTURE ME BUILT A TIME MACHINE AND CAME TO HELP ON MY PROJECT.
HELLO, YOU MISERABLE PILE OF SOLID SEWERAGE.
3/22/00 © 2000 United Feature Syndicate, Inc.
YOU ALWAYS GOT BAD ASSIGNMENTS AFTER TODAY.

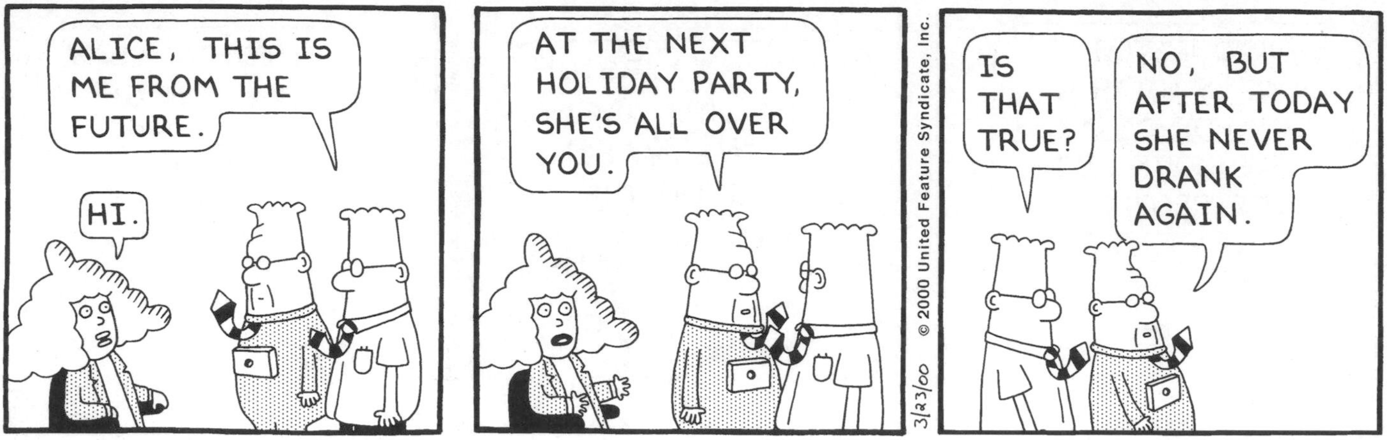
ALICE, THIS IS ME FROM THE FUTURE.
HI.
AT THE NEXT HOLIDAY PARTY, SHE'S ALL OVER YOU.
3/23/00 © 2000 United Feature Syndicate, Inc.
IS THAT TRUE?
NO, BUT AFTER TODAY SHE NEVER DRANK AGAIN.

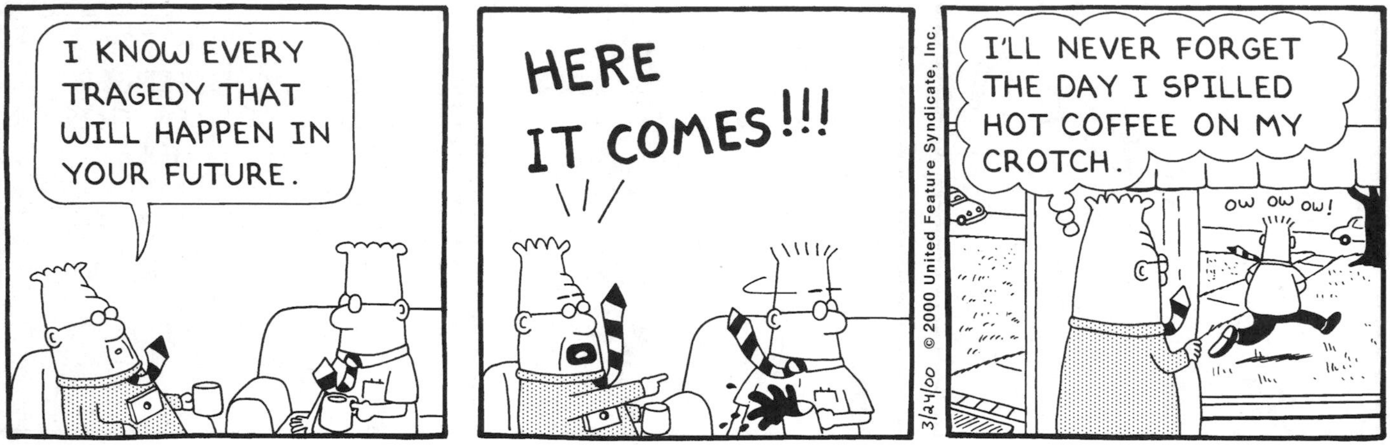
I KNOW EVERY TRAGEDY THAT WILL HAPPEN IN YOUR FUTURE.
HERE IT COMES!!!
3/24/00 © 2000 United Feature Syndicate, Inc.
I'LL NEVER FORGET THE DAY I SPILLED HOT COFFEE ON MY CROTCH.
OW OW OW!

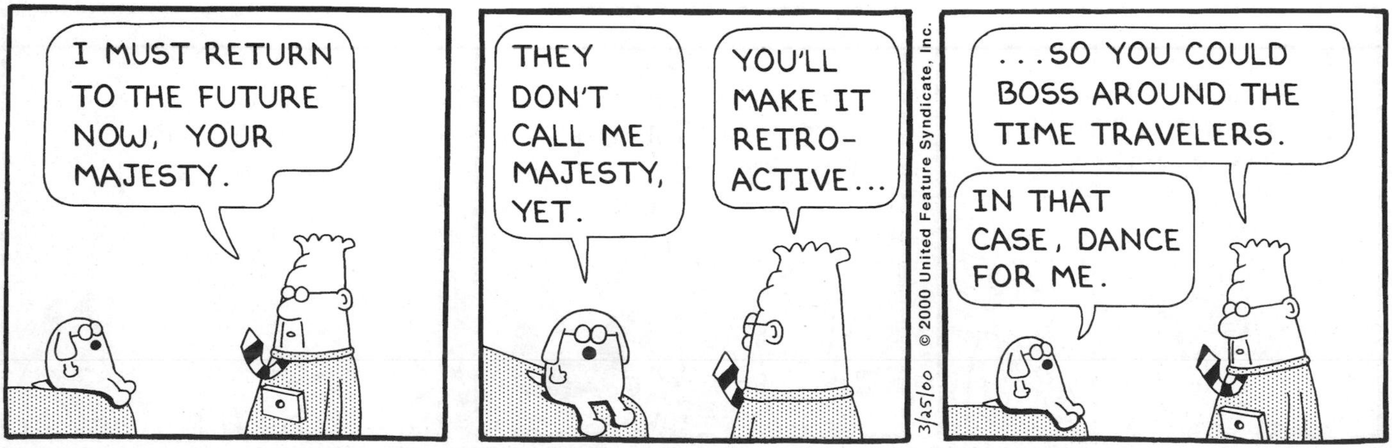
I MUST RETURN TO THE FUTURE NOW, YOUR MAJESTY.
THEY DON'T CALL ME MAJESTY, YET.
YOU'LL MAKE IT RETRO-ACTIVE...
3/25/00 © 2000 United Feature Syndicate, Inc.
...SO YOU COULD BOSS AROUND THE TIME TRAVELERS.
IN THAT CASE, DANCE FOR ME.

TINA, MOVE THAT TITLE...
...OVER HERE.
AAAGH!!
YOUR FINGER OIL IS ON MY SCREEN!!!
NOW I HAVE TO SPEND TEN MINUTES CLEANING IT...
...BECAUSE YOU DON'T UNDER-STAND HOW TO HOVER YOUR FINGER.
3/26/00 © 2000 United Feature Syndicate, Inc.
SEE?! THIS ISN'T HARD. YOU HOVER THE FINGER! DON'T TOUCH!
I HOPE I'M NOT LOSING MY AURA OF INFALLIBILITY.

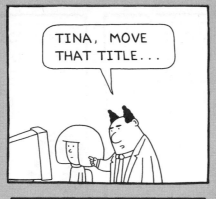

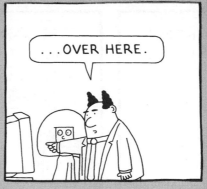

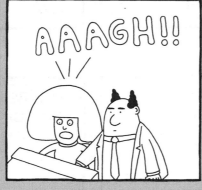

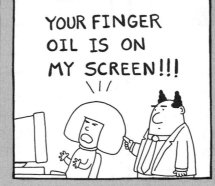

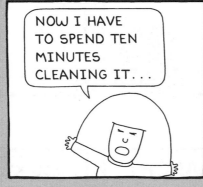

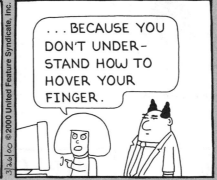

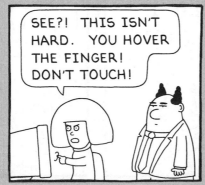

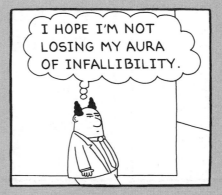

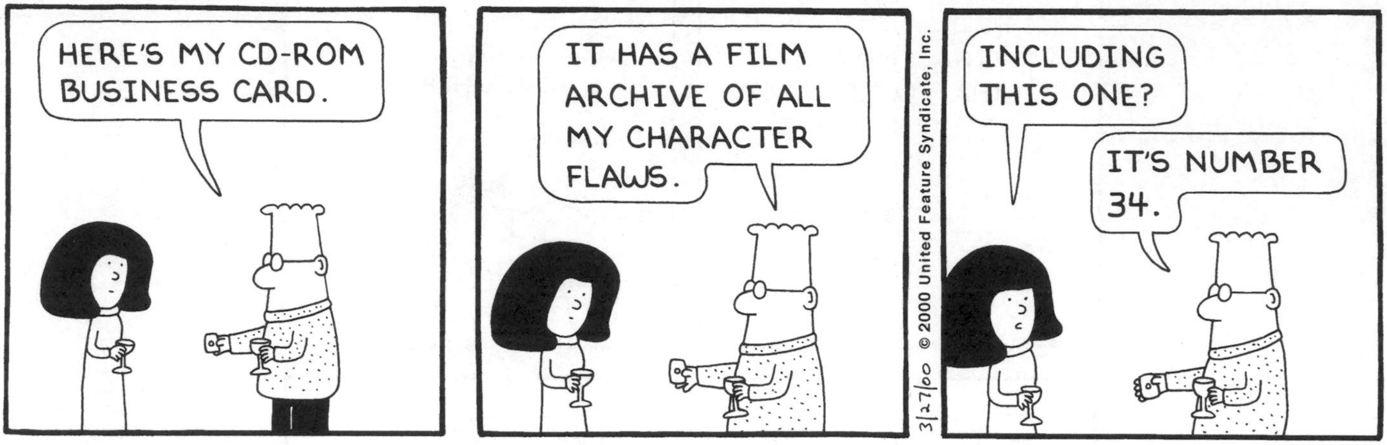
HERE'S MY CD-ROM BUSINESS CARD.
IT HAS A FILM ARCHIVE OF ALL MY CHARACTER FLAWS.
3/27/00 © 2000 United Feature Syndicate, Inc.
INCLUDING THIS ONE?
IT'S NUMBER 34.

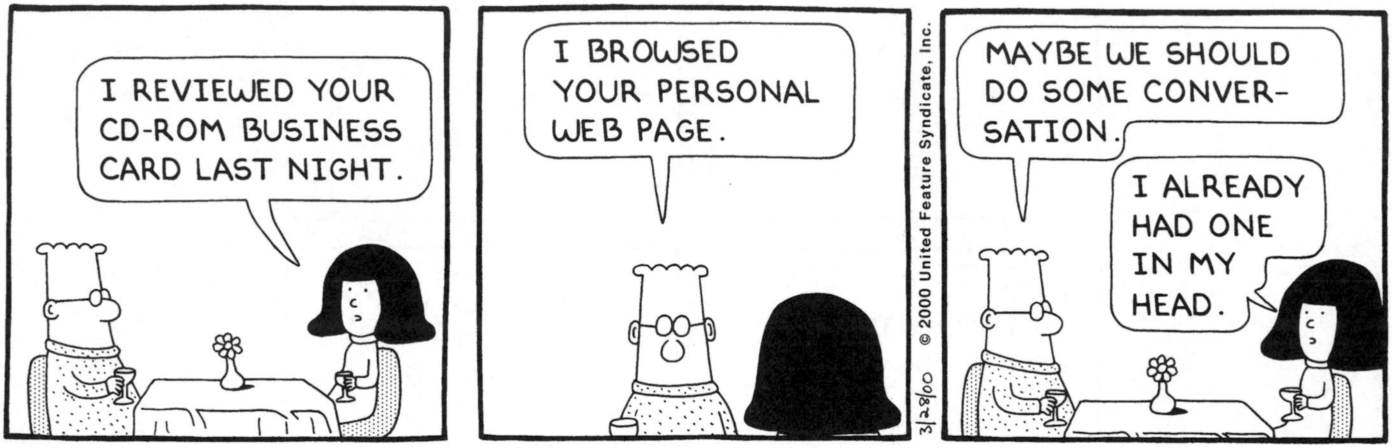
I REVIEWED YOUR CD-ROM BUSINESS CARD LAST NIGHT.
I BROWSED YOUR PERSONAL WEB PAGE.
3/28/00 © 2000 United Feature Syndicate, Inc.
MAYBE WE SHOULD DO SOME CONVER-SATION.
I ALREADY HAD ONE IN MY HEAD.

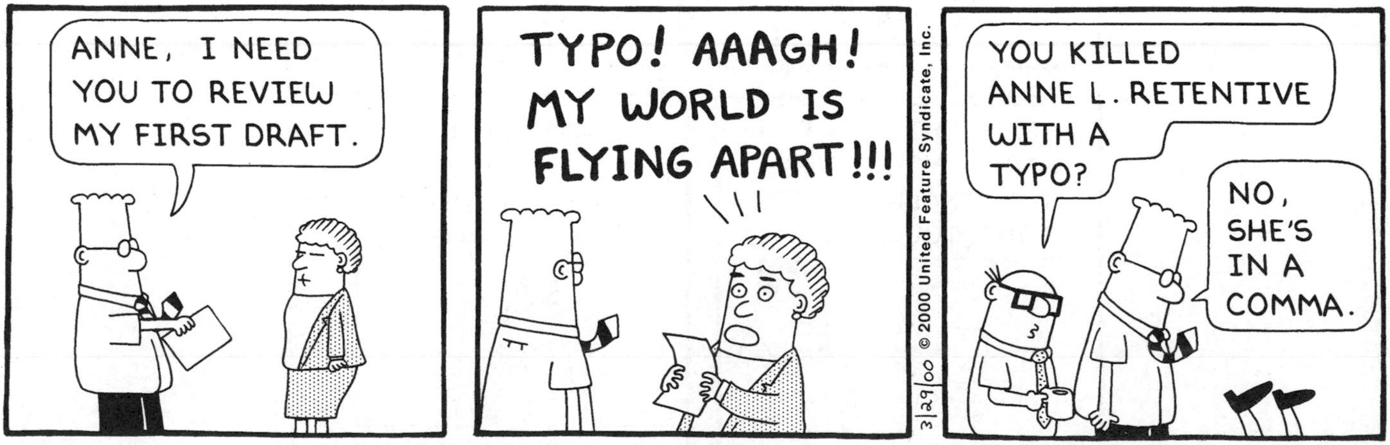
ANNE, I NEED YOU TO REVIEW MY FIRST DRAFT.
TYPO! AAAGH! MY WORLD IS FLYING APART!!!
3/29/00 © 2000 United Feature Syndicate, Inc.
YOU KILLED ANNE L. RETENTIVE WITH A TYPO?
NO, SHE'S IN A COMMA.

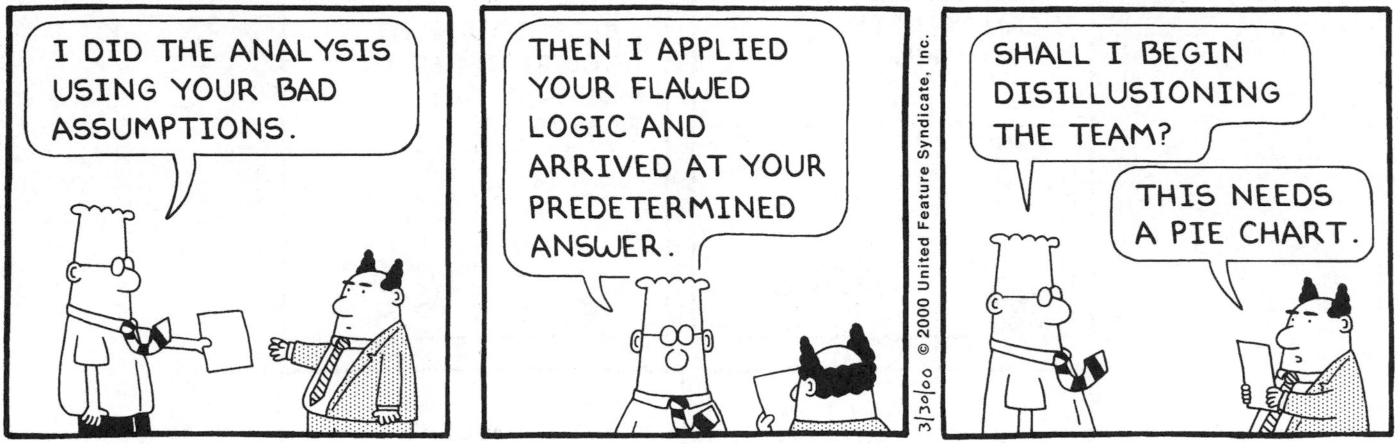
I DID THE ANALYSIS USING YOUR BAD ASSUMPTIONS.
THEN I APPLIED YOUR FLAWED LOGIC AND ARRIVED AT YOUR PREDETERMINED ANSWER.
3/30/00 © 2000 United Feature Syndicate, Inc.
SHALL I BEGIN DISILLUSIONING THE TEAM?
THIS NEEDS A PIE CHART.

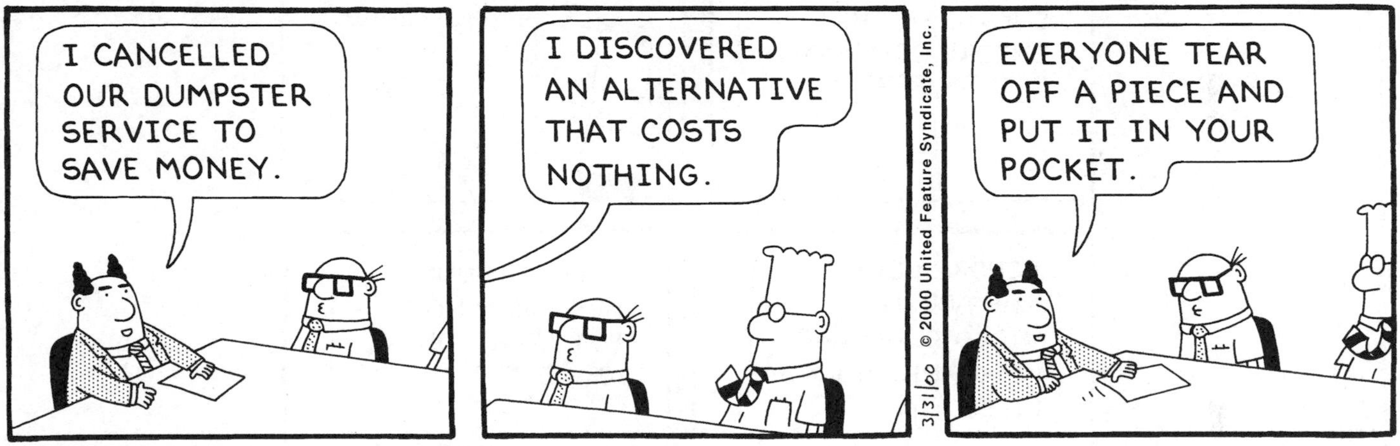
I CANCELLED OUR DUMPSTER SERVICE TO SAVE MONEY.
I DISCOVERED AN ALTERNATIVE THAT COSTS NOTHING.
3/31/00 © 2000 United Feature Syndicate, Inc.
EVERYONE TEAR OFF A PIECE AND PUT IT IN YOUR POCKET.

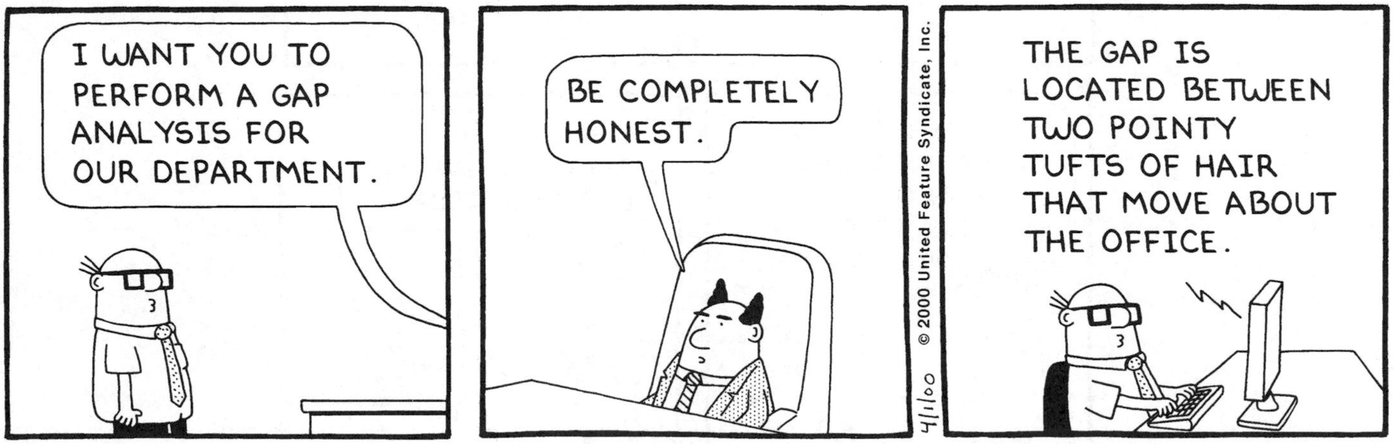
I WANT YOU TO PERFORM A GAP ANALYSIS FOR OUR DEPARTMENT.
BE COMPLETELY HONEST.
4/1/00 © 2000 United Feature Syndicate, Inc.
THE GAP IS LOCATED BETWEEN TWO POINTY TUFTS OF HAIR THAT MOVE ABOUT THE OFFICE.

CAN YOU SING OR DANCE?
TED? I THOUGHT YOU RESIGNED IN DISGUST TWO WEEKS AGO.
WELL...I WROTE A HUGE RESIGNATION MANIFESTO THAT I PLANNED TO E-MAIL TO THE ENTIRE COMPANY.
BUT I THOUGHT IT NEEDED PICTURES.
BEFORE LONG I WAS ADDING VIDEO CLIPS AND HUMOROUS SOUND FILES.
© 2000 United Feature Syndicate, Inc.
4/2/00
THEN I THOUGHT, HEY, WHY NOT PUT IT ALL ON A WEB SITE?
NOW I'M TURNING THE WHOLE THING INTO AN OFF BROADWAY THEATRE PRODUCTION.
I SAW MY FIRST MOTIVATED EMPLOYEE TODAY.

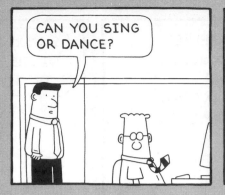

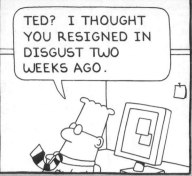

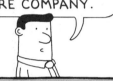

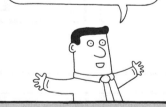

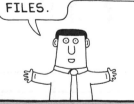

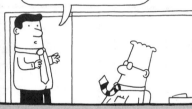

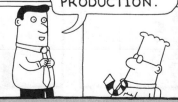

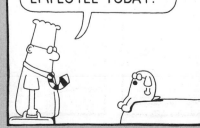

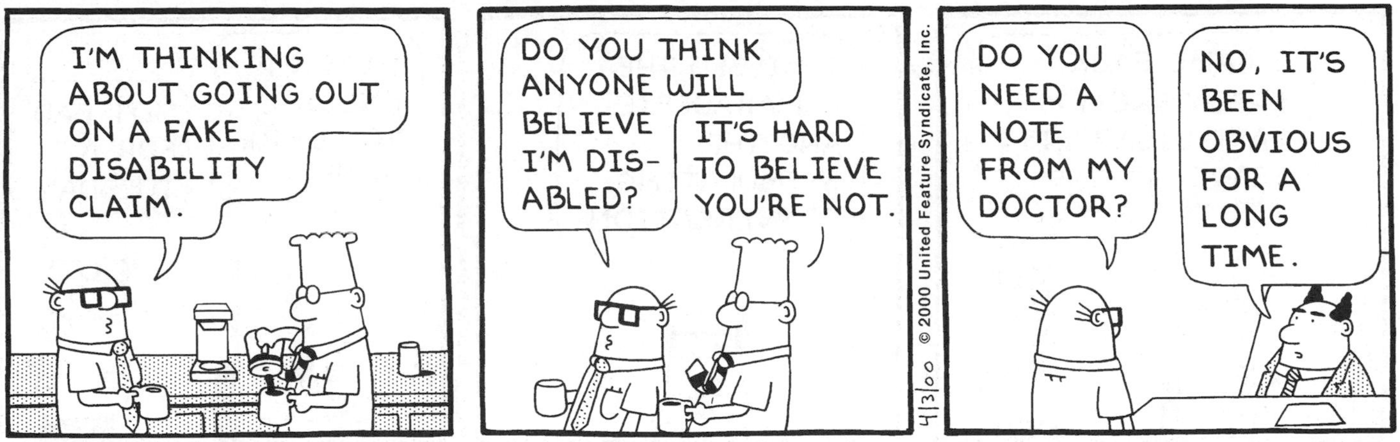
I'M THINKING ABOUT GOING OUT ON A FAKE DISABILITY CLAIM.
DO YOU THINK ANYONE WILL BELIEVE I'M DIS-ABLED?
IT'S HARD TO BELIEVE YOU'RE NOT.
4/3/00 © 2000 United Feature Syndicate, Inc.
DO YOU NEED A NOTE FROM MY DOCTOR?
NO, IT'S BEEN OBVIOUS FOR A LONG TIME.

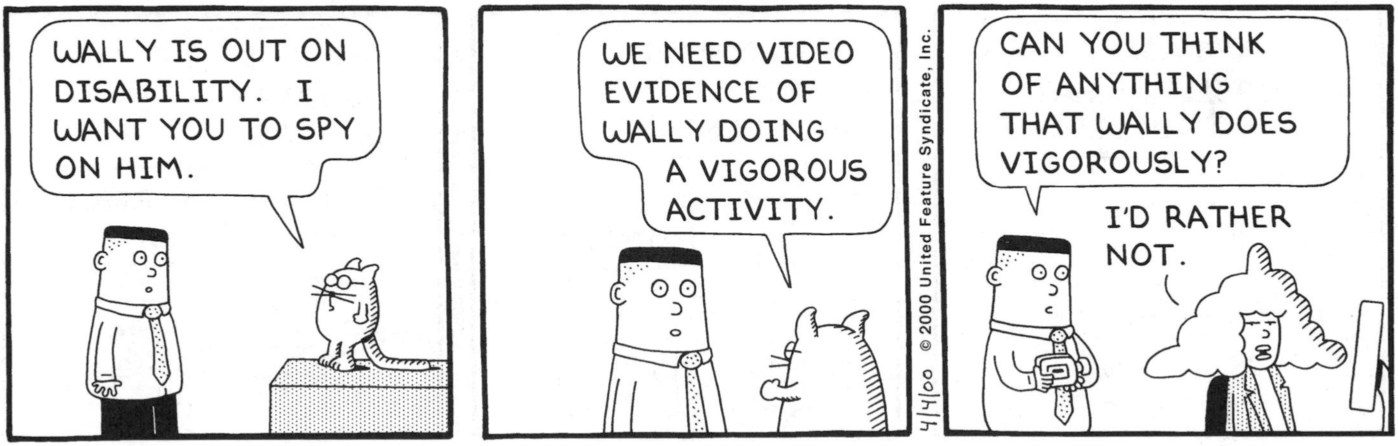
WALLY IS OUT ON DISABILITY. I WANT YOU TO SPY ON HIM.
WE NEED VIDEO EVIDENCE OF WALLY DOING A VIGOROUS ACTIVITY.
4/4/00 © 2000 United Feature Syndicate, Inc.
CAN YOU THINK OF ANYTHING THAT WALLY DOES VIGOROUSLY?
I'D RATHER NOT.

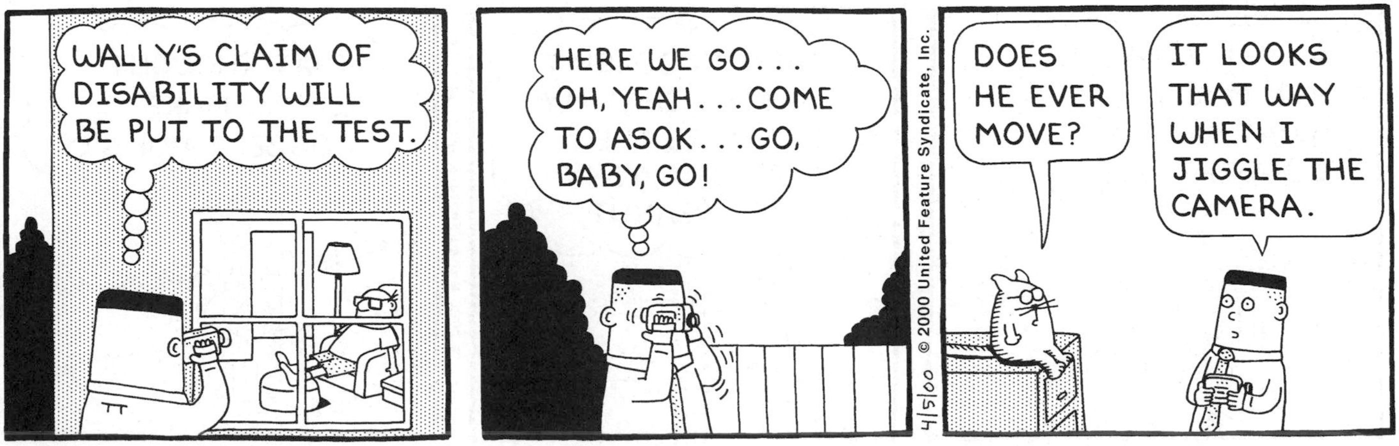
WALLY'S CLAIM OF DISABILITY WILL BE PUT TO THE TEST.
HERE WE GO... OH, YEAH...COME TO ASOK...GO, BABY, GO!
4/5/00 © 2000 United Feature Syndicate, Inc.
DOES HE EVER MOVE?
IT LOOKS THAT WAY WHEN I JIGGLE THE CAMERA.

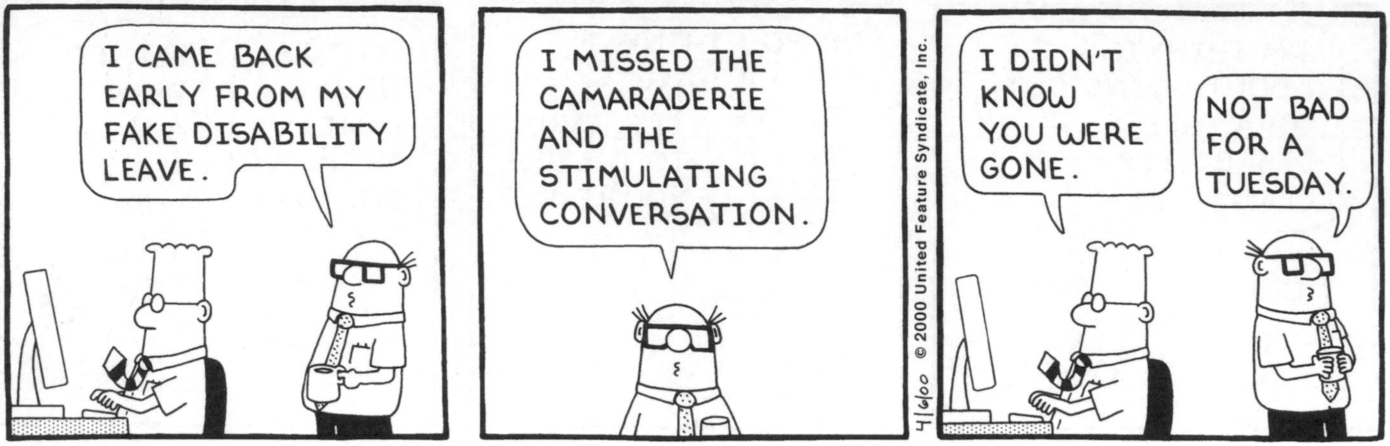
I CAME BACK EARLY FROM MY FAKE DISABILITY LEAVE.
I MISSED THE CAMARADERIE AND THE STIMULATING CONVERSATION.
4/6/00 © 2000 United Feature Syndicate, Inc.
I DIDN'T KNOW YOU WERE GONE.
NOT BAD FOR A TUESDAY.

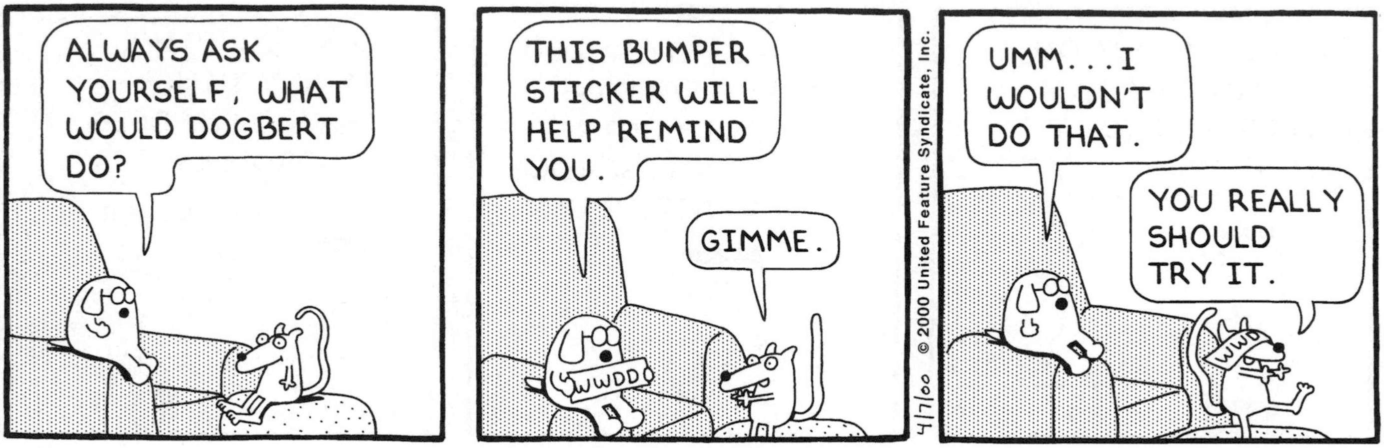
ALWAYS ASK YOURSELF, WHAT WOULD DOGBERT DO?
THIS BUMPER STICKER WILL HELP REMIND YOU.
WWDD
GIMME.
4/7/00 © 2000 United Feature Syndicate, Inc.
UMM. . . I WOULDN'T DO THAT.
YOU REALLY SHOULD TRY IT.

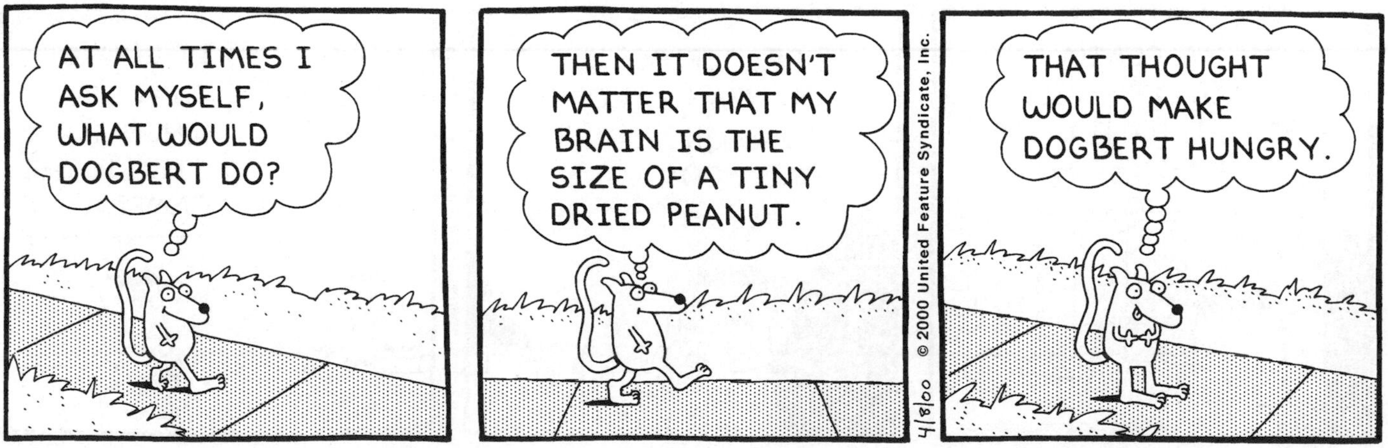
AT ALL TIMES I ASK MYSELF, WHAT WOULD DOGBERT DO?
THEN IT DOESN'T MATTER THAT MY BRAIN IS THE SIZE OF A TINY DRIED PEANUT.
4/8/00 © 2000 United Feature Syndicate, Inc.
THAT THOUGHT WOULD MAKE DOGBERT HUNGRY.

FLY TO AUSTIN AND ANSWER SOME QUESTIONS FOR A BIG CUSTOMER.
DOESN'T THIS CUSTOMER HAVE A TELEPHONE?
YOU DON'T CALL BIG CUSTOMERS!
UM... WHY NOT?
YOU HAVE TO GO IN PERSON TO SHOW THAT YOU CARE.
ACTUALLY, THAT WOULD SHOW THAT I DON'T UNDER-STAND THE CONCEPT OF THE TELEPHONE.
JUST GO.
DO THEY HAVE THESE WHERE YOU COME FROM?
4/9/00 ©2000 United Feature Syndicate, Inc.

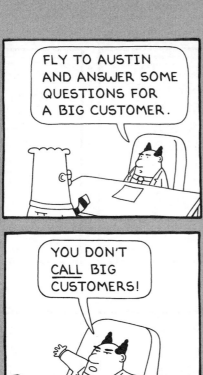

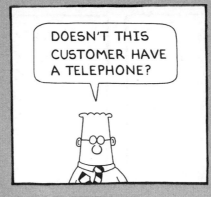

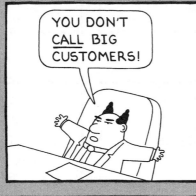

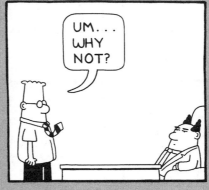

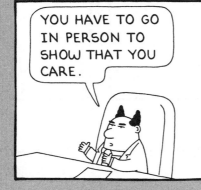

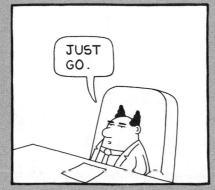

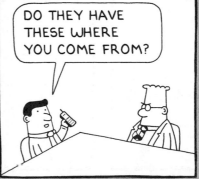

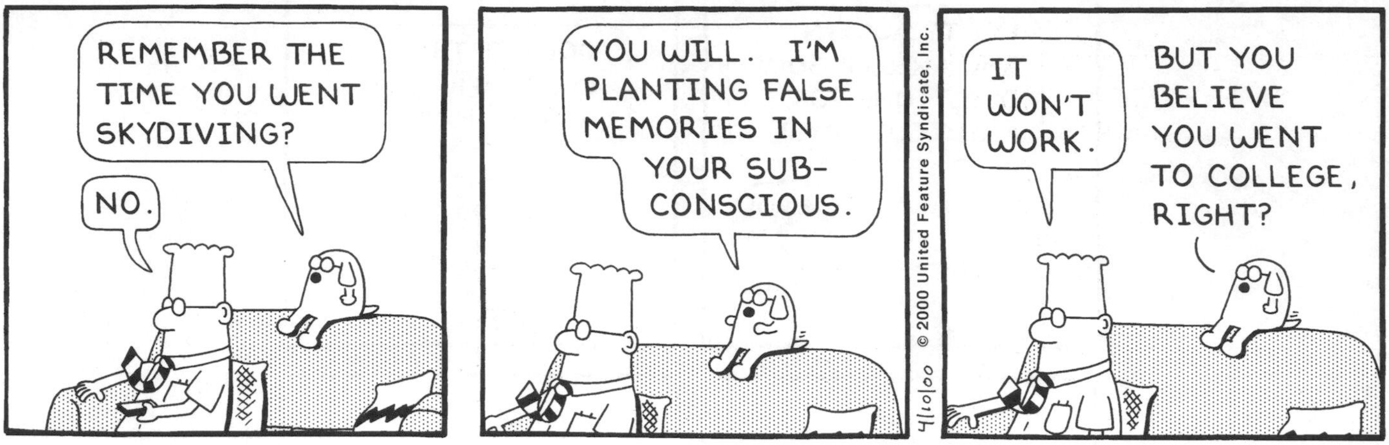
REMEMBER THE TIME YOU WENT SKYDIVING?
NO.
YOU WILL. I'M PLANTING FALSE MEMORIES IN YOUR SUB-CONSCIOUS.
© 2000 United Feature Syndicate, Inc.
4/10/00
IT WON'T WORK.
BUT YOU BELIEVE YOU WENT TO COLLEGE, RIGHT?

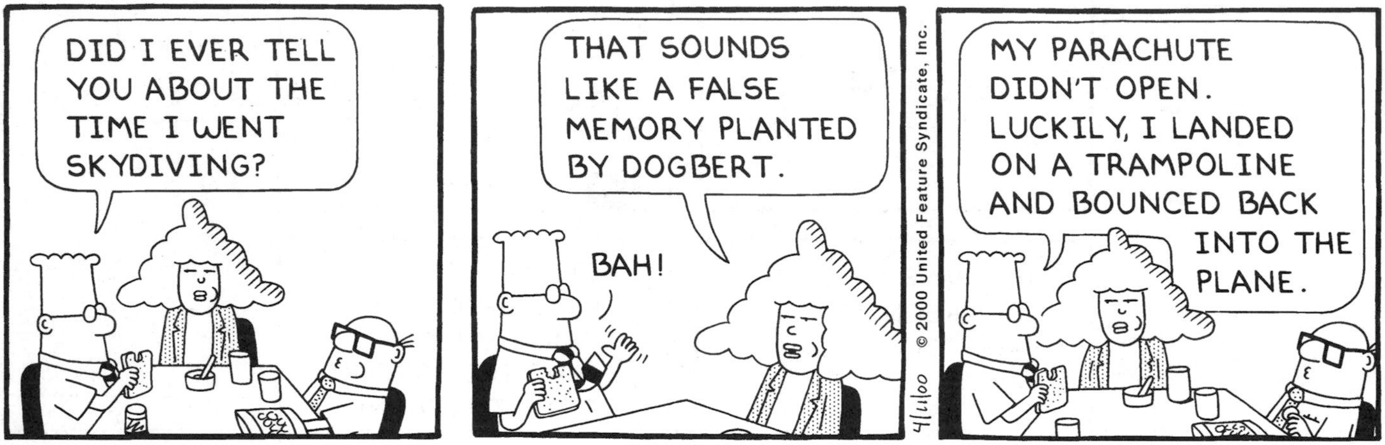
DID I EVER TELL YOU ABOUT THE TIME I WENT SKYDIVING?
THAT SOUNDS LIKE A FALSE MEMORY PLANTED BY DOGBERT.
BAH!
© 2000 United Feature Syndicate, Inc.
4/11/00
MY PARACHUTE DIDN'T OPEN. LUCKILY, I LANDED ON A TRAMPOLINE AND BOUNCED BACK INTO THE PLANE.

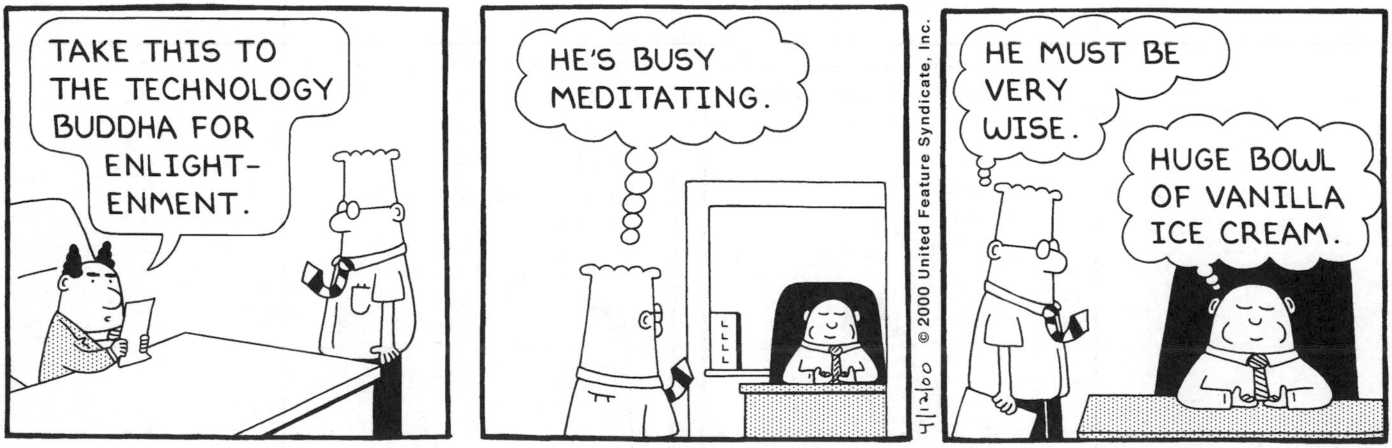
TAKE THIS TO THE TECHNOLOGY BUDDHA FOR ENLIGHT-ENMENT.
HE'S BUSY MEDITATING.
© 2000 United Feature Syndicate, Inc.
4/12/00
HE MUST BE VERY WISE.
HUGE BOWL OF VANILLA ICE CREAM.

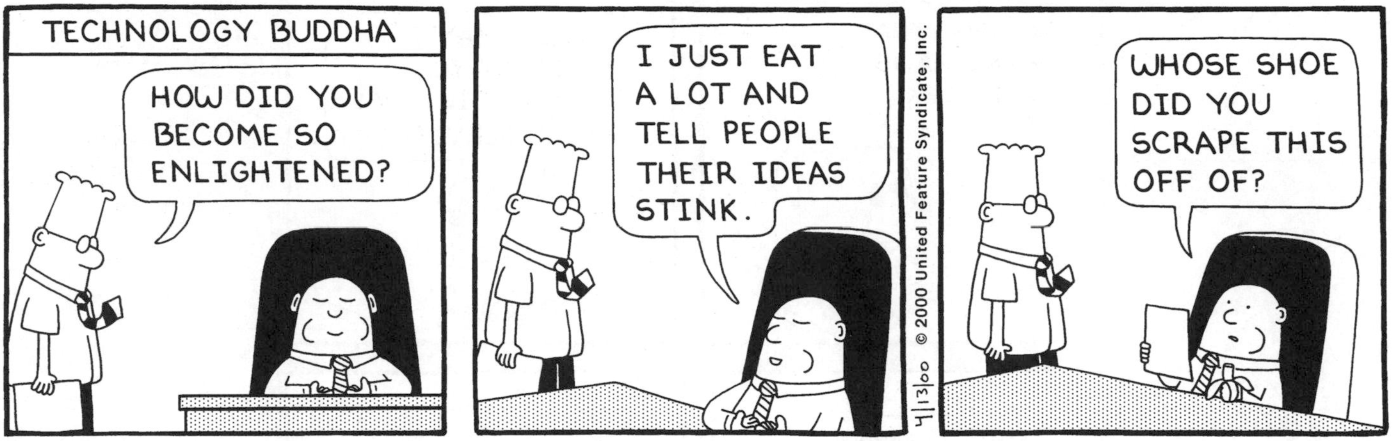
TECHNOLOGY BUDDHA
HOW DID YOU BECOME SO ENLIGHTENED?
I JUST EAT A LOT AND TELL PEOPLE THEIR IDEAS STINK.
4/13/00 © 2000 United Feature Syndicate, Inc.
WHOSE SHOE DID YOU SCRAPE THIS OFF OF?

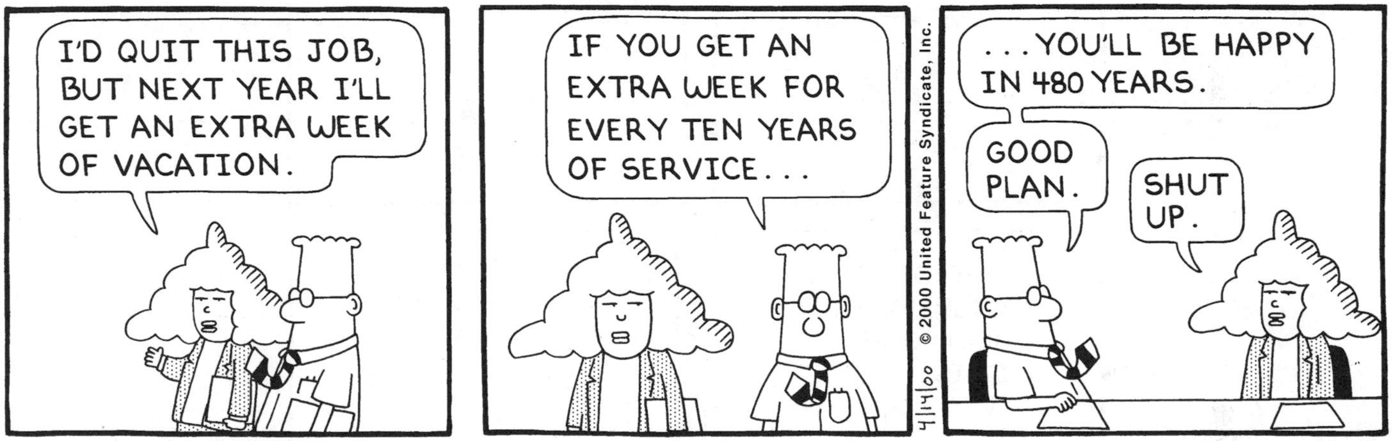
I'D QUIT THIS JOB, BUT NEXT YEAR I'LL GET AN EXTRA WEEK OF VACATION.
IF YOU GET AN EXTRA WEEK FOR EVERY TEN YEARS OF SERVICE . . .
4/14/00 © 2000 United Feature Syndicate, Inc.
. . . YOU'LL BE HAPPY IN 480 YEARS.
GOOD PLAN.
SHUT UP.

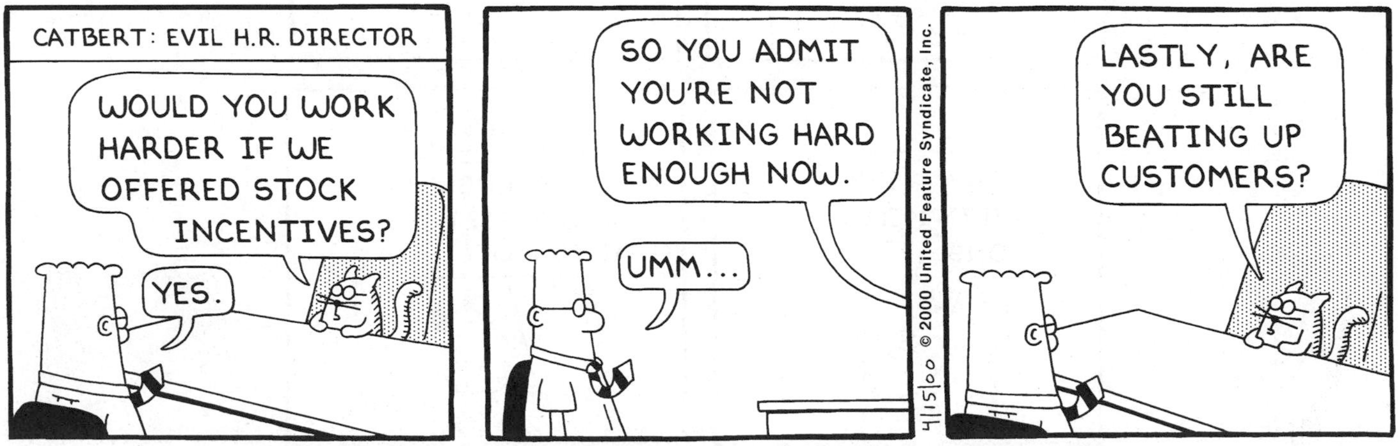
CATBERT: EVIL H.R. DIRECTOR
WOULD YOU WORK HARDER IF WE OFFERED STOCK INCENTIVES?
YES.
SO YOU ADMIT YOU'RE NOT WORKING HARD ENOUGH NOW.
UMM . . .
4/15/00 © 2000 United Feature Syndicate, Inc.
LASTLY, ARE YOU STILL BEATING UP CUSTOMERS?

AGAIN? THAT THING RANG LAST WEEK, TOO.
NEWS
RING RING
HELLO. MAY I INTEREST YOU IN LONG-DISTANCE PHONE SERVICE?
HOW LONG IS IT?
UMM... IT'S VERY LONG. EXTREMELY LONG.
I NEED TO KNOW EXACTLY HOW LONG IT IS!
IF IT'S TOO SHORT I'LL HAVE TO SHOUT THE LAST MILE!
I HATE THAT.
OKAY...IT'S FIFTY MILES LONG.
NO, THANKS.
I DON'T KNOW ANYONE FIFTY MILES AWAY.
©2000 United Feature Syndicate, Inc.
4/16/00

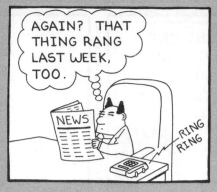

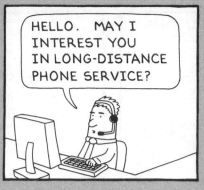

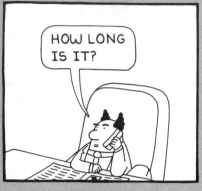

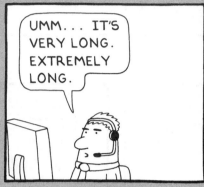

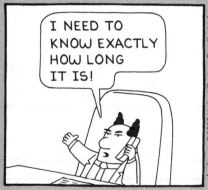

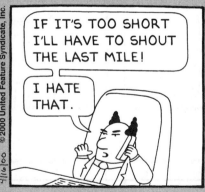

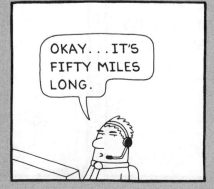

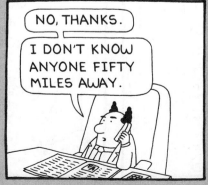

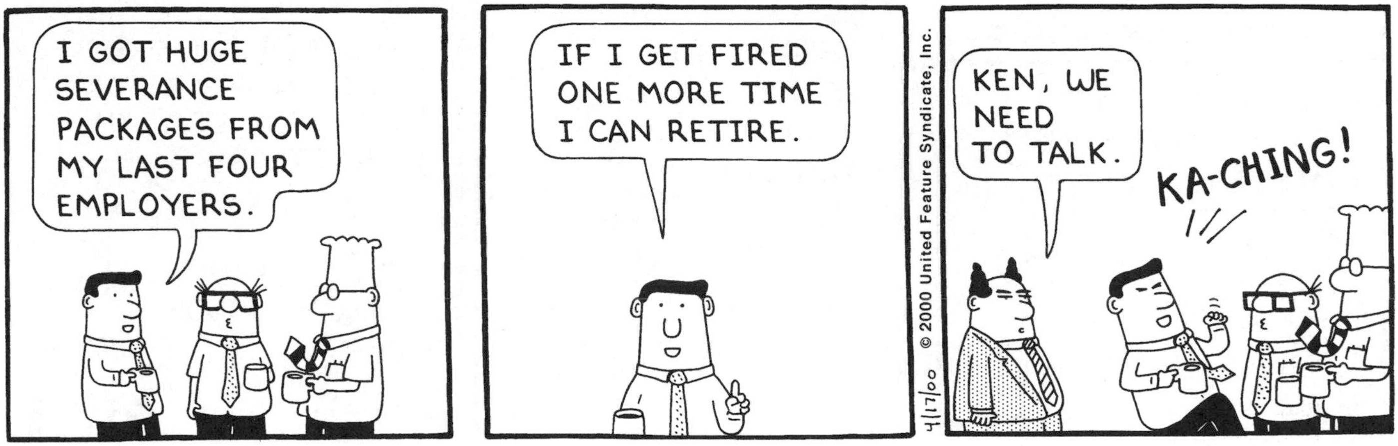
I GOT HUGE SEVERANCE PACKAGES FROM MY LAST FOUR EMPLOYERS.
IF I GET FIRED ONE MORE TIME I CAN RETIRE.
4/17/00 © 2000 United Feature Syndicate, Inc.
KEN, WE NEED TO TALK.
KA-CHING!

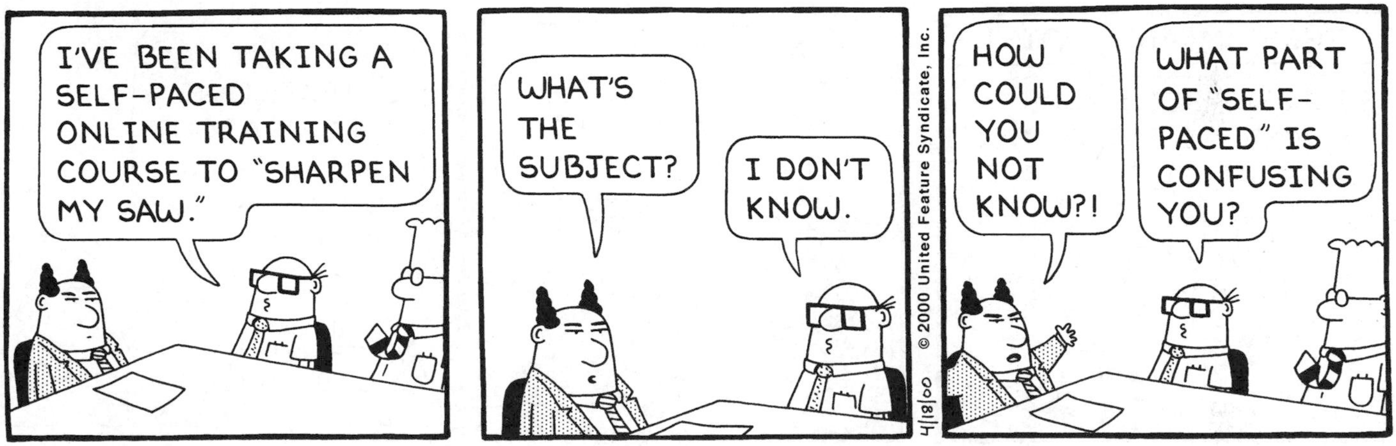
I'VE BEEN TAKING A SELF-PACED ONLINE TRAINING COURSE TO "SHARPEN MY SAW."
WHAT'S THE SUBJECT?
I DON'T KNOW.
4/18/00 © 2000 United Feature Syndicate, Inc.
HOW COULD YOU NOT KNOW?!
WHAT PART OF "SELF-PACED" IS CONFUSING YOU?

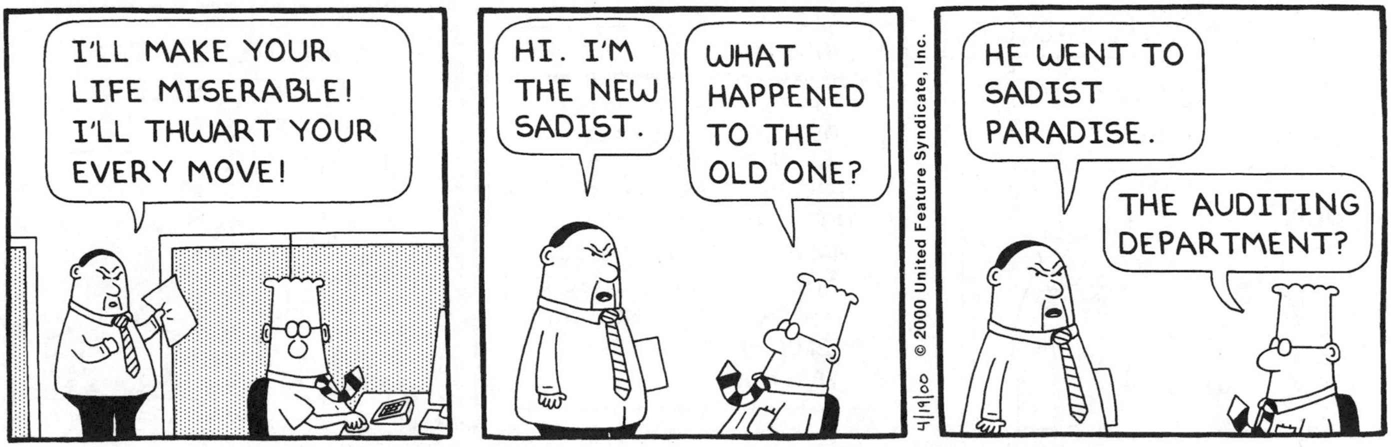
I'LL MAKE YOUR LIFE MISERABLE! I'LL THWART YOUR EVERY MOVE!
HI. I'M THE NEW SADIST.
WHAT HAPPENED TO THE OLD ONE?
4/19/00 © 2000 United Feature Syndicate, Inc.
HE WENT TO SADIST PARADISE.
THE AUDITING DEPARTMENT?

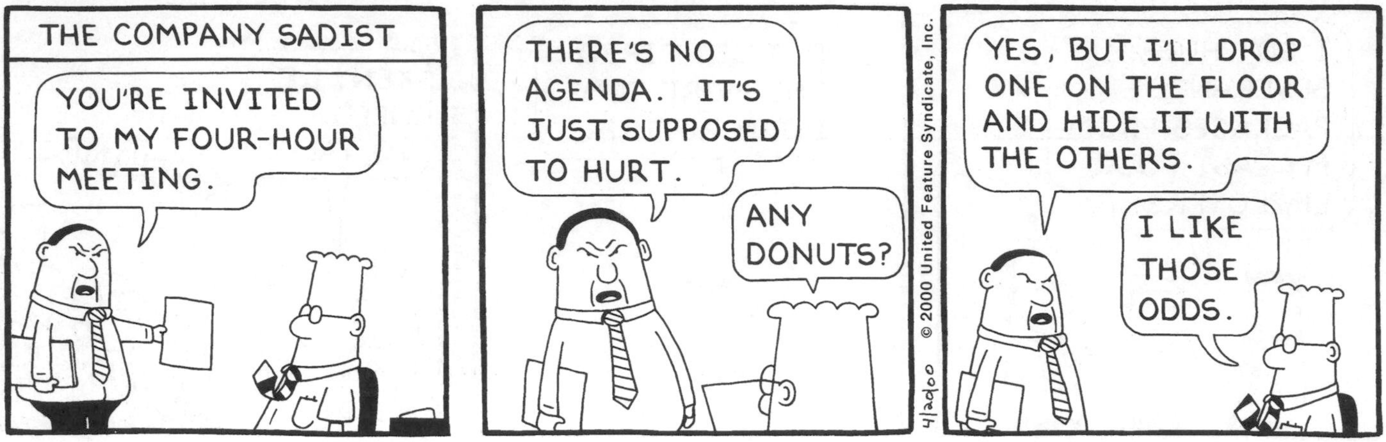
THE COMPANY SADIST
YOU'RE INVITED TO MY FOUR-HOUR MEETING.
THERE'S NO AGENDA. IT'S JUST SUPPOSED TO HURT.
ANY DONUTS?
YES, BUT I'LL DROP ONE ON THE FLOOR AND HIDE IT WITH THE OTHERS.
I LIKE THOSE ODDS.
© 2000 United Feature Syndicate, Inc.
4/20/00

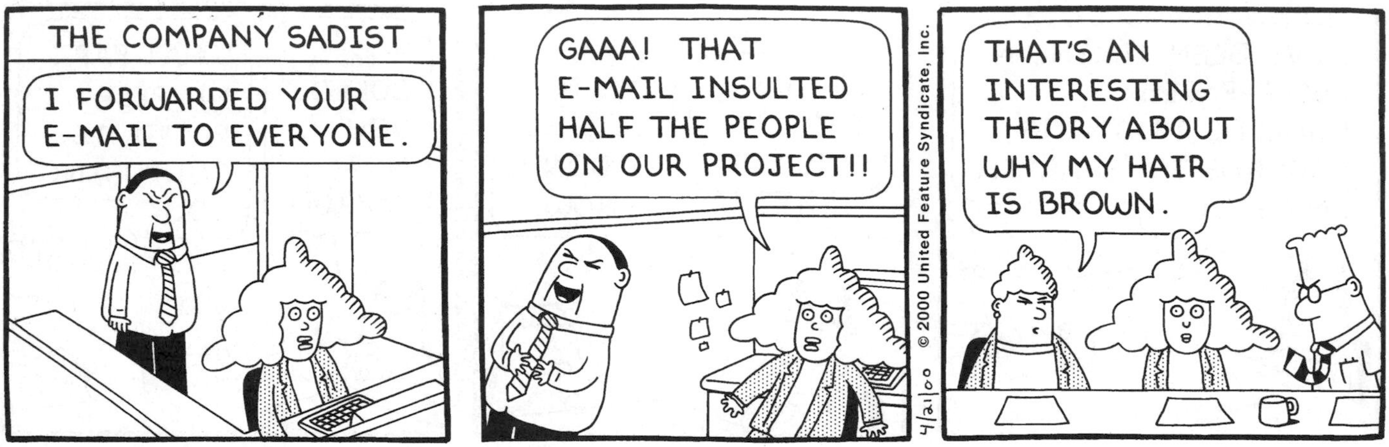
THE COMPANY SADIST
I FORWARDED YOUR E-MAIL TO EVERYONE.
GAAA! THAT E-MAIL INSULTED HALF THE PEOPLE ON OUR PROJECT!!
THAT'S AN INTERESTING THEORY ABOUT WHY MY HAIR IS BROWN.
© 2000 United Feature Syndicate, Inc.
4/21/00

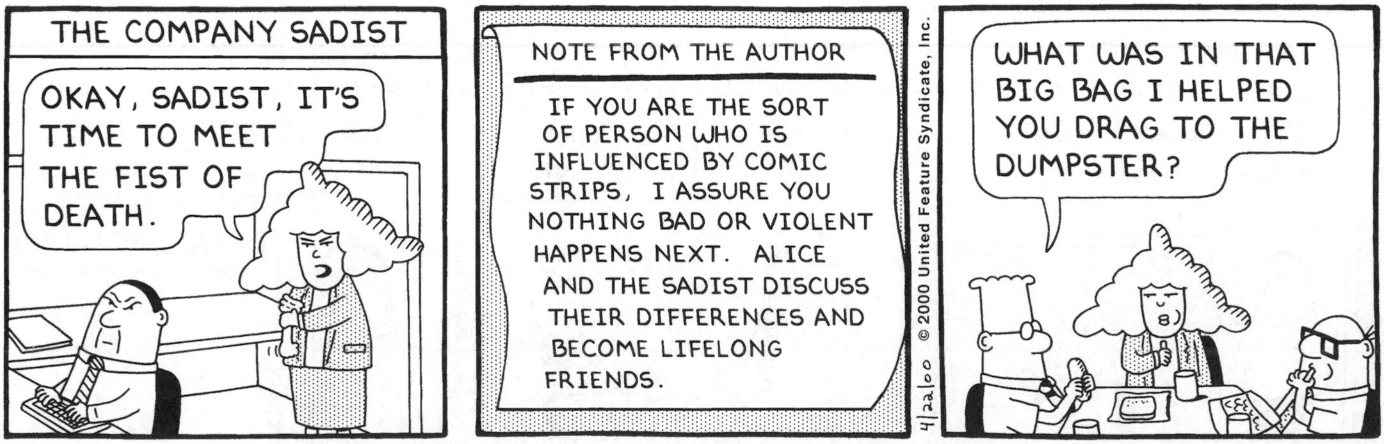
THE COMPANY SADIST
OKAY, SADIST, IT'S TIME TO MEET THE FIST OF DEATH.
NOTE FROM THE AUTHOR
IF YOU ARE THE SORT OF PERSON WHO IS INFLUENCED BY COMIC STRIPS, I ASSURE YOU NOTHING BAD OR VIOLENT HAPPENS NEXT. ALICE AND THE SADIST DISCUSS THEIR DIFFERENCES AND BECOME LIFELONG FRIENDS.
WHAT WAS IN THAT BIG BAG I HELPED YOU DRAG TO THE DUMPSTER?
© 2000 United Feature Syndicate, Inc.
4/22/00

ZZZZZ
BEEP BEEP BEEP
IT'S TIME TO COMPLAIN ABOUT MY WORKLOAD.
AN OUNCE OF PREVENTION IS WORTH A POUND OF ASSIGNMENTS.
I'M WORKING DAY AND NIGHT!
I'VE GOT PROJECTS, ASSIGNMENTS, DELIVERABLES, TASKS...
...MUST-DO ITEMS, ACTION ITEMS, FIRE DRILLS, AND DOG AND PONY SHOWS.
WALLY, I HAVE AN ASSIGNMENT FOR YOU.
!
I SOLVED MY GLARE PROBLEM.
4/23/00 © 2000 United Feature Syndicate, Inc.

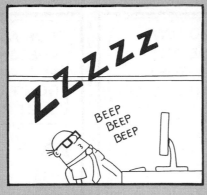

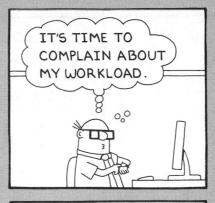

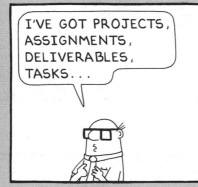

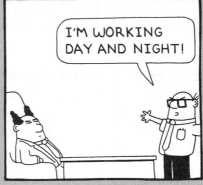

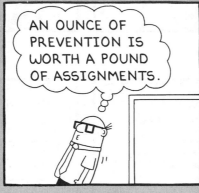

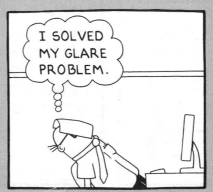

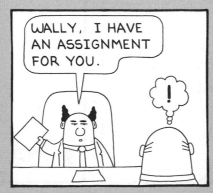

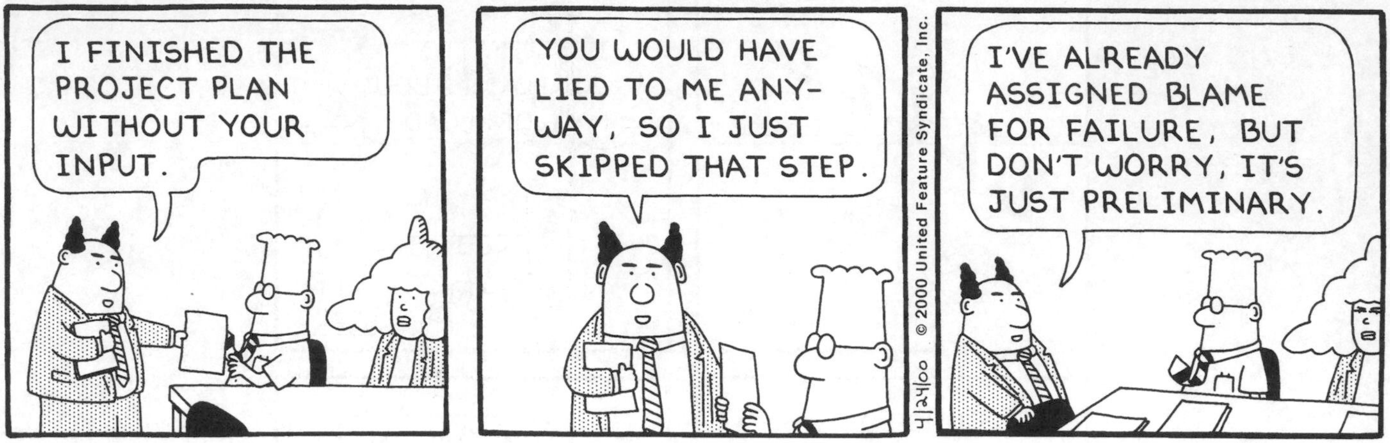
I FINISHED THE PROJECT PLAN WITHOUT YOUR INPUT.
YOU WOULD HAVE LIED TO ME ANYWAY, SO I JUST SKIPPED THAT STEP.
© 2000 United Feature Syndicate, Inc.
4/24/00
I'VE ALREADY ASSIGNED BLAME FOR FAILURE, BUT DON'T WORRY, IT'S JUST PRELIMINARY.

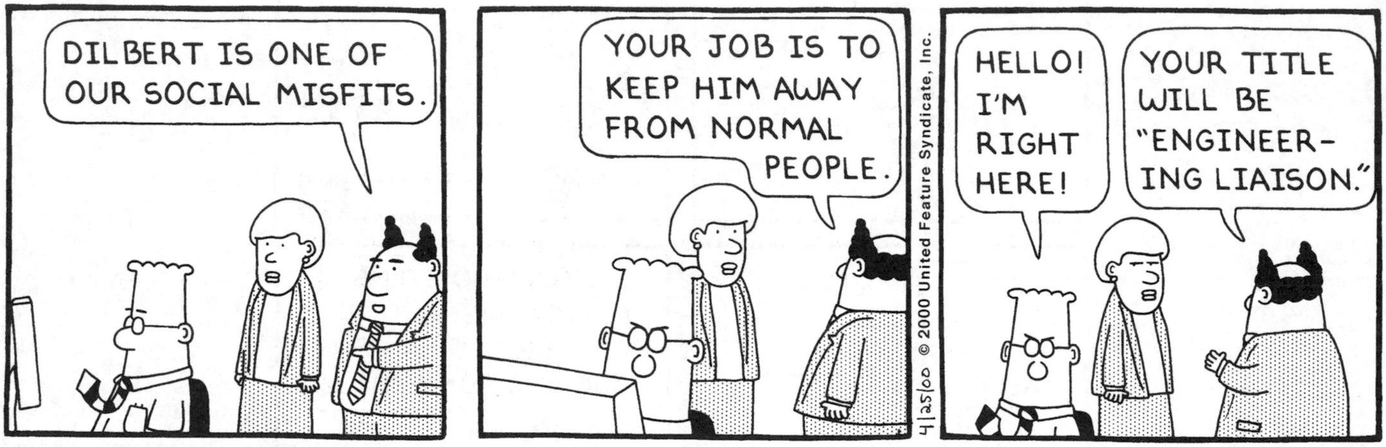
DILBERT IS ONE OF OUR SOCIAL MISFITS.
YOUR JOB IS TO KEEP HIM AWAY FROM NORMAL PEOPLE.
© 2000 United Feature Syndicate, Inc.
4/25/00
HELLO! I'M RIGHT HERE!
YOUR TITLE WILL BE "ENGINEERING LIAISON."

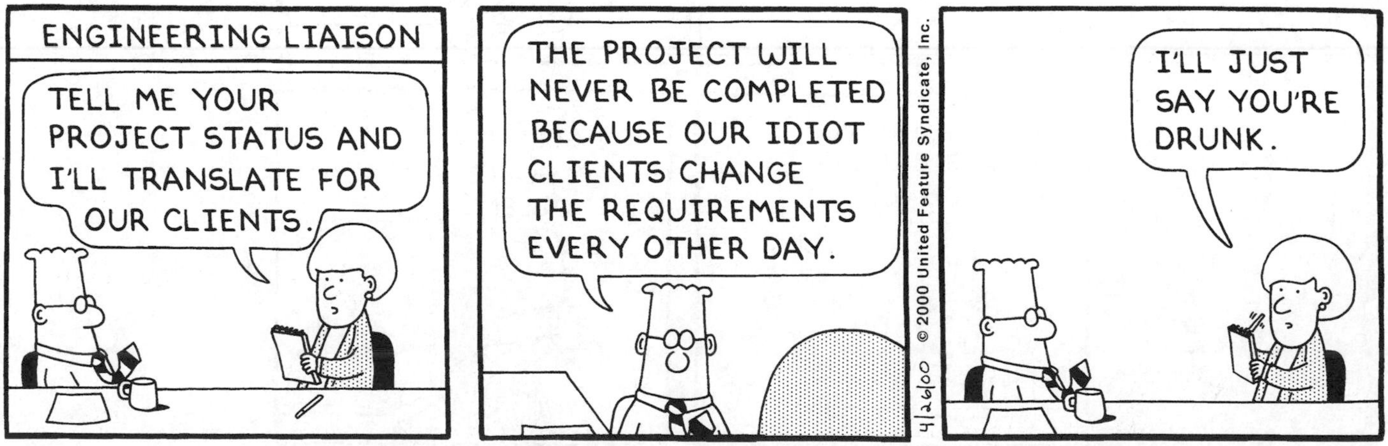
ENGINEERING LIAISON
TELL ME YOUR PROJECT STATUS AND I'LL TRANSLATE FOR OUR CLIENTS.
THE PROJECT WILL NEVER BE COMPLETED BECAUSE OUR IDIOT CLIENTS CHANGE THE REQUIREMENTS EVERY OTHER DAY.
© 2000 United Feature Syndicate, Inc.
4/26/00
I'LL JUST SAY YOU'RE DRUNK.

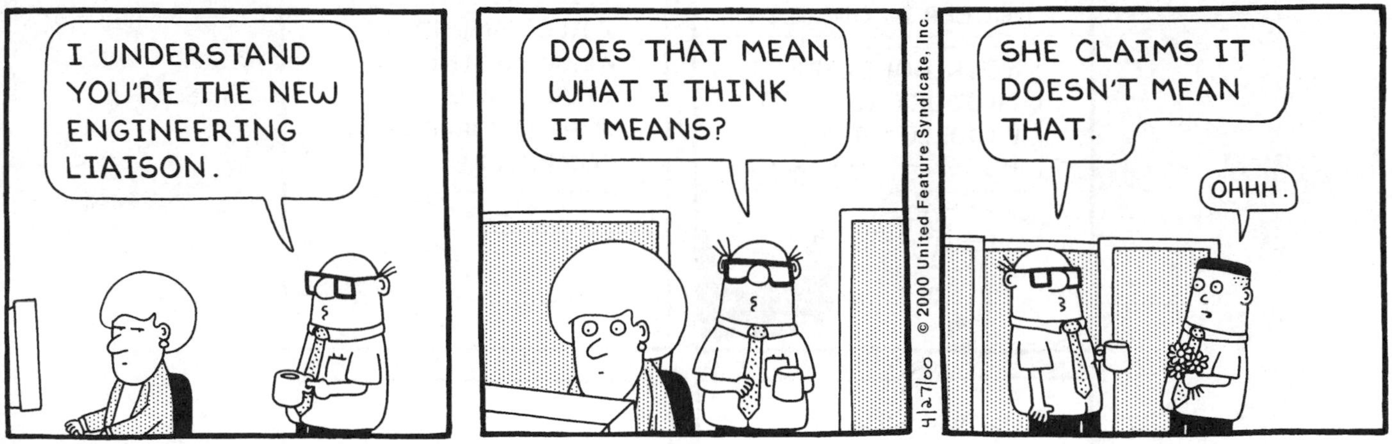
I UNDERSTAND YOU'RE THE NEW ENGINEERING LIAISON.
DOES THAT MEAN WHAT I THINK IT MEANS?
SHE CLAIMS IT DOESN'T MEAN THAT.
OHHH.
4/27/00 © 2000 United Feature Syndicate, Inc.

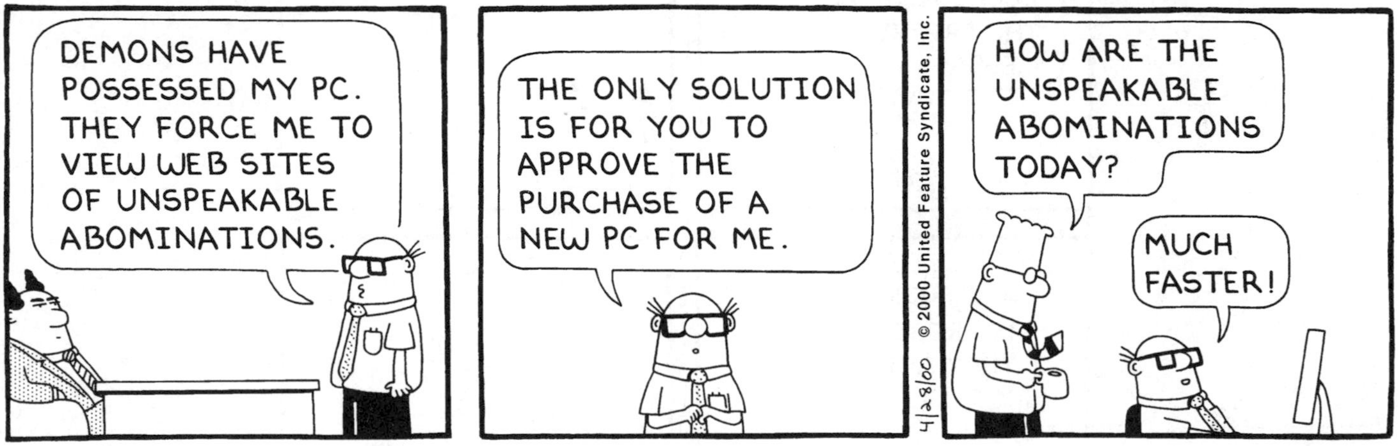
DEMONS HAVE POSSESSED MY PC. THEY FORCE ME TO VIEW WEB SITES OF UNSPEAKABLE ABOMINATIONS.
THE ONLY SOLUTION IS FOR YOU TO APPROVE THE PURCHASE OF A NEW PC FOR ME.
HOW ARE THE UNSPEAKABLE ABOMINATIONS TODAY?
MUCH FASTER!
4/28/00 © 2000 United Feature Syndicate, Inc.

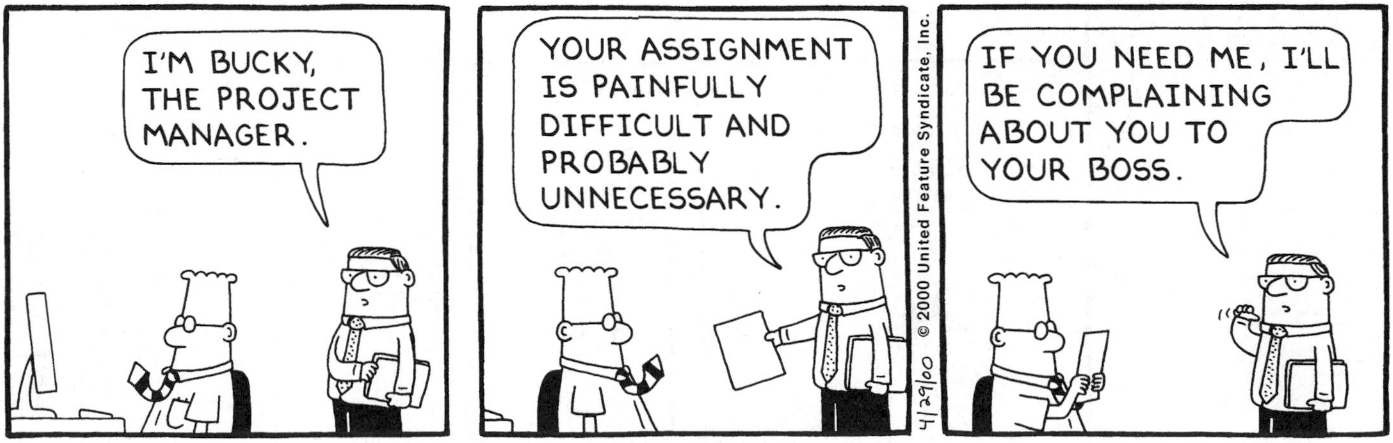
I'M BUCKY, THE PROJECT MANAGER.
YOUR ASSIGNMENT IS PAINFULLY DIFFICULT AND PROBABLY UNNECESSARY.
IF YOU NEED ME, I'LL BE COMPLAINING ABOUT YOU TO YOUR BOSS.
4/29/00 © 2000 United Feature Syndicate, Inc.

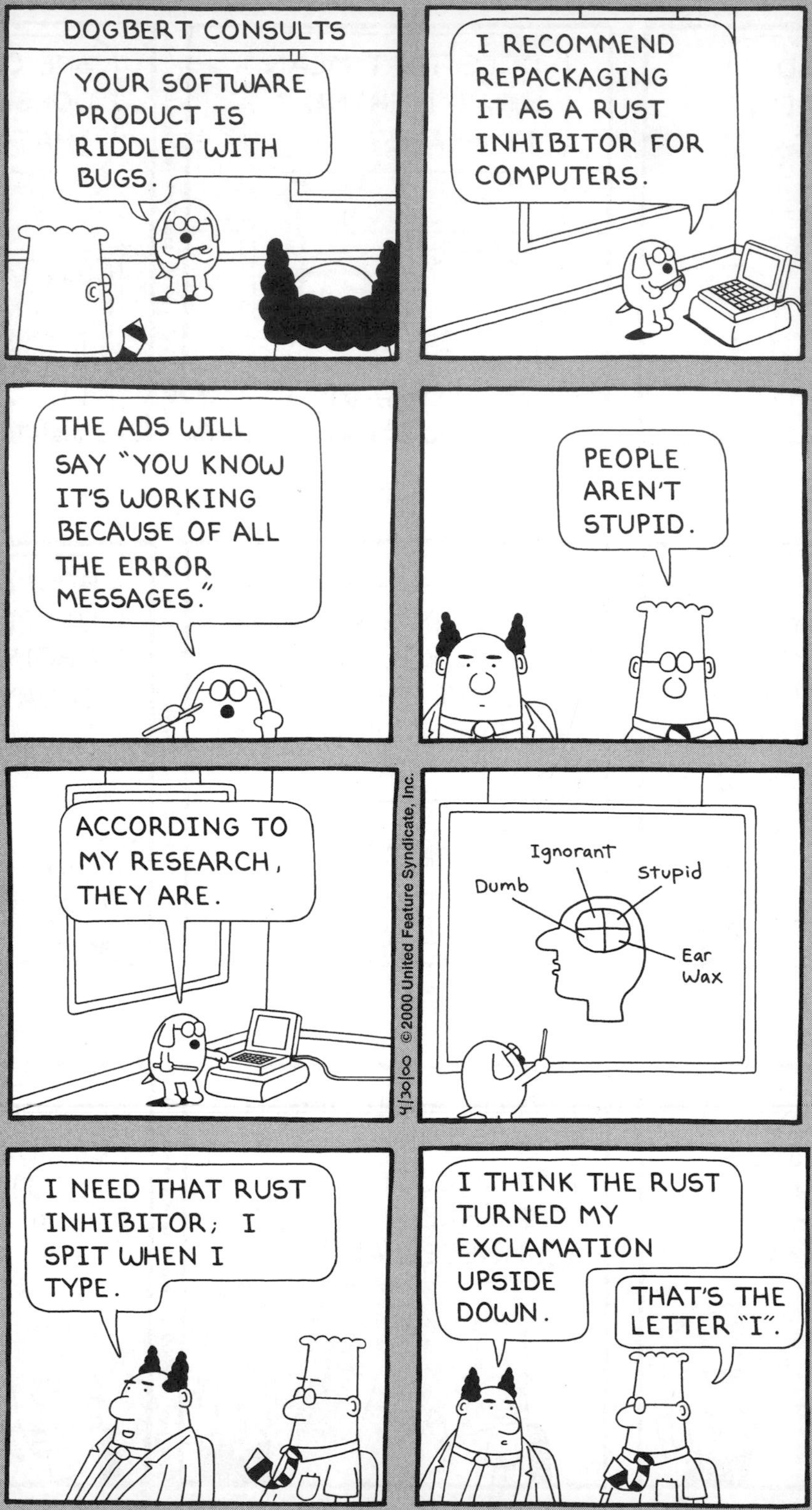
DOGBERT CONSULTS
YOUR SOFTWARE PRODUCT IS RIDDLED WITH BUGS.
I RECOMMEND REPACKAGING IT AS A RUST INHIBITOR FOR COMPUTERS.
THE ADS WILL SAY "YOU KNOW IT'S WORKING BECAUSE OF ALL THE ERROR MESSAGES."
PEOPLE AREN'T STUPID.
ACCORDING TO MY RESEARCH, THEY ARE.
Ignorant
Dumb
Stupid
Ear Wax
©2000 United Feature Syndicate, Inc.
4/30/00
I NEED THAT RUST INHIBITOR; I SPIT WHEN I TYPE.
I THINK THE RUST TURNED MY EXCLAMATION UPSIDE DOWN.
THAT'S THE LETTER "I".